SUPERCOLLIDER FOR THE CREATIVE MUSICIAN

Creating Technology for Music

Series Editor
V. J. Manzo, Associate Professor of Music Technology and
Cognition at Worcester Polytechnic Institute

SuperCollider for the Creative Musician: A Practical Guide
Eli Fieldsteel

SUPERCOLLIDER FOR THE CREATIVE MUSICIAN

A Practical Guide

Eli Fieldsteel

OXFORD
UNIVERSITY PRESS

Oxford University Press is a department of the University of Oxford. It furthers
the University's objective of excellence in research, scholarship, and education
by publishing worldwide. Oxford is a registered trade mark of Oxford University
Press in the UK and certain other countries.

Published in the United States of America by Oxford University Press
198 Madison Avenue, New York, NY 10016, United States of America.

© Oxford University Press 2024

All rights reserved. No part of this publication may be reproduced, stored in
a retrieval system, or transmitted, in any form or by any means, without the
prior permission in writing of Oxford University Press, or as expressly permitted
by law, by license, or under terms agreed with the appropriate reproduction
rights organization. Inquiries concerning reproduction outside the scope of the
above should be sent to the Rights Department, Oxford University Press, at the
address above.

You must not circulate this work in any other form
and you must impose this same condition on any acquirer.

Library of Congress Cataloging-in-Publication Data
Names: Fieldsteel, Eli, author.
Title: SuperCollider for the creative musician : a practical guide / Eli Fieldsteel.
Description: New York, NY : Oxford University Press, 2024. |
Series: Creating technology for music |
Includes bibliographical references and index.
Identifiers: LCCN 2023032483 (print) | LCCN 2023032484 (ebook) |
ISBN 9780197616994 (hardback) | ISBN 9780197617007 (paperback) |
ISBN 9780197617021 (epub) | ISBN 9780197617014 (updf)|
ISBN 9780197617038 (digital-online)| ISBN 9780197617045 (digital-online)
Subjects: LCSH: SuperCollider (Computer file) |
Computer composition (Music) | Software synthesizers.
Classification: LCC ML74.4.S86 F54 2024 (print) |
LCC ML74.4.S86 (ebook) | DDC 781.3/4536—dc23/eng/230718
LC record available at https://lccn.loc.gov/2023032483
LC ebook record available at https://lccn.loc.gov/2023032484

DOI: 10.1093/oso/9780197616994.001.0001

Paperback printed by Sheridan Books, Inc., United States of America
Hardback printed by Bridgeport National Bindery, Inc., United States of America

To Henry, my cat, who passed away shortly after I completed the first manuscript draft. He spent his last few weeks curled up in my lap listening to bleeps and bloops. He was an invaluable collaborator.

CONTENTS

ACKNOWLEDGMENTS   XI
ABOUT THE COMPANION WEBSITE   XIII
INTRODUCTION   XV

PART I   FUNDAMENTALS   1

CHAPTER 1   CORE PROGRAMMING CONCEPTS   3

- 1.1 Overview   3
- 1.2 A Tour of the Environment   3
- 1.3 An Object-Oriented View of the World   5
- 1.4 Writing, Understanding, and Evaluating Code   7
- 1.5 Getting Help   13
- 1.6 A Tour of Classes and Methods   17
- 1.7 Randomness   27
- 1.8 Conditional Logic   29
- 1.9 Iteration   32
- 1.10 Summary   34

CHAPTER 2   ESSENTIALS OF MAKING SOUND   35

- 2.1 Overview   35
- 2.2 Booting the Audio Server   35
- 2.3 Unit Generators   37
- 2.4 UGen Functions   42
- 2.5 Envelopes   51
- 2.6 Multichannel Signals   59
- 2.7 SynthDef and Synth   65
- 2.8 Alternate Expression of Frequency and Amplitude   71
- 2.9 Helpful Server Tools   72

PART II CREATIVE TECHNIQUES 77

CHAPTER 3 SYNTHESIS 79
- **3.1** Overview 79
- **3.2** Additive Synthesis 79
- **3.3** Modulation Synthesis 84
- **3.4** Wavetable Synthesis 93
- **3.5** Filters and Subtractive Synthesis 98
- **3.6** Modal Synthesis 106
- **3.7** Waveform Distortion 109
- **3.8** Conclusions and Further Ideas 113

CHAPTER 4 SAMPLING 115
- **4.1** Overview 115
- **4.2** Buffers 115
- **4.3** Sampling UGens 122
- **4.4** Recording UGens 129
- **4.5** Granular Synthesis 139

CHAPTER 5 SEQUENCING 146
- **5.1** Overview 146
- **5.2** Routines and Clocks 146
- **5.3** Patterns 156
- **5.4** Additional Techniques for Pattern Composition 170
- **5.5** Real-Time Pattern Control 176

CHAPTER 6 SIGNAL PROCESSING 183
- **6.1** Overview 183
- **6.2** Signal Flow Concepts on the Audio Server 183
- **6.3** Delay-Based Processing 198
- **6.4** Real-Time Granular Synthesis 204

CHAPTER 7 EXTERNAL CONTROL 211
- **7.1** Overview 211
- **7.2** MIDI 211
- **7.3** OSC 220
- **7.4** Other Options for External Control 227

CHAPTER 8 GRAPHICAL USER INTERFACES 233
- **8.1** Overview 233
- **8.2** Basic GUI Principles 233
- **8.3** Intermediate GUI Techniques 241
- **8.4** Custom Graphics 245

PART III LARGE-SCALE PROJECTS 249

CHAPTER 9 CONSIDERATIONS FOR LARGE-SCALE PROJECTS 251

- **9.1** Overview 251
- **9.2** waitForBoot 252
- **9.3** Asynchronous Commands 253
- **9.4** Initialization and Cleanup Functions 255
- **9.5** The Startup File 260
- **9.6** Working with Multiple Code Files 260

CHAPTER 10 AN EVENT-BASED STRUCTURE 263

- **10.1** Overview 263
- **10.2** Expressing Musical Events Through Code 263
- **10.3** Organizing Musical Events 266
- **10.4** Navigating and Rehearsing an Event-Based Composition 271
- **10.5** Indeterminacy in an Event-Based Composition 273

CHAPTER 11 A STATE-BASED STRUCTURE 278

- **11.1** Overview 278
- **11.2** Simple State Control 279
- **11.3** Composite States 282
- **11.4** Patterns in a State-Based Composition 285
- **11.5** One-Shots in a State-Based Composition 288
- **11.6** Signal Processing in a State-Based Composition 290
- **11.7** Performing a State-Based Composition 293

CHAPTER 12 LIVE CODING 298

- **12.1** Overview 298
- **12.2** A Live Coding Problem and Solution 299
- **12.3** NodeProxy 300
- **12.4** Additional NodeProxy Features 308
- **12.5** TaskProxy 314
- **12.6** Recording a Live Coding Performance 317

INDEX 321

ACKNOWLEDGMENTS

This book is the result of over a decade of using the SuperCollider programming language for music composition and experimental sound art, a journey that would not have been possible without the support of many others. My brother, Nathan, introduced me to SuperCollider in 2007 and provided the initial spark of interest. During my first year of graduate study in music composition, my peers L. Scott Price and Ilya Rostovtsev were creating code-based music that radically expanded the scope of my musical world. In 2010, I took a summer course with James Lipton and Ron Kuivila at Wesleyan University, which put so many missing pieces into place and allowed me to properly begin self-teaching. During my graduate studies, my advisor Russell Pinkston was an incredible teacher and an endless fount of knowledge. The Companion Code materials that accompany this book include audio samples from musicians who have enriched my life through collaborations, performances, and recording sessions, notably flutist Kenzie Slottow, percussionist Adam Groh, and saxophonist Nathan Mandel. A few close friends, colleagues, and former teachers—Jake Metz, Jon C. Nelson, and Stephen Taylor—generously volunteered their time to read and provide feedback on parts of the manuscript as it took shape. I also owe a great deal to the many gurus and developers of the SuperCollider community, who were always kind and helpful in online forums when I had questions. Finally, I am deeply grateful for my wife, Miriam, who is one of the most compassionate and supportive people I have ever met.

Thank you to everyone who helped me become the musician I am today.

ABOUT THE COMPANION WEBSITE

www.oup.com/us/supercolliderforthecreativemusician

We have created a website to accompany *SuperCollider for the Creative Musician: A Practical Guide.* Throughout this book, in-line examples of SuperCollider code appear in chapters, and additionally, each chapter pairs with one or more large-scale SuperCollider code projects. Collectively, these examples serve to amplify and augment concepts discussed in the book. The former (Code Examples) focus on bite-size ideas, while the latter (Companion Codes) explore broader topics in greater detail. All these examples are available on this website. When Companion Code files are referenced in the text, they are accompanied with Oxford's symbol ▶.

    The purpose of this website is to foster a hands-on learning approach, by enabling the reader to quickly explore code on their own, while avoiding the burden of having to copy code by hand into a computer. When engaging with a specific chapter, the reader is encouraged to download and open the corresponding Code Examples and Companion Codes in SuperCollider, so that they are readily accessible whenever the urge to experiment arises.

INTRODUCTION

Welcome to *SuperCollider for the Creative Musician: A Practical Guide*. I hope you'll find this book rewarding, ear-opening, and fun.

A little bit about myself: I've been a musician for most of my life. I took piano lessons when I was young, learned other instruments throughout middle school and high school, and became seriously interested in music composition when I was about 15 years old. At the same time, math and computer science were always among my strongest aptitudes. I took a handful of college math courses during my last year of high school, and I had studied the manual for my TI-83 calculator to the point where I was able to start coding semi-complex programs on my own. I dabbled in commercial audio software (GarageBand, mostly) in high school and college, but it wasn't until I'd started graduate studies in music composition that I began to realize the depth to which music and computational thinking could be artfully combined. Discovering SuperCollider and seeing/hearing what it could do opened creative doors that I didn't even know existed. Getting it to do what I wanted, however . . . was a different matter. I'd never had any formal training in computer programming beyond a few spontaneously taken college classes, and as coding platforms go, SuperCollider is quirky, so it was a slow uphill climb for me. After several years, as I finally began feeling competent and self-sufficient, I began taking notes on things I wish I'd known from day one. These notes evolved into a sort of curriculum, which manifested as an ongoing series of video tutorials published on YouTube, and now, this book.

Why use code to make music? Under the hood, all audio software is built with code, but often presented to the user as a rich graphical interface layer meant to provide an intuitive means of control, helping new users start making sounds quickly and easily, without really needing to know much about the underlying principles. It's wonderful that these tools exist, but for users wanting to get their hands deeper into the machine to do things that are more precise or customized, these tools can feel restrictive because the inner workings are "concealed" behind a thick graphical user interface. Programs like SuperCollider, which allow the user to work directly with code, provide far more direct control, power, and flexibility over the types of sounds that happen, when they happen, and how they happen. This book doesn't just present a series of cool sounds and techniques, it also attempts to unpack and dissect important details, show alternatives, illustrate common misunderstandings, and contextualize these techniques within a broader creative framework.

This book, and other teaching materials I've published, exist with a central goal of simplifying and accelerating the learning process for anyone who's recently discovered SuperCollider and feels a similar spark. Having taught music technology in higher education for several years, I've encountered several types of students for whom I think this book would be valuable. As the title suggests, it's a structured tutorial and reference guide for anyone wanting to create electronic music or experimental sound art with SuperCollider, and assumes readers fall somewhere on the continuum between musician and computer programmer.

Maybe you're a seasoned musician with a budding interest in coding, or maybe you're a software developer who creates electronic music as a side hustle. Whatever the case, if you have some familiarity with music and code—even just a little of each—you should be able to use this book to pick up the basics and get some new creative projects off the ground. Keep in mind, however, that this book isn't a formal substitute for an introduction to programming, digital audio principles, or music theory. These are very broad topics, beyond the scope of this publication. They are selectively discussed where relevant, but the overall focus of this book remains on using SuperCollider to develop creative audio projects.

This book divides into three parts: Part I covers the fundamentals of using the language, expressing ideas through code, writing basic programs, and producing simple sounds. Part II focuses on common practice techniques, including synthesis, sampling, sequencing, signal processing, external controllers, and graphical user interface design. In short, this second part details the "ingredients" that make up a typical project. Part III brings it all together and offers concrete strategies for composing, rehearsing, and performing large-scale projects.

It's hard to overstate the value of hands-on learning, especially for a sound-oriented coding language. To this end, each chapter includes numerous in-line SuperCollider code examples, and each chapter also pairs with one or more "Companion Code" files, which explore chapter topics in significantly greater depth. All of the Code Examples and Companion Codes are hosted on a companion website and referenced in the text with the following icon:

Use these resources! As you read, you'll (hopefully) get the urge to experiment. When you do, download these files, study their contents, and play around with them. These files exist to provide immediate, seamless access, avoiding the need to manually copy code from the book. Learning SuperCollider is a bit like learning a foreign language; reading a textbook is certainly a good idea, but if you want to become fluent, there's no proper substitute for immersing yourself in the language. You'll make some mistakes, but you'll also make important discoveries. It's all part of the learning process!

Before you begin reading, download the SuperCollider software, which (at the time of writing) is available at *supercollider.github.io*. You may also want to visit/bookmark the SuperCollider project page on GitHub (*github.com/supercollider/supercollider*), which includes a wiki, links to tutorials, and many other resources. I recommend working with a quality pair of headphones or loudspeakers, although built-in laptop speakers will work in a pinch. A good quality microphone and audio interface can be useful for exploring topics in Chapter 6, but there's plenty to keep you busy if you don't have access to these things, and a built-in laptop microphone will suffice for basic exploration. A standard MIDI keyboard controller will also be helpful (though not essential) for exploring some of the code examples in Chapters 7–8.

Finally, as you work through this book, keep an open mind and be patient with yourself. There's a lot to learn and it won't happen overnight, but with practice and dedication, you'll find that an amazing new world of sound will begin to reveal itself, which can be an incredibly exciting and liberating experience. Onward!

PART I
FUNDAMENTALS

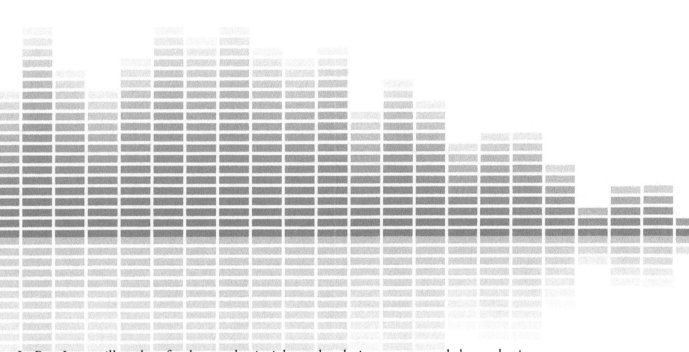

In Part I, we will explore fundamental principles and techniques meant to help you begin using SuperCollider at a basic level. Specifically, after completing these two chapters, you should be able to write simple programs and play simple sounds.

CHAPTER 1

CORE PROGRAMMING CONCEPTS

1.1 Overview

This chapter covers the essentials of programming in SuperCollider, such as navigating the environment, getting acquainted with basic terminology, understanding common data types, making simple operations, and writing/running simple programs. The goal is to become familiar with things you'll encounter on an everyday basis and develop a foundational understanding that will support you through the rest of this book and as you embark on your own SC journey.

Keyboard shortcuts play an important role in SC, as they provide quick access to common actions. Throughout this book, the signifier [cmd] refers to the command key on macOS systems, and the control key on Windows and Linux systems.

1.2 A Tour of the Environment

Before we start dealing with code, a good first step is to understand what we see when opening SC for the first time, as depicted in Figure 1.1.

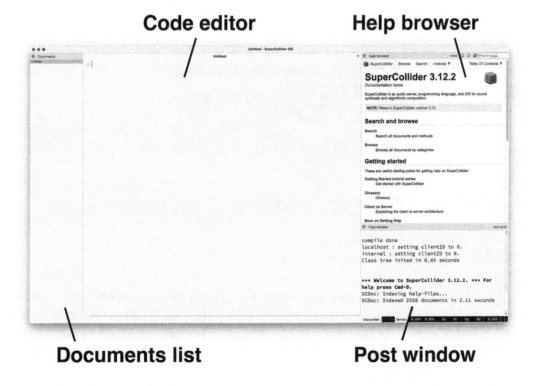

FIGURE 1.1 The SuperCollider environment.

SuperCollider for the Creative Musician. Eli Fieldsteel, Oxford University Press. © Oxford University Press 2024.
DOI: 10.1093/oso/9780197616994.003.0001

The centerpiece of the SC environment is the code editor, a large blank area that serves as your workspace for creating, editing, and executing code. Like a web browser, multiple files can be open simultaneously, selectable using the tab system that appears above the editor. Code files can be saved and loaded as they would be in any text editing or word processing software. SC code files use the file extension "scd" (short for SuperCollider document). The code editor is surrounded by three docklets: the post window, the help browser, and the documents list. The post window is where SC displays information for the user. Most often, this is the result of evaluated code, but may also include error messages and warnings. The help browser provides access to documentation files that detail how SC works. The documents list displays names of files that are currently open, offering a handy navigation option if many documents are open at once. Altogether, these and other features constitute the SC Integrated Development Environment, commonly known as the IDE. The IDE serves as a front-end interface for the user, meant to enhance workflow by providing things like keyboard shortcuts, text colorization, auto-completion, and more. The preferences panel, which is shown in Figure 1.2, is where some of these customizations can be made. The preferences panel is accessible in the "SuperCollider" drop-down menu on macOS, and the "Edit" drop-down menu on Windows/Linux.

FIGURE 1.2 The SuperCollider preferences panel.

The IDE is one of three components that make up the SC environment. In addition, there is the SC language (often called "the language" or "the client") and the SC audio server (often called "the server"). The technical names for these components are *sclang* and *scsynth*, respectively, and despite being integral parts of the environment, they remain largely invisible to the user.

The language is home to a library of objects, which are the basic building blocks of any program. It also houses the interpreter, a core component that interprets and executes code, translating it into action. The interpreter automatically starts when the IDE is launched, and a small status box in the lower-right corner of the IDE displays whether the interpreter is active. SC is an interpreted language, rather than a compiled language. In simple terms, this means that code can be executed selectively and interactively, on a line-by-line basis, rather than having to write the entirety of a program before running it. This is especially useful because SC is regularly used for real-time creative audio applications. In some musical scenarios (improvisation, for example), we won't know all the details in advance, so it's convenient to be able to interact with code "in the moment." This dynamism is featured in examples throughout this book (many of which are broken into separate chunks of code) and is on full display in the last chapter of this book, which discusses live coding.

The audio server is the program that handles calculation, generation, and processing of audio signals. Colloquially, it's the "engine" that powers SC's sound capabilities. It cannot be overstated that the server is fully detached and fundamentally independent from the language and IDE. The language and the server communicate over a network using a client-server model. For example, to play some audio, we first evaluate some code in the language. The language, acting as a client on the network, sends a request to the server, which responds by producing sound. In a sense, this setup is like checking email on a personal computer. An email client gives the impression that your messages are on your own machine, but in reality, you're a client user on a network, sending requests to download information stored on a remote server.

Often, the language and server are running on the same computer, and this "network" is more of an abstract concept than a true network of separate, interconnected devices. However, the client-server design facilitates options involving separate, networked machines. It's possible for an instance of the language on one computer to communicate with an audio server running on a different computer. It's equally possible for multiple clients to communicate with a single server (a common configuration for laptop ensembles), or for one language-side user to communicate with multiple servers. Messages passed between the language and server rely on the Open Sound Control (OSC) protocol, therefore the server can be controlled by any OSC-compliant software.[1] Most modern programming languages and audiovisual environments are OSC-compliant, such as Java, Python, Max/MSP, and Processing, to name a few. Even some digital audio workstations can send and receive OSC. However, using an alternative client doesn't typically provide substantial benefits over the SC language, due to its high-level objects that encapsulate and automatically generate OSC messages. In addition, the client-server divide improves stability; if the client application crashes, the server can play on without interruption while the client is rebooted.

Unlike the interpreter, the server does not automatically start when the IDE is launched and must be manually booted before we can start working with sound, which is the focus of the next chapter. For now, our focus is on the language and the IDE.

1.3 An Object-Oriented View of the World

The SC language is an object-oriented language. Though it's helpful to understand some core principles of object-oriented programming (OOP), a deep dive is not necessary from a musical perspective. This section conveys some essentials of OOP, relying primarily on analogies from the real world, avoiding a more theoretical approach.

1.3.1 OBJECTS AND CLASSES

Our world is full of *objects*, such as plants, animals, buildings, and vehicles. These objects exist within a hierarchy: some objects, like houses, supermarkets, and stadiums, are all members of the same category, or *class* of objects, called buildings. Applying some programming terminology to this example, buildings would be considered the parent class (or superclass) of houses, supermarkets, stadiums, and many others. Similarly, houses, supermarkets, and stadiums are each a child class (or subclass) of buildings. This hierarchy might extend further in either direction: we might have several subclasses of houses (cottages, mansions, etc.), while buildings, vehicles, plants, and animals might be subclasses of an even more all-encompassing superclass named "things." This organizational structure is tree-like, with a few large, broad branches near one end, and many smaller and more specific branches toward the other end.

Like the real world, the SC language is full of objects that exist within a similar class hierarchy, called the *class tree*. Classes of objects in SC include things like Integers, Floats, Strings, Arrays, Functions, Buttons, Sliders, and much more. When represented with code, a class name always begins with a capital letter, which is how SC distinguishes them. If some of these terms are foreign to you, don't worry. We'll introduce them properly later on.

1.3.2 METHODS AND INHERITANCE

Certain types of interactions make sense for certain types of objects. For example, it's reasonable to ask whether an animal is a mammal, but nonsense when applied to a vehicle. On the other hand, some types of queries make sense for all objects, like asking whether something is alive. The point is that a specific type of object "knows" how to respond to certain types of inquiries, to which it responds in a meaningful way. Such queries are called *methods* or *messages*.[2] For example, an integer knows how to respond to being "squared," (multiplied by itself). To a graphical slider, this method is meaningless. Further still, there are some methods that have meaning for both integers and sliders, such as one that asks, "are you an integer?"

If a method is defined for a class, all its subclasses automatically inherit that method and respond to it in a similar manner. It's also possible for the same method to produce different results when applied to different objects (this ability is called *polymorphism*). Consider the verb "to file." Semantically, what this means depends on the object being filed. To file a piece of paper means to organize it in a filing cabinet. To file a piece of metal, on the other hand, means to smooth it by grinding it down. Many examples of polymorphism exist within SC. The "play" method, for instance, is defined for many types of objects, but produces various results that may or may not involve sound production.

1.3.3 CLASSES VS. INSTANCES

There is an important distinction between a tangible object, and the abstract idea of that object. To illustrate, consider a house, compared to a blueprint for a house. The blueprint represents a house and provides a set of instructions for creating one. But it's not the same thing as the house itself. You can't live in a blueprint!

In this example, the blueprint functions similarly to the *class* of houses, while a physical house would be considered an *instance* of that class. You could, for example, use one blueprint to construct many houses. It might even be possible to construct several different houses using the same blueprint, by making a few tweaks to the instructions before each build. Generally, a class can conjure into existence a tangible version of what it represents, but it's usually these instances that we are interested in working with.

1.4 Writing, Understanding, and Evaluating Code

As we begin translating these abstract concepts into concrete code, bear in mind that writing computer code requires precision. Even the most seemingly minor details, like capitalization and spelling, are important. The interpreter will never try to "guess" what you mean if your code is vague or nonsensical. On the contrary, it will attempt to do exactly what you instruct and report errors if it can't comply.

Type the following into the code editor, exactly as it appears:

```
4.squared;
```

Then, making sure your mouse cursor is placed somewhere on this line, press [shift]+[return], which tells the interpreter to execute the current line. You'll see a brief flash of color over the code, and the number 16 will appear in the post window. If this is your first time using SC, congratulations! You've just run your first program. Let's take a step back and dissect what just happened.

1.4.1 A SINGLE LINE OF CODE, DECONSTRUCTED

The expression **4.squared** contains a member of the integer class and the "squared" method, which is defined for integers. We say that four is the *receiver* of the method. The period, in this context, is the symbol that applies the method to the receiver. This "receiver-dot-method" construction is commonly used to perform operations with objects, but there is a syntax alternative that involves placing the receiver in an enclosure of parentheses, immediately following the method:

```
squared(4);
```

Why choose one style over the other? This is ultimately dictated by personal preference and usually governed by readability. For example, an English speaker would probably choose **4.squared** instead of **squared(4)**, because it mimics how the phrase would be spoken.

The parentheses used to contain the receiver are one type of *enclosure* in SC. Others include [square brackets], {curly braces}, "double quotes," and 'single quotes.' Each type of enclosure has its own significance, and some have multiple uses. We'll address enclosures in more detail as they arise, but for now it's important to recognize than an enclosure always involves a pair of symbols: one to begin the enclosure, and another to end it. Sometimes, an enclosure contains only a few characters, while others might contain thousands of lines. If an opening bracket is missing its partner, your code won't run properly, and you'll likely see an error message.

The semicolon is the statement terminator. This symbol tells the interpreter where one expression ends and, possibly, where another begins. Semicolons are the code equivalent of periods and question marks in a novel, which help our brain parse the writing into discrete sentences. In SC, every code statement should always end with a semicolon. Omitting a semicolon is fine when evaluating only a single expression, but omitting a semicolon in a multi-line situation will usually produce an error.

In the case of either **4.squared** or **squared(4)**, the result is the same. On evaluation, the interpreter *returns a value* of 16. Returning a value is not the same thing as printing it in the post window. In fact, the interpreter always posts the value of the last evaluated line, which makes this behavior more of a byproduct of code evaluation than anything else. Returning a value is a deeper, more fundamental concept, which means the interpreter has taken your code and digested it, and is passing the result back to you. We can think of the expression `4.squared` or `squared(4)` as being an equivalent representation of the number 16. As such, we can treat the entire expression as a new receiver and chain additional methods to apply additional operations. For instance, Code Example 1.1 shows how we can take the reciprocal (i.e., one divided by the receiver) of the square of a number, demonstrated using both syntax styles:

CODE EXAMPLE 1.1: COMBINING MULTIPLE METHODS INTO A SINGLE STATEMENT, USING TWO DIFFERENT SYNTAX STYLES.

```
4.squared.reciprocal;

reciprocal(squared(4));
```

Methods chained using the "receiver-dot-method" style are applied from left to right. When using the "method(receiver)" syntax, the flow progresses outward from the innermost set of parentheses.

Unlike `squared` or `reciprocal`, some methods require additional information to return a value. For instance, the `pow` method raises its receiver to the power of some exponent, which the user must provide. Code Example 1.2 shows an expression that returns three to the power of four, using both syntax styles. In this context, we say that four is an *argument* of the pow method. Arguments are a far-reaching concept that we'll explore later in this chapter. For now, think of an argument as an input value needed for some process to work, such as a method call. Attempts to use `pow` without providing the exponent will produce an error. Note that when multiple items appear in an argument enclosure, they must be separated with commas.

CODE EXAMPLE 1.2: A CODE EXPRESSION INVOLVING A RECEIVER, METHOD, AND ARGUMENT, USING TWO DIFFERENT SYNTAX STYLES.

```
3.pow(4);

pow(3, 4);
```

1.4.2 MULTIPLE LINES OF CODE, DECONSTRUCTED

Suppose we continued chaining additional methods to one of the expressions in Code Example 1.1. After several dozen methods, the line would become quite long. It might run over onto a new line and would also become increasingly difficult to read and understand. For this reason, we frequently break up a series of operations into multiple statements, written on separate lines. To do this correctly, we need some way to "capture" a value, so that it can be referenced in subsequent steps.

A *variable* is a named container than can hold any type of object. One way to create a variable is to declare it using a **var** statement. A variable name must begin with a lowercase letter. Following this letter, the name can include uppercase/lowercase letters, numbers, and/or underscores. Table 1.1 contains examples of valid and invalid variable names.

TABLE 1.1 Examples of valid and invalid variable names.

Valid	Invalid
num	Num
myValue	my#$%&Value
sample_04	sample-04

Variable names should be short, but meaningful, striking a balance between brevity and readability. Once a variable is declared, an object can be assigned to a variable using the equals symbol. A typical sequence involves declaring a variable, assigning a value, and then repeatedly modifying the value and assigning each new result to the same variable, overwriting the older assignment in the process. This initially looks strange from a "mathematical" perspective, but the equals symbol doesn't mean numerical equality in this case; instead, it denotes a storage action. In Code Example 1.3, the expression **num = num.squared** could be translated into English as the following command: "Square the value currently stored in the variable named 'num,' and store the result in the same variable, overwriting the old value."

To evaluate a multi-line block, we need to learn a new technique and a new keyboard shortcut. The code in Code Example 1.3 has been wrapped in an enclosure of parentheses, each on its own line above and below. Here, we're already seeing that a parenthetical enclosure serves multiple purposes. In this case, it delineates a multi-line block: a modular unit that can be passed to the interpreter with a single keystroke. Instead of pressing [shift]+[return], place the cursor anywhere inside the enclosure and press [cmd]+[return].

CODE EXAMPLE 1.3: A MULTI-LINE BLOCK OF CODE.

```
(
var num;
num = 4;
num = num.squared;
num = num.reciprocal;
)
```

> ### TIP.RAND(); EVALUATING CODE
>
> Using the correct technique and keystroke for evaluating code can be a common point of confusion for new users. Even if your code is written correctly, misevaluation will produce errors that suggest otherwise, because it causes the interpreter to "see" your code incorrectly. Remember that there are two keyboard shortcuts for evaluating code: [shift]+[return] and [cmd]+[return]. Their behavior depends on the following conditions:
>
> - If any code is highlighted:
>   - either [cmd]+[return] or [shift]+[return] will evaluate the highlighted code.
> - If no code is selected, and the cursor is inside a multi-line block enclosure:
>   - [cmd]+[return] will evaluate the entire block.
>   - [shift]+[return] will evaluate the line on which the cursor is placed.
> - If no code is selected, and the cursor is not inside a multi-line block enclosure:
>   - either [cmd]+[return] or [shift]+[return] will evaluate the line on which the cursor is placed.
>
> Also note that in this context, the presence of return characters (rather than semicolons) determines what constitutes a "line" of code. For example, despite containing multiple statements, the following example is considered a single line, so either [cmd]+[return] or [shift]+[return] will evaluate it:
>
> ```
> var num; num = 4; num = num.squared; num = num.reciprocal;
> ```
>
> Conversely, the following example is considered to occupy multiple lines, despite containing only one statement. Thus, [shift]+[return] will not work unless the entire example is highlighted, and [cmd]+[return] will not work unless contained in a parenthetical enclosure.
>
> ```
> 4
> .squared;
> ```

Variables declared using a **var** statement are *local variables*; they are local to the evaluated code of which they are a part. This means that once evaluation is complete, variables created in this way will no longer exist. If you later attempt to evaluate **num** by itself, you'll find that it not only has lost its value assignment, but also produces an error indicating that the variable is undefined. Local variables are transient. They are useful for context-specific cases where there's no need to retain the variable beyond its initial scope.

If we need several local variables, they can be combined into a single declaration. They can also be given value assignments during declaration. Code Example 1.4 declares three variables and provides initial assignments to the first two. We square the first variable, take the reciprocal of the second, and return the sum, which is 49.2.

CODE EXAMPLE 1.4: A MULTI-LINE CODE BLOCK THAT DECLARES MULTIPLE LOCAL VARIABLES AND PROVIDES DEFAULT ASSIGNMENTS.

```
(
var thingA = 7, thingB = 5, result;
thingA = thingA.squared;
thingB = thingB.reciprocal;
result = thingA + thingB;
)
```

TIP.RAND(); NEGATIVE NUMBERS AS DEFAULT VARIABLE ASSIGNMENTS

If a variable is given a negative default value during declaration, there's a potential pitfall. The negative value must either be in parentheses or have a space between it and the preceding equals symbol. If the equals symbol and the minus symbol are directly adjacent, SC will mistakenly interpret the pair of symbols as an undefined operation. This same rule applies to a declaration of arguments, introduced in the next section. Of the following three expressions, the first two are valid, but the third will fail.

```
var num = -2;

var num =(-2);

var num =-2;
```

What if we want to retain a variable, to be used again in the future as part of a separate code evaluation? We can use an *environment variable*, created by preceding the variable name with a tilde character (~). Alternatively, we can use one of the twenty-six lowercase alphabetic characters, which are reserved as *interpreter variables*. Both environment and interpreter variables can be used without a local declaration, and both behave with global scope, that is, they will retain their value (even across multiple code documents) as long as the interpreter remains active. Interpreter variables are of limited use, since there are only twenty-six of them and they cannot have longer, more meaningful names. But they are convenient for bypassing declaration when sketching out an idea or quickly testing something. Environment variables are generally more useful because we can customize their names. The two blocks of code in Code Example 1.5 are each equivalent to the code in Code Example 1.3, but in either case, the variable will retain its assignment after evaluation is complete.

CODE EXAMPLE 1.5: USAGE OF INTERPRETER AND ENVIRONMENT VARIABLES (RESPECTIVELY).

```
(
n = 4;
n = n.squared;
n = n.reciprocal;
)

(
~num = 4;
~num = ~num.squared;
~num = ~num.reciprocal;
)
```

1.4.3 POSTING A VALUE

The `postln` method has the effect of printing its receiver to the post window, followed by a new line. This method simply returns its receiver, so it is "neutral" in the sense that it does not modify the object to which it applies. This method is useful for visualizing values partway through a multi-line block, perhaps to check for correctness. On evaluating the code in Code Example 1.6, we will see the value 16 appear in the post window (the result of `postln`), followed by 0.0625 (the result of the interpreter posting the result of the last evaluated line).

CODE EXAMPLE 1.6: USE OF THE `postln` METHOD.

```
(
~num = 4;
~num = ~num.squared.postln;
~num = ~num.reciprocal;
)
```

1.4.4 COMMENTS

A comment is text that the interpreter ignores. Comments are typically included to provide some information for a human reader. The imagined reader might be someone else, like a friend or collaborator, but it also might be you! Leaving notes for yourself is a good way to jog your memory if you take a long break from a project and don't quite remember where you left off.

There are two ways to designate text as a comment. For short comments, preceding text with two forward slashes will "comment out" the text until the next return character. To create larger comments that include multiple lines of text, we enclose the text in another type of enclosure, beginning with a forward slash–asterisk, and ending with an asterisk–forward slash. These styles are depicted in Code Example 1.7.

CODE EXAMPLE 1.7: USAGE OF TWO DIFFERENT COMMENT STYLES.

```
(
/*
this is a multi-line comment, which might
be used at the top of your code in order
to explain some features of your program.
*/
var num = 4; // a single-line comment: declare a variable
num = num.squared;
num = num.reciprocal;
)
```

1.4.5 WHITESPACE

Whitespace refers to the use of "empty space" characters, like spaces and new lines. Generally, SC is indifferent to whitespace. For example, both of the following statements are considered syntactically valid and will produce the same result:

```
4.squared+2;
```

```
4 . squared + 2;
```

The use of whitespace is ultimately a matter of taste, but a consensus among programmers seems to be that there is a balance to be struck. Using too little whitespace cramps your code and doesn't provide enough room for it to "breathe." Too much whitespace, and code spreads out to the point of being similarly difficult to read. The whitespace choices made throughout this book are based on personal preference and years of studying other programmers' code.

1.5 Getting Help

The IDE includes resources for getting help on a number of topics. This section focuses on accessing and navigating these resources.

1.5.1 THE HELP BROWSER

The help browser is the primary resource for getting help within the IDE. It provides access to all of SC's documentation, which includes overviews, reference files, guides, a few tutorials, and individual help files for every object.[3] It includes a search feature, as well as browse option for exploring the documentation by category. It's a good idea to spend some time browsing to get a sense of what's there. Keep in mind that the documentation is not structured as a comprehensive, logically sequenced tutorial (if it were, there'd be less need for books such as this); rather, it tends to be more useful as a quick reference for checking some specific detail.

There are two keystrokes for quickly accessing a page in the help browser: [cmd]+[d] will perform a search for the class or method indicated by the current location of the mouse cursor, and [shift]+[cmd]+[d] invokes a pop-up search field for querying a specific term. If there is an exact class match for your query (capitalization matters), that class's help file will appear. If not, the browser will display a list of results that it thinks are good matches. Try it yourself! Type "Integer" into the editor, and press [cmd]+[d] to bring up the associated help file.

The structure of a class help file appears in Figure 1.3. In general, these files each begin with the class name, along with its superclass lineage, a summary of the class, and a handful of related classes and topics. Following this, the help file includes a detailed description, class methods, instance methods, and often some examples that can be run directly in the browser and/or copied into the text editor.

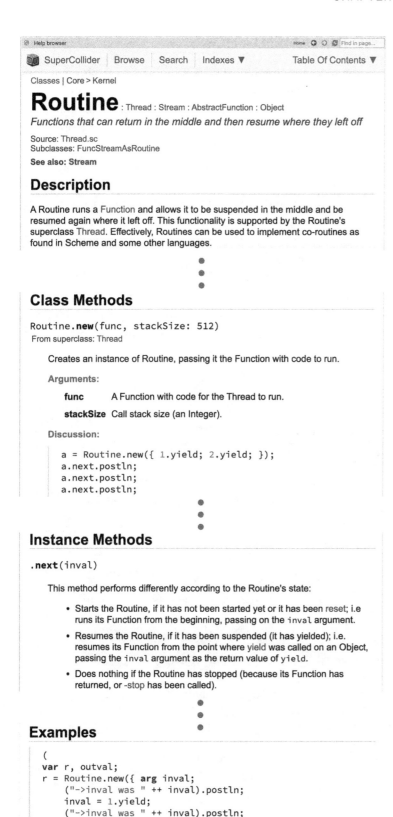

FIGURE 1.3 The structure of a class help file. Vertical ellipses represent material omitted for clarity and conciseness.

1.5.2 SEARCHING FOR IMPLEMENTATIONS

The help browser is the primary resource for new users, but as you get more comfortable with SC, you may want to look directly at the source code for a class or method. Additionally, because SC is an open-source project in active development, there are cases where the content of a help file may not be completely consistent with the behavior of the object it describes. The source code, on the other hand, lets us see exactly how something works.

There are two keystrokes for looking up implementations of class or method: [cmd]+[i] will perform a search for all the source code implementations of the class or method indicated by the current location of the mouse cursor, and [shift]+[cmd]+[i] will bring up a search bar. When you enter your search term, a list of source code files in which that term appears will populate a list (see Figure 1.4). Selecting one will open the source file and automatically scroll to the relevant spot. Just be sure not to edit anything!

To try this yourself, press [shift]+[cmd]+[i], type "play" in the search bar, and press enter to see a list of classes that implement this method. Click one of these items and press enter to open the source code for that class. If the source code looks totally incomprehensible to you, don't worry! Being able to read these files isn't essential, but as you get more comfortable with SC, you may find yourself digging around in these files more often.

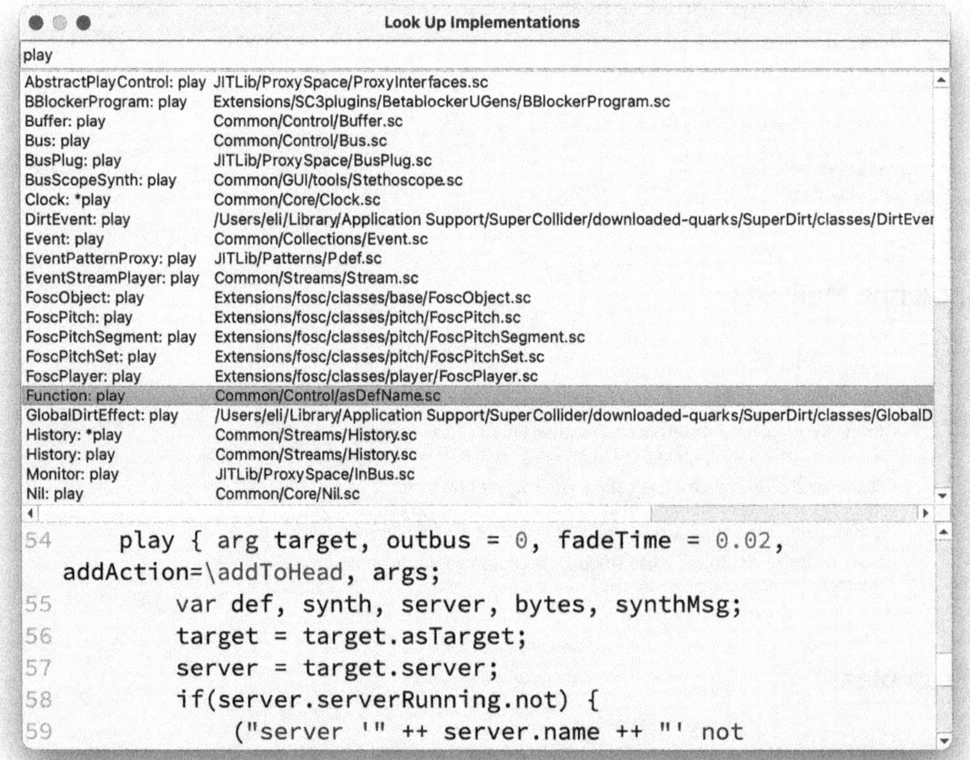

FIGURE 1.4 The search window for looking up implementations of methods.

1.5.3 THE CLASS BROWSER

The class browser is a graphical tool for browsing the class tree. The **browse** method can be applied to any class name (e.g. **Array.browse**), which invokes the browser and displays information for that class. The class browser, shown in Figure 1.5, displays a class's superclass, subclasses, methods, and arguments. Buttons near the top of the browser can be used for navigating backward and forward (like a web browser), as well as navigating to a class's superclass, or bringing up source code files. You can also navigate to a subclass by double-clicking it in the list in the bottom-left corner.

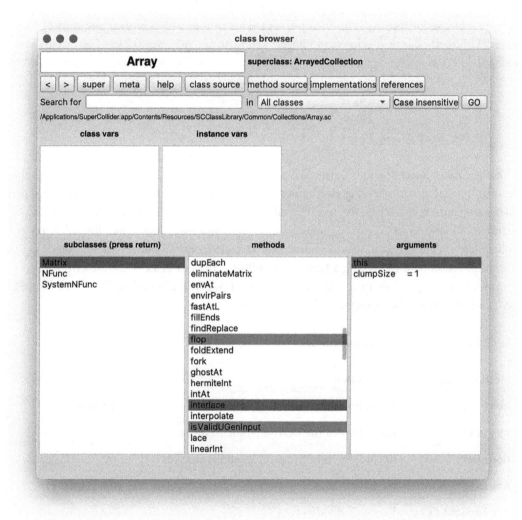

FIGURE 1.5 The class browser.

1.6 A Tour of Classes and Methods

With a basic understanding of writing and evaluating code behind us, we're ready to take a more detailed look at some commonly used classes and methods, to get a better sense of the operations we're likely to regularly encounter.

1.6.1 INTEGERS AND FLOATS

The **Integer** and **Float** classes represent numerical values. We've already encountered integers, which are whole numbers that can be positive, negative, or zero. A float, on the other hand, is a number that includes a decimal point, like 9.02 and -315.67. Even the number 1.0 is a float, despite being quantitatively equal to one. Some programming languages are quite particular about the distinction between integers and floats, balking at certain operations that attempt to combine them, but SC is flexible, and will typically convert automatically as needed. Integers and floats are closely related on the class tree and therefore share many methods, but there are a few methods which apply to one and not the other.

We'll begin our tour by introducing the **class** method, which returns the class of its receiver. This method is not exclusive to integers and floats; in fact, every object knows how to respond to it! However, it's relevant here in showing the classes to which different numbers belong.

```
4.class; // -> Integer

4.0.class; // -> Float
```

There are many methods that perform mathematical operations with numbers. Those that perform an operation involving two values are called *binary operators*, while those that perform an operation on a single receiver, like taking the square root of a number, are called *unary operators*. Most operations exist as method calls (e.g., **squared**), but some, like addition and multiplication, are so commonly used that they have a direct symbolic representation (imagine if multiplication required typing **12.multipliedBy(3)** instead of **12 * 3**). Descriptive lists of commonly used operators appear in Tables 1.2 and 1.3. A more complete list can be found in a SC overview file titled "Operators."

TABLE 1.2 List of common unary operators.

Method Usage	Description
abs(x);	Absolute value. Non-negative value of *x*, i.e., distance from zero.
ceil(x);	Round up to the nearest whole number.
floor(x);	Round down to the nearest whole number.
neg(x);	Negation. Positive numbers become negative and vice-versa.
reciprocal(x);	Return 1 divided by *x*.
sqrt(x);	Return the square root of *x*.
squared(x);	Return *x* raised to the power of 2.

TABLE 1.3 List of common binary operators.

Name	Method Usage	Symbolic Usage	Description
Addition	N/A	**x + y;**	
Subtraction	N/A	**x - y;**	

TABLE 1.3 Continued.

Name	Method Usage	Symbolic Usage	Description
Multiplication	N/A	x * y;	
Division	N/A	x / y;	
Exponentiation	x.pow(y);	x ** y;	Return *x* raised to the power of *y*.
Modulo	x.mod(y);	x % y;	Return the remainder of *x* divided by *y*.
Rounding	x.round(y);	N/A	Return *x* rounded to the nearest multiple of *y*.

"Order of operations" refers to rules governing the sequence in which operations should be performed. In grade school, for example, we typically learn that in the expression 4 + 2 * 3, multiplication should happen first, and then addition. SC has its own rules for order of operations, which may surprise you. If an expression includes multiple symbolic operators, SC will apply them from left-to-right, without any precedence given to any operation. If an expression includes a combination of method calls and symbolic operators, SC will apply the method calls first, and then the symbolic operators from left-to-right. Parenthetical enclosures have precedence over method calls and symbolic operators (see Code Example 1.8). In some cases, it can be good practice to use parentheses, even when unnecessary, to provide clarity for readers.

> **CODE EXAMPLE 1.8. EXAMPLES OF HOW PRECEDENCE IS APPLIED TO COMBINATIONS OF METHODS, SYMBOLIC BINARY OPERATORS, AND PARENTHETICAL ENCLOSURES.**
>
> ```
> // symbolic operators have equal precedence, applied left-to-right:
> 4 + 2 * 3; // -> 18
>
> // parentheses have precedence over symbolic operators:
> 4 + (2 * 3); // -> 10
>
> // methods have precedence over symbolic operators:
> 4 + 2.pow(3); // -> 12
>
> // parentheses have precedence over methods:
> (4 + 2).pow(3); // -> 216
>
> // parentheses first, then methods, then binary operators:
> 1 + (4 + 2).pow(3); // -> 217
> ```

1.6.2 STRINGS

A string is an ordered sequence of characters, delineated by an enclosure of double quotes. A string can contain any text, including letters, numbers, symbols, and even non-printing characters like tabs and new lines. Strings are commonly used to represent text and may be used to provide names or labels for certain types of objects. Several examples appear in Code Example 1.9.

Certain characters need special treatment when they appear inside a string. For example, what if we want to put a double quotation mark inside of a string? If not done correctly, the internal quotation mark will prematurely terminate the string, likely causing the interpreter to report a syntax error. Special characters are entered by preceding them with a backslash, which in this context is called the *escape character*. Its name refers to the effect it has on the interpreter, causing it to "escape" the character's normal meaning.

CODE EXAMPLE 1.9: EXAMPLES OF STRINGS AND USAGE OF THE ESCAPE CHARACTER.

```
// a typical string
"Click the green button to start.";

// using the escape character to include quotation marks
"The phrase \"practice makes perfect\" is one I try to remember.";

// using the escape character to include new lines
"This string\nwill print on\nmultiple lines.";
```

We know the plus symbol denotes addition for integers and floats, but it also has meaning for strings (the usage of one symbol for multiple purposes is called *overloading* and is another example of polymorphism). A single plus will return a single string from two strings, inserting a space character between them. A double plus does nearly the same thing but omits the space. These and a handful of other string methods appear in Code Example 1.10.

CODE EXAMPLE 1.10: COMMON STRING METHODS AND OPERATIONS.

```
"Hello" + "there!"; // -> "Hello there!"

"Some" ++ "times"; // -> "Sometimes"

"I'm a string.".size; // return the number of characters in the string

"I'm a string.".reverse; // reverse the order of the characters

"I'm a string.".scramble; // randomize the order of the characters

"I'm a string.".drop(2); // remove the first two characters

"I'm a string.".drop(-2); // remove the last two characters
```

1.6.3 SYMBOLS

A symbol is like a string, in that it's composed of a sequence of characters and commonly used to name or label things. Where a string is used, a symbol can often be substituted, and vice-versa. A symbol is written in one of two ways: by preceding the sequence of characters with a backslash (e.g., **\freq**), or by enclosing it in single quotes (e.g., **'freq'**). These styles are largely interchangeable, but the quote enclosure is the safer option of the two. Symbols that begin with or include certain characters will trigger syntax errors if using the backslash style. Unlike a string, a symbol is an irreducible unit; it is not possible to access or manipulate the individual characters in a symbol, and all symbols return zero in response to the **size** method. It is, however, possible to convert back and forth between symbols and strings using the methods **asSymbol** and **asString** (see Code Example 1.11). Symbols, being slightly more optimized than strings, are the preferable choice when used as names or labels for objects.

CODE EXAMPLE 1.11: CONVERSION FROM STRING TO SYMBOL AND VICE-VERSA.

```
"hello".asSymbol.class; // -> Symbol

\hello.asString.class; // -> String
```

1.6.4 BOOLEANS

There are exactly two instances of the Boolean class: **true** and **false**. These values are special keywords, meaning we can't use either as a variable name. If you type one of these keywords into the code editor, you'll notice its text will change color to indicate its significance. Booleans play a significant role in conditional logic, explored later in this chapter.

Throughout SC, there are methods and binary operators that represent true-or-false questions, and which return a Boolean value that represents the answer. These include less-than/greater-than operations, and various methods that begin with the word "is" (e.g., **isInteger**, **isEmpty**), which check whether some condition is met. Some examples appear in Code Example 1.12, and a list of common binary operators that return Booleans appears in Table 1.4.

CODE EXAMPLE 1.12: EXAMPLES OF CODE EXPRESSIONS THAT RETURN BOOLEAN VALUES.

```
1 < 2; // -> true

1 > 2; // -> false

1.isInteger; // -> true

1.0.isInteger; // -> false

"hello".isEmpty; // -> false

"".isEmpty; // -> true
```

TABLE 1.4 Common binary operators that return Boolean values.

Symbolic Usage	Description
x == y	Return **true** if *x* and *y* are equal, **false** otherwise.
x != y	Return **true** if *x* and *y* are not equal, **false** otherwise.
x > y	Return **true** if *x* is greater than *y*, **false** otherwise.
x < y	Return **true** if *x* is less than *y*, **false** otherwise.
x >= y	Return **true** is *x* is greater than or equal to *y*, **false** otherwise.
x <= y	Return **true** is *x* is less than or equal to *y*, **false** otherwise.

1.6.5 NIL

Like true and false, **nil** is a reserved keyword in the SC language, and is the singular instance of the **Nil** class. Most commonly, it represents the value of a variable that hasn't been given a value assignment, or something that doesn't exist. We rarely use nil explicitly, but it shows up frequently, so it's helpful to be familiar. The **isNil** method, demonstrated in Code Example 1.13, can be useful for confirming whether a variable has a value (attempting to call methods on an uninitialized variable is a common source of error messages).

CODE EXAMPLE 1.13: USAGE OF THE isNil METHOD.

```
(
var num;
num.isNil.postln; // check the variable — initially, it's nil
num = 2; // make an assignment
num.isNil.postln; // check again — it's no longer nil
)
```

1.6.6 ARRAYS

An array is an ordered collection of objects. Syntactically, objects stored in an array are separated by commas and surrounded by an enclosure of square brackets. Arrays are like strings in that both are ordered lists, but while strings can only contain text characters, an array can contain anything. In fact, arrays can (and often do) contain other arrays. Arrays are among the most frequently used objects, because they allow us to express an arbitrarily large collection as a singular unit. Arrays have lots of musical applications; we might use one to contain pitch information for a musical scale, a sequence of rhythmic values, and so on.

As shown in Code Example 1.14, we can access an item stored in an array by using the **at** method and providing the numerical index. Indices begin at zero. As an alternative, we can follow an array with a square bracket enclosure containing the desired index.

> **CODE EXAMPLE 1.14: ACCESSING ITEMS STORED IN AN ARRAY.**
>
> ```
> x = [4, "freq", \note, 7.5, true];
>
> x.at(3); // -> 7.5 (return the item stored at index 3)
>
> x[3]; // alternate syntax
> ```

Most unary and binary operators defined for numbers can also be applied to arrays, if they contain numbers. Several examples appear in Code Example 1.15. If we apply a binary operator to a number and an array, the operation is applied to the number and each item in the array, and the new array is returned. A binary operation between two arrays of the same size returns a new array of the same size in which the binary operation has been applied to each pair of items. If the arrays are different sizes, the operation is applied to corresponding pairs of items, but the smaller array will repeat itself as many times as needed to accommodate the larger array (this behavior is called "wrapping").

> **CODE EXAMPLE 1.15: BEHAVIOR OF ARRAYS IN RESPONSE TO COMMON UNARY AND BINARY OPERATIONS.**
>
> ```
> [50, 60, 70].squared;      // -> [2500, 3600, 4900]
>
> 1 + [50, 60, 70];          // -> [51, 61, 71]
>
> [1, 2, 3] + [50, 60, 70];  // -> [51, 62, 73]
>
> [1, 2] + [50, 60, 70];     // -> [51, 62, 71]
> ```

The **dup** method, defined for all objects, returns an array of copies of its receiver. An integer, provided as an argument, determines the size of the array. The exclamation mark can also be used as a symbolic shortcut (see Code Example 1.16).

> **CODE EXAMPLE 1.16: USAGE OF dup AND ITS SYMBOLIC SHORTCUT, THE EXCLAMATION MARK.**
>
> ```
> 7.dup; // -> [7, 7] (default size is 2)
>
> 7.dup(4); // -> [7, 7, 7, 7]
>
> 7 ! 4; // -> [7, 7, 7, 7] (alternate syntax)
> ```

Arrays are a must-learn feature, rich with many convenient methods and uses—too many to squeeze into this section. Companion Code 1.1 provides an array "cheat sheet," covering many of these uses.

1.6.7 FUNCTIONS

We'll inevitably write some small program that performs a useful task, like creating chords from pitches or converting metric values to durations. Whatever this code does, we certainly don't want to be burdened with copying and pasting it all over our file—or worse, typing it out multiple times—because this consumes time and space. Functions address this problem by encapsulating some code and allowing us to reuse it easily and concisely. Functions are especially valuable in that they provide an option for modularizing code, that is, expressing a large program as smaller, independent code units, rather than having to deal with one big messy file. A modular program is generally easier to read, understand, and debug.

A function is delineated by an enclosure of curly braces. If you type the function that appears in Code Example 1.17 from top to bottom, you'll notice the IDE will automatically indent the enclosed code to improve readability. If you write your code in an unusual order, the auto-indent feature may not work as expected, but you can always highlight your code and press the [tab] key to invoke the auto-indentation feature. Once a function is defined, we can evaluate it with **value**, or by following it with a period and a parenthetical enclosure. When evaluated, a function returns the value of the last expression it contains.

CODE EXAMPLE 1.17: DEFINING AND EVALUATING A FUNCTION.

```
(
f = {
    var num = 4;
    num = num.squared;
    num = num.reciprocal;
};
)

f.value; // -> 0.0625

f.(); // alternate syntax for evaluating
```

The function in Code Example 1.17 is not particularly useful, because it produces the same result every time. Usually, we want a function whose output depends on some user-provided input. For instance, suppose we want our function to square and take the reciprocal of an arbitrary value.

We've already seen similar behavior with **pow** (which is, itself, a sort of function). We provide the exponent as an argument, which influences the returned value. So, in our function, we can declare an argument of our own using an **arg** statement. Like a variable, an argument is a named container that holds a value, but which also serves as an input to a function, allowing a user-specified value to be "passed in" at the moment of execution. If no value is provided at execution time, the default value of the argument (defined in the declaration) will be used. Providing default values for arguments is not required, but often a good idea.

CODE EXAMPLE 1.18: DEFINING AND EVALUATING A FUNCTION WITH AN ARGUMENT.

```
(
f = {
    arg input = 4;
    var num;
    num = input.squared;
    num = num.reciprocal;
};
)

f.(5); // -> 0.04 (evaluate, passing in a different value as the input)

f.(); // -> 0.0625 (evaluate using the default value)
```

Code Example 1.19 shows a syntax alternative that replaces the **arg** keyword with an enclosure of vertical bar characters (sometimes called "pipes") and declares multiple arguments, converting the code from Code Example 1.4 into a function. When executing a function with multiple arguments, the argument values must be separated by commas, and will be interpreted in the same order as they appear in the declaration.

CODE EXAMPLE 1.19: DEFINING AND EVALUATING A FUNCTION WITH MULTIPLE ARGUMENTS, DECLARED USING THE "PIPE" SYNTAX.

```
(
g = { |thingA = 7, thingB = 5|
    var result;
    thingA = thingA.squared;
    thingB = thingB.reciprocal;
    result = thingA + thingB;
};
)

g.(3, 2); // -> 9.5 (thingA = 3, thingB = 2);
```

> **TIP.RAND(); ARGUMENTS AND VARIABLES**
>
> New users may wonder about precise differences between arguments and variables, and what "rules" might apply. In some respects, they're similar: each is a named container that holds a value. Variables are ordinary, named containers that provide the convenience of storing and referencing data. An argument, on the other hand, can only be declared at the very beginning of a function, and serves the specific purpose of allowing some input that can be passed or routed into the function during execution. Variable declarations can only occur at the beginning of a parenthetically enclosed multi-line code block, or at the beginning of a function. If a function declares arguments and variables, the argument declaration must come first. It's not possible to spontaneously declare additional variables or arguments somewhere in the middle of your code.

1.6.8 GETTING AND SETTING ATTRIBUTES

Objects have attributes. As a simplified real-world example, a car has a color, a number of doors, a transmission that may be manual or automatic, etc. In SC, we interact with an object's attributes by applying methods to that object. Retrieving an attribute is called *getting*, and changing an attribute is called *setting*. To get an attribute, we simply call the method that returns the value of that attribute. For setting an attribute, there are two options: we can follow the getter method with an equals symbol to assign a new value to it, or we can follow the getter method with an underscore and the new value enclosed in parentheses. The following pseudo-code demonstrates essential syntax styles for getting and setting, which reappear throughout this book. Note that an advantage of the underscore syntax is that it allows us to chain multiple setter calls into a single expression.

```
x = Car.new; // make a new car

x.color = "red"; // set the color

x.numDoors_(4).transmission_("manual"); // set two more attributes

x.numDoors; // get the number of doors (returns 4)
```

1.6.9 LITERALS

In Section 1.3.3, we compared a house to a blueprint of a house to better understand the conceptual difference between classes and instances. If this example were translated into SC code, it might look something like this:

```
x = House.new(30, 40); // create a house with specific dimensions

x.color_("blue"); // set the color

x.hasGarage_(true); // set whether it has a garage
```

In this imaginary example, we make a new house, paint it blue, and add a garage. This general workflow—creating a new thing, storing it in a variable, and interacting with it through instance methods—is quite common. In fact, most of the objects we'll introduce from this point forward will involve a workflow that follows this basic pattern. We won't necessarily use **new** in every case (some classes expect different creation methods), but the general idea is the same.

Interestingly, we haven't been using this workflow for the classes introduced in this section. For example, we don't have to type **Float.new(5.2)** or **Symbol.new(\freq)**. Instead, we just type the object as is. Classes like these, which have a direct, syntactical representation through code, are called *literals*. When we type the number seven, it is literally the number seven. But an object like a house can't be directly represented with code; there is no "house" symbol in our standard character set. So, we must use the more abstract approach of typing **x = House.new**, while its literal representation remains in our imagination.

Integers, floats, strings, symbols, Booleans, and functions are all examples of literals. Arrays, for the record, exist in more of a grey area; they have a direct representation via square brackets, but we may sometimes create one with **Array.new** or a related method. There is also a distinction between literal arrays and non-literal arrays, but which is not relevant to our current discussion. The point is that many of the objects we'll encounter in this book are not literals and require creation via some method call to their class.

> ### TIP.RAND(); OMITTING THE "NEW" METHOD
>
> The **new** method is so commonly used for creating new instances of classes that we can usually omit it, and the interpreter will make the right assumption. For example, using our imaginary "house" class, we could write **x = House(30, 40)** instead of **x = House.new(30, 40)**. However, if creating a new instance without providing any arguments, we can omit **new** but cannot omit the parentheses, even if they are empty. For example, **x = House.new()** and **x = House()** are both valid, but **x = House** will be problematic. In this third case, the interpreter will store the house class, instead of a new house instance.

1.7 Randomness

Programming languages are quite good at generating randomness. Well, not exactly—programming languages are good at producing behavior that humans find convincingly random. Most random algorithms are pseudo-random; they begin with a "seed" value, which fuels a deterministic supply of numbers that feel acceptably random. Regardless of how they're generated, random values can be useful in musical applications. We can, for example, spawn random melodies from a scale, shuffle metric values to create rhythmic variations, or randomize the stereophonic position of a sound.

1.7.1 PICKING FROM A RANGE

The **rrand** method (short for "ranged random") returns a random value between a minimum and maximum, with a uniform distribution, meaning every value in the range is equally likely to appear. If the minimum and maximum are integers, the result will be an integer. If either boundary is a float, the result will be a float. The **exprand** method also returns a value within a range, but approximates an exponential distribution, which means that on average, the output values will tend toward the minimum. This method always returns a float, and the minimum and maximum value must have the same sign (both positive or both negative, and neither can be zero). These methods are demonstrated in Code Example 1.20. This book favors the "method(receiver)" syntax for these methods because it highlights their ranged nature more clearly.

CODE EXAMPLE 1.20: RETURNING A RANDOM NUMBER FROM A RANGE.

```
rrand(1, 9);            // random integer between 1 - 9,
                        // uniform distribution

rrand(40.0, 90.0);      // random float between 40 - 90,
                        // uniform distribution

exprand(1, 100);        // random float between 1 - 100,
                        // exponential distribution
```

Which of these two methods should you use? It depends on what the output will be used for. A dice roll or coin flip, in which all outcomes are equally probable, can be accurately simulated with **rrand**. However, our ears perceive certain musical parameters nonlinearly, such as frequency and amplitude. Therefore, using a uniform distribution to generate values for these parameters may produce a result that sounds unbalanced. Consider, for example, generating a random frequency between 20 and 20,000 Hz. If using **rrand**, then the output will fall in the upper half of this range about half the time, (between approximately 10,000 and 20,000 Hz). This may seem like a wide range, but from a musical perspective, it's only one octave, and a very high-pitched octave at that! The other half of this range spans approximately 9 octaves, so the sonic result would appear saturated with high frequencies, while truly low frequencies would be rare. By contrast, **exprand** would provide a more natural-sounding distribution. So, don't just pick one of these two methods at random (no pun intended)! Instead, think about how the values will be used, and make an informed decision.

1.7.2 RANDOMLY PICKING FROM A COLLECTION

We sometimes want to select a random value from a collection, instead of a range. If the possible outcomes are stored in an array, we can use **choose** to return one of them (see Code Example 1.21). This method doesn't remove the item from the collection; it simply reports a selection while leaving the collection unaltered.

CODE EXAMPLE 1.21: SELECTING A RANDOM ITEM FROM A COLLECTION.

```
(
var scale, note;
scale = [0, 2, 4, 5, 7, 9, 11, 12];
note = scale.choose;
)
```

Suppose we have a bag of 1,000 marbles. 750 are red, 220 are green, and 30 are blue. How would we simulate picking a random marble? We could create an array of 1,000 symbols and use **choose**, but this is clumsy. Instead, we can use **wchoose** to simulate a weighted choice, shown in Code Example 1.22. This method requires an array of weight values, which must sum to one and be the same size as the collection we're choosing from. To avoid doing the math in our heads, we can use **normalizeSum**, which scales the weights so that they sum to one, while keeping their relative proportions intact.

CODE EXAMPLE 1.22: WEIGHTED RANDOMNESS.

```
(
var bag, pick;
bag = [\red, \green, \blue];
pick = bag.wchoose([750, 220, 30].normalizeSum);
)
```

1.7.3 GENERATING AN ARRAY OF RANDOM VALUES

As we've seen, **dup** returns an array of copies of its receiver and can be used to generate an array of random values. However, there is a catch: if we simply call **dup** on a method that generates a random choice, it will duplicate the result of that random choice. The workaround involves enclosing the random generator in curly braces—thus creating a function—and then duplicating that function. This works because the behavior of **dup** is slightly different when applied to a function. Instead of merely duplicating the function, **dup** will duplicate and evaluate each function copy it creates. Therefore, the random process will be performed once for each item that populates the returned array.

CODE EXAMPLE 1.23: USAGE OF dup WITH METHODS THAT GENERATE RANDOMNESS.

```
rrand(40, 90).dup(8); // 8 copies of 1 random value

{rrand(40, 90)}.dup(8); // 8 uniquely chosen random values
```

1.8 Conditional Logic

Life is full of choices based on certain conditions. If it's a nice day, I'll ride my bike to work. If ice cream is on sale, I'll buy two. In computer programming, conditional logic refers to mechanisms used for similar decision-making, with many possible musical applications. For example, if a section of a piece of music has been playing for at least three minutes, transition to the next section. If the amplitude of a sound is too high, reduce it. This section focuses on expressions of the form "if-then-else," which tend to be relatively common. Other conditional mechanisms are documented in a reference file called "Control Structures."

1.8.1 IF

One of the most common conditional methods is **if**, which includes three components: (1) an expression that represents the test condition, which must return a Boolean value, (2) a function to be evaluated if the condition is true, and (3) an optional function to be evaluated if false. Code Example 1.24 demonstrates the use of conditional logic to model a coin flip (a value of 1 represents "heads"), in three styles that vary in syntax and whitespace. The second style tends to be preferable to the first, because it places the "if" at the beginning of the expression, mirroring how the sentence it represents would be spoken in English. Because the entire expression is somewhat long, the multi-line approach can improve readability. Note that in the first expression, the parentheses around the test condition are required to give precedence to the binary operator **==** over the **if** method. Without parentheses, the **if** method is applied to the number 1 instead of the full Boolean expression, which produces an error.

CODE EXAMPLE 1.24: USAGE OF if TO MODEL A COIN FLIP.

```
// "receiver-dot-method" syntax:
([0, 1].choose == 1).if({\heads.postln}, {\tails.postln});

// "method(receiver)" syntax:
if([0, 1].choose == 1, {\heads.postln}, {\tails.postln});

// structured as a multi-line block:
(
if(
    [0, 1].choose == 1,
    {\heads.postln},
    {\tails.postln}
);
)
```

1.8.2 AND/OR

The methods **and** and **or** (representable using binary operators **&&** and **||**), allow us to check multiple conditions. For example, if ice cream is on sale, and they have chocolate, then I'll buy two. Code Example 1.25 models a two-coin flip in which both must be "heads" for the result to be considered true. Again, parentheses around each conditional test are required to ensure correct order of operations.

CODE EXAMPLE 1.25: USAGE OF THE BINARY OPERATOR && TO MODEL A TWO-COIN FLIP.

```
(
if(
    ([0, 1].choose == 1) && ([0, 1].choose == 1),
    {"both heads".postln},
    {"at least one tails".postln}
);
)
```

1.8.3 CASE AND SWITCH

Say we roll a six-sided die and want to perform one of six unique actions depending on the outcome. A single **if** statement is insufficient because it envisions only two outcomes. If we insisted on using **if**, we'd need to "nest" several **if**'s inside of each other. Even with a small handful of possible outcomes, the code quickly spirals into an unreadable mess. Alternatively, a **case** statement (see Code Example 1.26) accepts an arbitrary number of function pairs. The first function in each pair must contain a Boolean expression, and the second function contains code to be evaluated if its partner function is true. If a test condition is false, the interpreter moves onto the next pair and tries again. As soon as a test returns true, the interpreter executes the partner function and exits the **case** block, abandoning any remaining conditional tests. If all tests are false, the interpreter returns **nil**.

CODE EXAMPLE 1.26: USAGE OF case TO SIMULATE A SIX-SIDED DIE ROLL.

```
(
var roll = rrand(1, 6);
case(
    {roll == 1}, {\red.postln},
    {roll == 2}, {\orange.postln},
    {roll == 3}, {\yellow.postln},
    {roll == 4}, {\green.postln},
    {roll == 5}, {\blue.postln},
    {roll == 6}, {\purple.postln}
);
)
```

A **switch** statement is similar to **case**, but with a slightly different syntax, shown in Code Example 1.27. We begin with some value—not necessarily a Boolean—and provide an arbitrary number of value-function pairs. The interpreter will check for equality between the starting value and each of the paired values. For the first comparison that returns true, the corresponding function is evaluated.

CODE EXAMPLE 1.27: USAGE OF `switch` TO SIMULATE A SIX-SIDED DIE ROLL.

```
(
var roll = rrand(1, 6);
switch(
    roll,
    1, {\red.postln},
    2, {\orange.postln},
    3, {\yellow.postln},
    4, {\green.postln},
    5, {\blue.postln},
    6, {\purple.postln}
);
)
```

1.9 Iteration

One of the most attractive aspects of computer programming is its ability to handle repetitive tasks. Iteration refers to techniques that allow a repetitive task to be expressed and executed concisely. Music is full of repetitive structures and benefits greatly from iteration. More generally, if you ever find yourself typing a nearly identical chunk of code many times over, or relying heavily on copy/paste, this could be a sign that you should be using iteration.

Two general-purpose iteration methods, **do** and **collect**, often make good choices for iterative tasks. Both are applied to some collection—usually an array—and both accept a function as their sole argument. The function is evaluated once for each item in the collection. A primary difference between these two methods is that **do** returns its receiver, while **collect** returns a modified collection of the same size, populated using values returned by the function. Thus, **do** is a good choice when we don't care about the values returned by the function, and instead simply want to "do" some action a certain number of times. On the other hand, **collect** is a good choice when we want to modify or interact with an existing collection and capture the result. At the beginning of an iteration function, we can optionally declare two arguments, which represent each item in the collection and its index as the function is repeatedly executed. By declaring these arguments, we give ourselves access to the collection items within the function.

In Code Example 1.28(a), we iterate over an array of four items, and for each item, we post a string. In this case, the items in the array are irrelevant; the result will be the same as long as the size of the array is four. Performing an action some number of times is so common, that **do** is also defined for integers. When **do** is applied to some integer **n**, the receiver will be interpreted as the array **[0, 1, ... n−1]**, thus providing a shorter alternative, depicted in Code Example 1.28(b). In Code Example 1.28(c), we declare two arguments and post them, to visualize the values of these arguments.

> **CODE EXAMPLE 1.28: USAGE OF do TO PERFORM SIMPLE ITERATIVE TASKS.**
>
> (a)   `[30, 40, 50, 60].do({"this is a test".postln});`
>
> (b)   `4.do({"this is a test".postln});`
>
> (c)   `[30, 40, 50, 60].do({|item, index| [item, index].postln});`

A simple usage of **collect** appears in Code Example 1.29. We iterate over the array, and for each item, return the item multiplied by its index. **collect** returns this new array.

> **CODE EXAMPLE 1.29: USAGE OF collect TO ITERATE OVER AN ARRAY AND RETURN A NEW ARRAY.**
>
> ```
> x = [30, 40, 50, 60].collect({|item, index| item * index});
> // -> the array [0, 40, 100, 180] is now stored in x
> ```

Numerous other iteration methods exist, several of which are depicted in Code Example 1.30. The **isPrime** method is featured here, which returns true if its receiver is a prime number, and otherwise returns false.

> **CODE EXAMPLE 1.30: EXAMPLES OF ADDITIONAL ITERATION METHODS.**
>
> ```
> x = [101, 102, 103, 104, 105, 106, 107];
>
> // return the subset of the array for which the function
> returns true:
> x.select({ |n| n.isPrime }); // -> [101, 103, 107]
>
> // return the first item for which the function returns true:
> x.detect({ |n| n.isPrime }); // -> 101
>
> // return true if the function returns true for at least one item:
> x.any({ |n| n.isPrime }); // -> true
>
> // return true if the function returns true for every item:
> x.every({ |n| n.isPrime }); // -> false
>
> // return the number of items for which the function returns true:
> x.count({ |n| n.isPrime }); // -> 3
> ```

1.10 Summary

The topics presented in this chapter provide foundational support throughout the rest of this book, and hopefully throughout your own explorations with SC. Due to the fundamental nature of these concepts, some of the code examples in this chapter may feel a bit dry, abstract, or difficult to fully digest. If you don't fully understand how and why these techniques might apply in a practical setting, that's reasonable. As you continue reading, these concepts will arise again and again, reflected through applications in synthesis, sampling, sequencing, and composition. For now, to provide some practical context, Companion Code 1.2 explores one possible application that ties several of these concepts together: creating a function that converts a pitch letter name and octave to the corresponding MIDI note number.

Notes

1. Matthew J. Wright and Adrian Freed, "Open SoundControl: A New Protocol for Communicating with Sound Synthesizers," in *Proceedings of the 1997 International Computer Music Conference*, Proceedings of the International Computer Music Association (San Francisco: International Computer Music Association, 1997). More information about OSC can be found at https://opensoundcontrol.stanford.edu/.
2. Technically, "method" and "message" are not synonymous, though they are closely related. A message is a more abstract concept of requesting an operation to be performed on an object. A method is a more concrete concept that encompasses the name and description of how a message should be implemented for an object. In a practical context, it is within reason to use these terms interchangeably.
3. At the time of writing, the documentation files are also available on the web at https://doc.sccode.org/.

CHAPTER 2

ESSENTIALS OF MAKING SOUND

2.1 Overview

In this chapter, we'll move beyond the basics of the SC language and begin focusing on sound-specific features. Primarily, we'll introduce core classes and methods explicitly designed to support audio, as well as some auxiliary methods and tools that enhance the creative workflow.

2.2 Booting the Audio Server

Before making sound, it's good to ensure your audio hardware setup is configured properly. If you're using headphones, plug them into your computer. If you're using an external audio interface, it should be connected and powered on. You can use your computer's built-in speakers, but they tend not to reproduce low frequencies well. If you're on macOS or Windows, set your operating system to use your preferred output device, and SC will automatically adopt your selection. If you're on Linux, you'll need to boot the JACK audio server before booting the SC server.[1] Additional information regarding hardware setup can be found in a documentation file titled "Audio device selection."

On the topic of things to do before booting the server, there are several options for configuring the server, like the number of output channels your hardware setup provides, the amount of real-time memory the server is allowed to allocate, and so on. These are all accessible through the **ServerOptions** class. Any changes applied through this class will only take effect after the server is rebooted. In most cases, there's no need to meddle with server configuration. Some examples of server reconfigurations appear throughout Chapter 6, and the **ServerOptions** help file contains additional examples and information.

Once you're all set, you can launch the server by evaluating:

```
s.boot;
```

By default, the keyboard shortcut [cmd]+[b] will also boot the server. As you run this line, information will appear in the post window. If the boot is successful, the numbers in the server status bar in the bottom-right corner of the IDE will turn green, and the post window should look like the image in Figure 2.1. If the server numbers don't turn green, the server has not successfully booted. Boot failures are relatively uncommon, but when they do occur, they are rarely cause for alarm and almost always quickly rectifiable. For example, if you're using separate hardware devices for audio input/output, the server will not boot if these devices are running at different sample rates. Alternatively, if a running server is unexpectedly interrupted (e.g., if the USB cable for your audio interface becomes unplugged), an attempt to reboot may produce an error that reads "Exception in World_OpenUDP: unable to bind udp socket," or "ERROR: server failed to start." This message appears because there is likely a hanging instance of the audio server application that must be destroyed, which can be done by evaluating **Server.killAll** before rebooting. In rarer cases, a boot failure may be resolved by recompiling the SC class library, quitting and reopening the SC environment, or—as a last resort—restarting your computer.

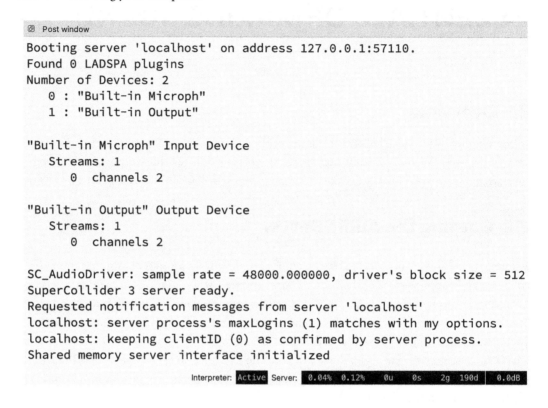

FIGURE 2.1 The post window and status bar after the server has successfully booted.

We know that the lowercase letters a through z are available as interpreter variables, but we didn't store anything in **s**. So, how does **s.boot** work? When we launch the SC environment, a reference to the server is automatically assigned to this variable. Evaluate it, and you'll see that the interpreter returns "localhost," the default name of your local server application. This assignment is a convenience to the user, providing access to the server through a single character. If you accidentally overwrite this variable, you can remake the assignment manually, by evaluating:

```
s = Server.local;
```

The server can also be booted by evaluating:

```
Server.local.boot;
```

Or, you can click the server numbers in the status bar to access a pop-up menu, from which the server can be booted. You can quit the server from this same pop-up menu, or by evaluating one of the following two expressions:

```
s.quit;
```

```
Server.local.quit;
```

Some examples in this book omit `s.boot` and assume your server is already running. If you attempt to work with sound while the server is offline, the post window will display a friendly warning that the server is not running.

2.3 Unit Generators

Unit generators (`UGens`) are objects that represent digital signal calculations on the audio server. They are the basic building blocks for sound processes, akin to modules on an analog synthesizer. Each UGen performs a specific task, like generating a sawtooth wave, applying a low-pass filter, playing back an audio file, and so on. Table 2.1 displays a roughly categorized list of some of the simplest and most commonly used UGens. The purposes of some UGens are obvious from their names (`WhiteNoise` generates white noise), while others, like `Dust`, are more cryptic. The documentation includes a guide file titled "Tour of UGens."

TABLE 2.1 A selection of commonly used UGens.

Category	UGens
Oscillators	`SinOsc, Pulse, Saw, Blip, LFPulse, LFSaw, LFTri, VarSaw`
Noise Generators	`LFNoise0, LFNoise1, PinkNoise, WhiteNoise`
Envelopes	`Line, XLine, EnvGen`
Filters	`LPF, HPF, BPF, BRF`
Triggers	`Impulse, Dust, Trig`
Sound File Players	`PlayBuf, BufRd`
Stereo Panners	`Pan2, Balance2`

Musical fluency doesn't demand intimate familiarity with every UGen. UGens are a means to an end, so you'll only need to get acquainted with those that help achieve your goals. This book focuses on a core set of UGens that are broadly applicable in synthesis, sampling, and signal processing.

2.3.1 A QUICK REVIEW OF DIGITAL AUDIO CONCEPTS

A digital audio signal is represented as a sequence of samples. A sample, in this context, is a number—specifically, a float—that represents signal value at an instantaneous moment in time. All digital audio software and hardware devices operate at a sample rate, which determines the number of samples that occur in one second. Thus, a UGen can generally be viewed as a number that is rapidly and constantly changing. Your hardware is likely running at 44,100 or 48,000 samples per second, two of the most common rates. When the server boots, it will adopt the sample rate of your system.

The sample rate of a system determines the highest frequency that can be accurately represented, called the Nyquist frequency. It is equal to half the sample rate, because two samples per cycle is the bare minimum for capturing the essential cyclic behavior of a periodic signal. If the frequency of a signal exceeds the Nyquist frequency, the system doesn't have enough samples per cycle to faithfully represent it. The result is usually an erroneous measurement, producing a signal whose frequency is lower than the Nyquist frequency. This phenomenon is called aliasing, or foldover, depicted in Figure 2.2.

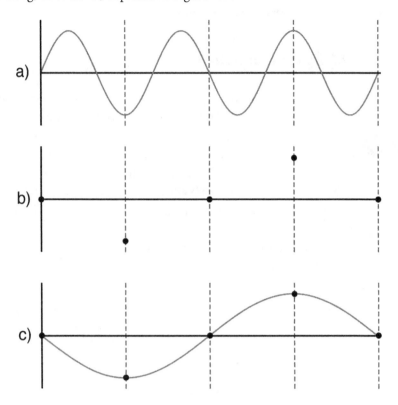

FIGURE 2.2 A simplified diagram of aliasing, including (a) a continuous periodic signal whose frequency exceeds the Nyquist frequency, (b) the result of sampling this periodic signal, and (c) the erroneous attempt to reconstruct the original signal using sample data. Dashed lines indicate moments when samples are taken.

Digital audio is processed in blocks of samples, rather than one-by-one. Block processing is less taxing in terms of processing power but introduces a small amount of latency (an entire block must be computed before it can be rendered). The size of a block varies but is almost always a power of two. As block size increases, CPU load decreases and latency increases, and vice-versa. Like samples and sample rates, the concept of sample blocks is not unique to SC; it is ubiquitous throughout the digital audio realm. In SC, a block of samples is usually called a "control block" or "control cycle."

Assuming you've already booted the server, you can check the sample rate and block size by evaluating the following expressions:

```
s.sampleRate;
```

```
s.options.blockSize;
```

2.3.2 UGEN RATES

A UGen runs at a particular rate, depending on the class method used to create the instance. Instead of using **new** to create a UGen instance, we use **ar**, **kr**, or **ir**, which represent audio rate, control rate, and initialization rate.

An audio rate UGen produces output values at the sample rate, which is the highest-resolution signal available to us. If you want to hear a signal through your speakers, it must run at the audio rate. Generally, if you require a high frequency signal, a fast-moving signal, or anything you want to monitor directly, you should use **ar**.

Control rate UGens run at the control rate. This rate is equal to sample rate divided by block size. If the sample rate is 48,000 and the block size is 64, then the control rate calculates 48,000 ÷ 64 = 750 samples per second, outputting one at the start of each control cycle. Control rate UGens have a lower resolution but consume less processing power. They are useful when you need a relatively slow-moving signal, like a gradual envelope or a low-frequency oscillator. Because the control rate is a proportionally reduced sample rate, the Nyquist frequency is similarly reduced. In this case, the highest control rate frequency that can be faithfully represented is 750 ÷ 2 = 375 Hz. Therefore, if you require an oscillator with a frequency higher than 375 Hz, **kr** is a poor choice. In fact, signal integrity degrades as the frequency of a signal approaches the Nyquist frequency, so **ar** is a good choice even if a UGen's frequency is slightly below the Nyquist frequency.

Consider a sine oscillator with a frequency of 1 Hz, used to control the cutoff frequency of a filter. It's possible to run this oscillator at the audio rate, but this would provide more resolution than we need. If using the control rate instead, we'd calculate 750 samples per cycle, which is more than enough to visually represent one cycle of a sine wave. In fact, as few as 20 or 30 points would probably be enough to "see" a sinusoidal shape. This is an example in which we can take advantage of control rate UGens to reduce the server's processing load, without sacrificing sound quality. Figure 2.3 depicts a 120 Hz sine oscillator running at the audio rate and the control rate. If you're unsure of which rate to use in a particular situation, **ar** is usually the safer choice.

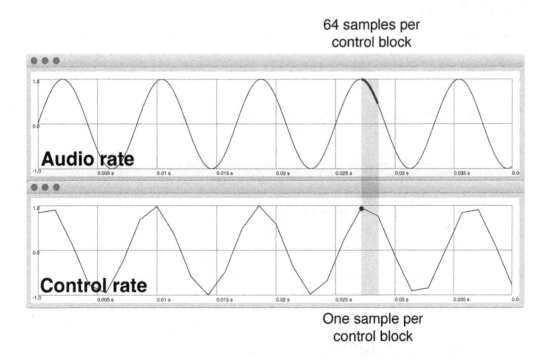

FIGURE 2.3 A few centiseconds of a 120 Hz sine wave running at the audio rate and control rate.

Initialization rate UGens are the rarest of the three. In fact, many UGens won't understand the **ir** method. A UGen at the initialization rate produces exactly one sample when created and holds that value indefinitely. So, the initialization rate is not really a rate at all; it's simply a means of initializing a UGen so that it behaves like a constant. The CPU savings **ir** provides are obvious, but what's the point of a signal that's stuck on a specific value? There are a few situations in which this choice makes sense. One example is the **SampleRate** UGen, a UGen that outputs the sample rate of the server. In some signal algorithms, we need to perform a calculation involving the sample rate, which may vary from one system to another. Generally, the sample rate does not (and should not) change while the server is booted, so it's inefficient and unnecessary to repeatedly calculate it.

2.3.3 UGEN ARGUMENTS

In the previous chapter, we observed that some methods, like **pow**, require arguments to function correctly. UGens are no different. The expression **SinOsc.ar()** produces no errors, but questions remain. What is the frequency of this sine oscillator? What is its amplitude? The specific arguments that **ar**, **kr**, and **ir** accept, and their default values, depend on the type of UGen.

In the "Class Methods" section of the **SinOsc** help file (shown in Figure 2.4), we see that this UGen can run at the audio or control rate, and the arguments are the same for both methods. Four input values are expected: **freq**, **phase**, **mul**, and **add**. **freq** determines the frequency of the oscillator, measured in Hz. **phase** controls an offset amount, measured in radians, used to make the oscillator begin at a specific point within its cycle. **mul** is a value that is multiplied by every sample in the output signal, and **add** is a value added to every sample in the output signal.

Class Methods

```
SinOsc.ar(freq: 440.0, phase: 0.0, mul: 1.0, add: 0.0)

SinOsc.kr(freq: 440.0, phase: 0.0, mul: 1.0, add: 0.0)
```

Arguments:

freq Frequency in Hertz. Sampled at audio-rate.

phase Phase in radians. Sampled at audio-rate.

> **NOTE:** phase values should be within the range +-8pi. If your phase values are larger then simply use .mod(2pi) to wrap them.

mul Output will be multiplied by this value.

add This value will be added to the output.

FIGURE 2.4 A screenshot of the class methods section of the **SinOsc** help file.

TIP.RAND(); WORKING WITH pi

In the case of **SinOsc**, one cycle is equal to 2π radians. In SC, we use the special keyword **pi** to represent π. Expressions such as **pi/4**, **3pi/2**, etc., are valid.

freq and **phase** are relatively specific to **SinOsc**. Most oscillator UGens have a frequency argument, but not all have a phase argument. Those that do might measure it using a different scale. The triangle wave oscillator **LFTri**, for example, expects a phase value between 0 and 4. The pulse wave generator **Pulse** has no phase input but has a **width** argument that determines its duty cycle (the percentage of each cycle that is "high" vs. "low"). Further still, a noise generator like **PinkNoise** has neither a frequency nor a phase argument.

By contrast, **mul** and **add** are nearly ubiquitous throughout the UGen family, and almost always occur as the last two arguments. Most UGens are either bipolar or unipolar; the default output range of a bipolar UGen is -1 to +1, while the default range of a unipolar UGen is bounded between 0 and +1. These ranges are considered "nominal," and register at or near 0 decibels on a digital signal meter. This is the highest level that can be represented in a digital system, so you should envision a nominal signal as being quite loud!

By virtue of its multiplicative behavior, **mul** corresponds to signal amplitude. The default **mul** value is one, which has no effect. A **mul** value of 0.5, for example, reduces amplitude by half. Specifying a **mul** value greater than one will push signal amplitude past representational limits, and distortion may occur. When directly monitoring the output of a UGen, a **mul** value around 0.05 or 0.1 is a good "ballpark" range, which is sufficiently loud without being unpleasant, and which provides ample headroom.

> ### TIP.RAND(); CALIBRATING YOUR HARDWARE SETUP
>
> The discussion of **mul** brings up important considerations regarding monitoring level and loudness. When using SC (or any digital audio platform, really), it's smart to calibrate your system volume before you start creating. First, turn your system volume down so it's almost silent, then run the following line of code, which plays a two-channel pink noise signal:
>
> ```
> {PinkNoise.ar(mul: 1) ! 2}.play;
> ```
>
> As the noise plays, slowly turn up your system volume until the noise sounds strong and healthy. It shouldn't be painful, but it should be unambiguously loud, perhaps even slightly annoying. Once you've set this volume level, consider your system "calibrated" and don't modify your hardware levels again. This configuration will encourage you to create signal levels in SC that are comfortable and present a minimal risk of distorting.
>
> By contrast, a bad workflow involves setting your system volume too low, which encourages compensation with higher **mul** values. This configuration gives the misleading impression that your signal levels are low, when they're actually quite high, with almost no headroom. In this setup, you'll inevitably find yourself in the frustrating situation of having signals that seem too quiet, but with levels that are constantly "in the red."

add defaults to zero, in which case it (like **mul**) has no effect on a UGen's output signal. When playing a UGen through your speakers, it's generally not useful or recommended to specify a non-zero **add** value. If **add** is non-zero, the entire waveform vertically shifts, so that its point of "equilibrium" no longer coincides with true zero. A vertically shifted signal may not sound any different to the human ear, but if routed through a loudspeaker, the speaker cone will vibrate asymmetrically, which may fatigue or stress the loudspeaker over long periods of time, possibly degrading its integrity and lifespan.

These "rules" for **mul** and **add** apply mainly to situations in which we're directly listening to a UGen. There are other cases, such as modulating one signal with another, where it's desirable to specify custom **mul/add** values.

> **TIP.RAND(); ORDER OF OPERATIONS WITH mul/add**
>
> When specifying **mul/add** values, keep in mind that these operations always occur in a specific order: The multiplication happens first, then the addition.

The main takeaway from this discussion is that each UGen is unique, not only in its purpose, but also in terms of the input arguments it accepts, their default values, and their expected ranges. As you start working with sound, don't guess or make assumptions! Take the time to read the help files and make sure the values you provide are consistent with what the UGen expects. Few things in this world are quite as startling as accidentally supplying a frequency value for an amplitude argument! For additional context, you may find it helpful to read the first few paragraphs of the "UGen" class help file, as well as a guide file titled "Unit Generators and Synths."

2.4 UGen Functions

2.4.1 PLAYING AND STOPPING SIMPLE SOUNDS

Function-dot-play refers to a simple code structure that allows us to quickly make sound. This construct involves a function that contains one or more UGens and receives the **play** method. In Code Example 2.1, we have an audio rate sine UGen with user-specified arguments. If you evaluate this line, you should hear a 300 Hz tone in your left speaker.

> **CODE EXAMPLE 2.1: AN EXAMPLE OF USING FUNCTION-DOT-PLAY TO CREATE SOUND.**
>
> ```
> {SinOsc.ar(300, 0, 0.1, 0)}.play;
> ```

Press [cmd]+[period] to stop the sound. Take a moment to memorize this keyboard shortcut! Incorporate it into your muscle memory. Carve it into your bedroom walls. Dream about it at night. It's your trusty panic button.

Let's unpack the expression in Code Example 2.1 and examine some variations. First, let's acknowledge that listening to sound in only one speaker can be uncomfortable, particularly on headphones. SC interprets an array of UGens as a multichannel signal. So, if the function contains an array of two **SinOsc** UGens, the first signal will be routed to the left speaker, and the second to the right. The duplication shortcut, shown in Code Example 2.2, is a quick way to create such an array. Multichannel signals will be explored later in this chapter.

> **CODE EXAMPLE 2.2:** USING OBJECT DUPLICATION TO CREATE A TWO-CHANNEL SOUND.
>
> ```
> {SinOsc.ar(300, 0, 0.1, 0) ! 2}.play;
> ```

We know that **SinOsc** expects four arguments, and we've provided four values. The frequency is 300, the phase is zero, and so on. When provided this way, we're responsible for the correct order. SC isn't clever enough to determine which is which if we mix things up. An experienced user may remember what these numbers mean, but for a newcomer, this minimal style may involve a lot of back-and-forth between the code and the help files. Code Example 2.3 depicts an alternative, using a more verbose style:

> **CODE EXAMPLE 2.3:** SPECIFICATION OF ARGUMENT VALUES USING A VERBOSE "KEYWORD" STYLE.
>
> ```
> {SinOsc.ar(freq: 300, phase: 0, mul: 0.1, add: 0) ! 2}.play;
> ```

This longer but more descriptive approach of specifying argument values applies to all methods, not just those associated with UGens. Companion Code 2.1 details some variations and rules to be aware of when using this keyword style.

2.4.2 CHANGING A SOUND WHILE PLAYING

Suppose we want to change the frequency of an oscillator while it's playing. To enable real-time changes to a sound, we need to make a few changes to the examples in the previous section. First, we must declare an argument at the beginning of the UGen function (just as we did with ordinary functions in the previous chapter) and incorporate it into the appropriate UGen. Argument names are flexible, and don't have to match the name of the UGen argument for which they're being used. However, "freq" is certainly a good choice, because it's short and meaningful at a glance. It's also wise to provide a default value in the declaration.

When calling **play**, we must assign the resulting sound process to a variable, so that we can communicate with it later. While the sound is playing, we can alter it using the **set** method and providing the name and value of the parameter we want to change. Code Example 2.4 shows this sequence of actions.

CODE EXAMPLE 2.4: PLAYING A UGEN FUNCTION AND USING set TO CHANGE THE SOUND.

```
(
x = { |freq = 300|
    SinOsc.ar(freq, mul: 0.1) ! 2;
}.play;
)

x.set(\freq, 400); // change the frequency
```

We can declare as many arguments as we need. Code Example 2.5 adds a second argument that controls signal amplitude and demonstrates a variety of **set** messages.

CODE EXAMPLE 2.5: USE OF set MESSAGES WITH A UGEN FUNCTION CONTAINING MULTIPLE ARGUMENTS.

```
(
x = { |freq = 300, amp = 0.1|
    SinOsc.ar(freq, mul: amp) ! 2;
}.play;
)

x.set(\freq, 400, \amp, 0.4); // modify both arguments

x.set(\amp, 0.05, \freq, 500); // order of name/value pairs doesn't matter

x.set(\freq, 600); // modify only one argument
```

It's often desirable to separate creating and playing a UGen function into two discrete actions. In Code Example 2.6, we define a UGen function and store it in the interpreter variable **f**. Then, we play it, storing the resulting sound process in the interpreter variable **x**. The former is simply the object that defines the sound, while the latter is the active sound process that understands **set** messages. It's important not to confuse the two.

CODE EXAMPLE 2.6: THE FUNCTION-DOT-PLAY CONSTRUCT, SEPARATED INTO TWO DISCRETE ACTIONS OF DEFINING AND PLAYING THE SOUND.

```
(
// define the sound
f = { |freq = 300, amp = 0.1|
    SinOsc.ar(freq, mul: amp) ! 2;
};
)

x = f.play; // play the sound

x.set(\freq, 400, \amp, 0.3); // change the sound

f.set(\freq, 500, \amp, 0.05); // no effect if applied to the function
```

Even if arguments in a UGen function have default values, we can override them when playing the function. The **play** method has an **args** argument, which accepts an array of name-value pairs, shown in Code Example 2.7.

CODE EXAMPLE 2.7: OVERRIDING ARGUMENT VALUES WHEN CALLING play ON A UGEN FUNCTION.

```
(
f = { |freq = 300, amp = 0.1|
    SinOsc.ar(freq, mul: amp) ! 2;
};
)

x = f.play(args: [freq: 800, amp: 0.2]); // override default arguments

x.set(\freq, 600, \amp, 0.05); // set messages work normally
```

2.4.3 OTHER WAYS TO STOP A SOUND

The [cmd]+[period] shortcut is useful for stopping sound, but it's indiscriminate. As an alternative, we can **free** a sound process. With this method, we can have multiple sound processes playing simultaneously, and remove them one-by-one, shown in Code Example 2.8. This example also highlights the value of defining a function and playing it separately; specifically, we can spawn multiple sound processes from one function.

> **CODE EXAMPLE 2.8:** USING free TO STOP SOUND PROCESSES INDIVIDUALLY.
>
> ```
> (
> f = { |freq = 300, amp = 0.1|
>     SinOsc.ar(freq, mul: amp) ! 2;
> };
> )
>
> x = f.play(args: [freq: 350]);
>
> y = f.play(args: [freq: 450]);
>
> y.free;
>
> x.free;
> ```

Like [cmd]+[period], freeing a sound process also results in a hard stop, which may not be what we want. When using function-dot-play, we can also use **release** to create a gradual fade, optionally providing a fade duration measured in seconds (see Code Example 2.9).

> **CODE EXAMPLE 2.9:** USE OF release TO FADE OUT A SOUND CREATED BY FUNCTION-DOT-PLAY.
>
> ```
> (
> f = { |freq = 300, amp = 0.1|
>     SinOsc.ar(freq, mul: amp) ! 2;
> };
> )
>
> x = f.play;
>
> x.release(2);
> ```

2.4.4 MATH OPERATIONS WITH UGENS

We've already established that a UGen is essentially a sequence of numbers, therefore most math operations defined for floats and integers can also be applied to UGens. Signal summation, for example, is a fundamental technique that forms the basis of audio mixing and additive synthesis. When two signals are summed, their corresponding samples are summed, and the result is a new waveform in which both signals can usually be perceived. Code Example 2.10 and Figure 2.5 depict the summation of a sine wave with pink noise.

CODE EXAMPLE 2.10: USING ADDITION TO MIX A SINE WAVE WITH PINK NOISE.

```
(
x = {
    var sig;
    sig = SinOsc.ar(300, mul: 0.15);
    sig = sig + PinkNoise.ar(mul: 0.1);
    sig = sig ! 2;
}.play;
)

x.release(2);
```

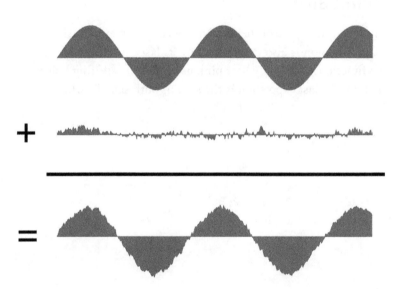

FIGURE 2.5 A graphical depiction of summing a sine wave with pink noise.

When a binary operator is used between a number and a UGen, the operation is applied to the number and every sample value produced by the UGen. This being the case, multiplication and addition can be used instead of providing argument values for **mul** and **add**. Code Example 2.11 rewrites the code from Code Example 2.10 using this approach.

CODE EXAMPLE 2.11: USE OF BINARY OPERATORS AS AN ALTERNATIVE TO SPECIFYING mul AND add.

```
(
x = {
    var sig;
    sig = SinOsc.ar(300) * 0.15;
    sig = sig + (PinkNoise.ar * 0.1);
    sig = sig ! 2;
}.play;
)

x.release(2);
```

TIP.RAND(); A UGEN FUNCTION PLAYS THE LAST EXPRESSION

Just as ordinary functions return the value of their last expression when evaluated, the output signal from a UGen function is also determined by its last expression. In the first of the following two functions, we'll only hear pink noise, despite creating a sine wave. In the second function, the last expression is the sum of both signals, which is what we hear.

```
(
{
    var sig0, sig1;
    sig0 = SinOsc.ar(300, mul: 0.15) ! 2;
    sig1 = PinkNoise.ar(mul: 0.1) ! 2;
}.play;
)

(
{
    var sig0, sig1;
    sig0 = SinOsc.ar(300, mul: 0.15) ! 2;
    sig1 = PinkNoise.ar(mul: 0.1) ! 2;
    sig0 + sig1;
}.play;
)
```

Multiplying one signal by another is also common. The code in Code Example 2.12 multiplies pink noise by a low-frequency sine wave, producing a sound like ocean waves. This is a simple example of signal modulation, which involves the use of one signal to influence some aspect of another. A phase value of $3\pi/2$ causes the sine oscillator to begin at the lowest point in its cycle, and the multiplication/addition values scale and shift the output values to a new range between 0 and 0.2. The effects of these argument values are visualized in Figure 2.6.

CODE EXAMPLE 2.12: MODULATING THE AMPLITUDE OF PINK NOISE WITH A LOW-FREQUENCY OSCILLATOR.

```
(
x = {
    var sig, lfo;
    lfo = SinOsc.kr(freq: 1/5, phase: 3pi/2, mul: 0.1, add: 0.1);
    sig = PinkNoise.ar * lfo;
    sig = sig ! 2;
}.play;
)

x.release(2);
```

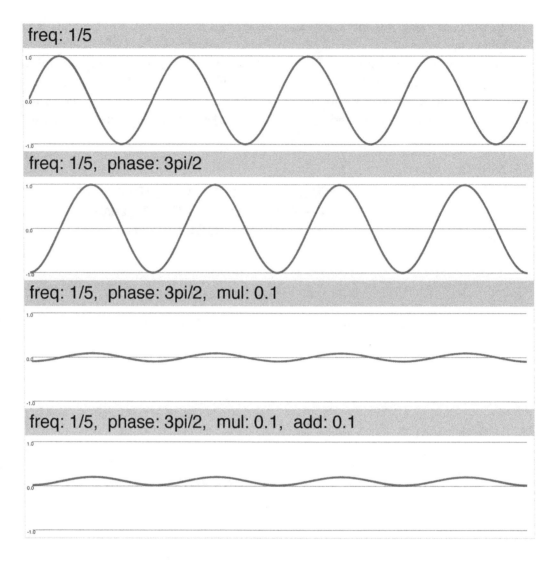

FIGURE 2.6 An incremental visualization of how argument values influence the waveform of a **SinOsc** UGen.

When we want a UGen's output to range between some arbitrary minimum and maximum, using **mul/add** sometimes involves cumbersome mental math. Even worse, the actual range of the UGen isn't immediately clear from looking at the code. A better approach involves using one of several range-mapping methods, such as **range**, demonstrated in Code Example 2.13. This method lets us explicitly provide a minimum and maximum, avoiding the need to deal with **mul/add**. Table 2.2 lists some common range-mapping methods.

CODE EXAMPLE 2.13: USE OF range TO SPECIFY CUSTOM OUTPUT BOUNDARIES OF A UGEN.

```
(
x = {
    var sig, lfo;
    lfo = SinOsc.kr(freq: 0.2, phase: 3pi/2).range(0, 0.2);
```

```
    sig = PinkNoise.ar * lfo;
    sig = sig ! 2;
}.play;
)

x.release(2);
```

TABLE 2.2 Common UGen range-mapping methods.

Method	Description
`.range(x, y)`	Linearly map the output range between *x* and *y*.
`.exprange(x, y)`	Exponentially map the output range between *x* and *y*. Arguments must be either both positive or both negative, and neither can be 0.
`.curverange(x, y, n)`	Map the output range between *x* and *y* using a custom warp value *n*. Positive values create exponential-like behavior, negative values create logarithmic-like behavior.
`.unipolar(x)`	Map the output range between 0 and *x*.
`.bipolar(x)`	Map the output range between ±*x*.

> **TIP.RAND(); RANGE-MAPPING VS. MUL/ADD**
>
> Range-mapping methods are designed as alternatives to **mul/add** arguments, and they assume the range of the UGen to which they apply has not been previously altered. You can specify a UGen's range using one approach or the other, but you should never apply both approaches at the same time. If you do, a range-mapping operation will be applied twice in a row, producing erroneous numbers and possibly startling sound!

As you start exploring UGen functions of your own, remember that just because a math operation can be used doesn't necessarily mean it should. Dividing one signal by another, for example, is dangerous! This calculation may involve division by some extremely small value (or even zero), which is likely to generate a dramatic amplitude spike, or something similarly unpleasant. Experimentation is encouraged, but you should proceed with purpose and mindfulness. Mute or turn your system volume down first before you try something unpredictable.

2.5 Envelopes

If we play a function containing some oscillator or noise generator, and then step away for a coffee, we'd return sometime later to find that sound still going. In music, an infinite-length sound isn't particularly useful. Instead, we usually like sounds to have definitive beginnings and ends, so that we can structure them in time.

An *envelope* is a signal with a customizable shape and duration, typically constructed from individual line segments joined end-to-end. Envelopes are often used to control the amplitude of another signal, enabling fades instead of abrupt starts and stops. By using **release**, we've already been relying on a built-in envelope that accompanies the function-dot-play construct. When controlling signal amplitude, an envelope typically starts at zero, ramps up to some positive value, possibly stays there for a while, and eventually comes back down to zero. The first segment is called the "attack," the stable portion in the middle is the "sustain," and the final descent is the "release." Many variations exist; an "ADSR" envelope, for example, has a "decay" segment between the attack and sustain (see Figure 2.7).

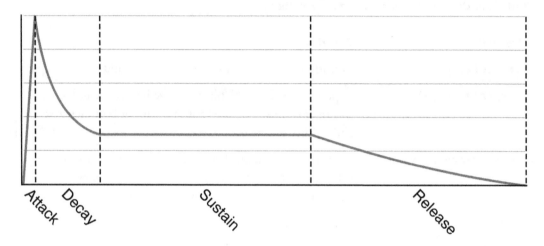

FIGURE 2.7 A visualization of an ADSR envelope.

It's important to recognize that the ADSR envelope is just one specific example that happens to be useful for modeling envelope characteristics of many real-world sounds. Ultimately, an envelope is just a signal with a customizable shape, which can be used to control any aspect of a signal algorithm, not just amplitude.

2.5.1 LINE AND XLINE

The UGens **Line** and **XLine** provide simple envelope shapes. **Line** generates a signal that travels linearly from one value to another over a duration in seconds. **XLine** is similar but features an exponentially curved trajectory. Like the **exprand** and **exprange** methods, the start and end values for **XLine** must have the same sign and neither can be zero. Code Example 2.14 and Figure 2.8 depict the usage and visual results of using these UGens as amplitude envelopes. Note that **XLine** cannot end at zero, but it can get close enough that the difference is unnoticeable.

CODE EXAMPLE 2.14: USAGE OF Line AND XLine AS SIMPLE AMPLITUDE ENVELOPES.

```
(
{
    var sig, env;
    env = Line.kr(start: 0.3, end: 0, dur: 0.5);
    sig = SinOsc.ar(350) * env;
    sig = sig ! 2;
}.play;
)

(
{
    var sig, env;
    env = XLine.kr(start: 0.3, end: 0.0001, dur: 0.5);
    sig = SinOsc.ar(350) * env;
    sig = sig ! 2;
}.play;
)
```

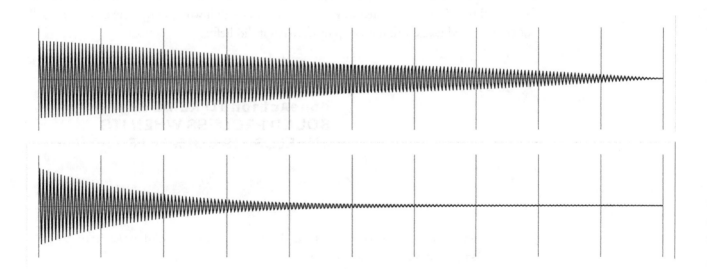

FIGURE 2.8 Visual result of **Line** (top) and **XLine** (bottom) when used as amplitude envelopes for an oscillator signal.

2.5.2 DONEACTIONS

Line and **XLine** include an argument, named **doneAction**, which appears in UGens that have an inherently finite duration. In SC, a doneAction represents an action that the audio server takes when the UGen that contains the doneAction has finished. These actions can be specified by integer, and a complete list of available actions and their meanings appears in the help file for the **Done** UGen. Most of the descriptions in this table may look completely meaningless to you, but if so, don't worry. In practice, we rarely employ a doneAction other than zero (do nothing) or two (free the enclosing synth). The default doneAction is zero, and while taking no action sounds harmless, it carries consequences. To demonstrate, evaluate either of the two code examples in Code Example 2.14 many times in a row. As you do, you'll notice your CPU usage will gradually creep upwards.

Why does this happen? Because a doneAction of zero tells the server to do nothing when the envelope is complete, the envelope remains active on the server and continues to output its final value indefinitely. These zero or near-zero values are multiplied by the sine oscillator, which results in a silent or near-silent signal. The server is indifferent to whether a sound process is silent; it only knows that it was instructed to do nothing when the envelope finished. If you evaluate this code over and over, you'll create more and more non-terminating sound processes. Eventually, the server will become overwhelmed, and additional sounds will start glitching (if you've followed these instructions and ramped up your CPU numbers, now is a good time to press [cmd]+[period] to remove these "ghost" sounds).

From a practical perspective, when our envelope reaches its end, we consider the sound to be totally finished. So, it makes sense to specify 2 for the doneAction. When running the code in Code Example 2.15, the server automatically frees the sound when the envelope is done. Evaluate this code as many times as you like, and although it won't sound any different, you'll notice that CPU usage will not creep upwards as it did before.

CODE EXAMPLE 2.15: USE OF A TERMINATING doneAction TO REMOVE A SOUND PROCESS WHEN ITS ENVELOPE IS COMPLETE.

```
(
{
    var sig, env;
    env = XLine.kr(start: 0.3, end: 0.0001, dur: 0.5, doneAction: 2);
    sig = SinOsc.ar(350) * env;
    sig = sig ! 2;
}.play;
)
```

Knowing which doneAction to specify is an important skill, essential for automating the cleanup of stale sounds and optimizing usage of the audio server's resources.

2.5.3 ENV AND ENVGEN

Lines are useful for simple envelopes, but don't provide much flexibility. Once a **Line** or **XLine** starts, it cannot be restarted, modified, or looped; it merely travels from start to end, and triggers a doneAction when finished. In most cases, it's preferable to use the more flexible **EnvGen**. The shape of an **EnvGen** is determined by an instance of a language-side class called **Env**, provided as the envelope signal's first argument. An instance of **Env** created with **new** expects three arguments: an array of level values, an array of segment durations, and an array of curve specifications. We can also **plot** an **Env** to visualize its shape. Code Example 2.16 and Figure 2.9 demonstrate the creation of an **Env** and its visual appearance.

CODE EXAMPLE 2.16: CREATING AND PLOTTING AN INSTANCE OF Env.

```
(
e = Env.new(
    levels: [0, 1, 0],
    times: [1, 3],
    curve: [0, 0]
);

e.plot;
)
```

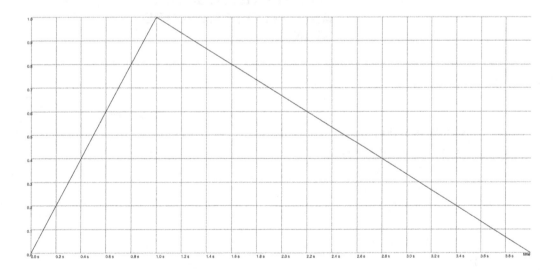

FIGURE 2.9 Visualization of the **Env** from Code Example 2.16.

Let's unpack the meaning of the numbers in Code Example 2.16. The first array contains envelope levels, which are values that the envelope signal will visit as time progresses: the envelope starts at 0, travels to 1, and returns to 0. The second array specifies durations of the segments between these levels: the attack is 1 second long, and the release is 3 seconds. The final array determines segment curvatures. Zero represents linearity, while positive/negative values will "bend" the segments. Note that when an **Env** is created this way, the size of the first array is always one greater than either of the other two arrays. Take a moment to modify the code from Code Example 2.16, to better understand how the numbers influence the envelope's shape. Code Example 2.17 illustrates how **EnvGen** and **Env** work together to create an envelope signal in a UGen function. Keywords are used for clarity. Because it is inherently finite, **EnvGen** accepts a doneAction. As before, it makes sense to specify a doneAction of 2 to automate the cleanup process.

> **TIP.RAND(); UNDERSTANDING ENVELOPE CURVES**
>
> When using numbers to specify segment curves, it can be hard to remember how a segment will bend depending on the sign of the number. The rule is: positive values cause a segment to be more horizontal at first, and more vertical toward the end. Negative values cause the segment to be more vertical at first, becoming more horizontal toward the end.
>
> Certain symbols can also be used to specify a segment curve, such as **\lin**, **\exp**, **\sin**, and others. A table of valid options appears in the **Env** help file, under the section that explains the class method **new**.

CODE EXAMPLE 2.17: USAGE OF Env AND EnvGen TO CREATE A CUSTOM AMPLITUDE ENVELOPE SIGNAL.

```
(
{
    var sig, env;
    env = EnvGen.kr(
        envelope: Env.new(
            levels: [0, 1, 0],
            times: [1, 3],
            curve: [0, 0]
        ),
        doneAction: 2
    );
    sig = SinOsc.ar(350) * 0.3;
    sig = sig * env;
    sig = sig ! 2;
}.play;
)
```

Envelopes can be divided into two categories: those with fixed durations, and those that can be sustained indefinitely. The envelopes we've seen so far belong to the first category, but in the real world, many musical sounds have amplitude envelopes with indefinite durations. When a violinist bows a string, we won't know when the sound will stop until the bow is lifted. An envelope that models this behavior is called a gated envelope. It has a parameter, called a "gate," which determines how and when the envelope signal progresses along its trajectory. When the gate value transitions from zero to positive, the envelope begins and sustains at a point along the way. When the gate becomes zero again, the envelope continues from its sustain point and finishes the rest of its journey. Like a real-world gate, we describe this parameter as being open (positive) or closed (zero).

To create a sustaining envelope, we can add a fourth argument to **Env.new()**: an integer representing an index into the levels array, indicating the value at which the envelope will sustain. In SC terminology, this level is called the "release node." In Code Example 2.18, the release node is 2, which means the envelope signal will sustain at a level of 0.2 while the gate remains open. Because **gate** is a parameter we'd like to change while the sound is playing, it must be declared as an argument, and supplied to the **EnvGen**. In effect, this example creates an ADSR envelope, similar to Figure 2.7: the attack travels from 0 to 1 over 0.02 seconds, the decay drops to a level of 0.2 over the next 0.3 seconds, and the signal remains at 0.2 until the gate closes, which triggers a one-second release.

CODE EXAMPLE 2.18: USAGE OF Env AND EnvGen TO CREATE A GATED ENVELOPE.

```
(
f = { |gate = 1|
    var sig, env;
    env = EnvGen.kr(
        envelope: Env.new(
            [0, 1, 0.2, 0],
            [0.02, 0.3, 1],
            [0, -1, -4],
            2
        ),
        gate: gate,
        doneAction: 2
    );
    sig = SinOsc.ar(350) * 0.3;
    sig = sig * env;
    sig = sig ! 2;
};
)

x = f.play;

x.set(\gate, 0);
```

In some cases, we may want to retrigger an envelope, opening and closing its gate at will, to selectively allow sound to pass through. If so, a doneAction of 2 is a poor choice, because we don't necessarily want the sound process to be destroyed if the envelope reaches its end. Instead, a 0 doneAction (the default) is the correct choice, demonstrated in Code Example 2.19, which causes the envelope to "idle" at its end point until it is retriggered.

It's worth being extra clear about the specific behavior of an envelope in response to gate changes when a release node has been specified:[2]

- A zero-to-positive gate transition causes the envelope to move from its current level to the second level in the levels array, using its first duration and first curve value. Note that the envelope never revisits its first level, which is only used for initialization.
- A positive-to-zero gate transition causes the envelope to move from its current value to the value immediately after the release node, using the duration and curve values at the same index as the release node.

CODE EXAMPLE 2.19: A RETRIGGERABLE GATED ENVELOPE.

```
(
f = { |gate = 1|
    var sig, env;
    env = EnvGen.kr(
        Env.new(
            [0, 1, 0.2, 0],
            [0.02, 0.3, 1],
            [0, -1, -4],
            2
        ),
        gate
    );
    sig = SinOsc.ar(350) * 0.3;
    sig = sig * env;
    sig = sig ! 2;
};
)

x = f.play;

x.set(\gate, 0); // fade to silence but do not free

x.set(\gate, 1); // reopen the gate to restart the envelope

x.set(\gate, 0); // fade to silence again

x.free; // free when finished
```

This retriggering ability may also be useful for fixed-duration envelopes. It's possible but clumsy to retrigger a fixed-duration envelope with a standard gate argument, because it requires manually closing the gate before reopening. As a solution, we can precede the gate argument name with **t_**, which transforms it into a "trigger-type" argument, which responds differently to **set** messages. When a trigger-type argument is set to a non-zero value, it holds that value for a single control cycle, and then almost immediately "snaps" back to zero. It's like a real-world gate that's been augmented with a powerful spring, slamming shut immediately after being opened. Code Example 2.20 depicts the use of trigger-type arguments. Note that the default gate value is zero, which means the envelope will idle at its starting level (zero) until the gate is opened.

CODE EXAMPLE 2.20: USE OF TRIGGER-TYPE ARGUMENTS TO CREATE A RETRIGGERABLE FIXED-DURATION ENVELOPE.

```
(
x = { |t_gate = 0|
    var sig, env;
    env = EnvGen.kr(
        Env.new(
            [0, 1, 0],
            [0.02, 0.3],
            [0, -4],
        ),
        t_gate,
    );
    sig = SinOsc.ar(350) * 0.3;
    sig = sig * env;
    sig = sig ! 2;
}.play;
)

x.set(\t_gate, 1); // evaluate repeatedly

x.free; // free when finished
```

EnvGen, in partnership with **Env**, is one of the more complex UGens in the class library, with many variations and subtleties. Both help files contain additional information, and Companion Code 2.2 explores additional uses and features of envelopes.

2.6 Multichannel Signals

Spatial perception is a central component of the human auditory system. Our ability to localize the origin of a sound in our environment is instinctual; we naturally turn our head toward something unexpected. This ability derives from having two ears at two different points on our head. Unless a sound source is on the vertical plane that symmetrically divides the body, a propagating sound wave reaches one ear slightly before it reaches the other, creating a binaural time delay that is interpreted by the brain to create a sense of spatial awareness. Sound localization is not solely determined by this time delay (spectrum and amplitude discrepancies between the ears provide additional information), but it is a significant factor.

Music would be much less interesting without the ability to simulate the illusion of physical space. In the process of mixing a recording of an ensemble, it's desirable to "place" instruments at specific locations, giving the listener the impression of being physically present at a live performance. Similarly, in electronic music, creative spatial choices can have exciting, immersive effects. The process of manipulating a signal to change its perceived spatial location is usually called "panning."

The illusion of space is achieved using multichannel audio signals, reproduced through multiple loudspeakers. In a stereophonic format, we start with two signals, which were perhaps recorded by two microphones positioned at slightly different points in space. On reproduction, the two signals are individually routed to left and right loudspeakers. If we are seated equidistantly from the speakers, and neither too close nor too far from them, we experience the auditory illusion of a "phantom image" that appears to emanate from the space between the speakers.

The stereophonic format is convenient because it approximates our natural listening experience reasonably well, and only requires two audio channels. But there's no reason to stop there! There are several standardized multichannel formats involving speakers that surround the listener, as well as newer, emerging formats for encoding three-dimensional "sound fields," such as Ambisonic formats.[3] Realistically, if you have *n* speakers, then you can use them to reproduce an *n*-channel signal, and you can position these speakers however you like. Build a tower of speakers, arrange them in a long line, hang them from the ceiling, mount them on giant robotic arms that flail wildly. There are no rules!

SC can easily express and manipulate arbitrarily large multichannel signals. With a short line of code and a reasonably powerful CPU, you can create a 500-channel signal in a matter of seconds. Even if you don't have 500 speakers to hear this signal in its true form, there are UGens capable of mixing multichannel signals down to formats with fewer channels. The bottom line is that the audio server interprets an array of UGens as a multichannel signal and will attempt to route the individual channels to a contiguous block of output channels.

2.6.1 MULTICHANNEL EXPANSION

In this section, it will be helpful to take a sneak peek at the server meters, a built-in graphical tool that allows us to visually monitor output levels. We can access the meters by booting the server and evaluating **s.meter**. Keeping the meters visible while you work is useful in general, not just for this section.

Earlier, we noted that an individual UGen produces a one-channel signal, heard in only one speaker. We can now run the following line and visually confirm the channel size on the server meters (see Figure 2.10).

```
{SinOsc.ar(300, mul: 0.1)}.play;
```

When applied to a UGen, the **dup** method (or its symbolic shortcut) returns an array of UGen copies, interpreted as a multichannel signal. When we run the following line, level will appear on both output meters.

```
{SinOsc.ar(300, mul: 0.1) ! 2}.play;
```

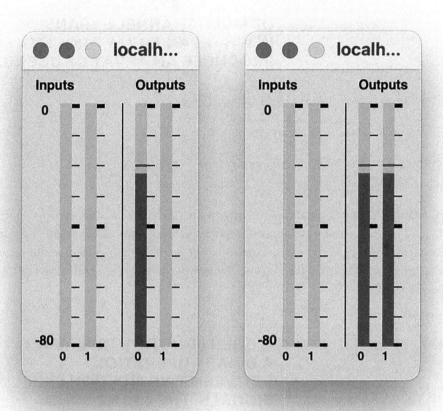

FIGURE 2.10 One- and two-channel signals displayed on the server meters.

When the last line of a UGen function is an array of signals, SC attempts to route the signal at index 0 to the lowest-numbered hardware output channel, and the item at index 1 to the next-highest hardware output channel, and so forth, for every signal in the array. If you are using your computer's built-in sound card, output channels 0 and 1 correspond to your built-in speakers or headphones. If you are using an external audio interface, these channels correspond to the two lowest-numbered outputs on that interface. Some external interfaces are capable of handling more than two simultaneous output channels. SC can (and should) be configured so that its number of input/output channels matches your hardware setup. Input/Output configuration is discussed more extensively in Chapter 6.

When we provide an array of numbers for a UGen argument, that UGen will transform into an array of UGens, distributing each number to the corresponding UGen. This transformational behavior is called *multichannel expansion* and is one of SC's most unique and powerful features. Consider the chain of code statements in Code Example 2.21, which depicts how multichannel expansion behaves on a step-by-step basis. In particular, note how the array **[350, 353]** causes the UGen to "expand" into an array of UGens. The result is a 350 Hz tone in the left speaker, and a 353 Hz tone on the right.

CODE EXAMPLE 2.21: A STEP-BY-STEP DEPICTION OF MULTICHANNEL EXPANSION, IN WHICH AN ARRAY ARGUMENT PRODUCES AN ARRAY OF UGENS.

```
{SinOsc.ar([350, 353]) * 0.2}.play;

{[SinOsc.ar(350), SinOsc.ar(353)] * 0.2}.play;

{[SinOsc.ar(350) * 0.2, SinOsc.ar(353) * 0.2]}.play;
```

When performing a binary operation involving two multichannel signals, as depicted in Code Example 2.22, the operations are applied to corresponding pairs of channels. If one multichannel signal is larger than the other, the smaller signal will "wrap" its channels to accommodate the larger signal. These are the same behaviors we've already seen with arrays of numbers in the previous chapter.

CODE EXAMPLE 2.22: A UGEN FUNCTION INVOLVING A BINARY OPERATION BETWEEN TWO MULTICHANNEL SIGNALS. THE 450 HZ TONE IS MODULATED BY A 1 HZ OSCILLATOR, AND THE 800 HZ TONE IS MODULATED BY A 9 HZ OSCILLATOR.

```
(
{
    var sig, mod;
    sig = SinOsc.ar([450, 800]);
    mod = SinOsc.kr([1, 9]).range(0, 1);
    sig = sig * mod;
    sig = sig * 0.2;
}.play;
)
```

When applying multichannel expansion to a deterministic UGen, it doesn't matter whether we duplicate an argument, or the UGen itself; the result is the same either way. However, this is not the case with stochastic UGens, such as noise generators. When we apply duplication to a stochastic UGen, we create an exact copy of the generator. When played, the same signal is sent to both speakers, creating the illusion of a single source directly between the speakers. On the contrary, when we duplicate a stochastic UGen's argument, multichannel expansion produces multiple unique instances of that UGen, which each produce a uniquely random signal. The sonic result in this case has a more pronounced sense of width and space. Code Example 2.23 shows the difference between these two versions of multichannel expansion.

CODE EXAMPLE 2.23: DUPLICATING A UGEN VS. A UGEN ARGUMENT, WHICH PRODUCES DIFFERENT BEHAVIORS WHEN APPLIED TO STOCHASTIC SIGNALS.

```
// these two expressions produce the same signal:
{SinOsc.ar(300 ! 2, mul: 0.1)}.play;
{SinOsc.ar(300, mul: 0.1) ! 2}.play;

// these two expressions produce different signals:
{PinkNoise.ar(mul: 0.2) ! 2}.play; // "point" source between the speakers
{PinkNoise.ar(mul: 0.2 ! 2)}.play; // "wide" source between the speakers
```

You may remember that we've seen a similar version of this behavior in the previous chapter, when creating arrays of random numbers:

```
rrand(1, 9) ! 8; // eight copies of one random number
```

```
{ rrand(1, 9) } ! 8; // eight uniquely generated random numbers
```

2.6.2 A COMMON MULTICHANNEL PITFALL

It's easy to fall into the knee-jerk habit of appending ! 2 to your signals so that something plays through both speakers. For a one-channel signal, this is fine, but it is problematic when applied to a signal that is already a multichannel signal.

CODE EXAMPLE 2.24: ERRONEOUSLY APPLYING DUPLICATION TO A MULTICHANNEL SIGNAL.

```
(
{
    var sig;
    sig = [SinOsc.ar(300), PinkNoise.ar];
    sig = sig * 0.1;
    sig = sig ! 2;
}.play;
)
```

In Code Example 2.24, we begin with a two-channel signal containing a sine wave in the left channel and pink noise in the right. This signal is scaled down to produce a comfortable monitoring level, and then erroneously duplicated, producing an array of arrays, written here in a simplified pseudo-code style:

```
[[SinOsc, PinkNoise], [SinOsc, PinkNoise]]
```

How should SC react to this? At the outermost layer, the audio server sees an array that contains two items, and so it tries to play the 0th item in the left speaker, and the 1st item in the right speaker. But, each of these items is an array, each containing two UGens. The result, for better or worse, is that the server sums the UGens in each internal array, resulting in the following (again written as pseudo-code):

```
[[SinOsc + PinkNoise], [SinOsc + PinkNoise]]
```

So, we hear both UGens in both speakers, and our intended stereo separation of these two signals is lost. The takeaway here is to be mindful of the channel size of your signals at every step of a UGen function, and only apply multichannel operations when it is appropriate to do so.

2.6.3 MULTICHANNEL UGENS

Some UGens are specifically designed to process signals such that their channel size is altered. One of the simplest is **Pan2**, an equal-power stereo panner that accepts a one-channel input signal, and outputs a two-channel signal based on a **pan** argument. When this argument is negative or positive 1, the signal is present in only one of the two output channels (i.e., panned "hard left" or "hard right"). When 0, the signal is equally present in both channels. Code Example 2.25 provides an example in which the pan position is modulated by an LFO, producing a sound that seems to "bounce" back and forth.

CODE EXAMPLE 2.25: USE OF Pan2 TO "MOVE" A SOUND IN THE STEREOPHONIC FIELD.

```
(
{
    var sig, pan;
    pan = SinOsc.kr(0.5) * 0.8;
    sig = PinkNoise.ar * 0.2;
    sig = Pan2.ar(sig, pan);
}.play;
)
```

Pan2 should always receive a one-channel input signal. If it receives a multichannel input signal, the output signal will be an array of arrays, similar to the pitfall illustrated in the previous section.

What happens if we create a multichannel signal with more than two channels? In Code Example 2.26, we create a 50-channel signal consisting of sine waves with random frequencies. If we play this signal as-is, we'll hear only the first two channels, because under typical conditions there are only two channels that correspond to loudspeakers.

> **CODE EXAMPLE 2.26: AN ATTEMPT TO PLAY A 50-CHANNEL SIGNAL. ONLY THE LOWEST TWO CHANNELS WILL BE HEARD.**
>
> ```
> (
> {
>     var sig, freq;
>     freq = {exprand(200, 2000)} ! 50;
>     sig = SinOsc.ar(freq) * 0.1;
> }.play;
> )
> ```

Splay, demonstrated in Code Example 2.27, is a UGen that mixes a multichannel signal to a two-channel format in which the input channels are "placed" at equidistant points from left-to-right. It's a convenient option for hearing every channel of an arbitrarily large multichannel signal.

> **CODE EXAMPLE 2.27: USE OF Splay TO MIX 50 CHANNELS TO A TWO-CHANNEL FORMAT.**
>
> ```
> (
> {
>     var sig, freq;
>     freq = {exprand(200, 2000)} ! 50;
>     sig = SinOsc.ar(freq) * 0.1;
>     sig = Splay.ar(sig);
> }.play;
> )
> ```

Exploring variations is left as an open exercise for the reader. It's possible to create intricate multichannel sounds with these simple principles, and we'll encounter many such sounds throughout this book. You may also want to read the guide file titled "Multichannel Expansion" to refine your understanding.

2.7 SynthDef and Synth

The "function-dot-play" approach is a shortcut for the more formal and flexible process of making sound, which involves the use of **SynthDef** and **Synth**. A SynthDef is a sort of "recipe" for a signal algorithm, while a Synth is an object that executes that algorithm. When we play a UGen function, the returned object is actually a Synth, which we've been referring to as a "sound process" up to this point. As an analogy for using these two classes, consider baking a cake. A SynthDef is like a recipe book, containing instructions for baking a variety of cakes. A Synth is like a cake, created by following a recipe from the book. From this single book, it's possible to create lots of different cakes, but the book itself is not a cake (and not nearly as delicious). If you wanted to make twenty cakes, you wouldn't need twenty books. In other words, two copies of the same book are redundant, but two identical cakes are not necessarily redundant (maybe your guests are extra hungry). Like a good recipe book, a SynthDef should be maximally flexible, so that it can be used to spawn a maximally diverse collection of tangible results. If a SynthDef is poorly designed (i.e., with a limited set of recipes), the sounds that can be produced will be similarly limited. Flexible SynthDef design primarily involves declaring plenty of arguments, so that numerous UGen parameters can be customized and controlled.

For short examples and quick tests, function-dot-play is convenient and saves time. However, in cases where reuse and flexibility of signal algorithms are of greater importance, it's preferable to use SynthDef and Synth. In fact, using Synth and SynthDef is the only way to create sound in SuperCollider. When we invoke function-dot-play, a SynthDef and Synth are created for us in the background.

2.7.1 CREATING A SYNTHDEF

CODE EXAMPLE 2.28: A SIMPLE UGEN FUNCTION USED TO ILLUSTRATE THE PROCESS OF CONVERSION TO A SYNTHDEF.

```
(
x = {
    var sig;
    sig = SinOsc.ar([350, 353]);
    sig = sig * 0.2;
}.play;
)
x.free;
```

Consider the UGen function in Code Example 2.28. We can change it into a SynthDef using a few simple steps, summarized here and detailed below:

1. Provide a name and UGen function.
2. Specify the output signal and destination.
3. 'add' the SynthDef.

A new SynthDef expects two arguments: a symbol, which represents the SynthDef's name, and a UGen function that defines its signal algorithm. Most algorithms, particularly those that generate or process a signal, produce some output signal. When this is the case, we must explicitly designate the output signal and its destination, by including an output UGen in the function. There are several types of output UGens, but **Out** is quite common. The first argument of **Out** indicates the destination bus (0 corresponds to your lowest-numbered hardware channel, usually your left speaker). The second argument is the signal to be sent to that bus. If the output signal is a multichannel signal, additional channels will be routed to busses with incrementally higher bus indices. For example, if **Out** is used to send a two-channel signal to bus 0, the channels will be routed to busses 0 and 1. Finally, we close the SynthDef.new enclosure, and use the **add** method to make the SynthDef available to the audio server. Code Example 2.29 depicts the result of this process.

CODE EXAMPLE 2.29: A SYNTHDEF CREATED FROM THE UGEN FUNCTION IN CODE EXAMPLE 2.28.

```
(
SynthDef(\test, {
    var sig;
    sig = SinOsc.ar([350, 353]);
    sig = sig * 0.2;
    Out.ar(0, sig);
}).add;
)
```

Once a SynthDef has been added, it will remain available as long as the SC environment remains open and the server remains booted. If you want to make changes to the SynthDef, you can re-evaluate the code, and the new definition will overwrite the old one. There can only be one SynthDef with a specific name, so if you have multiple SynthDefs, be sure to give them unique names.

2.7.2 CREATING A SYNTH

We can execute a SynthDef algorithm by instantiating a Synth. At minimum, the Synth needs to know the name of the SynthDef to be used. If we assign the Synth to a variable, we can communicate with it at a point in the future (see Code Example 2.30). Note that we don't need to explicitly "play" a Synth; simply creating a Synth puts it in an active state on the audio server.

CODE EXAMPLE 2.30: CREATING AND FREEING A SYNTH.

```
x = Synth(\test);

x.free;
```

When we use function-dot-play, SC not only creates a SynthDef and Synth in the background but also adds a few conveniences. If our function does not include a gated envelope, SC creates one automatically, with an argument named "gate." The **release** method, when applied to a Synth, assumes there is a "gate" argument used to control a sustaining envelope. Additionally, SC adds an **Out** UGen if one does not already exist.

When using SynthDef and Synth ourselves, no such conveniences are applied. Instead, we get exactly what we specify. If we don't include an amplitude envelope, the **release** method will have no effect. Similarly, if we don't include an output UGen, the Synth will not make any sound.

2.7.3 SYNTHDEF ARGUMENTS

Continuing our cake-baking analogy, the SynthDef from the previous section is like a cookbook with exactly one cake recipe. Every **\test** Synth sounds exactly the same. A better design choice involves declaring arguments for parameters we'd like to control. Doing so makes the SynthDef slightly more computationally expensive, but offers vastly more flexibility. Code Example 2.31 augments the SynthDef with an amplitude envelope and declares arguments for nearly all modulatable parameters.

CODE EXAMPLE 2.31: A MORE FLEXIBLY DESIGNED SYNTHDEF WITH NUMEROUS ARGUMENTS.

```
(
SynthDef.new(\test, {
    arg freq = 350, amp = 0.2, atk = 0.01, dec = 0.3,
    slev = 0.4, rel = 1, gate = 1, out = 0;
    var sig, env;
    env = EnvGen.kr(
        Env.adsr(atk, dec, slev, rel),
        gate,
        doneAction: 2
    );
    sig = SinOsc.ar(freq + [0, 1]);
    sig = sig * env;
    sig = sig * amp;
    Out.ar(out, sig);
}).add;
)

x = Synth(\test);

x.set(\freq, 450);

x.set(\amp, 0.5);

x.set(\gate, 0, \rel, 3);
```

To instantiate a Synth whose initial argument values differ from the SynthDef defaults, we provide an array of name-value argument pairs, depicted in Code Example 2.32, similar to the approach shown in Code Example 2.7. The array is the second argument that **Synth.new()** expects, so no **args:** keyword is needed.

> **CODE EXAMPLE 2.32:** CREATING A SYNTH WITH CUSTOM INITIAL ARGUMENT VALUES.
>
> ```
> x = Synth(\test, [freq: 800, amp: 0.1, atk: 4, slev: 1]);
>
> x.set(\gate, 0);
> ```

It's difficult to overstate the value of arguments in a SynthDef. Even if you declare an argument but never manipulate it, the fact that it exists provides the flexibility to do so, if you change your mind. If you want your cake frosting to be sometimes vanilla and sometimes chocolate, you'll need to declare a flavor argument.

At this point, we're able to start making somewhat interesting and musical sounds, for example, by using iteration to create tone clusters. A short example appears in Code Example 2.33. Modifying this example is left as an open exercise to the reader.

> **CODE EXAMPLE 2.33:** A PAIR OF CODE EXPRESSIONS THAT GENERATE AND FADE A TONE CLUSTER.
>
> ```
> (
> // return an array of four Synths, assigned to x
> x = [205, 310, 525, 700].collect({ |f|
>     Synth.new(\test, [\freq, f, \amp, 0.1]);
> });
> )
>
> // fade out each Synth
> x.do({ |n| n.set(\gate, 0, \rel, 5) });
> ```

Despite all its arguments, this SynthDef represents a relatively small book of recipes. It won't allow us to play an audio sample or add a reverb effect. However, no one SynthDef should be designed to produce every imaginable sound, just as no single recipe book will provide you with every cake recipe known to humankind. Indeed, as your projects become more complex, they will necessitate a modest collection of SynthDefs, each with a different purpose, just as you might accumulate a library of cake cookbooks over time. Creating SynthDefs flexible enough to produce a wide variety of sounds, but not so complex that they become unwieldy, is a skill that develops over time. Nevertheless, there are no hard rules, and there may be situations that call for an unusually large/complex SynthDef, and others that call for more minimal design.

> **TIP.RAND(); RANDOMNESS IN A SYNTHDEF**
>
> We have seen that randomness can be used inside of a UGen function to create interesting results (for example, in Code Examples 2.26 and 2.27). The language-side methods **rrand** and **exprand** can be used inside of a SynthDef, but it's usually better to use the UGens **Rand** and **ExpRand**. The language-side methods generate a random value exactly once, when the SynthDef is first added, but the UGens will generate a new random value every time a Synth is created from that SynthDef. Note also that the UGens **Rand** and **ExpRand** use the creation method **new** instead of **ar/kr/ir**, which can also be omitted. The following code demonstrates the difference between these two approaches:
>
> ```
> (
> SynthDef(\rand_lang, {
>     var sig = SinOsc.ar({exprand(200, 2000)} ! 30);
>     sig = Splay.ar(sig) * 0.05;
>     Out.ar(0, sig);
> }).add;
> )
>
> Synth(\rand_lang); // same randomness every time
>
> (
> SynthDef(\rand_ugen, {
>     var sig = SinOsc.ar({ExpRand(200, 2000)} ! 30);
>     sig = Splay.ar(sig) * 0.05;
>     Out.ar(0, sig);
> }).add;
> )
>
> Synth(\rand_ugen); //unique randomness every time
> ```

2.8 Alternate Expression of Frequency and Amplitude

Oscillators with a frequency parameter expect a value in Hertz. When thinking about musical pitch, Hertz isn't always the preferred unit of measurement. Using MIDI note numbers can be a convenient alternative. In this system, 60 corresponds to middle C (roughly 261.6 Hz), and an increment/decrement of one corresponds to a semitone shift in 12-tone equal temperament. We can convert from MIDI to Hertz using **midicps** and convert in the other direction with **cpsmidi**. Non-integer MIDI note numbers are valid and represent a pitch proportionally between two equal-tempered semitones.

```
60.midicps; // -> 261.6255653006

500.cpsmidi; // -> 71.213094853649
```

midiratio and **ratiomidi** are similarly useful methods that convert back and forth between an interval, measured in semitones, and the frequency ratio that interval represents. For example, **3.midiratio** represents the ratio between an F and the D immediately below it, because these two pitches are three semitones apart. Negative semitone values represent pitch movement in the opposite direction.

```
// the ratio that raises a frequency by one semitone

1.midiratio; // -> 1.0594630943591

// the ratio 8/5 is slightly more than 8 equal-tempered semitones

(8/5).ratiomidi // -> 8.1368628613517
```

Similarly, when expressing signal amplitude, a normalized range between zero and one isn't always the most intuitive choice. The **ampdb** method converts a normalized amplitude to a decibel value and **dbamp** does the opposite. A value of zero dB corresponds to a nominal amplitude value of one. If your audio system is properly calibrated, a decibel value around -20 dB should produce a comfortable monitoring level, and a typical signal will become inaudible around -80 dB.

```
-15.dbamp; // -> 0.17782794100389

0.3.ampdb; // -> -10.457574905607
```

For efficiency reasons, it is preferable not to build these methods into a SynthDef, and instead call them when creating or modifying a Synth, so that the server does not have to repeatedly perform these calculations. A few examples appear in Code Example 2.34.

CODE EXAMPLE 2.34: USAGE OF FREQUENCY AND AMPLITUDE CONVERSION METHODS.

```
(
SynthDef.new(\test, {
    arg freq = 350, amp = 0.2, atk = 0.01, dec = 0.3,
    slev = 0.4, rel = 1, gate = 1, out = 0;
    var sig, env;
    env = EnvGen.kr(
        Env.adsr(atk, dec, slev, rel),
        gate,
        doneAction: 2
    );
    sig = SinOsc.ar(freq + [0, 1]);
    sig = sig * env;
    sig = sig * amp;
    Out.ar(out, sig);
}).add;
)

x = Synth(\test, [freq: 60.midicps, amp: -20.dbamp]);

x.set(\freq, 62.midicps); // increase pitch by 2 semitones

x.set(\amp, -12.dbamp); // increase level by 8 dB

x.set(\gate, 0);
```

2.9 Helpful Server Tools

Working with sound in a code-based interface can feel intimidating, especially in the absence of graphical tools to help visualize your work. Thankfully, there are several built-in tools that provide such assistance (we introduced the server meters in Section 2.6.1). Several of these tools are accessible from the "Server" drop-down menu, and also by clicking on the server status bar in the lower-right corner of the IDE. Figure 2.11 displays several of these tools.

2.9.1 POLLING A UGEN

We can **poll** any UGen, which prints its output values in the post window while it's running, shown in Code Example 2.35. It's a troubleshooting tool, like **postln**, but for UGens. Obviously, we can't (and shouldn't) print every value that comes out of a UGen, which is tens of thousands of numbers per second. Just ten values or so per second can be enough to get the information we need. Still, polling a UGen, even at a low frequency, is relatively taxing on your CPU, and should only be used for debugging. The first argument of **poll** is the frequency at which the UGen value is sampled and displayed, which rarely needs to be greater than 20. Excessively high values may cause SC to become unresponsive.

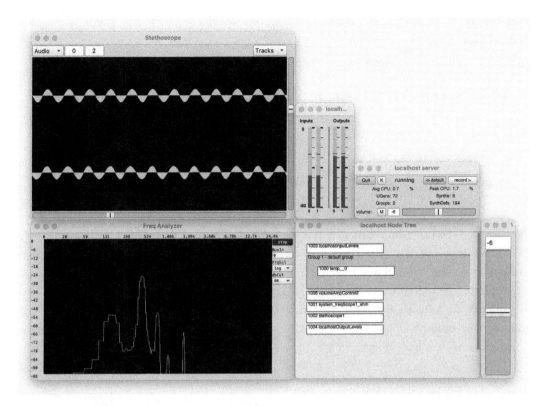

FIGURE 2.11 Several graphical server tools. Clockwise from upper left: Stethoscope, Server Meters, Server GUI, Volume Slider, Node Tree, and FreqScope (also called Spectrum Analyzer or Frequency Analyzer).

```
CODE EXAMPLE 2.35: POLLING A UGEN.

(
x = {
    var sig, freq;
    freq = SinOsc.kr(0.2).exprange(200, 800).poll(20);
    sig = SinOsc.ar(freq);
    sig = sig * 0.2;
    sig = sig ! 2;
}.play;
)
```

2.9.2 PLOTTING A UGEN FUNCTION

A UGen function's output signal can be visualized by calling **plot** instead of **play**, and providing a duration argument (see Code Example 2.36). This is a real-time feature, which means an amount of time equal to the specified duration must elapse before the plot is displayed, so longer plots are increasingly impractical. Plotting is a great way to visually learn more about the behavior of a UGen you're unfamiliar with, without the risk of unexpectedly loud sounds. If the output of the UGen is a multichannel signal, the result will be a multichannel plot.

> **CODE EXAMPLE 2.36: PLOTTING UGEN FUNCTIONS.**
>
> ```
> {SinOsc.ar(110)}.plot(0.05); // 0.05 seconds of a 110 Hz sine wave
>
> {SinOsc.ar([110, 220, 330, 440])}.plot(0.05); // multichannel plot
> ```

Plotting a UGen function returns an instance of a class named **Plotter**, a graphical display that responds to a variety of methods that alter its appearance. These changes can be invoked through code, but it is simpler to rely on a handful of keyboard shortcuts, enabled when a signal plot is the topmost window. A list of keyboard shortcuts appears in the **Plotter** help file. If a plot contains an especially large number of data points, attempts to move or resize the window may produce sluggish behavior. UGen plots are most nimble and useful when plotting a relatively small set of data.

2.9.3 STETHOSCOPE

The **Stethoscope** class provides a real-time digital oscilloscope, useful for visually monitoring the shape and behavior of a signal. Assuming the server is booted, this tool can be created by evaluating:

```
s.scope;
```

By default, the oscilloscope monitors audio busses 0 and 1. In a typical setup, anything sent to loudspeakers will appear on the scope. Like **Plotter**, a **Stethoscope** instance responds to methods that alter its behavior and appearance, most of which can be invoked through mouse interaction or keyboard shortcuts. A table of these shortcuts appears in the **Stethoscope** help file.

Periodic signals may appear to be unstable or jumpy, or to move forward/backward on the oscilloscope. This is an example of the "wagon wheel effect," which is the same phenomenon that causes tires to appear as if they are spinning backward or standing still in car commercials. The illusion results from two periodic processes being superimposed. In our case, the frame rate of the scope interferes with the apparent frequency of the signal. You can attempt to bring these two periodic processes into harmony by adjusting horizontal zoom level using the bottom slider. When properly "tuned," the signal movement will appear to stand still, and it becomes much easier to understand its shape and behavior.

2.9.4 FREQSCOPE

The **FreqScope** class is like **Stethoscope** but provides a real-time spectral analyzer instead of a waveform display. This tool is created by evaluating:

```
FreqScope.new;
```

A `FreqScope` can only monitor one channel at a time and analyzes audio bus zero by default. It's possible to monitor a different bus using the number box on the right-hand side of the analyzer window.

2.9.5 MAIN VOLUME SLIDER

`Volume` is a class that the audio server uses for adjusting the overall level of its output. It includes a built-in graphical component that makes this functionality available to the user via a slider and number box, which can be created by evaluating:

```
s.volume.gui;
```

If you adjust this slider and then close the slider window, the volume change will remain in effect.

2.9.6 RECORDING TO AN AUDIO FILE

Some users may wish to use SC for its rich algorithmic capabilities, and use a DAW for composition, assembly, mixing, and mastering. This is a reasonable thing to do, considering that DAW environments are specifically tailored for this type of work. To use a DAW-related term, it is possible to "bounce" sounds from SC and render them as an audio file. To do this, we can first materialize a graphical window that represents the server's status:

```
s.makeGui;
```

Clicking the "record" button will cause SC to begin recording any signal that plays on busses 0 and 1. When clicked again, recording will stop and an audio file will be written to your hard drive. The post window displays the path to the newly created audio file, and the location of your default recording directory can be printed by evaluating:

```
Platform.recordingsDir;
```

Your recording may include a second or two of silence at the beginning of the file, on account of time passing between clicking the button and running your sound code, but this silence is easily trimmed in any waveform editor. The recording process can also be started and stopped by evaluating **s.record** and **s.stopRecording**.

2.9.7 THE NODE TREE

The node tree is a real-time graphical representation of active processes on the audio server. It can be invoked by evaluating:

```
s.plotTree;
```

When a Synth is created, it will be represented by a white box that appears on the node tree window (try this yourself!). The node tree can be useful for sleuthing out certain types of problems. For instance, if you're trying to create a sound but don't hear anything, check the node tree. If you see the white box that represents your Synth, you can be fairly certain the problem is related to something in your SynthDef function. If you don't see a white box, then it means the problem is related to the code meant to create the Synth.

Notes

1 At the time of writing, detailed instructions for installing SC and its software dependencies on Linux systems can be found on the SC GitHub page: https://github.com/supercollider/supercollider/wiki/Installing-SuperCollider-from-source-on-Ubuntu.
2 It is also possible to designate a point earlier in the envelope as the "loop node." When a loop node is specified in addition to a release node, the envelope will loop the section between these two nodes as long as the gate remains open. The envelope behavior described here assumes that only a release node has been specified. See the Env help file for more information on setting a loop node.
3 "Ambisonics" refers to a mathematical framework for encoding sound information in a three-dimensional format, irrespective of any particular loudspeaker setup. It was chiefly pioneered by Michael Gerzon during the 1970s. The Ambisonic Toolkit, developed by researchers at DXARTS at the University of Washington, provides a set of additional tools and classes for working with Ambisonic sound in SC: https://www.ambisonictoolkit.net/.

PART II
CREATIVE TECHNIQUES

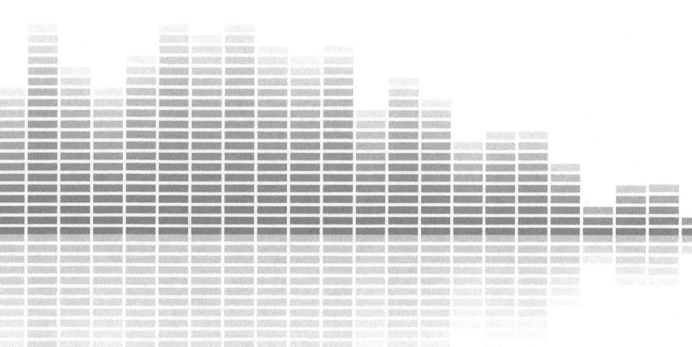

In this second part, we move beyond the fundamentals of interacting with SuperCollider and take a closer look at well-established techniques and workflows that are often cornerstones of electronic music-making and creative sound design projects. Specifically, the next several chapters discuss synthesis, sampling, sequencing, signal processing, options for external control, and graphical user interface design. These topics can be thought of as the component parts that constitute large-scale creative works, and they should provide you with lots of ideas to play with.

CHAPTER 3

SYNTHESIS

3.1 Overview

Synthesis refers to creative applications of combining and interconnecting signal generators, typically relying on oscillators and noise, with a goal of building unique timbres and textures. This chapter explores synthesis categories, many of which are accompanied by Companion Code files designed to promote further exploration and deeper understanding.

3.2 Additive Synthesis

Additive synthesis implies summation of two or more waveforms, producing a new waveform with a unique shape and spectrum. Each sample value in a sum waveform is equal to the sum of the samples of all component waveforms at that specific point in time. Figure 3.1 illustrates a simple example.

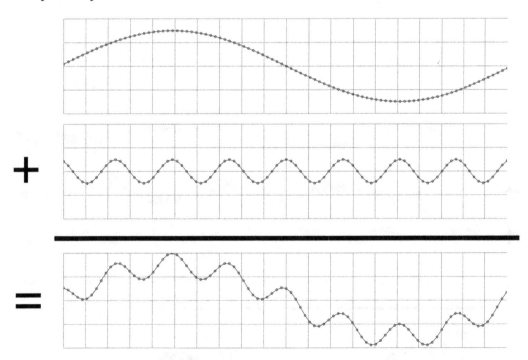

FIGURE 3.1 An illustration of additive synthesis involving two sine waves.

Traditionally, additive synthesis refers to summation of sine waves. The advantage and popularity of the sine wave is related to the fact that any periodic vibration can be expressed as a sum of sines provided with the proper frequencies, amplitudes, and phases. Thus, we can view the sine wave as the fundamental "building block" of more complex periodic waveforms.

When we sum a collection of sine waves whose frequencies are all integer multiples of a common value, the result is a waveform in which the component sines perfectly align with one another. In this case, the tones coalesce and become more difficult to perceive on an individual basis, and we tend to experience a sense of pitch determined by this common multiple, called the fundamental frequency.

The simplest way to approach additive synthesis in SC is to manually sum several signals together, demonstrated in Code Example 3.1, and the first 0.01 seconds of the code in this example are visualized in Figure 3.2.

CODE EXAMPLE 3.1: ADDITIVE SYNTHESIS BY WAY OF MANUAL SIGNAL SUMMATION.

```
(
{
    var sig;
    sig = SinOsc.ar(200, mul: 0.2);
    sig = sig + SinOsc.ar(400, mul: 0.1);
    sig = sig + SinOsc.ar(600, mul: 0.05);
    sig = sig + SinOsc.ar(800, mul: 0.025);
    sig = sig ! 2;
}.play;
)
```

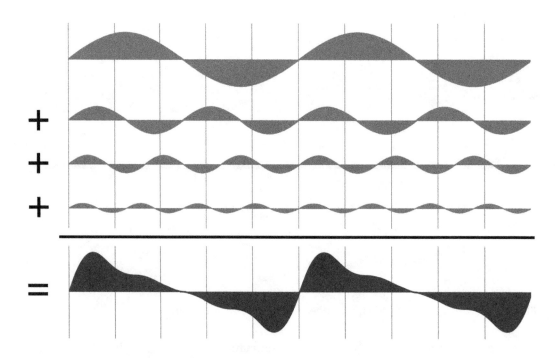

FIGURE 3.2 A visualization of the summation process in Code Example 3.1.

Although summation of non-sinusoidal waveforms may not be considered additive synthesis in the classical sense, it is nonetheless an interesting and fruitful creative pathway. Generally, combining sounds through summation is a fundamental and far-reaching concept. Mixing, a focal point in audio engineering, relies on waveform summation to achieve a desirable musical balance. Organ stops can be adjusted to control airflow through combinations of pipes, producing a particular tone color. The vibrations from acoustic instruments in an ensemble blend in the air, which the ear experiences as a singular sum of pressure variations. At their core, these examples are all based on the fundamental idea of signal summation. Companion Code 3.1 continues this discussion of the basics of additive synthesis with some additional examples.

When summing signals, peak amplitude of the sum waveform tends to be greater than that of any of its individual components, so distortion is a concern in additive synthesis. In Code Example 3.1, for example, if all four **mul** values are one, the sum has a peak amplitude close to four, which exceeds 0 dBFS and yields a loud, possibly distorted result. As a general rule, the largest "safe" amplitude for an individual signal in an additive sum is the reciprocal of the number of waveforms being summed (in Code Example 3.1, this value is 0.25), although scaling this value down even further is sensible to promote a comfortable monitoring level and leave headroom for the possibility of additional sounds to be mixed in later.

3.2.1: ADDITIVE SYNTHESIS AND ITERATION

Code Example 3.1 is an example of a repetitive task that can be expressed more concisely with iteration. Code Examples 3.2 and 3.3 rewrite this example using **do** and **collect**. Note that because **do** returns its receiver, we must initialize **sig** as zero and explicitly store each sum operation within the iteration function. By contrast, because **collect** returns a new collection of **SinOsc** UGens, we can simply call **sum** on this result. Despite this difference, both are preferable to the manual approach shown in Code Example 3.1, because adding more sines now only requires enlarging the **freqs** array, rather than typing entirely new lines of code. Companion Code 3.2 explores additional ideas involving iteration.

CODE EXAMPLE 3.2: USING do TO REWRITE THE ADDITIVE SYNTHESIS EXAMPLE IN CODE EXAMPLE 3.1.

```
(
{
    var sig = 0, freqs = [200, 400, 600, 800];
    freqs.do({ |f, i|
        sig = sig + SinOsc.ar(f, mul: 0.2 / 2.pow(i));
    });
    sig = sig ! 2;
}.play;
)
```

CODE EXAMPLE 3.3: USING `collect` TO REWRITE THE ADDITIVE SYNTHESIS EXAMPLE IN CODE EXAMPLE 3.1.

```
(
{
    var sig, freqs = [200, 400, 600, 800];
    sig = freqs.collect({ |f, i|
        SinOsc.ar(f, mul: 0.2 / 2.pow(i));
    });
    sig = sig.sum;
    sig = sig ! 2;
}.play;
)
```

3.2.2 OTHER ADDITIVE SYNTHESIS UGENS

A few UGens offer alternative interfaces for additive synthesis, typically providing efficiency or simplification at the cost of some flexibility.

Blip, demonstrated in Code Example 3.4, outputs the sum of a contiguous block of harmonics that always includes the fundamental. All harmonics have equal amplitudes, and the number of harmonics can be dynamically changed. When the number of harmonics changes, **Blip** avoids harsh clicks by ensuring new sines start at zero crossings, but the entrances and exits of individual harmonics are still slightly audible. **Blip** is an anti-aliasing oscillator (automatically reducing the number of harmonics if necessary), which boasts a relatively efficient design but offers little in terms of controlling individual harmonics.

CODE EXAMPLE 3.4: USE OF `Blip` TO GENERATE AN ADDITIVE SPECTRUM. THE NUMBER OF HARMONICS IS CONTROLLED BY A TRIANGLE WAVE.

```
(
{
    var sig, harm;
    harm = LFTri.kr(0.1, 3).range(1, 50);
    sig = Blip.ar([80, 81], harm);
    sig = sig * 0.1;
}.play;
)
```

Klang represents a bank of summed sine oscillators. The frequencies are fixed, but the design is more computationally efficient than creating individual sines. **Klang** provides arguments that scale and shift the frequencies, but these values are fixed once the Synth is created. **Klang** is a slightly unusual UGen in that the oscillator parameters must be specified as a **Ref** array containing three internal arrays for frequencies, amplitudes, and phases. The general purpose of a **Ref** array in the context of UGen functions is to prevent the multichannel expansion that would ordinarily occur. A **Ref** can be created using **new**, or the backtick character can be used as a syntax shortcut:

```
Ref.new([[200, 400, 600, 800], [0.4, 0.2, 0.1, 0.05], [0, 0, 0, 0]]);

`[[200, 400, 600, 800], [0.4, 0.2, 0.1, 0.05], [0, 0, 0, 0]];
```

DynKlang is a version of **Klang** in which the oscillator parameters can be dynamically controlled, but which is no more efficient than manually creating individual **SinOsc** generators. Code Examples 3.5 and 3.6 demonstrate the use of **Klang** and **DynKlang**. In the second example, the frequencies and amplitudes are scaled by noise generators, which creates a continually shifting additive spectrum.

CODE EXAMPLE 3.5: AN ADDITIVE SYNTHESIS EXAMPLE USING Klang.

```
(
{
    var sig;
    sig = Klang.ar(
        `[// <- note the backtick character
            Array.exprand(40, 50, 8000).sort,
            Array.exprand(40, 0.001, 0.05).sort.reverse,
            Array.rand(40, 0, 2pi)
        ]
    );
    sig = sig ! 2;
}.play;
)
```

CODE EXAMPLE 3.6: AN ADDITIVE SYNTHESIS EXAMPLE USING DynKlang.

```
(
{
    var sig, freqs, amps, phases;
    freqs = Array.exprand(40, 50, 8000).sort;
    amps = Array.exprand(40, 0.005, 0.2).sort.reverse;
    phases = Array.rand(40, 0, 2pi);
    sig = DynKlang.ar(`[ // <- note the backtick character
        freqs * LFNoise1.kr(0.02 ! 40).exprange(0.25, 2),
        amps * LFNoise1.kr(1 ! 40).exprange(0.02, 1),
        phases
```

```
    ]);
    sig = sig ! 2;
}.play;
)
```

3.3 Modulation Synthesis

Modulation refers to the process of controlling some signal parameter using the output of another signal. Frequency modulation, amplitude modulation, and ring modulation are among the most firmly established types, but modulation synthesis is a broad term that characterizes any configuration in which one signal influences a parameter of another. In the simplest setup, modulation synthesis calls for two signals: a carrier (the signal being influenced), and a modulator (the signal doing the influencing). Larger, more complex networks of interconnected signals are possible, such as multiple carriers/modulators, modulators arranged in series or parallel, and a carrier may even serve as its own modulator. With purposeful creative decisions, modulation synthesis can produce exciting results.

Implementing modulation synthesis in SC involves supplying UGens as input values for other UGens. One common approach involves using an LFO to modulate the cutoff frequency of a low-pass filter as it processes some spectrally rich sound (demonstrated in Code Example 3.7), thus periodically attenuating higher frequencies and creating a familiar "wah-wah" effect.

CODE EXAMPLE 3.7: MODULATING THE FREQUENCY OF A LOW-PASS FILTER TO CREATE A "WAH-WAH" EFFECT.

```
(
{
    var sig, mod;
    mod = SinOsc.ar(4, 3pi/2).range(0, 3000);
    sig = Pulse.ar([90, 91]);
    sig = LPF.ar(sig, 200 + mod);
    sig = sig * 0.1;
}.play;
)
```

A word of caution: In modulation synthesis, the sine wave is frequently favored as a modulator because of its spectral simplicity, smooth shape, and predictable behavior. Other waves, such as sawtooth, pulse, and triangle waves, have hard corners and/or abrupt changes in their wave shape. When one of these signals is used as a modulator, certain configurations may produce gritty, glitchy results, which may include clicks, pops, and other types of digital noise. The desirability of these sounds is subjective, but the issue is further compounded by mathematical nuances of backend UGen design. For example, it is not uncommon for the frequency of a carrier oscillator to become negative when modulated. **SinOsc** has a stable response to negative frequencies, equivalent to inverting the polarity of the waveform (e.g. multiplication by negative one). By contrast, the amplitude of **Pulse** substantially increases as its frequency approaches zero, and **Saw** accumulates positive DC offset as its frequency becomes negative. Even worse, the output of **LFTri**, **LFCub**, and **LFPar** will rapidly approach negative infinity when their frequency argument is negative. Most filter UGens exhibit similarly explosive behavior when their frequency argument is near or below zero. The takeaway is that UGens are not freely interchangeable! These discrepancies underscore that using a programming language to create sound demands a measure of caution. When dealing with experimental modulation configurations, you should take steps to avoid harming your speakers/ears, such as using UGens that filter out DC bias and limit amplitude (e.g., **LeakDC** and **Limiter**), and turning down your system volume before evaluating dubious code.

> ### TIP.RAND(); LeakDC AND Limiter
>
> Working with chaotic or unpredictable signals? **LeakDC** and **Limiter** can help tame them. **LeakDC** is essentially a high-pass filter with a very low cutoff frequency, which brings a signal's center of gravity back to zero if it starts to shift in the positive or negative direction. **Limiter**, as its name suggests, limits amplitude to a user-provided argument, which defaults to one. Generally, both UGens can be applied to a signal at the end of a UGen function with no risk and minimal overhead. The following pseudo-code provides an example:
>
> ```
> (
> {
>     var sig;
>     sig = ...some chaotic/unpredictable signal...
>     sig = Limiter.ar(sig);
>     sig = LeakDC.ar(sig);
> }.play;
> )
> ```

3.3.1 AMPLITUDE MODULATION AND RING MODULATION

Classic amplitude modulation (AM) refers to a configuration in which the carrier and modulator are sine waves, and the modulator causes the carrier amplitude to fluctuate between zero and one. At low modulator frequencies, AM produces a *tremolo* effect. As the modulator frequency increases beyond 20 Hz, a spectral transformation occurs, in which a pair of additional sine waves appear at frequencies equal to the carrier frequency ± modulator frequency. These additional spectral components are called sidebands.

A slowly increasing modulator frequency demonstrates this sonic metamorphosis in Code Example 3.8, and Figure 3.3 displays waveform and spectrum information when the modulator frequency is 150 Hz.

CODE EXAMPLE 3.8: AMPLITUDE MODULATION WITH A GRADUALLY INCREASING MODULATOR FREQUENCY.

```
(
{
    var sig, mod, modHz;
    modHz = XLine.kr(1, 150, 10);
    mod = SinOsc.ar(modHz).range(0, 1);
    sig = SinOsc.ar(750, mul: mod);
    sig = sig * 0.2 ! 2;
}.play;
)
```

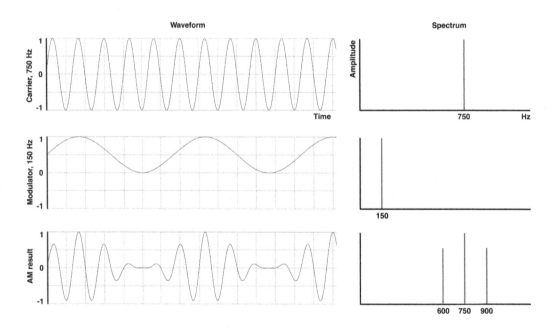

FIGURE 3.3 Waveforms and spectra corresponding to Code Example 3.8, at the moment when the modulator frequency reaches its peak.

Ring modulation (RM) is a nearly identical variation of AM. In RM, the output range of the modulator is bounded between ±1. The spectral consequence of this change is that the carrier is no longer present in the output spectrum. Similar examples appear in Code Example 3.9 and Figure 3.4. Although "classic" AM and RM involve sine waves, these modulation techniques can theoretically be applied to any two signals. In either case, we are essentially multiplying one signal by another, and the results may vary significantly, depending on the types of signals involved. Companion Code 3.3 explores additional ideas related to amplitude modulation.

> **CODE EXAMPLE 3.9:** **RING MODULATION WITH A GRADUALLY INCREASING MODULATOR FREQUENCY.**
>
> ```
> (
> {
>     var sig, mod, modHz;
>     modHz = XLine.kr(1, 150, 10);
>     mod = SinOsc.ar(modHz).range(-1, 1);
>     sig = SinOsc.ar(750, mul: mod);
>     sig = sig * 0.2 ! 2;
> }.play;
> )
> ```

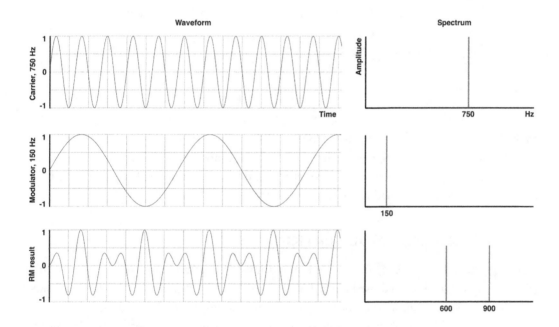

FIGURE 3.4 Waveforms and spectra corresponding to Code Example 3.9, at the moment when the modulator frequency reaches its peak.

In modulation contexts, it may be tempting to use a control-rate modulator to conserve CPU power, since this signal quite literally "controls" another. However, the quality of a control rate oscillator degrades if its frequency is too high (recall the principles surrounding the Nyquist frequency, introduced in Chapter 2). If you play the examples in Code Example 3.10, you'll notice that they sound quite different, despite all the numbers being the same.

CODE EXAMPLE 3.10: DISCREPANCIES IN AUDIO QUALITY BETWEEN USING AN AUDIO RATE MODULATOR VS. A CONTROL RATE MODULATOR.

```
(
{
    var sig, mod;
    mod = SinOsc.ar(1050).range(0, 1); // audio rate modulator
    sig = SinOsc.ar(750);
    sig = sig * mod * 0.2 ! 2;
}.play;
)

(
{
    var sig, mod;
    mod = SinOsc.kr(1050).range(0, 1); // control rate modulator
    sig = SinOsc.ar(750);
    sig = sig * mod * 0.2 ! 2;
}.play;
)
```

Even if the frequency of a modulator is low, using an audio rate modulator is a perfectly reasonable choice. Doing so will ensure that the carrier and modulator have equal mathematical precision and help guarantee the highest-quality sound. Audio rate signals require more CPU power, but the additional load is rarely consequential.

3.3.2 FREQUENCY MODULATION

Compared to AM and RM, frequency modulation (FM) offers a greater range of results without requiring additional oscillators. FM is a widely used, flexible, and well-documented technique, and is the foundation for many hardware synthesizers and software plug-ins.

At its core, FM involves a carrier oscillator whose frequency is offset by the output of a modulator oscillator. The amplitude of an FM modulator is typically greater than an AM/RM modulator in order to audibly influence the carrier frequency. At low modulator frequencies, FM produces a slow fluctuation in pitch known as *vibrato*. As the modulator frequency increases, a spectral transformation occurs in which multiple sideband pairs appear on either side of the carrier frequency, at intervals determined by the modulator frequency. The number of audible sideband pairs increases with modulator amplitude. Sidebands with "negative" frequencies are reflected across zero Hz into positive territory. Sideband amplitudes are determined by Bessel functions (an intermediate mathematical topic beyond the scope of this book), but for our purposes, it's sufficient to generalize that sideband amplitudes are, on average, lower than that of the carrier, and a sideband whose frequency is relatively distant from the carrier tends to have a lower amplitude than a sideband relatively close to the carrier.

Code Example 3.11 demonstrates a simple FM configuration. The carrier has a base frequency of 750 Hz, offset by a modulator with an amplitude of 300. Thus, the frequency of the carrier ranges from 450 to 1,050 Hz. The modulator frequency gradually increases over ten seconds, showcasing the spectral transformation that takes place. You can visualize this transformation by first opening the spectrum analyzer with `FreqScope.new`.

CODE EXAMPLE 3.11: A SIMPLE FM CONFIGURATION IN WHICH THE MODULATOR FREQUENCY GRADUALLY INCREASES.

```
(
{
    var sig, mod, modHz;
    modHz = XLine.kr(1, 150, 10);
    mod = SinOsc.ar(modHz, mul: 300);
    sig = SinOsc.ar(750 + mod);
    sig = sig * 0.2 ! 2;
}.play;
)
```

How many audible sideband pairs can we expect in a particular FM configuration? In the simple case of one sine wave modulating the frequency of another, the ratio of modulator amplitude to modulator frequency (called the index of modulation) provides a rough estimate. The number of sideband pairs we perceive tends to be equal to or slightly higher than this ratio. When the modulator frequency in Code Example 3.11 reaches its peak, the ratio of modulator amplitude to frequency is 300:150 = 2:1, so we can expect approximately to hear two (or possibly three or four) audible sideband pairs, keeping in mind that whether a sideband is "audible" is subjective. Table 3.1 summarizes the spectral consequences of altering FM parameters, and Figure 3.5 provides a corresponding graphical depiction.

TABLE 3.1 Summary of behavioral characteristics of FM parameters.

Parameter	Change	Description
modulator amplitude	+	number of audible sidebands increases
	−	number of audible sidebands decreases
modulator frequency	+	spacing of sidebands increases
	−	spacing of sidebands decreases
carrier frequency	+	entire spectrum shifts upward
	−	entire spectrum shifts downward

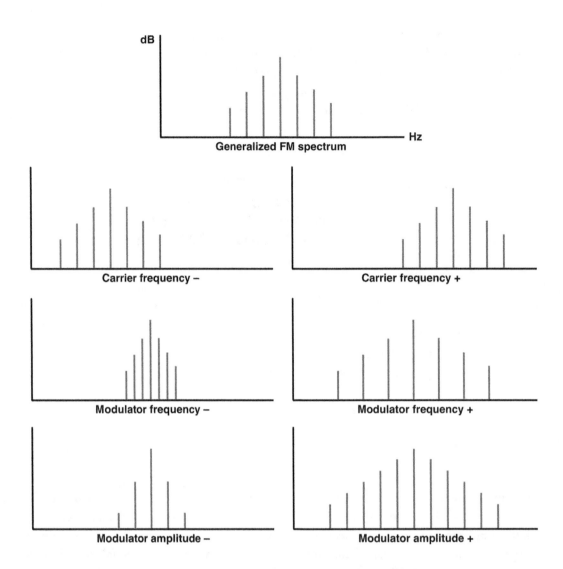

FIGURE 3.5 Graphical summary of behavioral characteristics of FM parameters.

The realm of possibilities expands when additional oscillators are incorporated into a modulation network. Two possible configurations include multiple modulators, arranged in series or in parallel. The former describes a chain of signals, in which a modulator influences another modulator, which in turn influences a carrier, and the latter describes a situation in which multiple modulators are summed before influencing a carrier. Code Example 3.12 provides an example of each configuration. In both examples, the frequency of one modulator is intentionally slow so that its influence is easily distinguished from the other modulator. Additional ideas for simple and complex FM modulation are featured in Companion Code 3.4 and 3.5.

> **CODE EXAMPLE 3.12:** **EXAMPLES OF FM SYNTHESIS WITH MODULATORS IN SERIES AND PARALLEL.**
>
> ```
> (
> {
>     var sig, mod1, mod2;
>     mod2 = SinOsc.ar(0.2, mul: 450);
>     mod1 = SinOsc.ar(500 + mod2, mul: 800);
>     sig = SinOsc.ar(1000 + mod1);
>     sig = sig * 0.2 ! 2;
> }.play;
> )
>
> (
> {
>     var sig, mod1, mod2;
>     mod2 = SinOsc.ar(0.2, mul: 450);
>     mod1 = SinOsc.ar(500, mul: 800);
>     sig = SinOsc.ar(1000 + mod1 + mod2);
>     sig = sig * 0.2 ! 2;
> }.play;
> )
> ```

3.3.3 ADDITIONAL MODULATION IDEAS

AM, RM, and FM are well-established practices, but modulation synthesis can apply to parameters beyond amplitude and frequency. Some UGens include a **width** parameter that alters the waveshape in a different manner. In the case of pulse waves, the width controls the duty cycle, that is, the proportion of each cycle that is "on" vs. "off." In the case of a variable-duty sawtooth wave, the width parameter will morph between sawtooth and triangle shapes. Code Example 3.13 provides two examples. The oscilloscope (**s.scope**) is useful for visualizing the results. Other UGens have unique parameters that can be modulated in interesting ways. You should always keep modulation in mind as a creative option that can be deployed quickly and relatively cheaply.

CODE EXAMPLE 3.13: TWO EXAMPLES OF WIDTH MODULATION.

```
(
{
    var sig, mod;
    mod = LFTri.ar(0.3).range(0, 1);
    sig = Pulse.ar(100, width: mod);
    sig = sig * 0.2 ! 2;
}.play;
)

(
{
    var sig, mod;
    mod = LFTri.ar(0.3).range(0, 1);
    sig = VarSaw.ar(200, width: mod);
    sig = sig * 0.2 ! 2;
}.play;
)
```

Modulation synthesis provides an opportunity to discuss the tangential topic of aliasing vs. anti-aliasing UGens. Some UGens have low-frequency (LF) counterparts, such as **Saw/LFSaw** and **Pulse/LFPulse**. Some, like **SinOsc**, have no LF counterpart. Others, like **LFTri**, have no non-LF counterpart.

What's the difference between LF and non-LF UGens? Simply, LF UGens are designed to run at low frequencies, often below 20 Hz. They will alias at high frequencies, but produce clean and geometrically precise waveshapes, and therefore make excellent low-frequency modulators. Non-LF UGens have internal design features which prevent or filter out aliasing at higher frequencies. These UGens produce a clean sound throughout the entire audible spectrum, but their waveshapes may have geometrical quirks or irregularities that reduce their value as modulators. In Code Example 3.14, the frequency of an anti-aliasing pulse wave increases over ten seconds. If this instance of **Pulse** is replaced with **LFPulse**, the sound will alias at higher frequencies, producing a distinctive fluttering sound.

CODE EXAMPLE 3.14: A DEMONSTRATION OF ALIASING USING Pulse AND LFPulse.

```
(
{
    var sig, freq;
    freq = XLine.kr(20, 8000, 10, doneAction: 2);
    sig = Pulse.ar(freq); // replace with LFPulse and notice the
                             difference
```

```
        sig = sig * 0.2 ! 2;
    }.play;
    )
```

The takeaway is that anti-aliasing UGens are not freely substitutable with their LF counterparts. UGens prone to aliasing tend to make better modulators, while anti-aliasing UGens make better carriers, although there are some exceptions (`SinOsc` makes a fine carrier or modulator at all frequencies). Table 3.2 provides a list of common oscillators categorized by waveshape and whether they will exhibit aliasing.

TABLE 3.2 A list of common oscillators grouped by waveshape and aliasing behavior.

Waveshape	Anti-Aliasing	Aliasing
Sine and sine-like	`SinOsc, FSinOsc`	`LFCub, LFPar`
Sawtooth	`Saw`	`LFSaw, SyncSaw, VarSaw`
Pulse/Square	`Pulse`	`LFPulse`
Triangle	N/A	`LFTri, VarSaw`
Impulse	`Blip`	`Impulse`

3.4 Wavetable Synthesis

Wavetable synthesis begins with a table of sample values that represents information for creating a periodic waveshape. A wavetable oscillator produces a signal by cyclically reading these values at a particular frequency, while a waveshaper uses this data as a transfer function that maps input samples to output samples, transforming one waveform into another. The separation of oscillator from waveshape is a flexible model, in which multiple wavetable oscillators can use the same table, or one oscillator can interpolate between multiple tables.

Efficiency is a primary advantage of wavetable synthesis. Instead of relying on mathematical calculations with sample values, the signal data is stored in advance and merely retrieved, which is less computationally expensive. It's for this reason that many digital oscillators, such as `SinOsc`, are actually wavetable oscillators. One disadvantage of wavetable synthesis is that there is no inbuilt mechanism that prevents aliasing at higher frequencies. This problem can be circumvented by running the audio server at a higher sampling rate, creating wavetables with little or no high spectral content, or by creatively embracing some amount of aliasing.

In SC, wavetable data is stored in buffers. Buffers, discussed more thoroughly in Chapter 4, are commonly used to store recorded audio, but the data in a buffer is merely a sequence of floats and may represent a variety of information, such as wavetables, envelopes, musical scale information, and so on. For efficiency reasons, the number of samples in a wavetable must be a power of two, and a typical size ranges from 512 to 8192. There is a point of diminishing returns above which large wavetables do not produce audibly superior results. Wavetables with fewer values are less able to produce smooth waveshapes and are more likely to alias.

SC requires a buffer to be filled using a special format called "wavetable format," a modified version of raw wavetable data that is twice as large, and which uses the following mathematical formula, in which n_0, n_1, and so on represent sample values. This format improves efficiency at the cost of allocating a larger buffer.

```
raw format: [n0, n1, n2, n3, ...]

wavetable format: [2n0-n1, n1-n0, 2n1-n2, n2-n1, 2n2-n3, n3-n2, ...]
```

Why this unusual format? In the rare case where the frequency of an oscillator equals the sampling rate divided by the size of the wavetable, the process of generating a signal is simple: the oscillator simply retrieves one table value per sample. For other frequencies, table values will not align with the sample clock, and the oscillator must interpolate between successive wavetable values to approximate "in-between" values. By storing the data in wavetable format, some of the burden of calculation is lifted from the server. There are several ways to create raw wavetable shapes, but they must be converted to wavetable format (using **asWavetable** or **asWavetableNoWrap**) and stored in a buffer before they can be used by a wavetable UGen.

3.4.1 CREATING AND PLAYING WAVETABLES

The **Osc** UGen is a generic wavetable oscillator. It is virtually identical to **SinOsc** with the exception that its wavetable is ours to specify. The language-side class **Signal**, a relative of arrays, holds an ordered collection of floats that represent audio samples, and the **sineFill** method can be used to create a **Signal** instance composed of sums of harmonically related sines. This method expects three arguments: the wavetable size, an array of harmonic amplitudes, and an array of initial phases specified in radians. To make this data available to wavetable UGens, we must allocate a buffer and load the data in wavetable format. Once the wavetable is stored in a buffer on the audio server, we can play it with an instance of **Osc**. This process is depicted in Code Example 3.15. Note that buffers are server-side objects, so the server must be booted before buffers can be used.

CODE EXAMPLE 3.15: CREATING A WAVETABLE AND READING IT WITH A WAVETABLE OSCILLATOR. THE TABLE CONTAINS ONLY THE FUNDAMENTAL AT FULL AMPLITUDE WITH AN INITIAL PHASE OF ZERO RADIANS, AND REPRESENTS ONE CYCLE OF SINE WAVE.

```
(
~wt = Signal.sineFill(8192, [1], [0]).asWavetable;
b = Buffer.loadCollection(s, ~wt);
)

{ Osc.ar(b, 200) * 0.2 ! 2 }.play;
```

There is a limit to the number of buffers that can be allocated (the default is 1024). If **Buffer.loadCollection(s, ~wt)** is evaluated a second time, the server will allocate a new buffer, without deallocating the previous, even if the same wavetable and variable name are used. When you are finished with a buffer, it is sensible to free it with **b.free**. Quitting and rebooting the audio server has the side effect of deallocating all buffers. To conserve space, code examples omit a buffer-freeing expression; it's assumed that the user will handle this responsibility, if needed. Wavetable creation and playback techniques are explored in Companion Code 3.6.

3.4.2 BLENDED WAVETABLES

Once an oscillator begins reading through a custom wavetable, its output signal can be modified through math operations with numbers and other UGens, but we cannot easily apply smooth changes to the wavetable data itself. The contents of the buffer can be overwritten with a new wavetable, or we can tell a wavetable oscillator to read from a different buffer, but such a change will be abrupt.

VOsc is a UGen that retains the basic functionality of **Osc** but can also interpolate between two wavetables, creating a blended waveshape. **VOsc** requires multiple same-size wavetables stored in a block of buffers whose integer identifiers (called "bufnums") are consecutive. The **allocConsecutive** method can be used to guarantee bufnum adjacency.

When the **bufpos** argument of **VOsc** is an integer, the oscillator reads the wavetable stored in the buffer whose bufnum matches that integer. When this argument is a value between x and x + 1, the waveshape is determined by applying a weighted average to each pair of corresponding samples in wavetables with bufnums x and x + 1. For example, if the buffer position is 4.75, then the nth sample in the blended wavetable will be equal to:

```
(0.25 * nth sample in bufnum 4) + (0.75 * nth sample in bufnum 5)
```

Code Example 3.16 creates four consecutive wavetables and uses iteration to load and plot them. Note that **lace** is an array method that creates a new array by interleaving elements of multiple starting arrays, which in this case inserts zeroes between non-zero amplitudes, thus zeroing the amplitudes of even-numbered harmonics.

CODE EXAMPLE 3.16: CREATION OF MULTIPLE WAVE TABLES, STORED IN CONSECUTIVELY NUMBERED BUFFERS.

```
(
b = Buffer.allocConsecutive(4, s, 16384);

~wt = [
    Signal.sineFill(8192, 1 ! 4, 0 ! 4),
    Signal.sineFill(8192, 1 / (1..50), 0 ! 50),
    Signal.sineFill(
        8192,
        [1 / (1, 3..50), 0 ! 25].lace(50),
        0 ! 50
    ),
    Signal.sineFill(
        8192,
        Array.exprand(50, 0.001, 1).sort.reverse,
        {rrand(0, 2pi)} ! 50
    ),
];
```

```
            b.do({ |buf, i| buf.loadCollection(~wt[i].asWavetable) });
)

~wt.plot; // optional visualization
```

Using the wavetables in Code Example 3.16, we can morph from one to another with **VOsc**, demonstrated in Code Example 3.17. In this example, a sine wave modulates the buffer position index, which sweeps back and forth across these four tables every 20 seconds. Note that it's sensible to limit the buffer position so that it never equals the bufnum of the last buffer in the consecutive block, implemented by setting the upper boundary of **bufmod** as 2.999 instead of 3. If this value equals the highest bufnum, SC will attempt to access that buffer and the buffer whose bufnum is one greater, in order to calculate a weighted average between them. If no such buffer exists, **VOsc** will fail and its output signal will become silent. As an alternative to constraining the buffer index, we can allocate one extra buffer using **allocConsecutive**, but leave it empty. Companion Code 3.7 continues an exploration of **VOsc** techniques.

CODE EXAMPLE 3.17: PLAYING A WAVETABLE OSCILLATOR THAT MORPHS BETWEEN MULTIPLE WAVETABLES. THIS CODE ASSUMES THE CODE IN CODE EXAMPLE 3.16 HAS BEEN PREVIOUSLY EVALUATED.

```
(
{
    var sig, bufmod;
    bufmod = SinOsc.kr(0.05, 3pi/2).unipolar(2.999);
    sig = VOsc.ar(b[0].bufnum + bufmod, 200);
    sig = sig * 0.1 ! 2;
}.play;
)
```

3.4.3 WAVESHAPING

The **Shaper** UGen offers a variation on previously described techniques. In the case of **Osc** and **VOsc**, the internal process that reads wavetable data is a repeating linear ramp signal. We can indirectly influence this signal by modulating its phase, but we can't replace it with a different signal. **Shaper** allows this substitution, accepting a wavetable buffer and an arbitrary input signal. The input signal is used as an index into the wavetable, treated as a transfer function, which maps input samples onto new output samples. Transfer functions typically have an input and output range bounded between ±1.

The identity transfer function (the function that applies no change to its input signal) is represented by the Cartesian function **y = x**, where **x** is a sample value from the input signal, and **y** is the corresponding output sample. Other simple examples include the line **y = -x**, which inverts the input signal, and the line **y = x / 2**, which reduces amplitude by half. Nonlinear transfer functions produce more interesting results. For example, an S-shaped transfer function pushes input values closer to ±1 and therefore has a "soft-clipping" effect on an input waveform. These transfer functions are illustrated in Figure 3.6.

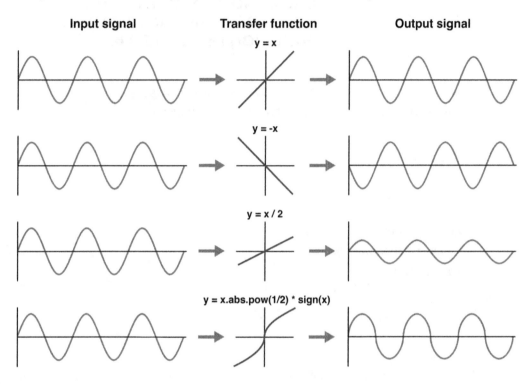

FIGURE 3.6 Sample-mapping behavior of various transfer functions.

The process of creating wavetables for **Shaper** is slightly different from that for other wavetable UGens. With **Osc/VOsc**, the wavetable is treated as a cyclic entity. Consequentially, the last and first table values are treated as "adjacent" when an interpolation calculation is needed between these values. However, with **Shaper**, the wavetable is treated as a static transfer function, rather than a repeating shape, which means interpolation between the first and last value is a meaningless operation that may produce unintended results. For this reason, one extra value is placed at the end of the transfer function, to facilitate correct interpolation behavior. In terms of implementation, the starting **Signal** should have a size that is a power of two plus one. Then, **asWavetableNoWrap** converts the data to wavetable format such that the final size is **2 * (signalSize - 1)** (see Code Example 3.18). When creating transfer functions, it is sensible to create a shape that passes through the point (0, 0), so that an input value of zero produces an output value of zero, which avoids problems related to DC offset. Companion Code 3.8 explores additional ideas related to **Shaper**.

CODE EXAMPLE 3.18: CREATION AND APPLICATION OF AN S-SHAPED TRANSFER FUNCTION TO CREATE A "SOFT-CLIPPED" SINE WAVE. THE WAVETABLE IS DERIVED FROM AN INSTANCE OF Env, CREATING AN S-CURVE SHAPE SIMILAR TO THE LAST TRANSFER FUNCTION IN FIGURE 3.6.

```
(
~wt = Env.new([-1, 0, 1], [1, 1], [4, -4]).asSignal(8193);
b = Buffer.loadCollection(s, ~wt.asWavetableNoWrap);
)

~wt.plot; // optional visualization

(
{
    var sig, index;
    index = SinOsc.ar(200);
    sig = Shaper.ar(b, index);
    sig = sig * 0.2 ! 2;
}.play;
)
```

Wavetable synthesis is a powerful tool, and serves as the basis for many synthesis platforms and plug-ins. Among its most appealing aspects is that it allows explicit creation of detailed, highly customized waveshapes, a process made considerably more difficult when restricted to mathematical operations on a small handful of standard waveshapes. In addition, wavetable synthesis tends to be relatively efficient in comparison to some other synthesis techniques, inviting rich, immersive timbres at relatively low cost.

3.5 Filters and Subtractive Synthesis

Any device capable of altering a signal's spectrum can be thought of as a filter. Filters exist in great variety and are exceptionally versatile, with applications throughout all aspects of composition and audio engineering. They are core features in hardware and software synthesizers, and they form the basis of equalizers and other tools for acoustic adjustments and corrections.

Protect your ears! Filters can be dangerous. They are relatively safe when tucked into a piece of commercial software, where potentially problematic parameters are locked behind restricted numerical ranges. This is not the case in SC, where it is easy to overlook a risky value, misplace a decimal point, omit a zero, and so on. Many filters "blow up" under certain conditions, producing a sudden loud sound. Usually, such an explosion stems from a frequency value that is negative, too close to zero, or above the Nyquist frequency. Additionally, practice good creative audio hygiene: before evaluating code in uncertain situations, apply a limiter, mute your system volume while watching the server meters, remove your headphones, and so on.

Subtractive synthesis is the audio equivalent of sculpting. A sculptor begins with a large, unformed mass of material, and selectively removes parts to produce a desired result. In a sense, subtractive synthesis is the opposite of additive synthesis, where we begin with nothing, and construct a spectrum, piece-by-piece. In subtractive synthesis, we begin with a spectrally rich signal, and use filters to attenuate certain frequency regions, so that only the desired content remains.

3.5.1 NOISE UGENS

Noise generators, illustrated in Code Example 3.19 and Figure 3.7, produce signals with relatively broad spectra and provide excellent starting points for subtractive synthesis. The term "white noise" colloquially refers to anything with a "shhh"-type sound, but in digital audio, white noise means something more specific. A white noise signal contains a uniform distribution of energy at all frequencies, just as white light is a combination of all colors in the visible spectrum. Because of our logarithmic perception of pitch (an exponential increase in frequency corresponds to a linear increase in semitones), white noise tends to sound bright and loud. This can be explained by the fact that higher octaves have larger frequency ranges, and therefore contain more energy. For example, the highest audible octave (10 to 20 kHz) contains an amount of energy equal to the combined amount of energy in all of the lower octaves (0 to 10 kHz). In its raw form, white noise has a distinct, aggressive sound, which most would agree is intolerable at high amplitudes.

Pink noise, by contrast, contains equal energy per octave, and the intensity of pink noise decreases by three decibels per octave. This distribution is more closely aligned with our logarithmic perception of pitch and produces a more psychoacoustically balanced sound. It is sometimes favored for acoustical testing, sleep aids, and other situations where the nuance of human perception is relevant.

The sample values in a brown noise signal follow Brownian motion, a pattern of movement sometimes described as a random or "drunk" walk. These samples are not fully random, but chart a meandering path, never deviating too far from the previous value. The result is a spectrum with even more low frequency energy than pink noise, and an intensity which decreases by six decibels per octave. The sound is reminiscent of standing close to a large waterfall.

CODE EXAMPLE 3.19: UGEN FUNCTIONS THAT PRODUCE VARIOUS TYPES OF NOISE SIGNALS.

```
{WhiteNoise.ar(0.1 ! 2)}.play;
{PinkNoise.ar(0.1 ! 2)}.play;
{BrownNoise.ar(0.1 ! 2)}.play;
```

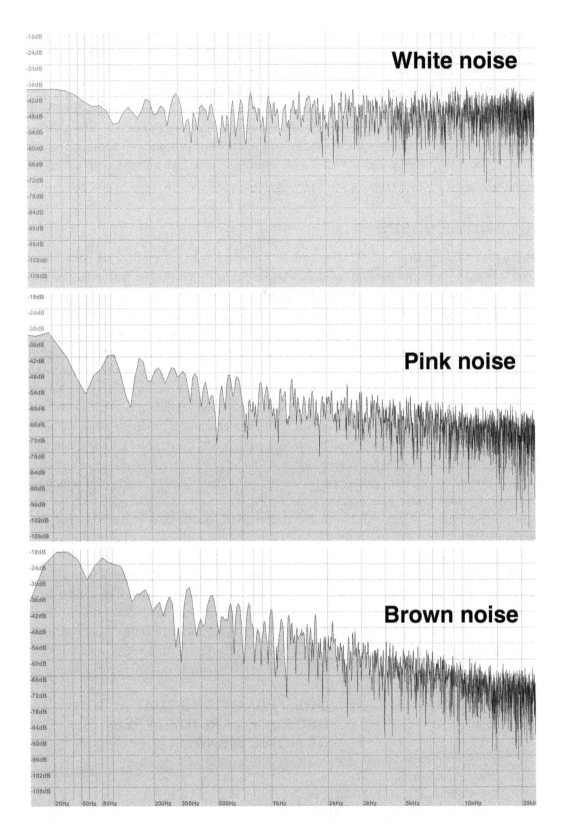

FIGURE 3.7 A spectrum analysis of white, pink, and brown noise, using a logarithmic frequency scale. REAPER is a registered trademark of Cockos Incorporated, used with permission.

SC also includes several low-frequency noise generators, whose waveforms are depicted in Figure 3.8. These UGens are commonly used as modulators for other signals but can also be used as audio-rate noise generators. Unlike white/pink/brown noise, these generators include a frequency argument, which determines the rate at which they select random values. **LFNoise0** is a non-interpolating noise generator, also called a "sample-and-hold" signal. Each time it selects a random value, it holds that value until the next is generated, producing a waveform with the appearance of a city skyline. **LFNoise1** linearly interpolates between random values to produce random ramps, and **LFNoise2** uses quadratic interpolation.[1]

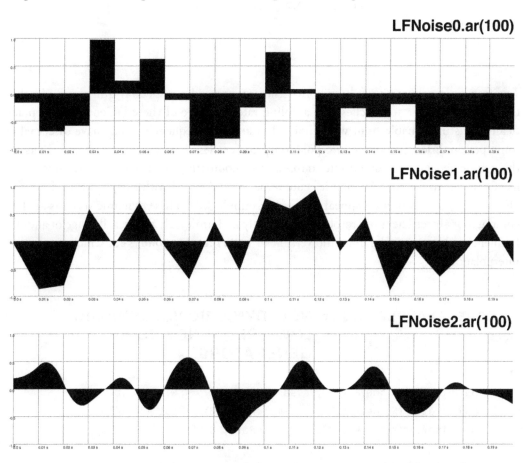

FIGURE 3.8 A 0.2-second plot of three different low-frequency noise generators running at 100 Hz.

A good way to hear the difference between these three types of noise generators is to use them as frequency inputs for periodic generators, as shown in Code Example 3.20. **LFNoise0** creates what could reasonably be called the quintessential "computer music" sound.

CODE EXAMPLE 3.20: LFNoise0 USED AS A FREQUENCY MODULATOR.

```
(
{
    var sig, freq;
    freq = LFNoise0.kr(8).exprange(150, 2000);
    sig = SinOsc.ar(freq) * 0.2 ! 2;
}.play;
)
```

The frequency argument of these noise generators provides a spectral dimension. As this frequency argument approaches the sampling rate, all three of these UGens become practically indistinguishable from white noise, but at lower frequencies, they have discernable sonic personalities. Smoother interpolation produces less high-frequency energy. If using these noise generators as audio-rate sources, or if modulating their frequency argument, it's usually better to use their "dynamic" counterparts (designated with a capital letter D in the UGen name). A comparison appears in Code Example 3.21. These dynamic versions are less computationally efficient but respond consistently and uniformly to the full range of audible frequencies. Note that the dynamic version of **LFNoise2** is **LFDNoise3**, which uses cubic interpolation.

CODE EXAMPLE 3.21: NON-DYNAMIC VS. DYNAMIC LOW-FREQUENCY NOISE GENERATORS.

```
{LFNoise0.ar(XLine.kr(100, s.sampleRate, 8)) * 0.1 ! 2}.play;
{LFNoise1.ar(XLine.kr(100, s.sampleRate, 8)) * 0.1 ! 2}.play;
{LFNoise2.ar(XLine.kr(100, s.sampleRate, 8)) * 0.1 ! 2}.play;

{LFDNoise0.ar(XLine.kr(100, s.sampleRate, 8)) * 0.1 ! 2}.play;
{LFDNoise1.ar(XLine.kr(100, s.sampleRate, 8)) * 0.1 ! 2}.play;
{LFDNoise3.ar(XLine.kr(100, s.sampleRate, 8)) * 0.1 ! 2}.play;
```

3.5.2 COMMON FILTER UGENS

Most digital filters belong to one of four basic categories depicted in Figure 3.9. The names of these categories describe the behaviors of filters that belong to them: low-pass and high-pass filters divide the audible spectrum at a cutoff frequency and "pass" one band while attenuating the other. Band-pass filters preserve a range of spectral content around a center frequency while attenuating spectral content outside of the band, and band-reject filters have the opposite effect.

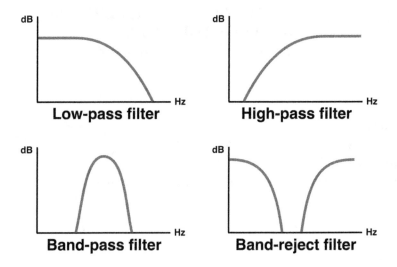

FIGURE 3.9 Frequency responses of four basic filter types.

The UGens **LPF**, **HPF**, **BPF**, and **BRF** provide an option for each of these four categories. **LPF** and **HPF** accept an input signal and a cutoff frequency. **BPF** and **BRF** accept input signal, a center frequency, and an additional argument named **rq**, short for "reciprocal quality." Quality, often shortened to "Q," is a measure of the selectivity of a filter, which correlates to its tendency to exhibit resonant behavior. In the case of band-pass and band-reject filters, Q is the ratio of center frequency to bandwidth. For example, if the center frequency is 1,000 Hz and the bandwidth is 100 Hz, the quality of the filter is 1,000/100 = 10. A higher quality means a narrower band and a more selective filter. In SC, filters expect this value to be specified as the reciprocal of Q (bandwidth divided by center frequency), a design choice which slightly increases UGen efficiency. An **rq** equal to one represents a nominal base quality, which increases as **rq** approaches zero. Code Example 3.22 includes code examples for each of these four filter UGens.

> ### TIP.RAND(); SAFE FILTER PARAMETERS
>
> The frequency parameter of a filter should always be within the audible spectrum, approximately 20 to 20,000 Hz. Reciprocal quality values should always be less than or equal to one, and greater than zero. Values outside of these ranges are unsafe and may result in explosive behavior.

CODE EXAMPLE 3.22: EXAMPLES OF BASIC FILTER UGENS USED TO PROCESS PINK NOISE. IN THE BAND-PASS/BAND-REJECT EXAMPLE, THE VERTICAL POSITION OF THE MOUSE CONTROLS FILTER QUALITY.

```
(
{
    var sig, cutoff;
    cutoff = LFTri.kr(0.1, 3).exprange(100, 10000);
    sig = PinkNoise.ar(1);
    sig = LPF.ar(sig, cutoff) * 0.25 ! 2; // replace with HPF
}.play;
)

(
{
    var sig, cutoff, rq;
    cutoff = LFTri.kr(0.1, 3).exprange(100, 10000);
    rq = MouseY.kr(0.01, 1, 1).clip(0.01, 1);
    sig = PinkNoise.ar(1);
    sig = BPF.ar(sig, cutoff, rq) * 0.25 ! 2; // replace with BRF
}.play;
)
```

In general, the output amplitude of a filtered signal may be noticeably different than the amplitude of the input signal, depending on the spectrum of the input signal, the type of filter being used, and the value of the cutoff/center frequency. In the context of mixing and audio engineering, filters are often used as corrective tools that remove problem frequencies. In such cases, there is rarely a need to compensate for what is lost. In creative contexts, however, filters may be used in bolder and more experimental ways. Particularly when the input signal is broadband noise, a filter may remove a significant amount of spectral content, which lowers the overall amplitude. It may be desirable to compensate for this loss by boosting the amplitude of the output signal. The exact amount of boost is context-sensitive and may rely on some trial-and-error guesswork. For example, when applying a band-pass filter to broadband noise, **rq** values close to zero will drastically reduce the amplitude. In this specific case, a sensible starting point for a compensation scalar is the reciprocal of the square root of **rq**. In Code Example 3.23, vertical mouse movements will alter the quality, but the overall amplitude remains stable.

CODE EXAMPLE 3.23: COMPENSATING FOR AMPLITUDE REDUCTION RESULTING FROM AGGRESSIVE FILTERING.

```
(
{
    var sig, cutoff, rq;
    cutoff = LFTri.kr(0.1, 3).exprange(100, 10000);
    rq = MouseY.kr(0.01, 1, 1).clip(0.01, 1);
    sig = PinkNoise.ar(1);
    sig = BPF.ar(sig, cutoff, rq, mul: 1 / rq.sqrt) * 0.5 ! 2;
}.play;
)
```

Filter copies can be applied in series to exaggerate their behavior and increase selectivity, which can be demonstrated by increasing the iteration count in Code Example 3.24. There is a point of diminishing returns above which additional filters will consume processing power without significantly improving the sound. With large numbers of filters in series, the output signal may begin to exhibit a substantial loss of amplitude, even within the "passed" spectral band.

CODE EXAMPLE 3.24: USE OF ITERATION TO APPLY COPIES OF A FILTER IN SERIES.

```
(
{
    var sig;
    sig = WhiteNoise.ar(1 ! 2);
    2.do({sig = LPF.ar(sig, 1000)}); // change to 3.do, 4.do, etc.
    sig = sig * 0.25;
}.play;
)
```

RLPF and **RHPF** are "resonant" variations of **LPF** and **HPF**. Like **BPF** and **BRF**, these UGens include a reciprocal quality parameter, capable of producing resonance at the cutoff frequency. As **rq** approaches zero, the resonant band narrows, selectivity increases, and the amplitude of spectral content near the cutoff frequency increases. Thus, it's important to be cautious with **rq** values close to zero, which may distort the output signal (a limiter may be appropriate).

RLPF and **RHPF** are useful in situations where spectral emphasis at the cutoff frequency is desired. By sweeping the cutoff frequency in certain ways, the output signal acquires a character that might be described as "wet," reminiscent of a water droplet falling into a bucket, or a continuous vocal morph between "ooh" and "ahh." A resonant low-pass filter is commonly used with an LFO to create a "wah-wah" effect, often found in synthesized basses and leads. An example appears in Code Example 3.25.

CODE EXAMPLE 3.25: MODULATING THE CUTOFF FREQUENCY OF A RESONANT LOW-PASS FILTER AS IT PROCESSES A PULSE WAVE.

```
(
{
	var sig, cutoff, freq, randseq;
	freq = LFNoise0.kr(1).range(25, 49).round(1).midicps;
	cutoff = VarSaw.kr(6, width: 0.1).exprange(50, 10000);
	sig = Pulse.ar(freq * [0.99, 1.01]);
	sig = RLPF.ar(sig, cutoff, 0.1);
	sig = sig * 0.1;
}.play;
)
```

3.5.3 SUBTRACTIVE SYNTHESIS TECHNIQUES

Subtractive synthesis is largely a matter of experimenting with basic examples and discovering interesting combinations of signals and filters. Low- and high-pass filters operate on relatively large spectral chunks, making them useful for broad timbral changes. Band-pass filters and resonant high/low-pass filters can create a sensation of pitch by emphasizing narrow frequency ranges, giving them a particular musical usefulness. Band-reject filters, while useful in engineering situations for removing problematic frequencies, tend to be the least musically useful; even with low Q values, their influence on a broadband signal is marginal. Companion Code 3.9 explores additional ideas related to subtractive synthesis.

3.6 Modal Synthesis

Physical objects vibrate when disturbed. Common musical examples include plucking a string or striking something with a mallet. The vibrational patterns of some objects, like bells and chimes, are composed of a complex sum of sinusoidal vibrations that decay over a relatively long duration. Other objects, like blocks of wood, exhibit periodic vibrations that decay almost instantly. Modal synthesis refers to the practice of creating (or recreating) the sound of a physical object by simulating its natural modes of vibration. Superficially, this technique is like additive synthesis, but involves injecting excitation signals into resonant filters, rather than summing sine generators.

Resonz and **Ringz**, demonstrated in Code Example 3.26, are resonant filters that provide an entryway into modal synthesis. **Resonz** is a band-pass filter with a constant gain at zero decibels. This means that as the bandwidth decreases, the sense of resonance increases, but spectral content at the center frequency will remain at its input level, while surrounding content is attenuated. It virtually indistinguishable from **BPF** in terms of usage and sound. **Ringz**, on the other hand, has a variable gain that depends on the bandwidth, specified indirectly as a 60 dB decay time. As this decay time increases, bandwidth narrows, a sense of resonance increases, and spectral content at the center frequency undergoes a potentially dramatic increase in amplitude. The difference between **Resonz** and **Ringz** is subtle but has significant consequences.

In terms of practical usage, because of its variable-gain design, **Ringz** is intended to be driven by single-sample impulses. Even an excitation signal a few samples long has the potential to overload **Ringz** and produce a distorted output signal. Longer signals, such as sustained noise, can technically be fed to an instance of **Ringz**, but the amplitude of the excitation signal and/or the output signal must be drastically reduced in order to compensate for the increase in level, particularly if the decay time is long. **Resonz**, by contrast, is designed to accept sustained excitation signals and is more likely to need an amplitude boost to compensate for low levels, particularly in narrow bandwidth situations. Feeding single-sample impulses into **Resonz** is fine, but the level of the output signal will likely be quite low.

CODE EXAMPLE 3.26: BASIC USAGE OF Ringz AND Resonz.

```
(
{
    var sig, exc;
    exc = Impulse.ar(1);
    sig = Ringz.ar(
        in: exc,
        freq: 800,
        decaytime: 1/3
    );
    sig = sig * 0.2 ! 2;
}.play;
)

(
{
    var sig, exc;
    exc = PinkNoise.ar(1);
    sig = Resonz.ar(
        in: exc,
        freq: 800,
        bwr: 0.001,
        mul: 1 / 0.001.sqrt
    );
    sig = sig * 0.5 ! 2;
}.play;
)
```

Klank and **DynKlank** encapsulate fixed and dynamic banks of **Ringz** resonators, offering a slightly more convenient and efficient option than applying multichannel expansion to an instance of **Ringz** (see Code Example 3.27). These UGens require a **Ref** array (see Section 3.2.2) containing internal arrays of frequencies, amplitudes, and decay times of simulated resonances. The frequencies can be scaled and shifted, and the decay times can also be scaled.

CODE EXAMPLE 3.27: USAGE OF **Klank** TO SIMULATE THE SOUND OF A PHYSICAL OBJECT WITH MULTIPLE RESONANT MODES OF VIBRATION.

```
(
{
    var sig, exc, freqs, amps, decays;
    freqs = [211, 489, 849, 857, 3139, 4189, 10604, 15767];
    amps = [0.75, 0.46, 0.24, 0.17, 0.03, 0.019, 0.002, 0.001];
    decays = [3.9, 3.4, 3.3, 2.5, 2.2, 1.5, 1.3, 1.0];
    exc = Impulse.ar(0.5);
    sig = Klank.ar(
        `[freqs, amps, decays], // <- note the backtick character
        exc,
    );
    sig = sig * 0.25 ! 2;
}.play;
)
```

As a practical example for further study, the end of Companion Code 3.10 uses modal synthesis techniques to recreate the sound of striking an orchestral triangle. The frequencies, amplitudes, and decay times were derived through methodical observation of real-time spectral analyses of a triangle sample (pictured in Figure 3.10), along with some visual guesswork.

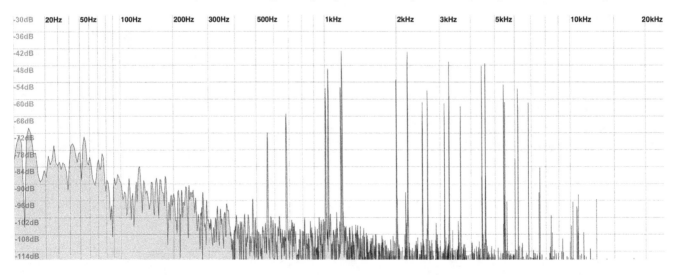

FIGURE 3.10 A spectrum analysis of a struck orchestral triangle. REAPER is a registered trademark of Cockos Incorporated, used with permission.

3.7 Waveform Distortion

Distortion means different things in different situations. It might refer to the gentle fuzziness of a vintage guitar amplifier or analog overdrive pedal, or it might refer to the harsh clipping that occurs when a digital audio signal exceeds zero decibels. The usefulness and appropriateness of distortion varies by context; it can add a sense of organic richness to an acoustic instrument, or utterly ruin an otherwise pristine recording. For the purposes of this section, distortion is treated as a broad, catch-all term, referring to a process that alters the shape of a waveform, typically through some relatively simple mathematical operation. Much in the same way that any device that alters a sound's spectrum can be viewed as a filter, it requires only a small stretch of the imagination to consider any waveshape-altering process as some flavor of distortion.

3.7.1 CLIPPING, FOLDING, AND WRAPPING

Clipping, folding, and wrapping are operations that constrain values within boundaries. They exist as language-side methods for numerical values (**clip/fold/wrap**), and also as UGens (**Clip/Fold/Wrap**). Each operation requires minimum/maximum boundary values, but they have different behaviors, depicted in Figure 3.11.

Clipping is a truncation operation; if an input value exceeds a boundary, it becomes equal to that boundary value. When applied to a waveform, regions beyond the boundaries become plateau-shaped. The audible byproducts of clipping are generally not subtle; even a small amount of clipping produces a rich cluster of harmonic activity, usually bringing drastic timbral changes. The effects of clipping are less noticeable in sounds which already have broad/chaotic spectra (e.g., white noise, dense FM textures), but the effects are obvious in relatively pure tones (e.g., sine waves, speech/singing). The purposeful use of clipping as a creative choice is uniquely challenging to execute, because it can easily sound unintentional.

When folding, boundaries act like reflective surfaces, causing out-of-range values to "rebound" by their excess amount. When applied to a waveform, folding does not create plateaus, but still introduces sharp corners, resulting in a cluster of higher harmonics, somewhat similar to clipping.

Wrapping establishes boundaries which are treated as adjacent. As a value exceeds one boundary, it appears at the opposite boundary. The concept is like east–west travel on a two-dimensional projection of the earth's surface; a trip along the equator superficially appears to be a journey from point A to B, but of course, we end up back where we started. Wrapping introduces large discontinuities into a waveshape, producing an especially harsh sound.

Code Example 3.28 demonstrates the use of **Clip** to distort a sine wave. The amplitude of the sine is modulated by another sine wave, which alters the amount of distortion applied. **Clip** can be substituted with **Fold** or **Wrap**.

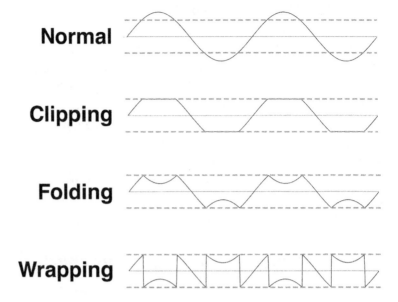

FIGURE 3.11 A visual depiction of waveform clipping, folding, and wrapping applied to a sine wave.

CODE EXAMPLE 3.28: BASIC USAGE OF `Clip` TO DISTORT A SINE WAVE.

```
(
{
    var sig, mod;
    mod = SinOsc.kr(0.1, 3pi/2).exprange(0.2, 4);
    sig = SinOsc.ar(300, mul: mod);
    sig = Clip.ar(sig, -1, 1); // replace with Fold.ar or Wrap.ar
    sig = sig * 0.2 ! 2;
}.play;
)
```

Used in isolation, these three waveform operations are coarse tools, relatively incapable of nuance. They tend to produce more satisfying results when used in combination with low-pass filters, which help soften the hard waveform corners and temper the high frequency content.

3.7.2 "GENTLE" DISTORTION

Clipping, folding, and wrapping have no effect on values within their boundaries, and a uniform effect on values outside of these boundaries. There is no smooth gradient applied to a signal as its value approaches a boundary. By contrast, **softclip**, **distort**, and **tanh** apply nonlinear math operations that provide gentler distortion algorithms. A visual reference and code example appear in Figure 3.12 and Code Example 3.29.

The **softclip** method has no effect on values between ±0.5, but applies the following operation to every input sample **n** whose absolute value is greater than 0.5:

```
(abs(n) * 4 - 1) / (abs(n) * 4) * n.sign;
```

The output is bounded between ±1 with reasonable smoothness. As the name implies, **softclip** is a gentler version of normal clipping. **distort** is a similar operation that uses the following formula, but affects all values:

```
(abs(n)) / (abs(n) + 1) * n.sign;
```

The results are again bounded between ±1, and a similarly gentle distortion curve is applied. Lastly, the hyperbolic tangent is a trigonometric function which behaves similarly to **softclip** and **distort**. It's not essential to understand the mathematical details of this operation, but it suffices to say that **tanh** is defined for all numbers between ±infinity, and has an output range bounded between ±1, making it a useful option for gentle distortion. All three methods result in additional higher spectral content, but not quite so aggressively as clipping, wrapping, and folding.

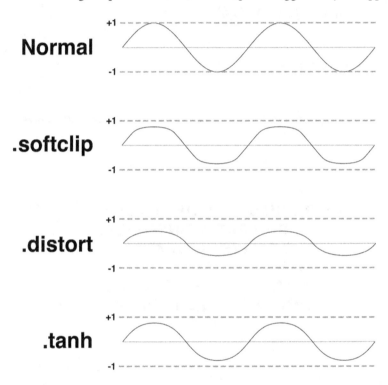

FIGURE 3.12 A visual depiction of **softclip**, **distort**, and **tanh** applied to a sine wave.

CODE EXAMPLE 3.29: BASIC USAGE OF softclip TO DISTORT A SINE WAVE.

```
(
{
    var sig, mod;
    mod = SinOsc.kr(0.1, 3pi/2).exprange(0.2, 4);
    sig = SinOsc.ar(300, mul: mod);
    sig = sig.softclip; // replace with 'distort' or 'tanh'
    sig = sig * 0.2 ! 2;
}.play;
)
```

3.7.3 DISTORTION VIA RANGE-MAPPING

The **lincurve** method maps values from a linear range to a curved range using a nonlinear algorithm, providing yet more options for warping waveform shapes in curious ways. This method takes five arguments: a pair of min/max input values, a pair of min/max output values, and a curve parameter, which behaves like **Env** curve values. Because of the vertical asymmetry of **lincurve**, it is sometimes a good idea to use **LeakDC** to compensate for DC offset. A visual depiction appears in Figure 3.13, and a code example appears in Code Example 3.30.

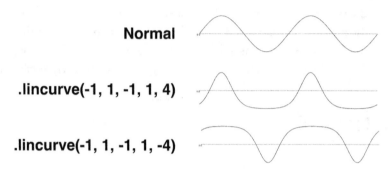

FIGURE 3.13 A visual depiction of **lincurve** applied to a sine wave, using positive and negative curve values.

CODE EXAMPLE 3.30: BASIC USAGE OF lincurve TO DISTORT A SINE WAVE. THE CURVE PARAMETER IS MODULATED, INSTEAD OF THE SOURCE SIGNAL'S AMPLITUDE.

```
(
{
    var sig, mod;
    mod = SinOsc.kr(0.2, 3pi/2).exprange(1, 15);
    sig = SinOsc.ar(300);
    sig = sig.lincurve(-1, 1, -1, 1, mod);
    sig = LeakDC.ar(sig) * 0.2 ! 2;
}.play;
)
```

3.7.4 BITCRUSHING

Bitcrushing has become something of a catch-all term that describes an artificial reduction of the resolution capabilities of a digital audio system. Technically, bitcrushing is a reduction in vertical resolution, that is, a reduction in the number of discrete amplitude values that can be assigned to individual samples. It is also possible to emulate a reduction in the sampling rate, which produces a loss of horizontal resolution. Both types of signal degradation generate additional high spectral content, but bitcrushing also alters a signal's dynamic range (making quiet sounds louder), while a sample rate reduction produces aliasing and tends to influence pitch.

An implementation of bitcrushing is surprisingly simple: we can **round** an audio signal to the nearest multiple of a value, imposing a "staircase" shape. To simulate a sample rate reduction, the **Latch** UGen can be used, which applies a sample-and-hold operation to its input signal whenever it receives a trigger. In both cases, the quality of the audio signal will degrade (possibly quite dramatically), but this type of sound may be stylistically appropriate in some situations.

CODE EXAMPLE 3.31: BASIC EXAMPLES OF BITCRUSHING AND SAMPLE RATE REDUCTION, APPLIED TO A SINE WAVE.

```
(
{
    var sig, mod;
    mod = SinOsc.kr(0.2, 3pi/2).exprange(0.02, 1);
    sig = SinOsc.ar(300);
    sig = sig.round(mod) * 0.2 ! 2;
}.play;
)

(
{
    var sig, mod;
    mod = SinOsc.kr(0.2, 3pi/2).exprange(SampleRate.ir/2, SampleRate.ir/100);
    sig = SinOsc.ar(300);
    sig = Latch.ar(sig, Impulse.ar(mod));
    sig = sig * 0.2 ! 2;
}.play;
)
```

Companion Code 3.11 explores creative applications of distortion techniques.

3.8 Conclusions and Further Ideas

In this chapter, we've focused our attention on synthesis techniques for creating compelling timbres and textures. Some techniques, like additive and wavetable synthesis, are inherently generative, while others, like subtractive synthesis and waveform distortion, are based on processing an existing signal with filters and mathematical operations. Keep these processing techniques in mind as you make your way through this book—they can just as easily be applied to sample-based sounds, explored in the next chapter.

A deep understanding of synthesis is useful, but ultimately just one ingredient in the compositional process. The next few chapters cover additional creative topics (sampling, sequencing, and signal processing), designed to provide a more comprehensive toolset. It's also worth recognizing that the compositional process is more than just the sum knowledge of these tools; it also involves important decisions about contrast, density, pace, symmetry, use of silence, and many other factors that determine the where, how, and why of a musical composition. A synthesized drone, an arpeggiated melody, or some other musical unit can rarely be considered a musical composition by itself, no matter how detailed and immersive it may be. What came before it? What comes after? How does its sonic material develop over time? How does it establish tension, and how does it resolve? What kind of interactive narrative is created through its existence with other musical elements?

These are questions that can only be answered through patience and self-discovery. For now, in the interest of providing one last practical application, Companion Code 3.12 brings together a few concepts from this chapter and synthesizes a few basic percussion sounds: a kick, snare, and hi-hat. These examples are intended as starting points for further study and experimentation.

Note

1 As a result of its quadratic algorithm, LFNoise2 occasionally overshoots its range boundaries. It can be a dangerous choice when used to control filter frequencies. Consider clipping its output or using a different UGen.

CHAPTER 4

SAMPLING

4.1 Overview

For the purposes of this chapter, sampling refers to creative practices that rely on recorded sound, typically involving modified playback of audio files stored in blocks of memory on the audio server. In a sense, sampling and synthesis are two sides of the same signal-generating coin. Synthesis relies on mathematical algorithms, while sampling is based on the use of content that has already been produced and captured, but most sound sources found throughout creative audio practices are rooted in one of these two categories.

Sampling opens a door to a world of sound that is difficult or impossible to create using synthesis techniques alone. Anything captured with a microphone and rendered to a file instantly becomes a wellspring of creative potential: a recording of wildlife can become a surreal ambient backdrop, or a recording of a broken elevator can be chopped into weird percussion samples. Instead of using dozens of sine waves or filters to simulate a gong, why not use the real thing?

Before loading sampled audio files into software, it's wise to practice good sample hygiene. Unnecessary silence should be trimmed from the beginnings and ends of the files, samples should be as free as possible from background noise and other unwanted sounds, and the peak amplitudes of similar samples should be normalized to a consistent level. Normalization level is partly a matter of personal preference, but –12 dBFS is usually a reasonable target, which makes good use of available bit depth while reserving ample headroom for mixing with other sounds.

4.2 Buffers

In order for a sampled audio file to be usable in SC, the server must be booted and the file must be loaded into a buffer, which is simply a block of allocated memory in which data can be stored. Buffers are server-side objects, but creation and interaction with buffers usually happens through the language-side **Buffer** class and its various methods. Although buffers typically store sample values of digital audio files, they are essentially multichannel arrays that hold floating point values, and therefore may contain data that represents other things, like envelopes, wavetables, or pitch collections. Once a buffer is allocated on the server, it remains there, globally accessible to all server processes, until it is explicitly freed (i.e., deallocated) or if you quit the server (pressing [cmd]+[period] has no effect on buffers). Buffers are a central class in SC, and a solid familiarity is essential for sampling-based work.

4.2.1 LOADING, PLAYING, AND INTERACTING WITH BUFFERS

The simplest way to read an audio file into a buffer begins with the class method **read**, which implicitly allocates an appropriately sized buffer and loads audio samples into it. This method needs to know the instance of the server on which the buffer will reside, and a string representing the path to the file. The format should be wav or aiff/aif, although compressed audio file formats, such as mp3, may also work on newer versions of SC). As a convenience, you can drag and drop a file into the code editor, and the appropriate string will be generated, which avoids the need to manually type long paths. After creation, a buffer can be auditioned using **play**. Buffers can be visually rendered with **plot**. This visualization is not nearly as sophisticated as that of a dedicated waveform editor, and the plot window may behave sluggishly for large buffers, but plotting remains a useful feature. A buffer can be deallocated with **free**. If multiple buffers have been created, it's possible to deallocate them all at once by evaluating **Buffer.freeAll**.

CODE EXAMPLE 4.1: LOADING, PLOTTING, PLAYING, AND FREEING A BUFFER. THE STRING MUST BE REPLACED WITH A STRING THAT REPRESENTS AN AUDIO FILE ON YOUR COMPUTER.

```
s.boot;

b = Buffer.read(s, "/Users/eli/Sounds/scaudio/drumsamples/Claps/clap1.aif");

b.plot;

b.play;

b.free;
```

The process of allocating a buffer and loading audio samples into it does not happen instantaneously. Attempts to create a buffer and access it within the same evaluation may fail. Buffers live on the server, but we interact with them from the language, which gives rise to timing-related nuances that may create confusing situations. For this reason, **read**, **plot**, and **play** are meant to be evaluated one after the other in Code Example 4.1. Executing these actions one-by-one is a primitive but effective way to avoid problems. More elegant options will be discussed in later sections of this book.

The standard download of SC includes a "Resources" folder, which contains two sound files whose primary purpose is to support interactive code examples in buffer-related help files. The paths to these files vary by operating system, but they can be accessed using **Platform**, a utility class that homogenizes cross-platform behavior and code expression. The built-in sound files can be loaded and played as shown in Code Example 4.2.

CODE EXAMPLE 4.2: LOADING AND PLAYING THE TWO BUILT-IN AUDIO FILES.

```
(
b = [
    Buffer.read(s, Platform.resourceDir ++ "/sounds/a11wlk01-44_1.aiff"),
    Buffer.read(s, Platform.resourceDir ++ "/sounds/a11wlk01.wav")
];
)

b[0].play;

b[1].play;
```

An allocated buffer has several attributes associated with it, which can be queried via language-side methods, shown in Code Example 4.3. Specifically, each buffer has a unique identifying integer called a *bufnum*. Although it's possible to manually specify buffer numbers as buffers are allocated, best practice is to allow automatic assignment. Buffers also have a frame count, equal to the number of samples divided by the number of channels. In the case of a one-channel buffer, the number of frames equals the number of samples. In a two-channel buffer, the sample count is twice the frame count, and so on. An illustration of the difference between frames and samples appears in Figure 4.1. Additional attributes include duration, number of channels, and the sample rate of the buffer (which may be different from the sampling rate of the audio server).

CODE EXAMPLE 4.3: LANGUAGE-SIDE METHODS FOR ACCESSING BUFFER ATTRIBUTES.

```
b = Buffer.read(s, Platform.resourceDir ++ "/sounds/a11wlk01.wav");

b.duration;

b.bufnum;

b.numFrames;

b.numChannels;

b.sampleRate;

b.query; // post several attributes
```

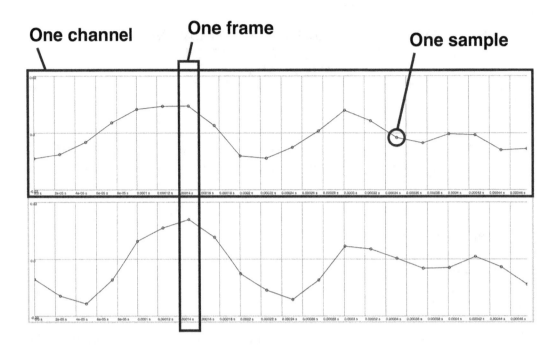

FIGURE 4.1 An illustration of the relationship between channels, frames, and samples in a two-channel buffer.

It's sometimes desirable to load only part of an audio file into a buffer. This can be done using the third and fourth arguments of **read**, which correspond to a starting frame index and a number of frames (**startFrame** and **numFrames**). However, a trial-and-error approach to finding the right frame range is often inferior to using dedicated waveform editing software to edit and export desired portions as new audio files, which can then be read into SC as is.

The two built-in samples are one-channel audio files. The **read** method automatically detects channel size and allocates a buffer with that many channels. However, we may want to read only one channel of a multichannel audio file, which can be handled with **readChannel**. This class method is similar to **read** but includes a **channels** argument, depicted in Code Example 4.4. This value should be an array of channel indices. If the path points to a stereo file, a value of **[0]** will read only the left channel, and a value of **[1]** will read only the right channel. Mixing a multichannel file to a monophonic format during this reading process is not easy and not recommended; it's better to deal with monophonic mixing using summation within a UGen function.

CODE EXAMPLE 4.4: USAGE OF readChannel TO READ AND PLAY ONE CHANNEL OF AN IMAGINARY STEREO FILE. THE STRING MUST BE REPLACED WITH A STRING THAT POINTS TO A TWO-CHANNEL FILE ON YOUR COMPUTER.

```
(
b = Buffer.readChannel(
    s,
```

```
        "path/to/some/stereo/file.aiff",
        channels: [0] // only read the left channel
    );
)

b.play;
```

For simplicity, the code examples in this chapter will rely on these built-in audio files, but substituting your own audio files is possible and encouraged. Supplementary audio files are included with Companion Code files for this chapter, for the sake of creating more interesting and varied examples, but substitutions can be made there as well.

4.2.2 BUFFER MANAGEMENT

For simple examples and quick testing, storing a buffer in an interpreter variable (as seen in several previous examples) is convenient. But, as sampling projects grow, it's not unusual to have dozens or even hundreds of buffers containing different sound files. For these projects, creating and naming buffers on an individual basis is inefficient and prone to duplicate or misspelled variable names. Furthermore, if audio files on your computer are added, moved, renamed, or deleted, your SC code will need to be updated to reflect these changes. An organized, systematic approach to buffer management is an essential first step in sampling projects.

Grouping buffers in collections, such as arrays (see Code Example 4.2), is a small step in the right direction. Using arrays avoids the need to assign a unique name to each buffer, and instead permits reference by numerical index (**b[0]**, **b[1]**, etc.). The main advantage of an array-based approach is that it is less prone to naming conflicts and human error. Situations involving categorical groups of samples can be improved using this approach, as demonstrated in Code Example 4.5. However, multiple problems remain unsolved: paths still need to be manually generated, and code must be modified to account for changes to the files themselves. In addition, an identifier such as **b[17]** is neither helpful nor descriptive.

CODE EXAMPLE 4.5: USING ARRAYS OF BUFFERS TO ORGANIZE CATEGORIES OF "DRONE" AND "CREAK" SAMPLES.

```
(
~drone = [
    Buffer.read(s, "/path/to/drone0.wav"),
    Buffer.read(s, "/path/to/drone1.wav"),
    Buffer.read(s, "/path/to/drone2.wav")
];

~creak = [
    Buffer.read(s, "/path/to/creak0.wav"),
    Buffer.read(s, "/path/to/creak1.wav"),
    Buffer.read(s, "/path/to/creak2.wav")
];
)
```

PathName is a utility class for accessing files and folders on your computer. In combination with iteration, **PathName** can automate the process of passing file paths to buffers and storing the buffers in a collection. We provide **PathName** with an absolute path to a folder, use **entries** to return an array of **PathName** instances that represent folder contents, and iteratively call **fullPath** on each instance to return each file's complete path string. This approach, demonstrated in Code Example 4.6, is especially convenient if all your audio files are stored in one folder.[1] In addition, this code will not need modification if audio files are added, renamed, or removed from their folder. However, if the folder contains any non-audio files or unrecognized file formats, this code will fail.

CODE EXAMPLE 4.6: USAGE OF PathName AND ITERATION TO CREATE AN ARRAY OF BUFFERS.

```
(
var folder = PathName.new("/path/to/folder/of/audio/files/");
b = folder.entries.collect({ |file| Buffer.read(s, file.fullPath) });
)

b[0].play;

b[1].play; // etc.
```

Access via numerical index is well-suited for audio files with similarly numerical file-naming schemes. In other cases, however, your sample library may already be organized into subfolders and sub-subfolders, and you may want to preserve this organizational structure as files are loaded into buffers. The **Event** class is a different type of collection, distantly related to arrays, which may be useful in this situation. An **Event** is an unordered collection, but each stored item is associated with a unique "key," designated as a symbol. An **Event** instance can be created with the **new** method, or by using an enclosure of parentheses. Basic usage (without involving buffers) is shown in Code Example 4.7.

CODE EXAMPLE 4.7: CREATING, FILLING, AND RETRIEVING DATA FROM AN Event.

```
(
b = (); // create an empty Event
b[\abc] = 17; // store three pieces of data in the Event
b[\jkl] = 30.2;
b[\xyz] = [2, 3, 4];
)

b[\jkl]; // retrieve the data stored at the key 'jkl'
```

The main advantage of storing buffers in an **Event** is the ability to use meaningful names, rather than numbers, to identify groups of audio files. An effective strategy is to store arrays of buffers in an event, pairing each array with a key named according to the immediate parent folder of each set of audio files. The example in Code Example 4.8 assumes there is a main folder, which contains some number of subfolders. We imagine these subfolders are named according to the source material of the audio files they contain, for example, "wood," "metal," and so on. After evaluation, the **Event** contains arrays of buffers, each stored at an appropriate symbol key (e.g., **\wood**, **\metal**).

CODE EXAMPLE 4.8: USAGE OF **PathName** AND ITERATION TO CREATE AN **Event** CONTAINING ARRAYS OF BUFFERS STORED AT KEYS THAT CORRESPOND TO AUDIO FILES' PARENT FOLDER NAMES.

```
(
var folder, subfolders;
b = ();
folder = PathName.new("/path/to/main/folder/");
subfolders = folder.entries; // array of PathName subfolders
subfolders.do({ |sub|
    // for each subfolder, iterate over the files
    // and load each one into a buffer
    var bufArray = sub.entries.collect({ |file|
        Buffer.read(s, file.fullPath);
    });
    // then, store the array in the Event, at a key
    // named according to the subfolder name
    b[sub.folderName.asSymbol] = bufArray;
});
)

b[\wood][0].play; // play the 0th file in the wood subfolder

b[\metal][3].play; // play the 3rd file in the metal subfolder, etc.
```

The code in Code Example 4.8 assumes there are exactly three hierarchical layers: the main folder, the subfolders, and the audio files within those subfolders. If the directory structure deviates from this model (e.g., if there are additional layers of subfolders, or if a folder contains a mix of files and folders, or if a folder contains a file in an invalid format), this code will fail. The Companion Code provided at the end of this chapter section illustrates additional refinements capable of anticipating such deviations.

One final problem remains unaddressed. All the previous examples rely on at least one absolute path. If one of these code examples were run on a different computer—even if the audio files were also moved to this computer—the absolute path would likely not represent a valid location. The solution is to identify the main folder using a relative path, rather than an absolute one.

A solid approach is to create a main project folder that contains all your assets, that is, your code and folder(s) of audio files. For example, if your project folder contains a code file and a folder named "audio" (which contains some number of subfolders of audio files), the expression:

```
"audio/".resolveRelative;
```

will return a valid absolute path that points to a folder named "audio," assumed to be present in the same directory as the code file. Therefore, the expression:

```
PathName.new("audio/".resolveRelative);
```

will return a valid instance of PathName through which all subfolders and files can be accessed. Thus, as long as the main project folder remains intact, code that relies on relative paths will work correctly on any computer. Companion Code 4.1 continues a discussion of buffer management strategies and concludes with a robust buffer-reading function that can be easily transplanted into any sample-based project.

4.3 Sampling UGens

Once a buffer has been allocated and loaded with audio samples, we can use UGens to read the contents of the buffer, generating an audio signal for further processing. **PlayBuf** and **BufRd** are the two primary options.

4.3.1 PLAYBUF

PlayBuf is a buffer-reading UGen that includes a modulatable playback rate, can be triggered to jump to a particular frame, and is capable of automatic looping. At minimum, to produce a signal, **PlayBuf** needs the number of audio channels of a buffer, along with its bufnum, demonstrated in Code Example 4.9. Note that many subsequent code examples in Section 4.3 assume the server is booted and that a one-channel buffer is loaded and stored in the interpreter variable **b**. In these examples, these steps may not be explicitly indicated.

CODE EXAMPLE 4.9: LOADING AND PLAYING A BUFFER USING PlayBuf.

```
b = Buffer.read(s, Platform.resourceDir ++ "/sounds/a11wlk01-44_1.aiff");

{PlayBuf.ar(b.numChannels, b.bufnum)}.play;
```

Using function-dot-play is useful for quickly auditioning a sound file, but offers few advantages over **b.play**. Creating a SynthDef offers reuse and flexibility, and helps highlight some common pitfalls. For instance, it may be tempting to declare arguments for the number of channels and the bufnum (see Code Example 4.10), but evaluating this code produces a "Non Boolean in test" error.

CODE EXAMPLE 4.10: **AN ATTEMPT TO CREATE A BUFFER-PLAYING SYNTHDEF WITH A CHANNEL SIZE ARGUMENT, WHICH FAILS.**

```
(
SynthDef(\playbuf, {
    arg nch = 1, buf = 0, out = 0;
    var sig = PlayBuf.ar(nch, buf);
    Out.ar(out, sig ! 2);
}).add;
)
```

Declaring a bufnum argument (here, named **buf**) is not related to this error. On the contrary, declaring a bufnum argument is almost always a good idea, as it allows us to specify an arbitrary buffer when creating a Synth. If we instead provided an integer or the expression **b.bufnum** inside **PlayBuf**, a static value would be hard-coded into the SynthDef, restricting playback to one (and only one) buffer.

The non-Boolean error seems strange at first, since nothing in the SynthDef seems to require a Boolean value. The error is the result of attempting to define the number of output channels as an argument. A fundamental design feature of the audio server is that all signals in a UGen function must have a fixed channel size when the SynthDef is created, so the **numChannels** argument must be a static value. In fairness, it appears at first glance that **nch** is a static value (it has been initialized to one). However, declared arguments are not static values—they are signals! Specifically, when an argument is declared, it automatically becomes an instance of a UGen belonging to a small family that includes **Control**, **AudioControl**, **TrigControl**, and a few others. These UGens are specifically designed to allow external control mechanisms to influence a signal algorithm, for example, through **set** messages. Because signals are dynamic entities whose value can change over time, the server is unable to determine an appropriate channel size for **PlayBuf** and reports an error. The solution is to explicitly specify the number of **PlayBuf** channels as an integer, as shown in Code Example 4.11. If your sample library includes a mix of mono and stereo files, a simple solution is to create two SynthDefs with different channel sizes. If you attempt to play a buffer with a number of channels that doesn't match the UGen channel size, SC will post a warning message and play however many channels it can accommodate (which may be fewer than expected).

CODE EXAMPLE 4.11: **CREATION OF A BUFFER-PLAYING SYNTHDEF AND SYNTH WITH A FIXED CHANNEL SIZE.**

```
(
SynthDef(\playbuf, {
    arg buf = 0, out = 0;
    var sig = PlayBuf.ar(1, buf); // fixed channel size
    Out.ar(out, sig ! 2);
}).add;
)

Synth(\playbuf, [buf: b.bufnum]);
```

Because the server automatically assigns bufnums, you should never make guesses or assumptions about which bufnum corresponds to which buffer. Instead, you should always provide the bufnum explicitly when creating a Synth, as demonstrated in the last line of Code Example 4.11.

Like **EnvGen**, **PlayBuf** has an inherently finite duration, and therefore includes a doneAction. If **PlayBuf** reaches the last frame of a buffer, and if its **loop** value is zero, it checks its doneAction. If the doneAction is two, the Synth will free itself. If **loop** is one, playback will loop and the doneAction will be ignored. A SynthDef argument can be used to dynamically modulate the loop behavior, shown in Code Example 4.12.

CODE EXAMPLE 4.12: **A BUFFER-PLAYING SynthDef WITH A MODULATABLE LOOP ARGUMENT.**

```
(
SynthDef(\playbuf, {
    arg buf = 0, loop = 1, out = 0;
    var sig = PlayBuf.ar(1, buf, loop: loop, doneAction: 2);
    Out.ar(out, sig ! 2);
}).add;
)

x = Synth(\playbuf, [buf: b.bufnum]); // looping is on by default

x.set(\loop, 0); // turn looping off
```

PlayBuf includes a **rate** parameter, which indirectly controls the position of an internal frame pointer, demonstrated in Code Example 4.13. This value is expressed as a ratio, so a value of two doubles playback speed while also shifting pitch up one octave and cutting playback duration in half. A rate of 0.5 has the opposite effects. Negative values reverse playback direction. A rate of zero freezes the playback pointer, producing silence and usually some amount of DC offset, depending on the value of the sample where the freeze occurred.

CODE EXAMPLE 4.13: MANIPULATING THE PLAYBACK RATE OF PlayBuf.

```
(
SynthDef(\playbuf, {
    arg buf = 0, rate = 1, loop = 1, out = 0;
    var sig = PlayBuf.ar(1, buf, rate, loop: loop, doneAction: 2);
    Out.ar(out, sig ! 2);
}).add;
)

x = Synth(\playbuf, [buf: b.bufnum]);

x.set(\rate, 2); // double speed

x.set(\rate, 0.5); // half speed

x.set(\rate, 0); // freeze frame pointer

x.set(\rate, -0.75); // backwards, three-quarter speed

x.set(\loop, 0); // free Synth when current playback cycle finishes
```

If the rate parameter is one, **PlayBuf** will read samples from the buffer at the audio server's sample rate. If the audio stored in a buffer was recorded at a different sample rate, it will be resampled to the server's rate and the perceived pitch of the audio will be altered. For example, if the buffer contains audio recorded at 44,100 samples per second, and the server is running at 48,000 samples per second, a **PlayBuf** with a rate value equal to one will play back audio with a pitch slightly higher than the original, by a ratio of 48,000 ÷ 44,100 (approximately 1.5 semitones). The most reliable way to guarantee that a rate value equal to one plays the sample at its original pitch is to scale the rate by an instance of **BufRateScale** (see Code Example 4.14), a UGen belonging to a family of buffer utility UGens designed to extract information from buffers. **BufRateScale** requires a bufnum and generates a signal whose value is the buffer's sample rate divided by the server's sample rate. When supplied as a rate value for **PlayBuf**, it compensates for potential shifts created by buffer/server sample rate mismatches. **BufRateScale** and its sibling UGens can run at the control rate or initialization rate. The control rate is more computationally expensive but able to track changes if one buffer is dynamically swapped with another using a **set** message. Table 4.1 lists various buffer utility UGens. Within a UGen function, these utility classes are usually a more flexible option than the language-side methods in Code Example 4.3.

TABLE 4.1 Names and descriptions of buffer utility UGens.

UGen	Description of Signal Output
BufChannels.kr(buf)	Number of channels in the buffer.
BufDur.kr(buf)	Duration of the buffer, in seconds.
BufFrames.kr(buf)	Number of frames in the buffer. Equal to the buffer duration multiplied by the buffer's sample rate.
BufRateScale.kr(buf)	A ratio equal to the sample rate of the buffer divided by the server's sample rate.
BufSampleRate.kr(buf)	The sample rate at which the buffer was recorded/created.
BufSamples.kr(buf)	The number of samples in the buffer. Equal to the number of channels multiplied by the number of frames.

CODE EXAMPLE 4.14: A SYNTHDEF THAT USES `BufRateScale` TO ENSURE CORRECT PLAYBACK RATE BEHAVIOR.

```
(
SynthDef(\playbuf, {
    arg buf = 0, rate = 1, loop = 1, out = 0;
    var sig;
    rate = rate * BufRateScale.kr(buf);
    sig = PlayBuf.ar(1, buf, rate, loop: loop, doneAction: 2);
    Out.ar(out, sig ! 2);
}).add;
)
```

It is possible to specify a frame index on which playback will start. When a trigger signal is received at **PlayBuf**'s trigger input, playback will instantaneously jump to the starting frame, demonstrated in Code Example 4.15. Note the use of a trigger-type argument, introduced in Chapter 2, which facilitates the ability to repeatedly trigger the frame jump.

CODE EXAMPLE 4.15: USE OF THE `trigger` AND `startPos` ARGUMENTS TO ENABLE AN INSTANTANEOUS JUMP TO AN ARBITRARY FRAME.

```
(
SynthDef(\playbuf, {
    arg buf = 0, rate = 1, t_trig = 1, start = 0, loop = 1, out = 0;
    var sig;
```

```
        rate = rate * BufRateScale.kr(buf);
        sig = PlayBuf.ar(1, buf, rate, t_trig, start, loop, doneAction: 2);
        Out.ar(out, sig ! 2);
}).add;
)

x = Synth(\playbuf, [buf: b.bufnum]);

// jump to the 0.5 second mark:
x.set(\start, s.sampleRate / 2, \t_trig, 1);

x.free;
```

Companion Code 4.2 explores additional creative options involving **PlayBuf**.

4.3.2 BUFRD

BufRd (short for "buffer read") serves the same general purpose as **PlayBuf**, but with a different design. Like **PlayBuf**, **BufRd** requires a static channel size and a bufnum. Whereas **PlayBuf** has several inputs that indirectly control the position of its internal frame pointer, **BufRd** has only a **phase** input, which is treated as an explicit frame pointer, and which must be an audio rate signal.

Line can be used as a frame pointer to create a simple "one-shot" player, which appears in Code Example 4.16. **BufFrames** and **BufDur** are useful for retrieving relevant buffer information. Because buffer frame indices begin with 0, the correct end value for Line is the number of frames minus 1. **BufRd** has no doneAction, and instead relies on its frame pointer or some other finite signal to provide an appropriate doneAction, when relevant.

CODE EXAMPLE 4.16: USE OF BufRd AND Line TO PLAY A BUFFER ONCE FROM START TO END.

```
(
SynthDef(\bufrd, {
    arg buf = 0, out = 0;
    var sig, phs;
    phs = Line.ar(0, BufFrames.kr(buf) - 1, BufDur.kr(buf),
        doneAction: 2);
    sig = BufRd.ar(1, buf, phs);
    Out.ar(out, sig ! 2);
}).add;
)

Synth(\bufrd, [buf: b.bufnum]);
```

Many new users may look at Code Example 4.16 and ask, "How do you make a Line UGen loop?" The answer is that **Line** cannot loop. Instead, a UGen capable of generating a repeating linear ramp, such as **Phasor**, is necessary. **Phasor**, demonstrated in Code Example 4.17, accepts a start and end value, and includes a rate argument, which represents a value increment per sample. A rate equal to one will cause **Phasor**'s output to increase by one for each sample, resulting in normal playback speed when the sample rates of the server and buffer are identical. **BufRateScale** should be used to compensate for potentially mismatched sample rates. Note that the end value of **Phasor** is the point at which the signal wraps back to the start value. The end value is never actually generated, so **BufFrames** is the correct end value, rather than the number of frames minus 1.

CODE EXAMPLE 4.17: USE OF BufRd AND Phasor TO CREATE A SAMPLE LOOPER.

```
(
SynthDef(\bufrd, {
    arg buf = 0, rate = 1, out = 0;
    var sig, phs;
    rate = rate * BufRateScale.kr(buf);
    phs = Phasor.ar(rate: rate, start: 0, end: BufFrames.kr(buf));
    sig = BufRd.ar(1, buf, phs);
    Out.ar(out, sig ! 2);
}).add;
)

Synth(\bufrd, [buf: b.bufnum]);
```

BufRd has a fourth argument named **loop**, which is often a source of confusion. Setting this value to 1 does not automatically cause looping behavior. Instead, **loop** determines how **BufRd** will respond if the frame index signal is outside of a valid range. If **loop** is 0, **BufRd** will clip frame values between 0 and the final frame index of its buffer. If **loop** is 1, **BufRd** will wrap out-of-range frame values between 0 and the final frame index. If frame pointer values are always within a valid range, the loop parameter is irrelevant.

The final argument of **BufRd** determines the type of sample interpolation that occurs if the phase signal points to a buffer location between frames, which commonly occurs when reading through a buffer faster or slower than normal. The default value of 2 corresponds to linear interpolation, which is fine for most cases. A value of 4 specifies cubic interpolation, producing a marginally cleaner sound at a marginally higher computational cost. A value of 1 disables interpolation altogether. Non-interpolation is advisable only in situations where the buffer and server have the same sample rate, and playback will never deviate from "normal" speed. Otherwise, the output signal will have an audible reduction in quality. For comparison, the sample interpolation of **PlayBuf** is always cubic, regardless of playback rate. Companion Code 4.3 explores additional creative options involving **BufRd**.

4.3.3 ADDITIONAL REMARKS ON BUFFER PLAYBACK

PlayBuf and **BufRd** have different interfaces but ultimately perform the same task. So, which is the right one to use? The answer, in many cases, is that either will suffice, and the decision partly depends on personal preference. If one of these two options intuitively feels easier to handle, then the choice is clear. There are, however, situations in which one UGen lends itself more readily to a task than the other.

Due to its built-in, automatically advancing frame pointer, **PlayBuf** offers convenience. If the goal is simply to initiate playback at some speed, and freely let that process live out its lifespan, then **PlayBuf** is a sensible choice, particularly when the circumstances don't require real-time management of frame pointer movement. In addition, its rate argument enables direct specification of pitch; for example, a value of **2.midiratio** returns a ratio that adjusts playback speed so that the perceived pitch increases by two semitones.

The need to create a second signal to drive **BufRd** is initially off-putting, but this separation makes **BufRd** quite nimble compared to **PlayBuf**. With simple substitutions, **BufRd** can be made to read through its buffer backward, exponentially, sinusoidally, randomly, and so on.

BufRd is an optimal choice for looping multiple audio files while keeping them synchronized. Consider two recordings of roughly the same length (e.g., four bars of drums and four bars of guitar), meant to be looped and played back simultaneously. If one recording is slightly longer—perhaps the tempo was slightly different or the audio files were sloppily trimmed—then two looping instances of **PlayBuf** will gradually drift out of phase. Synchronization in this case requires the awkward solution of scaling one rate by the ratio of the file lengths. On the other hand, two **BufRd** UGens driven by the same frame pointer signal will always remain perfectly phase-locked.

When dealing with especially long buffers (several minutes or more), **PlayBuf** is usually the better choice. **BufRd** relies on an explicit frame index, but the server cannot offer numerical precision beyond 2^{24} = 16,777,216. At a sampling rate of 44,100, a buffer with this many frames is just under six and a half minutes long (this duration decreases as sampling rate increases). Attempts to access frames at indices beyond this value will not succeed. **PlayBuf**, however, can handle relatively large audio files with no trouble.

When using either of these basic sampling UGens, it's important to keep in mind that musical pitch and time are inherently linked, just as they are on an analog tape player or vinyl turntable. When the speed of an audio-reading process increases, musical pitch proportionally increases, and durational aspects proportionally decrease (and vice-versa). DAWs, DJ software, and other commercial audio platforms have tools that give the impression that time and pitch are independently controllable, but this is not the case under normal circumstances. Decoupling pitch from time requires processing an audio signal in a more sophisticated way. Such processes may include granular synthesis, delay lines, or analysis/resynthesis based on the Fast Fourier Transform (FFT). Granular synthesis is explored later in this chapter, and a delay-based harmonizer is featured in Companion Code 6.2. Although not explored in this book, SC includes a large library of FFT-based UGens. A guide file titled "FFT Overview" provides detailed information.

4.4 Recording UGens

Just as some UGens read samples from a buffer in real-time, others can write sample data to buffers in real-time. **RecordBuf** and **BufWr** team up with **PlayBuf** and **BufRd** to provide this complementary function, and each have a design that roughly mirrors that of its partner. In some situations, your source materials will already exist as a collection of audio files, and your creative goals will revolve around playing those files in different ways. In this case, there's no need to mess around with recording UGens. However, combinations of recording/playback UGens give rise to new creative possibilities that tend to gravitate toward live delay effects and live looping.

In practice, a microphone signal is one of the most common things to feed into a recording/playback setup—for example, to gradually build up a layered, looped texture during a live performance. **SoundIn** provides access to microphone signals, but this UGen is best introduced alongside a discussion of how the server uses busses to pass signals from one Synth to another, so this topic is covered in Chapter 6. In this chapter, the signals we'll record into buffers will be generated using synthesis techniques, or by playing back other buffers.

4.4.1 RECORDBUF

RecordBuf resembles **PlayBuf**, with a few notable differences. At minimum, **RecordBuf** needs the signal that will be recorded, and the bufnum of the buffer in which recording will take place. The number of channels of the signal must match the number of channels in the buffer, or the recording process will fail. Like **PlayBuf**, **RecordBuf** has an internal frame pointer, but its rate cannot be fluidly manipulated. Instead, the pointer moves forward through a buffer at the sampling rate when **run** is positive, backward at the same speed when negative, and the pointer stops when **run** is 0. **RecordBuf** includes a doneAction, checked when the pointer is on the last frame, but ignored if **loop** is 1. When a trigger is received at the **trigger** input, the frame pointer jumps to frame 0. Unlike **PlayBuf**, the jump target is always frame 0 and cannot be modulated.

Basic uses of **RecordBuf** often begin with allocating an empty buffer via **alloc**, which needs the name of the server, a frame count, and a number of channels. To specify a duration in seconds, the frame count can be expressed by multiplying the duration by the sample rate. Once a buffer is allocated, a UGen function containing **RecordBuf** can be used to write a signal into it. Code Example 4.18 records an enveloped sine tone into a buffer. Note that signal attenuation occurs after recording, so that the signal is captured at full amplitude. The last line of code creates an attenuated, two-channel version of the signal, strictly for monitoring purposes, which has no impact on the recording process. **RecordBuf** needs no terminating doneAction, which is handled instead by the signal envelope. Once recording is complete, we can plot and play the buffer as we normally would. The **zero** method can be used to clear the contents of a buffer, replacing all samples with zeroes.

CODE EXAMPLE 4.18: AN EXAMPLE THAT ALLOCATES A BUFFER, RECORDS A 0.5-SECOND SINE TONE USING RecordBuf, AND THEN INTERACTS WITH THE BUFFER USING VARIOUS METHODS.

```
b = Buffer.alloc(s, s.sampleRate * 0.5, 1); // 1/2 sec mono buffer

(
{
    var sig = SinOsc.ar(ExpRand(200, 1200));
    sig = sig * Env.perc(0.01, 0.49).ar(2);
    RecordBuf.ar(sig, b);
    sig = sig * 0.25 ! 2;
```

```
    }.play;
)

b.plot;

{PlayBuf.ar(1, b, BufRateScale.kr(b), doneAction: 2) * 0.25 ! 2}.play;

b.zero; // clear the buffer

b.plot; // now empty
```

Note also in Code Example 4.18 that there's no need to capture the output signal of **RecordBuf** in a variable. The chief purpose of this UGen is to write a signal to a buffer, which happens regardless of whether it is stored in a variable.

Recording and monitoring are two separate, fully independent processes. We don't always want to record the signal we are monitoring, and vice-versa. Even if the UGen function outputs silence to loudspeakers (by adding a 0 as the final statement of the function), recording will still take place, as shown in Code Example 4.19.

CODE EXAMPLE 4.19: A DEMONSTRATION THAT RECORDING STILL OCCURS IF THE OUTPUT OF THE UGEN FUNCTION IS SILENT OR NONEXISTENT.

```
(
{
    var sig = SinOsc.ar(ExpRand(200, 1200));
    sig = sig * Env.perc(0.01, 0.49).ar(2);
    RecordBuf.ar(sig, b);
    sig = sig * 0.25 ! 2;
    0; // silent output
}.play;
)

b.play(mul: 0.25);
```

The **recLevel** and **preLevel** arguments can be configured to determine whether old buffer content is overwritten, or if new material is overdubbed (i.e., mixed with old content). These parameters can also be used to bypass recording. **recLevel** is a value multiplied by each sample of the input signal just before recording takes place, and **preLevel** is a value multiplied by each sample value that currently exists in the buffer, just before recording takes place. Technically, **RecordBuf** always overdubs, but by default, **recLevel** is 1 and **preLevel** is 0, which produces behavior indistinguishable from overwriting. If both arguments are equal to 1, new content is summed with existing content, and both will be heard on playback. If **recLevel** is 0 and **preLevel** is 1, the incoming signal is silenced and existing buffer content is untouched. Each time the UGen function in Code Example 4.20 plays, it overdubs a new random tone, while reducing the amplitude of the existing content by half. After evaluating the recording function several times, you'll hear several mixed tones when playing the buffer.

CODE EXAMPLE 4.20: USE OF `RecordBuf` TO OVERDUB NEW CONTENT INTO A BUFFER.

```
b.zero; // clear the buffer first

(
{ // evaluate this function 4-5 times
    var sig = SinOsc.ar(ExpRand(200, 1200));
    sig = sig * Env.perc(0.01, 0.49).ar(2);
    RecordBuf.ar(sig, b, recLevel: 1, preLevel: 0.5);
    sig = sig * 0.25 ! 2;
}.play;
)

{PlayBuf.ar(1, b, BufRateScale.kr(b), doneAction: 2) * 0.25 ! 2}.play;
```

The duration of a sound may not be known in advance of recording, so it's not always possible to allocate a buffer with the ideal size. To capture the entirety of a finite sound whose length is unknown, we can allocate a very large buffer (e.g., a minute or more), and use sample playback techniques that strategically avoid silence that remains at the end of the buffer. In other cases, it might only be necessary to capture a few seconds of an ongoing sound, in which case a shorter buffer can be allocated, and **RecordBuf** can be configured to loop through it, continuously overdubbing or overwriting as needed. A demonstration of taking a short recording of a longer sound is featured in Code Example 4.21. After the recording Synth is freed, the buffer will contain the last half-second of audio that occurred.

CODE EXAMPLE 4.21: USING A SHORT BUFFER AND `RecordBuf` TO CAPTURE AND PLAY BACK A FRAGMENT OF A LONGER SOUND.

```
b.zero; // clear the buffer first

(
x = {
    var sig, freq;
    freq = TExpRand.ar(200, 1200, Dust.ar(12));
    sig = SinOsc.ar(freq.lag(0.02));
    RecordBuf.ar(sig, b, loop: 1);
    sig = sig * 0.25 ! 2;
```

```
    }.play;
)

x.free;

y = {PlayBuf.ar(1, b, BufRateScale.kr(b), loop: 1) * 0.25 ! 2}.play;

y.release(2);
```

Recording and playback need not occur in separate UGen functions. Buffers are globally available on the server, so any number of processes can simultaneously interact with a buffer. For instance, we can move **PlayBuf** into the previous UGen function and configure **RecordBuf** for overdubbing. The result, demonstrated in Code Example 4.22, is a real-time accumulation of audio layers.

CODE EXAMPLE 4.22: USE OF RecordBuf AND PlayBuf TO CREATE A DELAY EFFECT.

```
b.zero; // clear the buffer first

(
x = {
    var sig, freq;
    freq = TExpRand.ar(200, 1200, Dust.ar(12));
    sig = SinOsc.ar(freq.lag(0.02));
    RecordBuf.ar(sig, b, recLevel: 1, preLevel: 0.5, loop: 1);
    sig = PlayBuf.ar(1, b, BufRateScale.kr(b), loop: 1) * 0.25 ! 2;
}.play;
)

x.release(2);
```

The **preLevel** attenuation acts as a stabilizing countermeasure that prevents the overall amplitude from spiraling out of control (values greater than 1 are dangerous and inadvisable). This combination of UGens is a simple model of a digital delay line, closely related to effects based on delay lines (slapback echo, multi-tap delay, flanger, chorus, reverb, and others). The multi-tap delay UGen **MultiTap** is, in fact, built using a combination of **PlayBuf** and **RecordBuf**.

The delay time in Code Example 4.22 can be changed by using a buffer with a different duration, and the decay time can be increased by setting **preLevel** closer to 1. When equal to 1, the decay time is infinite. It should be noted that using **PlayBuf/RecordBuf** in this manner is a somewhat roundabout way of creating a delay line, a task handled more efficiently by a family of dedicated delay UGens (explored in Chapter 6), although there is value in understanding this conceptual relationship. Companion Code 4.4 explores creative ideas involving **RecordBuf** and **PlayBuf**.

4.4.2 BUFWR

Like **RecordBuf**, **BufWr** requires a signal and the buffer in which recording should take place. The internal frame pointer of **BufWr** does not move automatically, but instead relies on an audio rate **phase** signal to determine where samples are recorded. **BufWr** has a **loop** argument, which (like **BufRd**) determines whether the UGen will clip or wrap frame indices that are out-of-range.

Basic usage of **BufWr** begins with allocating a buffer, after which a **Line** UGen can be used to advance the frame pointer, and also free the Synth when the process is complete, demonstrated in Code Example 4.23.

CODE EXAMPLE 4.23: AN EXAMPLE THAT ALLOCATES A TWO-CHANNEL BUFFER, RECORDS ONE SECOND OF A STEREO SINE TONE USING `BufWr`, AND THEN INTERACTS WITH THE BUFFER USING VARIOUS METHODS.

```
b = Buffer.alloc(s, s.sampleRate, 2); // a one-second stereo buffer

(
{
    var sig, phs;
    sig = SinOsc.ar([250, 252]);
    phs = Line.ar(0, b.numFrames - 1, b.duration, doneAction: 2);
    BufWr.ar(sig, b, phs);
    sig = sig * 0.25;
}.play;
)

b.play(mul: 0.25);

b.plot;
```

With freer control over the movement of the recording pointer, it may be tempting to vary the duration of **Line**, or perhaps use an entirely different UGen, to modulate the behavior of the recording process. However, **BufWr** cannot interpolate between samples like **BufRd**, and there is no way to record an input sample "in-between" two adjacent frames. If the speed of the recording process is varied such that the frame pointer does not align with buffer samples, **BufWr** will record each sample to the nearest available frame, either overwriting neighboring samples, or leaving tiny gaps of silence in the buffer.

For example, if the duration of **Line** is reduced, the frame pointer will move through the buffer more quickly, "stretching out" the input signal and resulting in a pitch reduction when played back at normal speed. In this case, fewer samples are recorded over the same amount of space, leaving a "breadcrumb trail" of zeroes (depicted in Figure 4.2 and Code Example 4.24). The expected pitch is audible when played back, but the sound is colored by harmonic distortion. Reducing the duration of **Line** by a factor of 9/10, for example, means that every ten buffer samples will contain one zero-value sample.

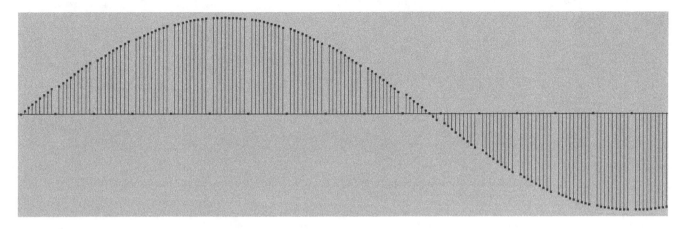

FIGURE 4.2 The visual result when using a slightly faster-than-normal frame pointer for **BufWr**.

CODE EXAMPLE 4.24: USING A SLIGHTLY FASTER-THAN-NORMAL FRAME POINTER FOR BufWr. ON REPRODUCTION, THE BUFFER CONTAINS HARMONIC DISTORTION.

```
b.zero; // clear the buffer first

(
{
    var sig, phs;
    sig = SinOsc.ar([250, 252]);
    phs = Line.ar(0, b.numFrames - 1, b.duration * 0.9,
    doneAction: 2);
    BufWr.ar(sig, b, phs);
    sig = sig * 0.25;
}.play;
)

b.play(mul: 0.25); // glitchy harmonic distortion
```

Increasing the duration of **Line** (thus reducing recording speed) has a similar effect, and the harmonic distortion is more noticeable with higher-frequency input signals. During the recording process, each sample written to the buffer may be overwritten by one or more subsequent samples before the recording pointer advances to the next frame. By upscaling the **Line** duration by a value of 3.7, we effectively lose 3.7 samples for every one sample that is successfully recorded (depicted in Figure 4.3). The result, once again, is a signal with a degraded quality, demonstrated in Code Example 4.25. The outcome is essentially identical to aliasing; something similar would occur if the sample rate of the server were reduced.

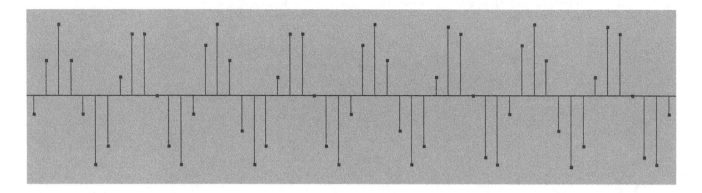

FIGURE 4.3 The visual result when using a slightly slower-than-normal frame pointer for **BufWr**.

CODE EXAMPLE 4.25: USING A SLIGHTLY SLOWER-THAN-NORMAL FRAME POINTER FOR BufWr. ON REPRODUCTION, THE BUFFER CONTAINS HARMONIC DISTORTION.

```
b.zero; // clear the buffer first

(
{
    var sig, phs;
    sig = SinOsc.ar([2000, 2010]);
    phs = Line.ar(0, b.numFrames - 1, b.duration * 3.7, doneAction: 2);
    BufWr.ar(sig, b, phs);
    sig = sig * 0.25;
}.play;
)

b.play(mul: 0.25); // glitchy harmonic distortion
```

Though it's technically possible to modulate the movement of the recording pointer, doing so is generally inadvisable, especially if accurate recording is the goal. The quality loss that results is likely part of the reason why the internal pointer of **RecordBuf** can only stand still or move at the sample rate. To create variations in the speed and pitch of recorded sound, it is better to capture these sounds at normal speed and vary their playback by manipulating **BufRd** or **PlayBuf**, taking advantage of their ability to interpolate between samples. Of course, there may be creative situations in which this glitchy flavor of harmonic distortion is appealing!

Phasor is an ideal choice for loop recording with **BufWr**. When the recording Synth in Code Example 4.26 is freed, the buffer will contain the last second of audio that occurred.

CODE EXAMPLE 4.26: **USING A SHORT BUFFER AND BufWr TO CAPTURE AND PLAY BACK A FRAGMENT OF A LONGER SOUND.**

```
b.zero; // clear the buffer first

(
x = {
    var sig, freq, phs;
    freq = TExpRand.ar(200, 1200, Dust.ar(12) ! 2);
    sig = SinOsc.ar(freq.lag(0.02));
    phs = Phasor.ar(0, BufRateScale.kr(b), 0, BufFrames.kr(b));
    BufWr.ar(sig, b, phs);
    sig = sig * 0.25;
}.play;
)

x.free;

y = {PlayBuf.ar(2, b, BufRateScale.kr(b), loop: 1) * 0.25}.play;

y.release(2);
```

BufRd and **BufWr** can simultaneously interact with the same buffer, shown in Code Example 4.27, creating a delay effect similar to Code Example 4.22. The playback pointer can be positioned behind the record pointer by subtracting some number of samples from the frame pointer signal. Note that the buffer playback signal is scaled down by a factor of 0.5 before being summed with the original signal to create a more convincing "echo" effect.

CODE EXAMPLE 4.27: **USE OF BufWr AND BufRd TO CREATE A DELAY EFFECT.**

```
b.zero; // clear the buffer first

(
x = {
    var sig, freq, phs, delay;
    freq = TExpRand.ar(200, 1200, Dust.ar(12) ! 2);
    sig = SinOsc.ar(freq.lag(0.02));
    phs = Phasor.ar(0, BufRateScale.kr(b), 0, BufFrames.kr(b));
    BufWr.ar(sig, b, phs);
    delay = BufRd.ar(2, b, phs - (SampleRate.ir / 3));
    sig = sig + (delay * 0.5);
    sig = sig * 0.25;
}.play;
)

x.release(2);
```

Overdubbing is possible with **BufWr**, though not as straightforward as it is with RecordBuf, due to a lack of explicit controls for amplitude levels of old/new buffer content. As demonstrated in Code Example 4.28, the process involves reading the buffer content, scaling down the amplitude (in this case, by a factor of 0.75), summing it with the live signal, and finally recording the sum signal into the buffer. **Line** applies a short fade-in to the source signal to prevent a click.

CODE EXAMPLE 4.28: OVERDUBBING WITH BufWr AND BufRd.

```
b.zero; // clear the buffer first

(
x = {
    var sig, freq, phs, delay;
    freq = TExpRand.ar(200, 1200, Dust.ar(12) ! 2);
    sig = SinOsc.ar(freq.lag(0.02), mul: 0.25);
    sig = sig * Line.kr(0, 1, 0.02);
    phs = Phasor.ar(0, BufRateScale.kr(b), 0, BufFrames.kr(b));
    sig = sig + (BufRd.ar(2, b, phs) * 0.75);
    BufWr.ar(sig, b, phs);
    sig = sig * 0.25;
}.play;
)

x.release(2);
```

Companion Code 4.5 explores creative options involving **BufWr** and **BufRd**.

4.4.3 ADDITIONAL REMARKS ON BUFFER RECORDING

RecordBuf and **BufWr** are designed to serve the same purpose, but one may be more appropriate than the other, depending on the circumstances. The native overdubbing feature of **RecordBuf** lends itself to accumulating multilayered textures, while the phase-locked nature of **BufWr** makes it well-suited for projects involving synchronized or tempo-driven music. **RecordBuf** is generally the better choice for long buffers, due to the limits of integer precision on the server (the same reason **PlayBuf** is superior to **BufRd** regarding long buffers).

Generating and outputting a signal is a primary function of most UGens, especially oscillators and noise generators. Yet the fact that **RecordBuf** and **BufWr** output a signal is more of a side-effect than an intentional design choice. **RecordBuf** outputs only the lowest channel of its input signal. At the time of writing, **BufWr** outputs its phase signal! These unusual behaviors reinforce that the main purpose of these UGens is to record a signal to a buffer, rather than to output some signal to be monitored. Generally, there's never any need to capture the output of a recording UGen in a variable.

4.5 Granular Synthesis

Granular synthesis involves breaking a sound into short segments called "grains," typically between 1 and 100 milliseconds long, and recombining them into a new sound, often quite different from the original. During the recombination process, parameters such as amplitude, playback speed, pan position, and others can be varied, usually on a grain-by-grain basis. Grains can be layered atop one another to create dense soundscapes or arranged more sparsely to create rhythmic/pointillistic textures. Grains can also be played backwards or reassembled in a random order. Because of its ability to manipulate sound at a "microscopic" level, granular synthesis is an especially flexible technique, capable of diverse effects that are more challenging to implement with basic recording/playback UGens. Among its most valuable assets is the ability to independently manipulate pitch and durational aspects of a sound, while introducing minimal artifacts.

Granular synthesis is sometimes associated with the term "microsound," a subject focusing on sounds that are shorter than what we normally think of as a "note." A central appeal of granular synthesis is based on the postulation that all sound is composed of, and can be represented by, elementary units of sound that cannot be further broken down. In a sense, granular synthesis is a molecular approach to creative audio; grains and other microsounds can be treated as sound particles, capable of yielding a tremendous variety of larger and more musically relevant sounds through precise recombinations.[2]

Why is a topic with the name "synthesis" included in a sampling chapter? Granular synthesis tends to elude categorization. Like other synthesis techniques, it is inherently generative. On the other hand, it draws upon ideas close to sampling, such as capturing and reproducing parts of an existing sound. Furthermore, granular synthesis can be seen as a means of processing an input signal and would perhaps find a home in a signal processing chapter. Finally, granular synthesis could be considered a category of its own. It's included here due to that fact that granular synthesis is frequently applied to recorded sound, and several of SC's granular UGens operate on audio stored in a buffer. Reliance on buffers provides flexibility with temporal grain rearrangement: UGens can "look ahead" in a buffer to extract future content but can't do the same with a live signal.

In SC, `GrainBuf`, `TGrains`, and `Warp1` granulate audio stored in a buffer. This section introduces all three, but a familiarity with one will accelerate a familiarity with the other two. Other granular UGens include `GrainSin` and `GrainFM`, which apply granular synthesis to sine tones and frequency-modulated sine tones, as well as `GrainIn`, which operates on a live signal. These additional UGens are similar in design but offer somewhat less flexibility on account of restrictions on types of input signals and an inability to look ahead.

All three of the granulators explored in this section require an input sound stored in a one-channel buffer. Attempts to granulate a multichannel buffer will fail by either producing silence or distorting the audio. Bear in mind that this requirement does not mean that the output signal of a granular UGen must also be monophonic! On the contrary, a grain pulled from a one-channel buffer can be panned in stereo or a higher multichannel format. Thus, multichannel audio files should be mixed to a monophonic format before being loaded into SC, or the `readChannel` method should be used to read only one of several channels into a buffer. True granulation of a stereo audio file requires two separate buffers containing left/right content, and two separate instances of a granular UGen (a setup concisely handled with multichannel expansion). However, such a setup is rarely needed in practice; most creative goals can be met by using only one channel or a mono mix of a multichannel source.

4.5.1 GRAINBUF

The first four arguments of **GrainBuf** determine the number of channels of the output signal, a trigger signal which schedules grain generation, the duration of each grain (checked whenever a grain is created), and the buffer containing the source signal.

Like **PlayBuf** and **BufRd**, the number of channels of **GrainBuf** must be a fixed positive integer and cannot be modulated. Bear in mind that this value corresponds to the number of audio channels that **GrainBuf** will output, rather than the number of channels in the source buffer, which must always be one. **Impulse** and **Dust** generate single-sample impulses and are sensible choices for generating rhythmic or arrhythmic triggers, respectively. If using the built-in file demonstrated in Code Example 4.29, the following code will produce a stream of eight noisy grains per second, each 50 milliseconds long. Subsequent examples in this section assume the server is booted and that a one-channel audio file has been loaded into a buffer, stored in the variable **b**, and therefore do not explicitly include these steps.

CODE EXAMPLE 4.29: SIMPLE GRANULATION OF AUDIO STORED IN A BUFFER USING GrainBuf.

```
b = Buffer.read(s, Platform.resourceDir ++ "/sounds/a11wlk01.wav");

(
{
    GrainBuf.ar(
        numChannels: 2,
        trigger: Impulse.kr(8),
        dur: 0.05,
        sndbuf: b
    );
}.play;
)
```

The fifth argument (**rate**) is a ratio that determines playback speed of individual grains, which behaves exactly like the rate argument of **PlayBuf**. **GrainBuf** and the other granular UGens discussed here automatically resample the audio, so that a rate value of one produces the original sound, regardless of the sample rate of the source file. Therefore, it should not be necessary to scale the rate using **BufRateScale**. The sixth argument (**pos**) is a normalized position value that determines the starting frame in the buffer from which grains are generated. Zero represents the beginning of the file, and one represents the end. If a relatively long grain begins near the end of the buffer, **GrainBuf** will wrap to the beginning of the buffer to complete the grain. In this case, the grain will contain a bit of the end and beginning of the source buffer, which may or may not be desirable. If your source audio file does not fade to zero at both ends, a click may be produced. This wrapping behavior cannot be changed. The code in Code Example 4.30 selects grains that begin halfway through the buffer and plays each grain at a speed that corresponds to an increase of seven semitones.

CODE EXAMPLE 4.30: USING `GrainBuf` TO GRANULATE A BUFFER WITH PITCH TRANSPOSITION AND AN OFFSET START POSITION.

```
(
{
    GrainBuf.ar(
        numChannels: 2,
        trigger: Impulse.kr(8),
        dur: 0.05,
        sndbuf: b,
        rate: 7.midiratio,
        pos: 0.5
    );
}.play;
)
```

A unifying feature of UGens is that, with few exceptions, their arguments can be controlled by other UGens, and granular UGens are no different. For example, the **Line** UGen provides an option for moving the frame pointer through the buffer, rather than holding it at a static position. Code Example 4.31 advances the grain pointer from start to end over the buffer duration.

CODE EXAMPLE 4.31: USING `GrainBuf` TO GRANULATE A BUFFER USING A DYNAMIC FRAME POINTER.

```
(
{
    GrainBuf.ar(
        numChannels: 2,
        trigger: Impulse.kr(8),
        dur: 0.05,
        sndbuf: b,
        rate: 7.midiratio,
        pos: Line.kr(0, 1, BufDur.ir(b))
    );
}.play;
)
```

The seventh argument (**interp**) determines the type of sample interpolation applied when the rate argument alters grain pitch. The behavior is identical to **BufRd**: 4 is cubic, 2 is linear, and 1 disables interpolation. The default is linear, which is usually a good compromise. The eighth argument (**pan**) determines the pan position of each grain, and it should be a number between negative and positive 1. When **numChannels** is 2, this value behaves as it does with **Pan2** (0 is centered, negative/positive values shift the image to the left/right).

The ninth argument, **envbufnum**, is a buffer number that determines the shape of the amplitude envelope applied to each grain. In general, if no amplitude envelope is applied to a grain, the grain may produce a hard click at its beginning and end. With a high grain density, this can drastically affect the spectrum and timbre of the overall granular texture. The default value is negative one, which uses a built-in envelope shaped like a bell curve, providing a smooth fade-in and fade-out for each grain. An alternate envelope can be created by calling **discretize** on an **Env** and loading the resulting values into a buffer. The duration of the **Env** in this case is largely irrelevant, because it will be rescaled based on the duration of each grain. A relatively high discretization value is sensible to ensure a sufficiently large buffer and therefore a sufficiently precise representation of the envelope. Code Example 4.32 establishes a percussive grain envelope, producing a clear, distinct articulation at the start of each grain. In addition, a noise generator randomizes the pan position of each grain.

CODE EXAMPLE 4.32: AN EXAMPLE OF GrainBuf THAT USES A CUSTOM PERCUSSIVE GRAIN ENVELOPE AND RANDOMIZED PAN POSITIONS.

```
(
var env = Env.new([0, 1, 0], [0.01, 1], [0, -4]);
~grainenv = Buffer.loadCollection(s, env.discretize(8192));
)

(
{
    GrainBuf.ar(
        numChannels: 2,
        trigger: Impulse.kr(8),
        dur: 0.05,
        sndbuf: b,
        rate: 7.midiratio,
        pos: Line.kr(0, 1, BufDur.ir(b)),
        interp: 2,
        pan: LFNoise1.kr(10),
        envbufnum: ~grainenv
    );
}.play;
)
```

In addition to **mul/add**, **GrainBuf** includes a non-modulatable **maxGrains** parameter, which determines the maximum number of grains that can overlap at one time. The default is 512, a generous value that is sufficient in most cases. If the number of simultaneous grains exceeds this limit, the excess grains will not generate, and a warning message will be posted.

4.5.2 TGRAINS

Overall, **TGrains** and **GrainBuf** are similar, with the following exceptions:

- Some arguments have slightly different names (**sndbuf/bufnum**, **pos/centerPos**, **mul/amp**) and appear in a slightly different order.
- The grain envelope in **TGrains** has a bell curve shape and cannot be altered.
- The argument **centerPos** determines the point in the buffer where the grain reaches its peak amplitude, rather than where it begins. This value is measured in seconds, instead of being normalized between 0 and 1.
- The **mul/add** arguments are absent from **TGrains**. An argument named **amp** replaces **mul** and has a default value of 0.1 instead of 1, which means the signal output may be quieter than expected if this parameter remains untouched.

Code Example 4.33 uses **TGrains** to create roughly the same type of sound produced by the previous **GrainBuf** example.

CODE EXAMPLE 4.33: AN EXAMPLE OF TGrains THAT IMITATES THE SOUND PRODUCED BY CODE EXAMPLE 4.32.

```
(
{
    TGrains.ar(
        numChannels: 2,
        trigger: Impulse.kr(8),
        bufnum: b,
        rate: 7.midiratio,
        centerPos: Line.kr(0, BufDur.ir(b), BufDur.ir(b)),
        dur: 0.05,
        pan: LFNoise1.kr(10),
        amp: 1,
        interp: 2
    );
}.play;
)
```

4.5.3 WARP1

Warp1 retains much of the same functionality as **GrainBuf** and **TGrains**, but its design is slightly different, as is the naming and order of its arguments. In a break with consistency, the **numChannels** argument of **Warp1** corresponds to the number of channels in the source buffer, rather than the desired number of output channels. Thus, if a one-channel buffer is supplied for **bufnum**, **numChannels** argument should be 1. **Warp1** has no pan argument, so the output signal will always be the same channel size as the source buffer.

Other arguments have behaviors that mimic **GrainBuf**:

- **pointer** is a normalized buffer position value, equivalent to **pos**.
- **freqScale** is a ratio that determines grain playback speed, equivalent to **rate**.
- **windowSize** is the length of each grain, measured in seconds, equivalent to **dur**.
- **envbufnum**, **interp**, and **mul/add** have the same names and behaviors as they do in **GrainBuf**.

The major design distinction of **Warp1** is that there is no explicit trigger signal that governs the timing of grain generation. Instead, the timing of each grain is a function of the grain duration and an **overlaps** parameter, which is the ratio between the duration of the grain and the duration between adjacent grain onsets. For example, if **overlaps** is 3, the next grain will generate when the previous grain is one-third complete. If overlaps is 0.5, there will be a gap of silence between consecutive grains equal to the duration of one grain. Lastly, **windowRandRatio** is a value between 0 and 1 that randomizes grain duration, which is useful in offsetting the otherwise rhythmic behavior of grain generation, and can help produce a more pleasantly irregular sound. Code Example 4.34 uses **Warp1** to approximate the results of **GrainBuf** in Code Example 4.32. As a side note, the implicit frequency at which grains occur can be calculated by dividing **overlaps** by **windowSize**, which in this case is eight grains per second (0.4 ÷ 0.05).

CODE EXAMPLE 4.34: AN EXAMPLE OF Warp1 THAT IMITATES THE SOUND PRODUCED BY CODE EXAMPLE 4.32.

```
(
{
    var sig;
    sig = Warp1.ar(
        numChannels: 1,
        bufnum: b,
        pointer: Line.kr(0, 1, BufDur.ir(b)),
        freqScale: 7.midiratio,
        windowSize: 0.05,
        envbufnum: -1,
        overlaps: 0.4,
        windowRandRatio: 0,
        interp: 2,
        mul: 0.5,
    );
    sig = Pan2.ar(sig, LFNoise1.kr(10));
}.play;
)
```

Granular synthesis is fertile soil for all sorts of creative experiments, some of which are explored in Companion Code 4.6.

Notes

1 When using iteration to read audio files into buffers, as pictured in Code Example 4.6, the files will be read in numerical/alphabetical order. If you want an array to be filled with buffers in a specific order, a good practice is to attach numerical prefixes to file names before reading them into buffers. For example, instead of snare.wav, kick.wav, hihat.wav, you may rename these files 00_snare.wav, 01_kick.wav, 02_hihat.wav to ensure they are loaded in this numerical order.
2 For more information on granular synthesis and microsound, see Curtis Roads, *Microsound* (Cambridge, Mass: MIT Press, 2001).

CHAPTER 5

SEQUENCING

5.1 Overview

Music is fundamentally rooted in time. Thus, music sequencing tools are an essential part of any creative audio platform. Indulging in some simplification, a musical composition can be viewed as a sequence of sections, a section as a sequence of phrases, and a phrase as a sequence of notes. Thinking in this modular way, that is, conceptualizing a project as smaller sequential units that can be freely combined, is an excellent way to approach large-scale projects in SC, and in programming languages more generally.

SC provides a wealth of sequencing options. The **Pattern** library, for example, is home to hundreds of classes that define many types of sequences, which can be nested and combined to form complex, composite structures. The **Stream** class is also a focal point, which provides sequencing infrastructure through its subclasses, notably **Routine** and **EventStreamPlayer**. **Clock** classes provide an implicit musical grid on which events can be scheduled, and play a central role in sequencing as well.

It's important to make a distinction between processes that define sequences, and processes that perform sequences. As an analogy, consider the difference between a notated musical score and a live musical performance of that score. The score provides detailed performance instructions, and the sound of the music can even be imagined by studying it. However, the score is not the same thing as a performance. One score can spawn an infinite number of performances, which may be slightly or significantly different from each other. In SC, a pattern or function can be used to define a sequence, while some type of stream is used to perform it.

5.2 Routines and Clocks

5.2.1 ROUTINE

When we evaluate a function, the encapsulated code statements are executed in order, but these executions occur so quickly that they seem to happen all at once. When the function in Code Example 5.1 is evaluated, three tones are produced, and we hear a chord.

CODE EXAMPLE 5.1: A FUNCTION THAT PRODUCES A THREE-NOTE CHORD WHEN EVALUATED.

```
s.boot;

(
~eventA = {SinOsc.ar(60.midicps ! 2) * Line.kr(0.1, 0, 1, 2)};
~eventB = {SinOsc.ar(70.midicps ! 2) * Line.kr(0.1, 0, 1, 2)};
~eventC = {SinOsc.ar(75.midicps ! 2) * Line.kr(0.1, 0, 1, 2)};

f = {
    ~eventA.play;
    ~eventB.play;
    ~eventC.play;
};
)

f.();
```

How would we play these tones one-by-one, to create a melody? The **Routine** class, introduced in Code Example 5.2, provides one option for timed sequences. A routine is a special type of state-aware function, capable of pausing and resuming mid-execution. A routine encapsulates a function, and within this function, either the **yield** or **wait** method designates a pause (**yield** is used throughout this section, but these methods are synonymous when applied to a number). Once a routine is created, we can manually step through it by calling **next** on the routine. On each **next**, the routine begins evaluation, suspends when it encounters a pause, and continues from that point when another **next** is received. If a routine has reached its end, **next** returns nil, but a routine can be **reset** at any time, which effectively "rewinds" it to the beginning.

CODE EXAMPLE 5.2: USING A ROUTINE AND THE next METHOD TO MANUALLY STEP THROUGH A SEQUENCE OF NOTES.

```
(
~eventA = {SinOsc.ar(60.midicps ! 2) * Line.kr(0.1, 0, 1, 2)};
~eventB = {SinOsc.ar(70.midicps ! 2) * Line.kr(0.1, 0, 1, 2)};
~eventC = {SinOsc.ar(75.midicps ! 2) * Line.kr(0.1, 0, 1, 2)};

f = {
    ~eventA.play;
    1.yield;
    ~eventB.play;
    1.yield;
    ~eventC.play;
    1.yield;
};
```

```
    r = Routine(f);
)

r.next; // evaluate repeatedly

r.reset; // return to the beginning at any time
```

Note that **yield** must be called from within a routine, so the function **f** in Code Example 5.2 cannot be evaluated by itself:

```
f.(); // -> ERROR: yield was called outside of a routine.
```

> ### TIP.RAND(); A SYNTAX SHORTCUT FOR ROUTINES
>
> The convenience method **r** can be applied to a function and will return a routine that contains that function. Thus, a routine can be written in any of the following ways:
>
> ```
> Routine({"hello".postln; 1.yield;});
>
> {"hello".postln; 1.yield;}.r;
>
> r({"hello".postln; 1.yield;});
> ```

When stepping through a routine, each **yield** returns its receiver, in the same way that calling **value** on a function returns its last expression. Thus, the returned value from each **next** call is equal to each yielded item (this is also why each **next** causes the number one to appear in the post window). In Code Example 5.2, the thing we yield is irrelevant, and we have no interest in it. It could be any object; the number one is chosen arbitrarily. In this example, we are more interested in the actions that occur between yields, specifically, the production of sound. However, the ability of a routine to return values illustrates another usage. Suppose we want a process that generates MIDI note numbers that start at 48 and increment by a random number of semitones between one and four, until the total range exceeds three octaves. We can do so by defining an appropriate function and yielding values of interest. A **while** loop is useful, as it allows us to repeatedly apply an increment until our end condition is met (see Code Example 5.3).

CODE EXAMPLE 5.3: USING A ROUTINE AND while LOOP TO GENERATE RANDOMLY INCREMENTED MIDI NOTE NUMBERS.

```
(
~noteFunc = {
    var num = 48;
    while({num < 84}, {
```

```
            num.yield;
            num = num + rrand(1, 4);
        });
    };

    ~noteGen = Routine(~noteFunc);
)

~noteGen.next; // evaluate repeatedly
```

Note that this sequence is not predetermined, because each **next** performs a new application of the **rrand** function. Thus, if **~noteGen** is reset, it will generate a new random sequence, likely different than the previous.

We often want a routine to advance on its own. A routine will execute automatically in response to **play**, shown in Code Example 5.4. In this case, yield values are treated as pause durations (measured in seconds, under default conditions). Iteration, demonstrated in Code Example 5.5, is a useful tool for creating timed repetitions.

CODE EXAMPLE 5.4: USING A ROUTINE AND THE play METHOD TO AUTOMATICALLY STEP THROUGH A SEQUENCE OF NOTES.

```
(
~eventA = {SinOsc.ar(60.midicps ! 2) * Line.kr(0.1, 0, 1, 2)};
~eventB = {SinOsc.ar(70.midicps ! 2) * Line.kr(0.1, 0, 1, 2)};
~eventC = {SinOsc.ar(75.midicps ! 2) * Line.kr(0.1, 0, 1, 2)};

f = {
    ~eventA.play;
    1.yield;
    ~eventB.play;
    1.yield;
    ~eventC.play;
    1.yield;
};

r = Routine(f);
)

r.play;
```

> **CODE EXAMPLE 5.5:** USING ITERATION INSIDE A ROUTINE TO CREATE REPETITIONS.
>
> ```
> (
> ~playTone = { |freq|
>     {SinOsc.ar(freq ! 2) * Line.kr(0.1, 0, 1, 2)}.play;
> };
>
> f = {
>     3.do({
>         ~playTone.(72.midicps);
>         0.2.yield;
>         ~playTone.(62.midicps);
>         0.4.yield;
>     });
> };
>
> r = Routine(f);
> )
>
> r.play;
> ```

When using iteration in a routine, **number.do** can be replaced with **loop** or **inf.do** (a special keyword that represents infinity) to repeat a block of code indefinitely, as pictured in Code Example 5.6. A playing routine can be stopped at any time using **stop**—particularly important to keep in mind if a routine has no end! Stopping all routines is also one of the side-effects of pressing [cmd]+[period]. Once a routine is stopped, it cannot be resumed with **play** or **next** unless it is first reset.

> **CODE EXAMPLE 5.6:** AN INFINITE-LENGTH ROUTINE.
>
> ```
> (
> ~playTone = { |freq|
>     {SinOsc.ar(freq ! 2) * Line.kr(0.1, 0, 0.2, 2)}.play;
> };
>
> r = Routine({
>     loop({
>         ~playTone.(72.midicps);
>         0.4.yield;
>         [62, 63, 64].do({ |n|
>             ~playTone.(n.midicps);
>             (0.4 / 3).yield;
>         });
>     });
> ```

```
    });
)

r.play;

r.stop;
```

> **TIP.RAND(); THE DANGER OF INFINITE LOOPS**
>
> When using **play** or **next** on an infinite-length routine, make sure there's at least one **yield/wait**! Executing an infinite routine with no built-in pauses will immediately overwhelm your CPU and may even crash the language. While stuck in a loop, SC will struggle to receive even the most basic types of input, like pressing [cmd]+[period] or clicking drop-down menus, and a forced quit may be necessary. Some versions of SC may attempt to auto-recover unsaved code in the event of a crash, but it's not wise to rely too heavily on this feature.

Routines can be nested inside other routines, which is a valuable asset when building modular musical structures. Here, an important distinction arises, related to whether multiple routines will play simultaneously (in parallel) or sequentially (in series). Code Example 5.7 begins with two functions (**~sub0** and **~sub1**), which define an "ABAB" pattern and "CCC" pattern. These subroutines are nested inside two parent routines, **~r_parallel** and **~r_series**.

When a routine is played, the resulting process exists in its own temporal space, called a thread, which is independent from the parent thread in which it was created. Thus, when multiple routines are played using back-to-back code statements (as they are in **~r_parallel**), each exists independently, unaware of the others' existences. However, when serial behavior is desired, **embedInStream** can be used instead of **play**, which situates the subroutine in the parent thread. In this case, the parent routine and the two subroutines are all part of the same thread and exist along one temporal continuum. Thus, each subroutine begins only when the previous subroutine has finished.

CODE EXAMPLE 5.7: NESTING ROUTINES INSIDE OF OTHER ROUTINES SO THAT THEY PLAY IN PARALLEL OR IN SERIES.

```
(
~playTone = { |freq|
    {SinOsc.ar(freq ! 2) * Line.kr(0.1, 0, 0.2, 2)}.play;
};

~sub0 = {
    2.do({
        ~playTone.(67.midicps);
        0.15.yield;
```

```
            ~playTone.(69.midicps);
            0.15.yield;
        });
        0.5.yield;
    };

    ~sub1 = {
        3.do({
            ~playTone.(75.midicps);
            0.5.yield;
        });
        1.yield;
    };

    ~r_parallel = Routine({
        Routine(~sub0).play;
        Routine(~sub1).play;
    });

    ~r_series = Routine({
        Routine(~sub0).embedInStream;
        Routine(~sub1).embedInStream;
    });
)

~r_parallel.play; // subroutines execute simultaneously

~r_series.play; // subroutines play one after the other
```

Modular thinking is important and valuable. Before setting out to build some glorious routines, take a moment to conceptualize the musical structure they'll represent. Break down your structures into the simpler units, build subroutines (perhaps sub-subroutines), and combine them appropriately. A large, unwieldy, irreducible routine is usually harder to debug than a routine built from modular parts.

5.2.2 TEMPOCLOCK

In the previous section, yield values are interpreted as durations, measured in seconds. Unless you're working at a tempo of 60 (or perhaps 120) beats per minute, specifying durations in seconds is inconvenient, and requires extra math. To determine the duration of an eighth note at 132 bpm, for example, we first divide 60 by the tempo to produce a value that represents seconds per beat. If a quarter note is considered one beat, we then divide by two to get the duration of an eighth note:

```
(60 / 132 / 2).yield; // an eighth rest at 132 bpm
```

Manual calculation of durations based on tempo is cluttered and does not do a good job of visually conveying metric structure. **TempoClock**, one of three clock objects (its siblings are

SystemClock and AppClock), provides an elegant solution. These three clocks handle the general task of scheduling things at specific times. AppClock is the least accurate of the three, but it can schedule certain types of actions that its siblings cannot, notably, interacting with graphical user interfaces. SystemClock and TempoClock are more accurate, but TempoClock has the additional benefit of being able to express time in terms of beats at a particular tempo. When the interpreter is launched or rebooted, a default instance of TempoClock is automatically created:

```
TempoClock.default;
```

The default TempoClock runs at 60 bpm, and the current beat can be retrieved via the **beats** method:

```
TempoClock.default.beats; // evaluate repeatedly
```

When a routine is played, it is scheduled on a clock. If no clock is specified, it plays on the default TempoClock. This is why, throughout the previous section, yield values can be treated as durations, even though they technically specify a number of beats.

When creating your own instance of TempoClock, the first argument is interpreted as a value in beats per second. If you want to specify tempo in beats per minute, divide that value by 60:

```
t = TempoClock(132/60); // a TempoClock running at 132 bpm

t.beats; // evaluate repeatedly to get the current beat
```

A routine can be scheduled on a specific clock by providing that clock as the first argument for **play**. In Code Example 5.8, yield times represent beat values, relative to the clock on which the routine plays. The tempo of a TempoClock can be changed at any time using the **tempo** method, also depicted in this same example. Note that tempo only affects durations between onsets and has no effect on the durations of the notes themselves (which in this case are determined by Line).

CODE EXAMPLE 5.8: A ROUTINE THAT PLAYS THREE NOTES IN SEQUENCE, WITH TIMINGS BASED ON BEAT DURATIONS AT A SPECIFIC TEMPO.

```
(
t = TempoClock(132/60);

~playTone = { |freq|
    {SinOsc.ar(freq ! 2) * Line.kr(0.1, 0, 1, 2)}.play;
};

r = Routine({
    [60, 70, 75].do({ |n|
```

```
        ~playTone.(n.midicps);
        (1/2).yield;
    });
});
)

r.play(t);

t.tempo = 112/60;

r.reset.play(t); // now eighth notes at 112 bpm
```

We often want to synchronize several timed processes, so that they begin together and/or exist in rhythmic alignment. Manual attempts to synchronize a routine with one that's already playing will rarely succeed. Even if both routines are played on the same clock, their performances are not guaranteed to align with each other. By default, when a routine is played on a clock, it begins immediately. To schedule a routine to begin on a certain beat, we can specify **quant** information along with the clock, shown in Code Example 5.9.

CODE EXAMPLE 5.9: RHYTHMIC QUANTIZATION OF TWO ROUTINES.

```
(
t = TempoClock(132/60);

~playTone = { |freq|
    {SinOsc.ar(freq ! 2) * Line.kr(0.1, 0, 0.2, 2)}.play;
};

~r0 = Routine({
    loop({
        [60, 63, 65, 67].do({ |n|
            ~playTone.(n.midicps);
            (1/2).yield;
        });
    });
});

~r1 = Routine({
    loop({
        [70, 72, 75, 77].do({ |n|
            ~playTone.(n.midicps);
            (1/2).yield;
```

```
        });
    });
});
)

~r0.play(t, quant: 4); // begin playing on next beat multiple of four

~r1.play(t, quant: 4); // will be beat-aligned with ~r0
```

In some cases, you may want a rhythmic process to be quantized to a particular beat but shifted in time to begin some number of beats after or before that beat. In this case, an array of two values can be provided for **quant**, seen in Code Example 5.10. The first value represents a beat multiple, and the second value represents a number of beats to shift along the timeline. Negative values result in earlier scheduling.

CODE EXAMPLE 5.10: RHYTHMIC QUANTIZATION OF TWO ROUTINES WITH BEAT OFFSETS. THESE TWO LINES RELY ON THE CODE IN CODE EXAMPLE 5.9 AND ARE MEANT TO BE SUBSTITUTED FOR THE LAST TWO LINES IN THAT EXAMPLE.

```
~r0.reset.play(t, quant: [4, 0]); // plays on the next beat
multiple of four

~r1.reset.play(t, quant: [4, 1]); // plays one beat after the
next beat multiple of four
```

As an alternative to stopping all routines individually, all actions scheduled on a **TempoClock** can be removed by calling **clear** on the clock:

```
t.clear;
```

When a large-scale routine is constructed as a singular entity composed of subroutines, there is less of a need to control quantization information, because the timing aspects can be configured in advance. However, quantization is essential for real-time applications, such as live coding, in which new components may be added spontaneously.

There is generally no harm in allowing a **TempoClock** to continue existing in the background (any outstanding clocks are destroyed when quitting SC), but a **TempoClock** can be stopped at any time with **stop**. This is a hard stop that destroys the clock, after which resuming or querying the current beat is no longer possible. To resume, a new clock must be created. By default, [cmd]+[period] will destroy all user-created clocks, but a clock can be configured to survive [cmd]+[period] by setting its **permanent** attribute to true, shown in Code Example 5.11.

> **CODE EXAMPLE 5.11:** CONFIGURING A CLOCK TO SURVIVE [CMD]+[PERIOD].
>
> ```
> t = TempoClock(132/60).permanent_(true);
>
> // press [cmd]+[period]...
>
> t.beats; // the clock remains
>
> t.permanent = false;
>
> // press [cmd]+[period]...
>
> t.beats; // the clock is destroyed
> ```

These chapter sections aim to convey the essentials of using routines and **TempoClock** to express and perform musical sequences. Though the sounds are simple, the actions in a routine can be replaced with other valid statements, such creating new Synths or sending **set** messages to existing Synths. Companion Code 5.1 explores further ideas involving these two classes, which may help expand your understanding.

5.3 Patterns

Patterns, which exist as a family of classes that all begin with capital P, provide flexible, concise tools for expressing musical sequences. A pattern defines a sequence but does not perform that sequence. To retrieve a pattern's output, we can use **asStream** to return a routine, which can then be evaluated with **next**. In contrast to creating such routines ourselves, patterns are simpler, pre-packaged units with known behaviors, and tend to save time.

Patterns are, in a sense, a language of their own within the SC language, and it takes time to get familiar. At first, it can be difficult to find the right pattern (or combination of patterns) to express an idea. But, when learning a foreign language, you don't need to memorize the dictionary to become fluent. You only need to learn a small handful of important words, enough to form a few coherent, useful sentences, and the rest will follow with practice and exposure. Patterns are among the most thoroughly documented classes, and there are multiple tutorials built into the help browser.[1]

5.3.1 VALUE SEQUENCES

Many patterns define sequences of values. Often, these values are numbers, but may be any type of data. Consider **Pseries**, depicted in Code Example 5.12, which represents an arithmetic sequence that begins at 50, repeatedly adds 7, and generates a total of six values. Creating this stream from scratch using a routine, shown in Code Example 5.13, requires considerably more labor.

CODE EXAMPLE 5.12: A PATTERN-GENERATED ARITHMETIC SEQUENCE.

```
(
~pat = Pseries(start: 50, step: 7, length: 6);
~seq = ~pat.asStream;
)

~seq.next; // evaluate repeatedly
```

CODE EXAMPLE 5.13: A ROUTINE-GENERATED ARITHMETIC SEQUENCE.

```
(
~pat = {
    var num = 50, inc = 7, count = 0;
    while({count < 6}, {
        num.yield;
        num = num + inc;
        count = count + 1;
    });
};

~seq = Routine(~pat);
)

~seq.next; // evaluate repeatedly
```

Patterns are described as "stateless." They represent a sequence but are distinct from and completely unaware of its actualization. To emphasize, observe the result when trying to extract values directly from a pattern:

```
~pat = Pseries(50, 7, 6);

~pat.next; // -> returns "a Pseries"
```

nextN returns an array of values from a sequence, and **all** returns an array containing all of them. To demonstrate, Code Example 5.14 also introduces **Pwhite**, which defines a sequence of random values selected from a range with a uniform distribution. Like **rrand**, **Pwhite** defines a sequence of integers if its boundaries are integers, and floats if either boundary is a float.

> **CODE EXAMPLE 5.14:** RETRIEVING AN ARRAY OF MULTIPLE VALUES FROM A SEQUENCE.
>
> ```
> (
> ~pat = Pwhite(lo: 48, hi: 72, length: 10);
> ~seq = ~pat.asStream;
> )
>
> ~seq.nextN(4); // evaluate repeatedly
>
> ~seq.reset;
>
> ~seq.all;
> ```

Infinite-length sequences are possible, shown in Code Example 5.15, created by specifying **inf** for the pattern length or number of repeats. Here, we introduce **Prand**, which randomly selects an item from an array.

> **CODE EXAMPLE 5.15:** A PATTERN-GENERATED SEQUENCE WITH AN INFINITE LENGTH.
>
> ```
> (
> ~pat = Prand(list: [4, 12, 17], repeats: inf);
> ~seq = ~pat.asStream;
> )
>
> ~seq.next; // an inexhaustible supply
> ```

> **TIP.RAND();** CALLING "ALL" ON AN INFINITE-LENGTH STREAM
>
> Like playing an infinite-length routine with no yields, calling **all** on an infinite-length stream will crash the program!

Table 5.1 provides a list of commonly encountered patterns used to generate numerical sequences. Note that some patterns, like Pseries and Pwhite, can only define sequences with numerical output, while others, like Pseq and Prand, output items from an array and can therefore define sequences that output any kind of data.

TABLE 5.1 A list of commonly encountered patterns for generating numerical sequences.

Pattern	Description
Pseq(list, repeats, offset)	Sequentially outputs values from **list** array, with an optional **offset** to a specific index.
Pwhite(lo, hi, length)	Random values between **lo** and **hi** with a uniform distribution.
Pexprand(lo, hi, length)	Random values between **lo** and **hi** with an exponential distribution.
Pbrown(lo, hi, step, length)	Random values between **lo** and **hi**, but never deviating from the previous value by more than ±**step**.
Prand(list, repeats)	Randomly outputs values from **list** array.
Pxrand(list, repeats)	Randomly outputs values from **list** array, but never selects the same item twice in a row.
Pwrand(list, weights, repeats)	Randomly outputs values from **list** array, according to a second array of **weights** that must sum to one.
Pseries(start, step, length)	Arithmetic series. Begins at **start** and incrementally adds **step**.
Pgeom(start, grow, length)	Geometric series. Begins at **start** and repeatedly multiplies by **grow**.

Mathematical operations and methods that apply to numbers can also be applied to patterns that specify numerical sequences. Imagine creating a sequence that outputs random values between ±1.0, but also wanting that sequence to alternate between positive and negative values. One solution involves multiplying one pattern by another, demonstrated in Code Example 5.16. The result is a composite pattern that defines a sequence in which corresponding pairs of output values are multiplied. Code Example 5.17 offers another solution, involving nesting patterns inside of another. When an array-based pattern (such as Pseq or Prand) encounters another pattern as part of its output, it embeds the entire output of that pattern before moving on to its next item (similar to the **embedInStream** method for routines).

CODE EXAMPLE 5.16: MULTIPLICATION OF ONE PATTERN BY ANOTHER.

```
(
~pat = Pwhite(0.0, 1.0, inf) * Pseq([-1, 1], inf);
~seq = ~pat.asStream.nextN(8);
)
```

> **CODE EXAMPLE 5.17: NESTING PATTERNS INSIDE OTHER PATTERNS.**
>
> ```
> (
> ~pat = Pseq([
>     Pwhite(-1.0, 0.0, 1),
>     Pwhite(0.0, 1.0, 1)
> ], inf);
> ~seq = ~pat.asStream.nextN(10);
> )
> ```

5.3.2 THE EVENT MODEL

Value patterns are useful for generating sequences of numbers and other data types, but more is required to generate sequences of sound. **Pbind**, introduced in the next section, is a pattern capable of defining sound sequences, which relies on the **Event** class, discussed only briefly in Chapter 4 as a storage device for buffers. As a reminder, an Event is a type of unordered collection in which each item is paired with a "key," specified as a symbol. An Event can be created with the **new** method, or with an enclosure of parentheses. The following code statements use an Event to model quantity and type of fish in an aquarium. We begin with five guppies and eight goldfish:

```
a = (guppy: 5, goldfish: 8);
```

If we acquire three fish of a new breed, we can update the Event by adding a new key-value association:

```
a[\clownfish] = 3;
```

If a sixth guppy appears, we can update the value at that key. Because each key in an Event is unique, this expression overwrites the previous key, rather than creating a second identical key:

```
a[\guppy] = 6;
```

To retrieve the number of goldfish, we access the item stored at the appropriate key:

```
a[\goldfish]; // -> 8
```

An Event is not just a storage device; it is commonly used to model an action taken in response to a **play** message, in which its key-value pairs represent parameters and values necessary to that action. Often, this action is the creation of a new Synth, but Events model other actions, like musical rests, **set** messages, or sending MIDI data. There are numerous pre-made Event types that represent useful actions, each pre-filled with sensible default values. A complete list of built-in Event types can be retrieved by evaluating:

```
Event.eventTypes.keys.postcs;\
```

> **TIP.RAND(); POST WINDOW TECHNIQUES**
>
> **postcs** (short for "post compile string") is useful for printing the entirety of a large body of text in the post window. By contrast, **postln** truncates its receiver if deemed too long. Additionally, by appending the empty symbol (a single backslash) after the semicolon, we can suppress the "double-posting" that sometimes occurs as a result of the interpreter always posting the result of the last evaluated statement. Compare the following four expressions:
>
> ```
> (0..999).postln; // truncated double-post
> (0..999).postln;\ // truncated single-post
> (0..999).postcs; // non-truncated double-post
> (0..999).postcs;\ // non-truncated single-post (ideal!)
> ```
>
> **postcs** is also useful for visualizing the internals of a function:
>
> ```
> (
> ~func = { |input|
>     input = input + 2;
> };
> )
>
> ~func.postcs;\ // print the entire function definition
>
> ~func.postln;\ // only prints "a Function"
> ```

Each Event type represents a different type of action and thus expects a unique set of keys. Most Event types are rarely used and largely irrelevant for creative applications. The most common, by far, is the **note** Event, which models the creation of a Synth. This is the default Event type if unspecified. The components and behaviors of the note Event are given default values that are so comprehensive, that even playing an empty Event generates a Synth and produces a sound, if the server is booted:

```
().play;
```

On evaluation, the post window displays the resulting Event, which looks roughly like this:

```
-> ('instrument': default, 'msgFunc': a Function,
'amp': 0.1, 'server': localhost, 'sustain': 0.8, 'isPlaying': true,
'freq': 261.6255653006, 'hasGate': true, 'id': [1000])
```

The default note Event includes a **freq** key with a value of approximately 261.6 (middle C), an **amp** key with a value of 0.1, and a few other items that are relatively unimportant at the moment. We can override these default values by providing our own. For example, we can specify a higher and slightly louder pitch:

```
(freq: 625, amp: 0.4).play;
```

Where does this sound come from? The **instrument** key specifies the SynthDef to be used, and there is a **\default** SynthDef, automatically added when the server boots. This default SynthDef is primarily used to support code examples in pattern help files, and can be found in the Event source code within the **makeDefaultSynthDef** method. When a SynthDef name is provided for an Event's **instrument** key, that SynthDef's arguments also become meaningful Event keys. Event keys that don't match SynthDef arguments and aren't part of the Event definition will have no effect. For example, the default SynthDef has a pan position argument, but no envelope parameters. Thus, in the following line, **pan** will shift the sound toward the left, but **atk** does nothing:

```
(freq: 625, amp: 0.3, pan: -0.85, atk: 0.5).play;
```

The default SynthDef is rarely used for anything beyond simple demonstrations. Code Example 5.18 uses an Event to create a Synth using a SynthDef adapted from Companion Code 3.9.

CODE EXAMPLE 5.18: USING AN EVENT TO PLAY A SOUND USING A CUSTOM SYNTHDEF. ON CREATION, KEY-VALUE PAIRS IN THE EVENT ARE SUPPLIED AS SYNTH ARGUMENTS.

```
(
SynthDef(\bpf_brown, {
    arg atk = 0.02, rel = 2, freq = 800,
    rq = 0.005, pan = 0, amp = 1, out = 0;
    var sig, env;
    env = Env([0, 1, 0], [atk, rel], [1, -2]).kr(2);
    sig = BrownNoise.ar(0.8);
    sig = BPF.ar(sig, freq, rq, 1 / rq.sqrt);
    sig = Pan2.ar(sig, pan, amp) * env;
    Out.ar(out, sig);
}).add;
)

(instrument: \bpf_brown, freq: 500, atk: 2, rel: 4, amp: 0.6).play;
```

A few additional details about internal Event mechanisms are worth discussing. Throughout earlier chapters, the argument names **freq** and **amp** were regularly used to represent the frequency and amplitude of a sound. We can technically name these parameters whatever we like, but these specific names are chosen to take advantage of a flexible system of pitch and volume specification built into the Event paradigm. In addition to specifying amplitude via **amp**, we can also specify amplitude as a value in decibels, using the **db** key:

```
(instrument: \bpf_brown, db: -3).play;

(instrument: \bpf_brown, db: -20).play;
```

How is this possible? Despite the fact that **db** is not one of our SynthDef arguments, the Event knows how to convert and apply this value correctly. We can understand this behavior more clearly by examining some internals of the Event paradigm:

```
Event.parentEvents.default[\db]; // default db value = -20.0

Event.parentEvents.default[\amp].postcs; // -> the function {~db.dbamp}
```

In the absence of user-provided values, the default **db** value of -20.0 is converted to a normalized amplitude of 0.1. If a **db** value is provided, that value is converted to an amplitude. If an **amp** value is directly provided, it "intercepts" the conversion process, temporarily overwriting the function that performs the conversion, such that the **amp** value is directly provided to the Synth. It's important to remember that this flexibility is only available if the SynthDef includes an argument named "amp" that is used in the conventional sense (as a scalar that controls output level). If, for example, our SynthDef used a variable named "vol" for amplitude control, then neither **amp** nor **db** would have any effect on the sound if provided in the Event, akin to misspelling a SynthDef argument name when creating a Synth. In this case, our only option for level control would be "vol," and we would not have access to this two-tier specification structure. To specify level as a decibel value, we would have to perform the conversion ourselves, for example:

```
(vol: -20.dbamp).play;
```

The situation with **freq** is similar, but with more options. If "freq" is declared as a SynthDef argument that controls pitch, then four layers of pitch specification become available. These four options are somewhat intertwined, but are roughly expressible as follows:

1. "degree," along with "scale" and "mtranspose," allows modal expression of pitch as a scale degree, with the possibility of modal transposition.
2. "note," along with "root," "octave," "gtranspose," "stepsPerOctave," and "octaveRatio," allows specification of pitch as a scale degree within an equal-tempered framework, with a customizable octave ratio and arbitrary number of divisions per octave.
3. "midinote," along with "ctranspose" and "harmonic," allows specification of pitch as MIDI note numbers (non-integers are allowed), with the option for chromatic transposition and specification of a harmonic partial above a fundamental.
4. "freq," along with "detune," allows specification of a frequency value measured in Hertz, with an optional offset amount added to this value.

A graphic at the bottom of the Event help file depicts this pitch hierarchy, and a slightly modified version of this graphic appears in Figure 5.1. The final internally calculated value, **detunedFreq**, is ultimately passed as the `freq` value for the created Synth. Code Example 5.19 provides examples of pitch specification using these four tiers.

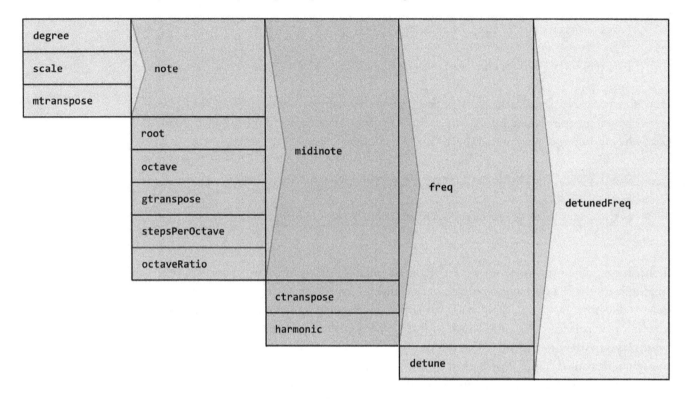

FIGURE 5.1 A visualization of the pitch specification hierarchy in the **Event** paradigm.

CODE EXAMPLE 5.19: USE OF FOUR DIFFERENT PITCH SPECIFICATIONS TO PLAY MIDDLE C, FOLLOWED BY THE D IMMEDIATELY ABOVE IT.

```
(degree: 0).play;
(degree: 1).play; // modal transposition by scale degree

(note: 0).play;
(note: 2).play; // chromatic transposition by semitones

(midinote: 60).play;
(midinote: 62).play; // MIDI note numbers

(freq: 261.626).play;
(freq: 293.665).play; // Hertz
```

> ### TIP.RAND(); FLATS AND SHARPS WITH SCALE DEGREES
>
> The **degree** key has additional flexibility for specifying pitch. Altering a degree value by ±0.1 produces a transposition by one semitone, akin to notating a sharp or flat symbol on a musical score:
>
> ```
> (degree: 0).play;
> (degree: 0.1).play; // sharp
> ```
>
> Similarly, "s" and "b" can be appended to an integer, which has the same result:
>
> ```
> (degree: 0).play;
> (degree: 0b).play; // flat
> ```

Again, these pitch options are only available if an argument named "freq" is declared in the SynthDef and used conventionally. In doing so, pitch information is specifiable at any of these four tiers, and calculations propagate through these tiers from "degree" to "detunedFreq." The functions that perform these calculations can also be examined:

```
Event.parentEvents.default[\degree]; // default = 0
Event.parentEvents.default[\note].postcs;
Event.parentEvents.default[\midinote].postcs;
Event.parentEvents.default[\freq].postcs;
Event.parentEvents.default[\detunedFreq].postcs;
```

Lastly, Code Example 5.20 demonstrates an interesting feature of Events. If a SynthDef includes a gated envelope, we must manually close the gate when creating a Synth, but the gate closes automatically when playing an Event.

CODE EXAMPLE 5.20: AUTOMATIC GATE CLOSURE WHEN USING AN EVENT TO CREATE A SYNTH WITH A GATED ENVELOPE.

```
(
SynthDef(\bpf_brown, {
    arg atk = 0.02, rel = 2, gate = 1, freq = 800,
    rq = 0.005, pan = 0, amp = 1, out = 0;
    var sig, env;
    env = Env.asr(atk, 1, rel).kr(2, gate);
    sig = BrownNoise.ar(0.8);
    sig = BPF.ar(sig, freq, rq, 1 / rq.sqrt);
    sig = Pan2.ar(sig, pan, amp) * env;
    Out.ar(out, sig);
}).add;
)
```

```
x = Synth(\bpf_brown, [freq: 500, amp: 0.2]);

x.set(\gate, 0); // manual gate closure

(instrument: \bpf_brown, freq: 500, amp: 0.2).play; // automatic
gate closure
```

The default note Event includes a **sustain** key, which represents a duration after which a (**\gate, 0**) message is automatically sent to the Synth. The sustain value is measured in beats, the duration of which is determined by the clock on which the Event is scheduled (if no clock is specified, the default TempoClock is used, which runs at 60 bpm). This mechanism assumes the SynthDef has an argument named "gate," used to release some sort of envelope with a terminating doneAction. If this argument has a different name or is used for another purpose, the Synth will become stuck in an "on" state, likely requiring [cmd]+[period]. The backend of the Event paradigm is complex, and perplexing situations (e.g., stuck notes) may arise from time to time. The Companion Code that follows the next section attempts to demystify common pitfalls. Although the Event paradigm runs deeper than discussed here, this general introduction should be enough to help you get started with Event sequencing using the primary Event pattern, **Pbind**. For readers seeking more detailed information on Event features and behaviors, the Event help file provides additional information, particularly in a section titled "Useful keys for notes." Relatedly, the code in Code Example 5.21 can be evaluated to print a list of keys that are built into the Event paradigm.

CODE EXAMPLE 5.21: CODE THAT PRINTS A COMPLETE LIST OF EVENT KEYS.

```
(
Event.partialEvents.keys.do({ |n|
    n.postln;
    Event.partialEvents[n].keys.postln;
    \.postln;
});\
)
```

5.3.3 EVENT SEQUENCES WITH PBIND

Pbind combines value patterns with Events, establishing a high-level framework for expressing musical sequences. A Pbind contains a list of pairs, each of which consists of an Event key and value pattern. When a stream is generated from a Pbind, and asked to perform its output, the result is a sequence of Events. Each Event contains keys from the Pbind, and each key is paired with the next value defined by its corresponding value pattern. This behavior of "binding" values to keys is what gives Pbind its name. Code Example 5.22 provides an example. To perform the Events, we convert the pattern to a stream, call **next** to yield an Event, and **play** it to generate a Synth. The only difference between this example and the stream examples from section 5.3.1 is that here, we must provide an empty starting Event to be populated (hence the additional set of parentheses inside of **next**).

CODE EXAMPLE 5.22: USING PBIND TO MANUALLY PLAY A SEQUENCE OF NOTE EVENTS.

```
(
p = Pbind(
    \midinote, Pseq([55, 57, 60], 2),
    \db, Pwhite(-20.0, -10.0, 6),
    \pan, Prand([-0.5, 0, 0.5], 6)
);
)

~seq = p.asStream;

~seq.next(()).play; // evaluate repeatedly, returns nil when finished

~seq.reset; // can be reset at any time
```

In Code Example 5.22, each internal value pattern specifies exactly six values, so the stream produces six Events. Because the Pbind does not specify otherwise, the created Events are note-type Events that use the default SynthDef. The "midinote" and "db" keys undergo internal calculations to yield "freq" and "amp" values, which are supplied to each Synth.

Manually extracting and playing Events one-by-one is rarely done, intended here as only an illustrative example. More commonly, we **play** a Pbind, which returns an **EventStreamPlayer**, a type of stream that performs an Event sequence. As demonstrated in Code Example 5.23, an EventStreamPlayer works by automating the Event extraction process, and scheduling the Events to be played on a clock, using the default TempoClock if unspecified, thus generating a timed musical sequence.

CODE EXAMPLE 5.23: USING PBIND TO GENERATE AN EVENTSTREAMPLAYER THAT PERFORMS A SEQUENCE OF NOTE EVENTS.

```
(
p = Pbind(
    \midinote, Pseq([55, 57, 60], 2),
    \db, Pwhite(-20.0, -10.0, 6),
    \pan, Prand([-0.5, 0, 0.5], 6)
);

~seq = p.play;
)
```

> **TIP.RAND(); DEBUGGING PATTERN VALUES**
>
> Visualizing a Pbind's output can be helpful for debugging code that doesn't work properly, and also for understanding pattern behavior in general. **postln** does not work in this context. Instead, **trace** can be applied to any pattern, which prints its output to the post window as a stream performs it:
>
> ```
> (
> p = Pbind(
>     \midinote, Pseq([55, 57, 60], 2).trace,
> );
>
> ~seq = p.play;
> )
> ```

The onset of each Synth occurs one second after the preceding onset. But where does this timing information originate? Timing information is typically provided using the **dur** key, which specifies a duration in beats and has a default value of one:

```
Event.partialEvents.durEvent[\dur]; // -> 1.0
```

We can provide our own timing information, which may be a value pattern, as shown in Code Example 5.24.

CODE EXAMPLE 5.24: USING THE dur KEY TO SPECIFY TIMING INFORMATION FOR AN EventStreamPlayer.

```
(
p = Pbind(
    \dur, Pseq([0.75, 0.25, 0.75, 0.25, 0.5, 0.5], 1),
    \midinote, Pseq([55, 57, 60], 2),
    \db, Pwhite(-20.0, -10.0, 6),
    \pan, Prand([-0.5, 0, 0.5], 6)
);

~seq = p.play;
)
```

Pbind can specify an infinite-length Event stream. If each internal value pattern is infinite, the Event stream will also be infinite. If at least one internal value pattern is finite, the length of the Event stream will be equal to the length of the shortest value pattern. If an ordinary number is provided for one of Pbind's keys, it will be interpreted as an infinite-length value stream that repeatedly outputs that number. An EventStreamPlayer can be stopped at any time with **stop**. Unlike routines, a stopped EventStreamPlayer can be resumed with

resume, causing it to continue from where it left off. Code Example 5.25 demonstrates these concepts: the **midinote** pattern is the only finite value pattern, which produces 24 values and thus determines the length of the Event stream. The **db** value –15 is interpreted as an infinite stream that repeatedly yields –15.

CODE EXAMPLE 5.25: STOPPING AND RESUMING AN EVENTSTREAMPLAYER WHOSE LENGTH IS MADE FINITE BY A FINITE-LENGTH INTERNAL VALUE PATTERN.

```
(
p = Pbind(
    \dur, Pseq([0.75, 0.25, 0.75, 0.25, 0.5, 0.5], inf),
    \midinote, Pseq([55, 57, 60], 8),
    \db, -15
);

~seq = p.play;
)

~seq.stop;

~seq.resume;
```

In a Pbind, only values or value patterns should be paired with Event keys. It may be tempting to use a method like **rrand** to generate random values for a key. However, this will result in a random value being generated once when the Pbind is created and used for every Event in the output stream, demonstrated in Code Example 5.26. Instead, the correct approach is to use the pattern or pattern combination that represents the desired behavior (in this case, Pwhite).

CODE EXAMPLE 5.26: AN INCORRECT APPROACH FOR CREATING RANDOMNESS IN AN EVENT STREAM.

```
(
p = Pbind(
    \dur, 0.2,
    \midinote, rrand(50, 90), // <- should use Pwhite(50, 90) instead
);

~seq = p.play;
)
```

Recalling techniques introduced in Section 5.2, an EventStreamPlayer can be scheduled on a specific TempoClock and quantized to a particular beat, demonstrated in Code Example 5.27.

CODE EXAMPLE 5.27: RHYTHMICALLY QUANTIZING TWO EVENTSTREAMPLAYERS ON A CUSTOM TEMPOCLOCK.

```
(
t = TempoClock(90/60);

p = Pbind(
    \dur, 0.25,
    \midinote, Pwhite(48, 60, inf),
);

q = Pbind(
    \dur, 0.25,
    \midinote, Pwhite(72, 84, inf),
);
)

~seq_p = p.play(t, quant:4); // scheduled on next beat multiple of 4

~seq_q = q.play(t, quant:4); // synchronizes with ~seq_p
```

Combined with a general understanding of Events, patterns, and streams, Pbind unlocks an endless supply of ideas for musical sequences. Companion Code 5.2 discusses additional details and includes a collection of more elaborate demonstrations.

5.4 Additional Techniques for Pattern Composition

As you explore musical sequences, you'll inevitably find yourself wanting to build larger ideas from smaller, individual patterns. This section covers a few relevant features of patterns, aiming to facilitate expression of more complex sequences.

5.4.1 THE REST EVENT

There are many types of pre-made Events, but so far, we've only been using note Events. In some cases, the note Event by itself is insufficient and awkward. Consider, for example, the musical phrase in Figure 5.2, which begins with a rest. How should we represent this phrase with patterns? The code in Code Example 5.28 is a poor choice, because it treats the phrase as if it begins on its first eighth note. Rhythmic misalignment would likely occur if we tried to quantize this pattern. A better approach involves using **rest** Events. A rest Event does exactly what its name suggests: when played, it does nothing for a specific number of beats. Event types are specified using the **type** key, and providing the type name as a symbol. A two-beat rest Event, for example, looks like this:

```
(type: \rest, dur: 2).play;
```

To employ rests in an Event sequence, we can embed instances of the **Rest** class in a Pbind's **dur** pattern. Each rest is given a duration, measured in beats, pictured in Code Example 5.29.

FIGURE 5.2 A notated musical phrase that begins with a rest.

CODE EXAMPLE 5.28: A RHYTHMICALLY PROBLEMATIC APPROACH FOR EXPRESSING THE MUSICAL PHRASE PICTURED IN FIGURE 5.2.

```
t = TempoClock.new(112/60);

(
Pbind(
    \dur, Pseq([1/2, 1/2, 1/2, 1/4, 1/2, 1/2, 1/2], 1),
    \sustain, 0.1,
    \degree, Pseq([4, 5, 7, 4, 5, 7, 8], 1),
).play(t);
)
```

CODE EXAMPLE 5.29: USE OF REST EVENTS IN A DURATION PATTERN TO EXPRESS THE MUSICAL PHRASE PICTURED IN FIGURE 5.2.

```
t = TempoClock.new(112/60);

(
Pbind(
    \dur, Pseq([
        Pseq([Rest(1/4), 1/4], 4), // bar 1
        Pseq([1/4, Rest(1/4), 1/4, Rest(1/4), 1/4, Rest(3/4)]) // bar 2
    ], 1),
    \sustain, 0.1,
    \degree, Pseq([
        0, 4, 0, 5, 0, 7, 0, 4, // bar 1
        5, 0, 7, 0, 8, 0, 0, 0 // bar 2
    ], 1),
).play(t);
)
```

When the code in Code Example 5.29 is quantized, the true downbeat of the phrase occurs on the target beat. Note that the pitch values nicely resemble the metric layout of the notated pitches. The pitch values that align with rest Events are ultimately meaningless since they do not sound. Zeroes are used for visual clarity, but any value is fine.

Other options exist for expressing a sequential mix of notes and rests. Rest Events can be generated by using a pattern to determine **type** values. This approach lets us use a constant **dur** value equal to the smallest beat subdivision necessary to express the rhythm, and the **type** pattern handles the determination of Event type (see Code Example 5.30). Another option involves supplying symbols for a pitch-related pattern (such as **degree**, **note**, **midinote**, or **freq**). If the pitch value of a note Event is a symbol, the Event becomes a rest Event. The simplest option is to use the empty symbol, expressed as a single backslash (see Code Example 5.31).

CODE EXAMPLE 5.30: PATTERN MANIPULATION OF THE type KEY TO EXPRESS THE MUSICAL PHRASE PICTURED IN FIGURE 5.2.

```
t = TempoClock.new(112/60);

(
Pbind(
    \type, Pseq([
        Pseq([\rest, \note], 4), // bar 1
        Pseq([\note, \rest], 2), \note, Pseq([\rest], 3) // bar 2
    ], 1),
    \dur, 1/4,
    \sustain, 0.1,
    \degree, Pseq([
        0, 4, 0, 5, 0, 7, 0, 4, // bar 1
        5, 0, 7, 0, 8, 0, 0, 0 // bar 2
    ], 1),
).play(t);
)
```

CODE EXAMPLE 5.31: USING SYMBOLS IN A PITCH PATTERN TO EXPRESS THE MUSICAL PHRASE PICTURED IN FIGURE 5.2.

```
t = TempoClock.new(112/60);

(
Pbind(
    \dur, 1/4,
```

```
    \sustain, 0.1,
    \degree, Pseq([
        \, 4, \, 5, \, 7, \, 4, // bar 1
        5, \, 7, \, 8, \, \, \  // bar 2
    ], 1),
).play(t);
)
```

Though it's possible to achieve a similar result by strategically providing zeroes in an amplitude pattern, this is less efficient. In this case, every Event will produce a Synth, and every Synth consumes some processing power, regardless of its amplitude.

5.4.2 LIMITING PATTERN OUTPUT WITH PFIN/PFINDUR

It's sometimes convenient to define an infinite length pattern but specify a finite output at performance time, therefore avoiding the need to manually stop the stream. Code Example 5.32 shows the use of **Pfin** to limit the number of values a pattern will output. **Pfindur** is similar, but instead of constraining based on Event quantity, Pfindur limits a stream based on the number of beats that have elapsed, shown in Code Example 5.33. The duration of one beat is, as usual, governed by the clock on which the stream plays.

CODE EXAMPLE 5.32: USING `Pfin` TO LIMIT THE OUTPUT OF AN EVENT STREAM TO 16 EVENTS.

```
(
p = Pbind(
    \dur, 1/8,
    \sustain, 0.02,
    \freq, Pexprand(200, 4000, inf),
);

q = Pfin(16, p);

~seq = q.play; // stops after 16 events
)
```

CODE EXAMPLE 5.33: USING `Pfindur` TO LIMIT THE OUTPUT OF AN EVENT STREAM TO THREE BEATS.

```
(
p = Pbind(
```

```
        \dur, 1/8,
        \sustain, 0.02,
        \freq, Pexprand(200, 4000, inf),
    );

    q = Pfindur(3, p);

    ~seq = q.play; // stops after 3 beats
)
```

Pfin and Pfindur are helpful in allowing us to focus on the finer musical details of a pattern during the compositional process, working in an infinite mindset and not concerning ourselves with total duration. When the sound is just right, we can simply wrap the pattern in one of these limiters to constrain its lifespan as needed.

5.4.3 COMPOSITE PATTERNS WITH PSEQ/PPAR/PTPAR

Once you have several Pbinds that represent musical phrases, a logical next step involves combining them into composite structures that represent longer musical phrases, large-scale sections, and perhaps eventually, an entire musical composition. Consider the code in Code Example 5.34, which represents a four-note sequence, and this same sequence shifted up by two scale degrees:

CODE EXAMPLE 5.34: TWO EVENT PATTERNS THAT REPRESENT SIMPLE MUSICAL PHRASES.

```
(
~p0 = Pbind(
    \dur, 1/6,
    \degree, Pseq([0, 2, 3, 5], 1),
    \sustain, 0.02,
);

~p1 = Pbind(
    \dur, 1/6,
    \degree, Pseq([2, 4, 5, 7], 1),
    \sustain, 0.02,
);
)
```

Suppose we wanted to play these phrases twice in sequence, for a total of four phrases. Pseq provides an elegant solution, pictured in Code Example 5.35, which demonstrates its ability to sequence Events, and not just numerical values. A composite pattern need not be deterministic; any value pattern that retrieves items from an array can be used for this purpose. If **Prand([~p0, ~p1], 4)** is substituted for Pseq, for example, the Event stream will play four phrases, randomly chosen from these two.

CODE EXAMPLE 5.35: USE OF `Pseq` TO PLAY EVENT PATTERNS IN SEQUENCE. THIS EXAMPLE RELIES ON THE TWO PATTERNS CREATED IN CODE EXAMPLE 5.34.

```
(
~p_seq = Pseq([~p0, ~p1], 2);
~player = ~p_seq.play;
)
```

To play these two phrases, we could simply enclose **~p0.play** and **~p1.play** in the same block and evaluate them with one keystroke, but this approach only sounds the patterns together—it does not express these two patterns as a singular unit. **Ppar** (see Code Example 5.36) is a better option, which takes an array of several Event patterns, and returns one Event pattern in which the individual patterns are essentially superimposed into a single sequence. Like Pseq, Ppar also accepts a **repeats** value. **Ptpar** is similar (see Code Example 5.37) but allows us to specify a timing offset for each individual pattern used to compose the parallel composite pattern.

CODE EXAMPLE 5.36: USE OF `Ppar` TO PLAY EVENT PATTERNS IN PARALLEL. THIS EXAMPLE RELIES ON THE TWO PATTERNS CREATED IN CODE EXAMPLE 5.34.

```
(
~p_par = Ppar([~p0, ~p1], 3);
~seq = ~p_par.play;
)
```

CODE EXAMPLE 5.37: USE OF `Ptpar` TO PLAY EVENT PATTERNS IN PARALLEL WITH INDIVIDUAL TIMING OFFSETS. THE SECOND PATTERN BEGINS ONE-TWELFTH OF A BEAT AFTER THE FIRST. THIS EXAMPLE RELIES ON THE TWO PATTERNS CREATED IN CODE EXAMPLE 5.34.

```
(
p = Ptpar([
    0, Pseq([~p1], 3),
    1/12, Pseq([~p0], 3)
```

```
    ], 1);

    ~seq = p.play;
)
```

As you may be able to guess from the previous examples, the composite patterns returned by Pseq, Ppar, and Ptpar retain the ability to be further sequenced into even larger composite patterns. In some cases, the final performance structure of a composition involves a parent Pseq, which contains Pseq/Ppar patterns that represent large-scale sections, which contain Pseq/Ppar patterns that represent sub-sections, and so forth, all the way down to note-level details. Companion Code 5.3 focuses on an example of how such a project might take shape. The central idea is that patterns should be treated as modular building blocks, which can be freely combined and may represent all sequential aspects of a composition. Conceptualizing time-based structures within the pattern framework provides great flexibility, allowing complex sequential ideas to be expressed and performed relatively easily.

5.5 Real-Time Pattern Control

Real-time control is an essential feature for performing electronic music. We've seen a simple example in previous chapters: a Synth argument can be "set" while it is running, which can influence its sound and behavior. It's also possible to manipulate characteristics of an EventStreamPlayer while it's playing, by swapping out one value pattern for another. This ability mostly relies on a handful of pattern objects that revolve around the concept of *proxies*. In SC, a proxy is a placeholder that references a piece of data we want to be able to change dynamically. Proxies enable fluid musical transitions and allow us to make spontaneous decisions on-the-fly, helping us avoid the need to prepare extensive sequential structures in advance.

The **PatternProxy** class provides core functionality for real-time pattern control, but in practice, we typically use one of its subclasses, such as **Pdefn**, **Pdef**, or **Pbindef**. These classes are part of a larger "def-type" family that includes **Ndef**, **Tdef**, **MIDIdef**, **OSCdef**, and others. These proxies share a common syntax by which they are created and referenced. On creation, a def-type object includes a name (provided as a symbol), followed by its data. The data can be dynamically overwritten and can be referenced by name. Code Example 5.38 provides a pseudo-code example. Proxies are the core element of live coding in SC, more fully explored in Chapter 12.

CODE EXAMPLE 5.38: A PSEUDO-CODE EXAMPLE OF CREATING, MANIPULATING, AND REFERENCING A PROXY OBJECT.

```
ThingDef(\name, data); // create proxy and provide initial data
ThingDef(\name, newData); // overwrite proxy with new data
ThingDef(\name); // reference current proxy data
```

5.5.1 PDEFN

Pdefn serves as a proxy for a single value pattern, deployed by wrapping it around the desired pattern. In Code Example 5.39, it serves as a placeholder for the **degree** pattern. While the EventStreamPlayer **~seq** is playing, the pitch information can be dynamically changed by overwriting the proxy data with a new value pattern.

CODE EXAMPLE 5.39: USING Pdefn TO CHANGE A VALUE PATTERN IN REAL-TIME.

```
(
p = Pbind(
    \dur, 0.2,
    \sustain, 0.02,
    \degree, Pdefn(\deg0, Pwhite(-4, 8, inf)),
);

~seq = p.play;
)

Pdefn(\deg0, Pseq([0, 2, 3], inf));
```

Note that if an infinite value pattern is replaced with a finite one, the EventStreamPlayer to which that pattern belongs also becomes finite. One practical application of this feature, pictured in Code Example 5.40, is to fade out an EventStreamPlayer by replacing its amplitude pattern with one that gradually decreases to silence or near-silence over a finite period of time.

CODE EXAMPLE 5.40: USING PDEFN TO FADE OUT AN EVENTSTREAMPLAYER.

```
(
p = Pbind(
    \dur, 0.2,
    \sustain, 0.02,
    \degree, Pwhite(-4, 8, inf),
    \db, Pdefn(\db0, -20),
);

~seq = p.play;
)

Pdefn(\db0, Pseries(-20, -1, 40));
```

Multiple Pdefn objects can be independently used and manipulated in the context of one Pbind. In this case, care should be taken to ensure that no two Pdefns share the same name. If they do, one will overwrite the other, much in the same way that an Event cannot contain two different pieces of data at the same key. It's also possible to deploy one Pdefn in several different places. A change to a Pdefn propagates through all its implementations, demonstrated in Code Example 5.41.

CODE EXAMPLE 5.41: USE OF MULTIPLE INSTANCES OF ONE PDEFN IN A MORE COMPLEX PATTERN STRUCTURE.

```
(
Pdefn(\deg0, Pseq([0, 4, 1, 5], inf));

p = Pbind(
    \dur, 0.2,
    \sustain, 0.02,
    \degree, Pdefn(\deg0),
);

q = Pbind(
    \dur, 0.2,
    \sustain, 0.02,
    \degree, Pdefn(\deg0) + 2,
);

~seq = Ppar([p, q]).play;
)

Pdefn(\deg0, Pseq([-3, -2, 0],inf));
```

Pdefn can be quantized using techniques similar to those previously discussed, but the syntax is slightly different, demonstrated in Code Example 5.42. Instead of specifying **quant** as an argument, each Pdefn has its own "quant" attribute, accessible by applying the **quant** method to the Pdefn and setting a desired value.

CODE EXAMPLE 5.42: QUANTIZING A PDEFN.

```
(
t = TempoClock(128/60);

p = Pbind(
    \dur, 1/4,
    \sustain, 0.02,
    \note, Pdefn(\note0, Pseq([0, \, \, \, 1, 2, 3, 4], inf)),
);
```

```
    ~seq = p.play(t, quant: 4);
)

(
Pdefn(\note0,
    Pseq([7, \, 4, \, 1, \, \, \], inf)
).quant_(4);
)
```

Pdefn "remembers" its quantization value, so it's unnecessary (but harmless) to re-specify this information for subsequent Pdefn changes meant to adhere to the same value. We can nullify a **quant** value by setting it to **nil**.

Code Example 5.43 shows a few additional techniques. Pdefn's data can be queried with **source** (optionally appending **postcs** for verbosity), and a Pdefn's data can be erased with **clear**. We can also iterate over all Pdefn objects to erase each one.

CODE EXAMPLE 5.43: RETRIEVING AND CLEARING A PDEFN'S DATA. THIS EXAMPLE RELIES ON CODE FROM THE PREVIOUS CODE EXAMPLE.

```
Pdefn(\note0).source; // -> a Pseq
Pdefn(\note0).source.postcs; // -> full Pseq code
Pdefn(\note0).clear; // erase Pdefn data
Pdefn(\note0).source; // -> nil
Pdefn.all.do({ |n| n.clear });
```

5.5.2 PDEF

Pdef, demonstrated in Code Example 5.44, is similar to Pdefn, and features many of the same techniques. The primary difference is that Pdef is a proxy for an Event pattern, rather than a value pattern. Typically, the data of a Pdef is a Pbind, but may also be a Pseq or Ppar that represents a composite of several Pbinds. When an Event pattern is encapsulated within a Pdef, any part of it can be changed while the Pdef is playing, without interruption of the Event stream. Pdef is generally useful in that it avoids the need to create multiple, independent Pdefns within a Pbind.

CODE EXAMPLE 5.44: USING **Pdef** TO CHANGE AN EVENT PATTERN IN REAL-TIME.

```
(
t = TempoClock(128/60);

Pdef(\seq,
    Pbind(
        \dur, 0.25,
        \sustain, 0.02,
        \degree, Pseq([0, 2, 4, 5], inf),
    )
).clock_(t).quant_(4);

Pdef(\seq).play;
)

(
Pdef(\seq, // swap the old Pbind for a new one
    Pbind(
        \dur, Pseq([0.5, 0.25, 0.25, 0.5, 0.5], inf),
        \sustain, 0.5,
        \degree, Pxrand([-4, -2, 0, 2, 3], inf),
    )
);
)
```

In Code Example 5.44, note that we set **clock** and **quant** attributes for the Pdef before playing it, which are retained and remembered whenever the Pdef's source changes. All the Pdefn methods shown in Code Example 5.43 are valid for Pdef as well.

5.5.3 PBINDEF

Pbindef is nearly the same as Pdef; it's a proxy for Event patterns, and it retains all the same methods and attributes of Pdef (in fact, Pbindef is a subclass of Pdef). These two classes even share the same namespace in which their data is stored, in other words, **Pdef(\x)** and **Pbindef(\x)** refer to the same object. The difference between these two classes is that Pbindef allows key-value pairs in its Event pattern to be modified on an individual basis, instead of requiring the entire Pbind source code to be present when a change is applied. Instead of placing a Pbind inside a proxy pattern, the syntax of a Pbindef involves "merging" Pdef and Pbind into a single entity, much in the same way that their names form a portmanteau.

Code Example 5.45 demonstrates various features of Pbindef, including changing one or more value-patterns in real-time, adding new value patterns, and substituting a finite value pattern to create a fade-out. Although this example does not use the **quant** and **clock** attributes, they can be applied to Pbindef using the same techniques that appear in Code Example 5.44.

CODE EXAMPLE 5.45: USING **Pbindef** TO CHANGE INDIVIDUAL PARTS OF AN EVENT PATTERN IN REAL-TIME.

```
(
Pbindef(\seqA,
    \dur, Pexprand(0.05, 2, inf),
    \degree, Prand([0, 1, 2, 4, 5], inf),
    \mtranspose, Prand([-7, 0, 7], inf),
    \sustain, 4,
    \amp, Pexprand(0.02, 0.1, inf),
).play;
)

// change degree pattern:
Pbindef(\seqA, \degree, Prand([0, 1, 3.1, 4.1, 5], inf));

// change dur and sustain pattern in one expression:
Pbindef(\seqA, \dur, 0.3, \sustain, Pseq([2, 0.02], inf));

// add a new value pattern:
Pbindef(\seqA, \pan, Pwhite(-0.8, 0.8, inf));

// fade out with finite amp pattern:
Pbindef(\seqA, \amp, Pgeom(0.05, 0.85, 30));
```

In Code Example 5.45, a finite Pgeom modifies the Event stream so that it ends after 30 Events. However, it's possible to restart the stream by playing the Pbindef again. In this case, it remembers its key-value pairs, and will generate another thirty Events with the same decreasing **amp** pattern. Of course, we can replace the amplitude pattern with an infinite value pattern before restarting playback, and the Event stream will continue indefinitely once more. The semi-permanence of Pbindef's key-value pairs can be a source of confusion, particularly if switching between different pitch or amplitude tiers. Consider the Pbindef in Code Example 5.46. It begins with explicit **freq** values, which override internal calculations that propagate upward from **degree** values. As a result, if we try to dynamically switch from frequency to degrees, the degree values will have no effect, because the Pbindef "remembers" the original frequency values. Thus, if we want to switch to specifying pitch in degrees, we also need to set the old frequency pattern to nil.

> **CODE EXAMPLE 5.46: A PITFALL RELATED TO THE SEMI-PERMANENCE OF PBINDEF'S KEY-VALUE PAIRS.**
>
> ```
> (
> Pbindef(\seqB,
>     \dur, 0.2,
>     \sustain, 0.02,
>     \freq, Pexprand(500, 1200, inf)
> ).play;
> )
>
> // degree values are ignored:
> Pbindef(\seqB, \degree, Pwhite(0, 7, inf));
>
> // degree values take effect
> Pbindef(\seqB, \freq, nil, \degree, Pwhite(0, 7, inf));
> ```

▶ Companion Code 5.4 explores additional creative ideas involving Pbindef.

Note

1 Two pattern-related tutorials are recommended as supplementary reading: (1) Understanding Streams, Patterns and Events, parts 1–7 (https://doc.sccode.org/Tutorials/Streams-Patterns-Events1.html) and (2) Patterns: A Practical Guide (https://doc.sccode.org/Tutorials/A-Practical-Guide/PG_01_Introduction.html).

CHAPTER 6

SIGNAL PROCESSING

6.1 Overview

Signal processing effects can add richness, depth, and cohesion to synthesis- and sampling-based sounds. In previous chapters, we've already seen simple examples of signal processing, for example, using an oscillator to modulate the frequency of another oscillator, applying a filter to alter a sound's spectrum, or using a value-constraining operation to bend and distort a waveform. However, these types of processing techniques are so closely tied to the signals on which they operate that we usually consider them an inseparable part of the signal-generating process. In this chapter, we will instead focus on signal processing techniques commonly applied to a large mix of several signals, such as delays and reverberation.

The concept of inserts versus auxiliary sends in DAW software is an apt analogy for this distinction. When a unique effect is needed for a specific audio track, such as an equalizer plug-in for correcting a spectral imbalance, it's easiest to insert the effect directly onto that track. However, when applying one effect to multiple tracks, it's tedious, inefficient, and redundant to insert identical copies of the effect on each source. At worst, these redundant effects can overwhelm your CPU. Additionally, when using a time-extending effect (such as echo or reverb) as an insert, it becomes slightly more difficult to adjust the level of the source signal without also affecting the level of the processing effect. The general solution to these problems is to establish an auxiliary send from one or more tracks and receive the signal mix on a separate auxiliary track, where the desired effect is applied as an insert.

In SC, the equivalent of an insert effect is to bundle signal-processing UGens into an existing SynthDef, such that the generative UGens and processing UGens are permanently intertwined as a single algorithm. The equivalent of an auxiliary send is to construct multiple SynthDefs in which the signal-generating and signal-processing code are fully separated. In this case, establishing the desired signal path involves placing multiple Synths on the server and ensuring that signal flows from one to the next.

6.2 Signal Flow Concepts on the Audio Server

To create custom signal paths and effect chains in SC, we first need to introduce some new classes, and discuss some details regarding how the audio server handles signal flow and sample processing.

6.2.1 BUSSES

In digital audio, a bus is a location where samples can be written and/or read, allowing signals to be mixed and shared between separate processes. Busses are not unique to SC—they are a staple of DAWs and also appear in other digital audio platforms. Busses also exist in analog contexts, such as analog mixers, where they serve the same general purpose.

We have already dealt with busses in a limited capacity. Each generative SynthDef we've created includes an output UGen, which specifies a bus destination, and the signal to be sent to that bus. In the usual case of stereo audio, output busses with indices 0 and 1 correspond to the main left/right outputs of your sound card or audio interface. This knowledge is sufficient for simple sounds but is only part of the bigger picture.

When the audio server boots, audio busses and control busses automatically become available for general signal routing needs, such as passing a source signal to an effect. Control signals can only be written to control busses. Audio signals can be written to either type of bus, but they will be downsampled to the control rate if necessary. Audio and control busses are stored in two separate global arrays and are addressable by numerical index. The default number of available busses can be accessed using the following code:

```
s.boot;

s.options.numAudioBusChannels; // returns # of audio busses

s.options.numControlBusChannels; // returns # of control busses
```

A contiguous block of audio busses, starting at index zero, are reserved and designated as "hardware" output busses, and are associated with output channels on your computer's sound card or external audio interface. A second, adjacent block of contiguous audio busses are reserved and designated as hardware input busses, associated with input channels on your sound card/audio interface. At the time of writing this book, the default is two hardware outputs and two hardware inputs. Thus, audio busses 0 and 1 represent output channels to speakers, and audio busses 2 and 3 represent hardware inputs, such as microphone connections. The remaining audio busses are deemed "private" audio busses, unassociated with physical audio hardware and freely available to the user for internal signal routing. These default values can also be retrieved:

```
s.options.numOutputBusChannels; // default = 2

s.options.numInputBusChannels; // default = 2

s.options.numPrivateAudioBusChannels; // default = 1020
```

This configuration determines the number of I/O level indicators on the server meter display, pictured in Figure 6.1. Under default conditions, although the window displays the input channels as having indices 0 and 1, the server internally views these channels as audio busses whose indices are immediately above the output bus indices.

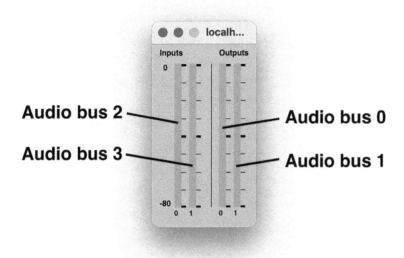

FIGURE 6.1 The server meter display of hardware input/output channels, and the internal audio busses they represent.

It's always a good idea to configure the server's hardware busses to mirror the input/output setup of your sound card/audio interface. For example, if you're using a multichannel interface, connected to four microphones and eight speakers, you should configure the server using the code in Code Example 6.1. These changes, like all server options, require a reboot to take effect. Once rebooted, the meter window will automatically reflect this change when closed and reopened.

CODE EXAMPLE 6.1: APPROPRIATE SERVER CONFIGURATION CODE IF YOUR AUDIO INTERFACE IS CONNECTED TO FOUR MICROPHONES AND EIGHT LOUDSPEAKERS.

```
(
s.options.numOutputBusChannels_(8);
s.options.numInputBusChannels_(4);
s.reboot;
)
```

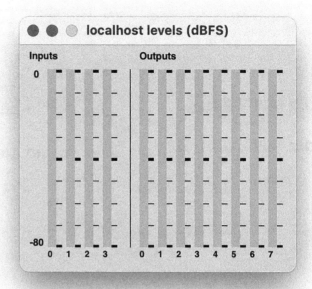

FIGURE 6.2 The appearance of the server meters after evaluating the code in Code Example 6.1 and re-opening the meter window.

After evaluating the code in Code Example 6.1, audio busses 0 through 7 will correspond to your eight loudspeakers, busses 8 through 11 correspond to your incoming microphone signals, and busses 12 through 1023 remain available as private busses for internal signal routing. Control busses, by contrast, are never associated with your computer's sound card. They are all considered "private" busses meant for internal routing of control signals, and there are no contiguous blocks reserved for special purposes. The remaining code in this chapter section assumes the server input/output configuration is in its default state, which can be done using the code in Code Example 6.2.

CODE EXAMPLE 6.2: CODE THAT RESETS THE SERVER'S HARDWARE I/O CONFIGURATION TO ITS DEFAULT STATE.

```
(
s.options.numOutputBusChannels_(2);
s.options.numInputBusChannels_(2);
s.reboot;
)
```

6.2.2 THE BUS CLASS

Referring to busses by numerical index is usually not preferable. If we build a complex network of signal paths and effects, we'll likely be dealing with multiple private busses that serve different purposes, such as a reverb bus, a delay bus, and others. It's more practical to refer to busses using meaningful names. A numerical approach can also be problematic when moving a project from one computer to another, because the configuration of output, input, and private busses may differ. This discrepancy could produce unexpected outcomes, like hearing a private audio channel in a loudspeaker.

The **Bus** class provides a simple, intuitive interface for reserving and naming busses. This class does not technically create or allocate busses on the server (which already exist when the server boots). Instead, the Bus class creates instances of language-side objects that reference specific server-side busses. The Bus class has a pair of internal counters that keep track of the lowest available private audio/control bus, starting at zero for control busses and the lowest-numbered private index for audio busses. These counters automatically increment as the user creates language-side bus references. In Code Example 6.3, the first eight private audio busses are referenced by **~mixerBus**, **~delayBus** references the next two, and **~reverbBus** references the next two. Under default conditions, these Bus objects address busses 4–11, 12–13, and 14–15. Code Example 6.3 also shows the use of **index** to get the lowest bus index from a Bus object.

CODE EXAMPLE 6.3: CREATION OF LANGUAGE-SIDE BUS OBJECTS THAT REFERENCE PRIVATE AUDIO BUSSES, AND THE USE OF index TO RETRIEVE THE LOWEST INDEX OF A BUS.

```
(
~mixerBus = Bus.audio(s, 8);
~delayBus = Bus.audio(s, 2);
~reverbBus = Bus.audio(s, 2);
)

~delayBus.index; // -> 12
```

Control busses behave similarly, as shown in Code Example 6.4. The internal bus counter begins at zero, thus the Bus objects in this example are associated with control busses 0–3, 4–5, and 6.

> **CODE EXAMPLE 6.4: CREATION OF LANGUAGE-SIDE BUS OBJECTS THAT REFERENCE CONTROL BUSSES, AND THE USE OF `index` TO RETRIEVE THE LOWEST INDEX OF A BUS.**
>
> ```
> (
> ~quadCtlBus = Bus.control(s, 4);
> ~stereoCtlBus = Bus.control(s, 2);
> ~monoCtlBus = Bus.control(s, 1);
> )
>
> ~monoCtlBus.index; // -> 6
> ```

As long as the server remains booted, busses only need to be reserved once. The availability of busses is not influenced by [cmd]+[period], freeing Synths, and so on. If any of the bus creation expressions in Code Examples 6.3 or 6.4 are evaluated a second time, the Bus class will reserve the next available bus or block of busses. If a global variable name is reused, the new reservation will overwrite the previous reference. The old block will still be considered "in use" by the bus allocator, but it will no longer be addressable by a variable name. So, if enough "accidental" re-evaluations occur, the bus allocator will exhaust its supply and post an error message. We can forcibly trigger this error using iteration:

```
1000.do({Bus.audio(s, 2)}); // -> "ERROR: failed to get an audio bus allocated."
```

The internal allocation counters of the Bus class can be reset by evaluating **s.newBusAllocators**. Therefore, it's usually a good idea to precede a chunk of bus-allocating code with this expression. As an example, no matter how many times the code in Code Example 6.5 is re-evaluated, the variables will always reference the same busses, and the allocator will never exhaust its bus supply.

> **CODE EXAMPLE 6.5: USE OF THE `newBusAllocators` METHOD TO RESET BUS ALLOCATION COUNTERS BEFORE RESERVING BUSSES.**
>
> ```
> (
> s.newBusAllocators; // reset bus counters
> ~mixerBus = Bus.audio(s, 8); // -> busses 4-11
> ~delayBus = Bus.audio(s, 2); // -> busses 12-13
> ~reverbBus = Bus.audio(s, 2); // -> busses 14-15
> )
> ```

6.2.3 INPUT/OUTPUT UGENS

In and **Out** are primary UGen choices for reading/writing signals to and from busses. **Out** writes an *n*-channel signal to a block of *n* busses. Code Example 6.6 writes a four-channel control-rate pink noise signal to busses 33 through 36, and our built-in oscilloscope provides a real-time display. Note that the controls at the top of the oscilloscope window can be manually adjusted to view any range of audio or control busses, as an alternative to expressing these adjustments through code.

CODE EXAMPLE 6.6: WRITING A MULTICHANNEL CONTROL SIGNAL TO FOUR CONTROL BUSSES AND VISUALIZING THE RESULT WITH THE OSCILLOSCOPE.

```
(
x = {Out.kr(33, PinkNoise.kr(1 ! 4))}.play;
s.scope(rate: \control, numChannels: 4, index: 33);
)

x.free;
```

Similarly, Code Example 6.7 writes a two-channel audio-rate sine wave to audio busses 14–15, also viewable using the oscilloscope. Under default conditions, we can see the signal on the scope, but we don't hear it nor see it on the meters because busses 14–15 are not associated with hardware channels.

CODE EXAMPLE 6.7: WRITING A MULTICHANNEL AUDIO SIGNAL TO TWO AUDIO BUSSES AND VISUALIZING THE RESULT WITH THE OSCILLOSCOPE.

```
(
x = {Out.ar(14, SinOsc.ar([150, 151], mul: 0.2))}.play;
s.scope(rate: \audio, numChannels: 2, index: 14);
)

x.free;
```

Technically, there is no such thing as a multichannel bus in SC. All busses have a channel size of one. When the allocator reserves an n-channel bus, it sets aside n monophonic busses. When using **Out** to write a multichannel signal to bus n, the first channel of the signal is written to bus n, the next channel is written to bus $n + 1$, and so on. There is nothing to prevent the user from accidentally writing to or reading from a bus that is already "in use." Proper use of the Bus class helps avoid these conflicts, but it's also the user's responsibility to make sure signal channel sizes and bus allocation sizes are consistent with each other. If you allocate a single bus, but write a stereo signal to it, the second channel of that signal will be written to the next-highest bus, which may produce unexpected results.

The **In** UGen accepts a bus index and a number of channels. Within a UGen function, **In** taps into one or more busses and becomes a source of the signal present on those busses. Code Example 6.8 creates two Synths: **~fader** reads an audio signal from **~bus**, attenuates the amplitude of that signal, and writes the modified signal to audio busses 0 and 1. **~src** generates a two-channel sine wave and writes it to **~bus**. Thus, we establish a basic signal flow in which samples are passed from one Synth to another.

CODE EXAMPLE 6.8: USING BUSSES AND INPUT/OUTPUT UGENS TO PASS A SIGNAL FROM ONE SYNTH TO ANOTHER.

```
(
s.newBusAllocators;
~bus = Bus.audio(s, 2);

SynthDef(\fader, { |in = 0, out = 0|
    var sig = In.ar(in, 2);
    sig = sig * 0.2;
    Out.ar(out, sig);
}).add;

SynthDef(\src, { |out = 0, freq = 150|
    var sig = SinOsc.ar(freq + [0, 1]);
    Out.ar(out, sig);
}).add;
)

(
~fader = Synth(\fader, [in: ~bus, out: 0]);
~src = Synth(\src, [out: ~bus]);
s.scope(rate: \audio, numChannels: 16, index: 0); // visualize bus activity
)

(
~src.free; // cleanup
~fader.free;
)
```

6.2.4 MICROPHONES AND SOUNDIN

> **TIP.RAND(); WATCH OUT FOR FEEDBACK!**
>
> There is always a risk of auditory feedback when working with a live microphone signal. If a mic signal is monitored through loudspeakers, the mic may capture the

loudspeaker output, cycle it back through your computer, and produce a horrible screeching sound. Using headphones, rather than loudspeakers, is one of the simplest and most reliable ways to avoid feedback. If headphones are not available, you should make sure your mic is placed sufficiently far away from your speakers, and also set the microphone input gain to be relatively low. Always be ready to press [cmd]+[period], if feedback starts to occur!

If you have an external microphone connected to your computer via an audio interface, or if you're using your computer's built-in sound card and mic, it's possible to read this live signal into SC for monitoring and/or processing. In this case, if you've configured SC's hardware I/O channels to be consistent with the I/O capabilities of your audio hardware, then you should see input channel activity on the server meter window when speaking into the mic. Under default conditions, if your mic is attached to the lowest-numbered input channel of your audio hardware, it will be accessible via audio bus 2. Code Example 6.9 reads the signal on audio bus 2, turns it into a two-channel signal via duplication, and writes it to audio busses 0 and 1, establishing a simple microphone pass-through.

CODE EXAMPLE 6.9: USING INPUT/OUTPUT UGENS TO CREATE A SIMPLE MICROPHONE PASS-THROUGH.

```
(
{// FEEDBACK WARNING — use headphones
    var sig = In.ar(bus: 2, numChannels: 1) ! 2;
    Out.ar(0, sig);
}.play;
)
```

A microphone signal is a signal like any other, and it can be processed in all the same ways. For example, Code Example 6.10 applies a random ring modulation effect to the mic signal.

CODE EXAMPLE 6.10: A MICROPHONE PASS-THROUGH WITH A RANDOM RING MODULATION EFFECT.

```
(
{// FEEDBACK WARNING — use headphones
    var sig, freq;
    sig = In.ar(2, 1) ! 2;
    freq = LFNoise0.kr([8, 7]).exprange(50, 2000);
    sig = sig * SinOsc.ar(freq);
    Out.ar(0, sig);
}.play;
)
```

By default, audio bus 2 refers to the lowest-numbered hardware input channel, but this may not always be the case, particularly if your hardware I/O configuration changes. For this reason, **SoundIn** is usually preferable to **In** for accessing a mic signal. SoundIn is a convenience UGen that automatically offsets the bus index by the number of hardware output busses, so that providing an index of 0 always corresponds to the lowest-numbered channel of your audio hardware device. The following two expressions are equivalent, assuming **n** is a valid bus index:

```
In.ar(n + s.options.numOutputBusChannels, 1);
```

```
SoundIn.ar(n, 1);
```

Code Example 6.11 rewrites the code from Code Example 6.9, substituting SoundIn for In.

CODE EXAMPLE 6.11: USING SoundIn TO CREATE A SIMPLE MICROPHONE PASS-THROUGH.

```
(
{// FEEDBACK WARNING — use headphones
    var sig = SoundIn.ar(bus: 0) ! 2;
    Out.ar(0, sig);
}.play;
)
```

SoundIn does not have an argument that represents a number of channels to read (its second and third arguments are **mul/add**). If, for example, you have two microphones in a stereo arrangement, connected to the lowest input channels on your audio interface, and want to read them into SC as a stereo signal, the **bus** for SoundIn should be the array **[0, 1]**.

6.2.5 ORDER OF EXECUTION

To pass a signal from Synth A to Synth B, sharing a bus is a necessary step, but this alone does not guarantee success. In addition, these Synths should also be placed on the server in the correct order. Synths on the server are processed from top to bottom, which in SC lingo is called "head to tail" (see Figure 6.3). On each control cycle, the server processes a block of samples for each Synth, starting at the head of the node tree and working downward. Thus, if the output of Synth A is used as an input signal for Synth B, then Synth B should exist below Synth A, closer to the "tail" of the node tree. "Order of execution" refers to how and where Synths are placed on the server, relative to the head/tail of the node tree, and relative to each other. As a reminder, the node tree visualizes Synth order, and can be invoked by evaluating **s.plotTree** after booting the server.

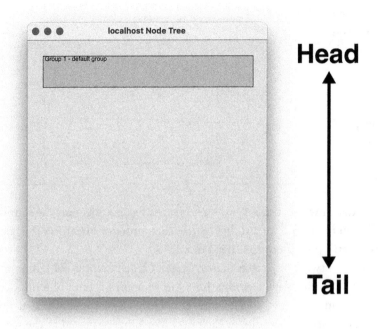

FIGURE 6.3 The orientation of the node tree as represented through its graphical utility.

Before exploring a detailed example of passing a signal from one Synth to another, let's first examine a simpler example involving two independent generative Synths. In Code Example 6.12, we hear both generative signals simultaneously, but the underlying process involves more than what meets the ear. By default, a new Synth is placed at the head of the node tree (technically, it is added to the head of the default group, discussed in the next section). Thus, when Synth ~a is created, it becomes the headmost Synth. Synth ~b is created next, at which point it becomes headmost, nudging the other Synth downward (two Synths cannot exist side-by-side). On each control cycle, SC first calculates 64 samples of ~b and writes the result to busses zero and one, then calculates 64 samples of ~a, and also writes to busses 0 and 1. By design, the **Out** UGen sums its output with bus content that already exists during the same control cycle. At the end of each control cycle, hardware bus content is sent out to audio hardware, and the process begins again for the next control block.

CODE EXAMPLE 6.12: CREATION OF TWO GENERATIVE SYNTHS.

```
(
SynthDef(\sine, { |gate = 1, out = 0|
    var sig = SinOsc.ar(250, mul: 0.1 ! 2);
    sig = sig * Env.asr.kr(2, gate);
    Out.ar(out, sig);
}).add;

SynthDef(\pink, { |gate = 1, out = 0|
    var sig = PinkNoise.ar(0.1 ! 2);
```

```
        sig = sig * Env.asr.kr(2, gate);
        Out.ar(out, sig);
}).add;
)


(
~a = Synth(\sine);
~b = Synth(\pink);
)
```

Because b + a = a + b, the order in which these Synths are created has no effect on the sound. Generally, if no Synth relies on the output of another Synth, then order of execution is irrelevant, even though Synths are still processed from head to tail.

Now, consider an example of two Synths that share a signal. Code Example 6.13 allocates a private two-channel audio bus and plays two Synths. One generates a tone blip approximately every three seconds, and the other applies a reverb effect to an input signal using **FreeVerb2**. Because the default behavior results in each new Synth being placed at the head of the node tree, this code produces a Synth order that is consistent with our desired signal flow (the reverb Synth ~b is created first, then the source Synth ~a is created). On each control cycle, the following steps occur:

1. 64 samples of Synth **~a** are generated.
2. These samples are written to **~bus**.
3. Synth **~b** reads 64 samples from **~bus**.
4. These samples are processed through a reverb UGen.
5. These 64 processed samples are written to busses zero and one.

CODE EXAMPLE 6.13: CREATION OF A GENERATIVE SYNTH AND A SYNTH THAT APPLIES A REVERB EFFECT TO THE GENERATED SIGNAL.

```
(
s.newBusAllocators;
~bus = Bus.audio(s, 2);

SynthDef(\pulses, { |out = 0, freq = 800, pulsefreq = 0.3|
    var sig = SinOsc.ar(freq + [0, 2], mul: 0.2);
    sig = sig * LFPulse.kr(pulsefreq, 0, 0.01);
    Out.ar(out, sig);
}).add;

SynthDef(\reverb, { |in = 0, out = 0, size = 0.97|
    var sig = In.ar(in, 2);
```

```
        sig = FreeVerb2.ar(sig[0], sig[1], mix: 0.2, room: size);
        Out.ar(out, sig);
    }).add;
)


(
~b = Synth(\reverb, [in: ~bus, out: 0]);
~a = Synth(\pulses, [out: ~bus]);
)
```

If the Synths in Code Example 6.13 were created in the reverse order, we would hear silence (press [cmd]+[period] and try this yourself). In this case, the following steps occur:

1. Synth **~b** reads 64 samples from **~bus**, currently empty.
2. These silent samples are processed by a reverb UGen, also producing silence.
3. These silent samples are written to busses 0 and 1.
4. 64 samples of Synth **~a** are generated.
5. These samples are written to **~bus**.

Thus, on each control cycle, this improper order yields a critical miscommunication between these two Synths.

6.2.6 GROUPS, TARGETS, AND ADDACTIONS

We have a few different options for ensuring proper Synth order on the node tree. Up until this point, we've only been specifying two arguments for new Synths, which determine the name of the SynthDef to be used and an array of argument values to be supplied. A new Synth accepts an additional pair of arguments, which are named **target** and **addAction**. The target of a new Synth represents an entity that already exists on the server, and the addAction represents how to add the new Synth relative to the target.

A **Group** is a type of object that helps organize Synths on the server, and is a common choice for a Synth target. Groups are a sibling class of Synths; both have the same parent class (**Node**), both are visualizable on the node tree, both are destroyed by [cmd]+[period], and both exist on the audio server in a specific order. Groups do not produce sound. Instead, they are merely containers for Synths and/or other Groups. When a new Group is created, it only needs to know its target and addAction. There is always one "default" Group that exists when the server is booted (visible in Figure 6.3), and it is immune to [cmd]+[period]. The default Group is accessible by evaluating:

```
s.defaultGroup;
```

When creating a new node (i.e., a new Synth or Group), its target can be a Synth, a Group, the server itself, or nil.[1] If the target is the server (specified as **s**), the target internally becomes the server's default Group. If the target is nil or unspecified, it becomes the default group on the default server. By default, the localhost server is the default server, but this can be confirmed with:

```
Server.default; // -> localhost
```

There are five possible addActions, usually specified as symbols: `\addToHead`, `\addToTail`, `\addBefore`, `\addToAfter`, and `\addReplace`. `\addToHead` and `\addToTail` assume the target is a Group and place the new Node at the head or tail of that Group. `\addBefore` and `\addAfter` place the new Node immediately before or after the target, which may be a Synth or Group. `\addReplace` removes the target, which can be a Synth or Group, and replaces it with the new Node. The default target and addAction are `Server.default.defaultGroup` and `\addToHead`. Thus, if these parameters are unspecified, a newly created Synth or Group will appear at the head of the default Group. Figure 6.4 shows the node trees that result from adding a new Synth using various combinations of targets and addActions.

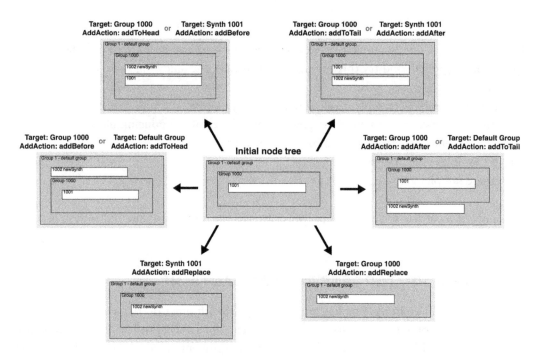

FIGURE 6.4 Node tree arrangements after adding a new Synth using different combinations of targets and addActions. Each outcome begins from the same tree configuration: a user-created Group (1000) inside the default Group, and a Synth (1001) inside that Group.

A primary application of Groups is to simplify the process of ensuring correct Synth order, demonstrated in Code Example 6.14. For example, if we have a source sound and an effect, we might create a "generative" Group and a "processing" Group. If these two Groups are in the correct order, we only need to make sure each Synth is placed into the correct Group, and we can create the two Synths in either order.

CODE EXAMPLE 6.14: USING GROUPS TO ORGANIZE SYNTHS AND FACILITATE CORRECT NODE ORDER. THIS EXAMPLE RELIES ON THE BUS AND SYNTHDEFS CREATED IN CODE EXAMPLE 6.13.

```
(
~genGrp = Group();
~fxGrp = Group(~genGrp, \addAfter);
~a = Synth(\pulses, [out: ~bus], ~genGrp);
~b = Synth(\reverb, [in: ~bus, out: 0], ~fxGrp);
)
```

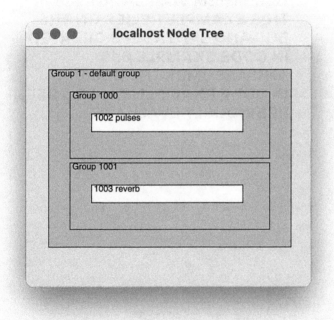

FIGURE 6.5 The Node tree after evaluating Code Example 6.14.

With this Group-based approach, we can freely add more generative Synths to **~genGrp**. If their output signals are routed to **~bus**, they will be processed by the reverb effect. The relative order of the generative Synths is unimportant; they only need to exist closer to the head of the node tree than the reverb Synth. Code Example 6.15 uses a routine that creates four additional source Synths. If a Group receives a **set** message, it relays that message to every node it contains, providing a convenient way to communicate with a large collection of Synths. If the Group contains another Group, the **set** message is applied recursively. If the **free** method is applied to a Group, it and all of the nodes it contains are destroyed. The **freeAll** method, by contrast, relays a **free** message to contained nodes, without freeing the Group itself. By freeing all the Synths in the generative Group, the source sounds are removed, but the reverb effect remains, allowing us to hear the complete decay of the reverb tail.

CODE EXAMPLE 6.15: PLACING SEVERAL ADDITIONAL SYNTHS INTO A GROUP AND COMMUNICATING WITH THEM VIA THAT GROUP. THIS EXAMPLE RELIES ON THE BUS AND SYNTHDEFS CREATED IN CODE EXAMPLE 6.13 AND ASSUMES THE CODE IN CODE EXAMPLE 6.14 HAS BEEN PREVIOUSLY EVALUATED.

```
(
Routine({
    4.do({
        Synth(\pulses, [freq: exprand(300, 3000), out: ~bus], ~genGrp);
        exprand(0.05, 1).wait;
    });
}).play;
)

~genGrp.set(\pulsefreq, 1); // set all Synths in ~genGrp

~genGrp.freeAll; // free all Synths in ~genGrp
```

Companion Code 6.1 puts these concepts into practice by emulating the basic signal flow of a simple analog mixer.

6.3 Delay-Based Processing

Delay lines are the basis of many effects commonly encountered throughout digital audio software, including echo, flanger, phaser, and chorus, as well as some reverberators and pitch-shifters. At their simplest, a delay-based effect typically mixes a signal with a delayed copy of itself. Long delay times produce discrete echoes, while very short delay times create interference patterns at the cycle- or sample-level, which influences the sound's spectrum. Digital delay lines work by writing input samples to memory and reading them back later. Thus, delay lines require the allocation of a buffer whose size determines the maximum possible delay time. A delay process treats its memory buffer "circularly," as if the beginning and end were connected. In other words, when either the reading or writing process of a delay reaches the end of its buffer, it wraps back to the beginning.

6.3.1 BASIC DELAYS

`DelayN` is one of the simplest delay UGens. It takes an input signal, along with a maximum delay time and an actual delay time, both measured in seconds. The maximum delay determines the size of the allocated memory buffer, and the actual delay time must be less than or equal to it. Code Example 6.16 passes a short noise burst through a half-second delay. The delayed signal is reduced by six decibels and summed with the original, producing an echo.

CODE EXAMPLE 6.16: USE OF `DelayN` TO CREATE A SIMPLE ECHO.

```
(
{
    var sig, delay;
    Line.kr(0, 0, 1, doneAction: 2);
    sig = PinkNoise.ar(0.5 ! 2) * XLine.kr(1, 0.001, 0.3);
    delay = DelayN.ar(sig, 0.5, 0.5) * -6.dbamp;
    sig = sig + delay;
}.play(fadeTime: 0);
)
```

A delay-based effect extends the durational lifespan of a sound process. In the previous example, it would be incorrect to give **XLine** a terminating doneAction. Doing so would free the Synth immediately after the source sound is complete and prevent the delay from sounding. For this reason, a separate terminating UGen (**Line**) with an appropriately long duration is needed. For the sake of brevity, most examples in this section bundle delay effects and the source signals they process into the same UGen function. In practice, a more sensible and efficient approach is to build separate SynthDefs for sound sources and processing effects, and route the signal from one Synth to the other using a bus, as demonstrated in Code Example 6.17.

CODE EXAMPLE 6.17: USE OF DELAYN TO CREATE A SIMPLE ECHO. THE SOURCE SIGNAL AND DELAY EFFECT ARE SPLIT INTO TWO SEPARATE SYNTHDEFS.

```
(
s.newBusAllocators;
~bus = Bus.audio(s, 2);

SynthDef(\del, {
    arg in = 0, out = 0, del = 0.5, amp = 0.5;
    var sig, delay;
    sig = In.ar(in, 2);
    delay = DelayN.ar(sig, 1, del) * amp;
    sig = sig + delay;
    Out.ar(out, sig);
}).add;

SynthDef(\src, {
    arg out = 0;
    var sig = PinkNoise.ar(0.5 ! 2);
    sig = sig * XLine.kr(1, 0.001, 0.3, doneAction: 2);
    Out.ar(out, sig);
}).add;
)

~del = Synth(\del, [in: ~bus, out: 0]); // create the echo effect

~src = Synth(\src, [out: ~bus]); // can be run repeatedly

~del.free;
```

DelayN automatically allocates a buffer using real-time memory. This allocation process is different from allocating a Buffer object on the server. In the case of DelayN, the memory buffer is inherently private to the delay UGen, and we cannot directly access it. There are limits to the total amount of delay time that real-time memory can accommodate. For example, if we attempt to instantiate a minute-long delay, the server will generate one or more "alloc failed" messages. On some older versions of SC, the server may crash and a reboot may be required:

```
{DelayN.ar(Silent.ar, 60, 60)}.play; // -> alloc failed
```

There are two limiting factors. The first is the amount of RAM your computer provides. It is impossible to allocate delays whose total duration corresponds to more real-time memory than your computer can provide. However, it is quite rare to need an amount of delay lines that exceeds your computer's real-time capabilities. Assuming four bytes per sample, eight gigabytes of RAM corresponds to about 11.5 hours of monophonic audio at a sampling rate of 48,000.

The second (more easily adjustable) factor is the amount of real-time memory that SC is allowed to access. This value, measured in kilobytes, is determined by a **ServerOptions** attribute named **memSize**. By default, this value is 8192, but can be modified like any other server attribute and applied with a server reboot, demonstrated in Code Example 6.18. A value of 2^{20} (roughly one gigabyte) is a value that works well in most cases, providing ample space for real-time buffer allocation while remaining well within the amount of real-time memory that most computers offer.

CODE EXAMPLE 6.18: MODIFICATION OF THE AMOUNT OF REAL-TIME MEMORY THAT THE AUDIO SERVER IS ALLOWED TO ACCESS.

```
(
s.options.memSize_(2.pow(20));
s.reboot;
)
```

BufDelayN, shown in Code Example 6.19, is a functionally identical alternative to DelayN. BufDelayN does not rely on real-time memory allocation and thus avoids its associated issues. The tradeoff is that the burden of buffer allocation and management falls to the user. Some additional attention to detail is required beyond simply allocating a buffer on the server and supplying it to BufDelayN. For efficiency reasons, the maximum number of samples that can be stored in a delay buffer is truncated to the next-lowest power of 2. Thus, if a one-second buffer is allocated with a sample rate of 48,000, the effective size of the buffer is only 32,768 samples. The **nextPowerOfTwo** method is helpful to ensure that delay buffers are sufficiently large.[2] Additionally, to delay an *n*-channel signal, BufDelayN requires an array of *n* monophonic buffers—a single multichannel buffer will not work correctly.

CODE EXAMPLE 6.19: USE OF **BufDelayN** TO CREATE A SIMPLE TWO-CHANNEL ECHO.

```
~buf = {Buffer.alloc(s, (s.sampleRate / 2).nextPowerOfTwo)} ! 2;

(
{
    var sig, delay;
    Line.kr(0, 0, 1, doneAction: 2);
    sig = PinkNoise.ar(0.5 ! 2) * XLine.kr(1, 0.001, 0.3);
    delay = BufDelayN.ar(~buf, sig, 0.5) * -6.dbamp;
    sig = sig + delay;
}.play(fadeTime: 0);
)
```

6.3.2 VARIABLE TIME DELAYS

The "N" in DelayN/BufDelayN stands for "non-interpolating." The delay time of one of these UGens is always quantized to the nearest control block, so dynamic changes to the delay time may produce glitchy artifacts. For delay-based processing with a fixed delay time, non-interpolating delays are perfectly fine. If the delay time is dynamic, however, an interpolating delay line is a better choice, such as **DelayL/DelayC**, which applies linear/cubic interpolation to delay time changes (**BufDelayL/BufDelayC** are analogous UGens). Cubic interpolation is smoother but more computationally expensive. Linear interpolation is a good compromise in most cases.

Consider a slow-moving sine oscillator, used to control the delay time of an interpolating delay line. While the sine wave is on a downward trajectory, the delay time is decreasing and the internal sample-reading pointer is moving closer to the internal recording pointer. As a side effect, the reading pointer temporarily traverses samples faster than normal, producing an increase in pitch. Likewise, when the modulating oscillator is on an upward trajectory, the delay time increases, the internal pointer momentarily reads samples more slowly, and a downward pitch shift occurs.

Common delay-based effects, such as flangers and phasers, exploit this pitch-shifting behavior. Code Example 6.20 passes a filtered sawtooth through an interpolating delay. The delay time is controlled by a low-frequency sine wave whose output ranges from one to ten milliseconds. Summing the original and delayed signals produces the effect, which exhibits a distinctive "sweeping" sound, characterized by a periodic pattern of phase interference.

CODE EXAMPLE 6.20: USE OF **DelayL** TO CREATE A FLANGER EFFECT.

```
(
{
    var sig, delay, lfo;
    lfo = SinOsc.kr(0.1, 3pi/2).range(0.001, 0.01);
    sig = LPF.ar(Saw.ar(100 ! 2, mul: 0.2), 2000);
    delay = DelayL.ar(sig, 0.01, lfo);
    sig = sig + delay;
}.play;
)
```

Companion Code 6.2 explores the application of dynamic delay lines to create chorus and harmonizer effects.

6.3.3 FEEDBACK DELAYS

DelayN and its sibling classes facilitate examples of feedforward delay, a configuration in which an input signal is summed with a delayed copy, but there is no signal path back to the effect's input. As a result, each UGen produces exactly one delayed signal copy. Creative options become more abundant when there is a feedback path, along which a delayed signal can be routed back to the input of the effect and delayed again (and again, and again). A comb filter, introduced in Code Example 6.21, is a delay line with feedback, available via **CombN** (along with **CombL/CombC** and also **BufCombN/BufCombL/BufCombC**). In addition to a maximum delay and actual delay time, these UGens also accept a decay time, measured in seconds, which determines the amount time after which the delayed signal level will have decreased by 60 decibels. A simple application of comb filters is to create a decaying series of echoes.

CODE EXAMPLE 6.21: USE OF CombN TO CREATE A SERIES OF DECAYING ECHOES.

```
(
{
    var sig, delay;
    Line.kr(0, 0, 10, doneAction: 2);
    sig = PinkNoise.ar(0.5 ! 2) * XLine.kr(1, 0.001, 0.3);
    delay = CombN.ar(sig, 0.1, 0.1, 9) * -6.dbamp;
    sig = sig + delay;
}.play(fadeTime: 0);
)
```

Why is it called a "comb" filter? With relatively large delay times, a comb filter is little more than a repetitive echo generator. But, when the delay times are very small, the feedback component of a comb filter exaggerates the phase interference patterns, creating resonance at frequencies whose periods are equal to the delay time (or an integer division of the delay time), because cycles of these frequencies will perfectly align with their delayed copies, and their amplitudes will sum to produce even greater amplitudes. In other words, the frequency equal to the inverse of the delay time, and all harmonics of that frequency, will resonate. If these repetitions occur frequently enough (about 20 repetitions per second or more), we will experience a sensation of pitch. The spectrum of this resonant behavior, demonstrated in Code Example 6.22, resembles the teeth of a comb, with prominent peaks at resonant frequencies and valleys of phase cancellation in-between.

CODE EXAMPLE 6.22: USE OF COMBN TO CREATE A RESONANT COMB FILTERING EFFECT.

```
(
SynthDef(\comb, { |freq = 4|
    var sig, delay;
    Line.kr(0, 0, 10, doneAction: 2);
    sig = PinkNoise.ar(0.5 ! 2) * XLine.kr(1, 0.001, 0.3);
    delay = CombN.ar(sig, 1, 1/freq, 9) * -6.dbamp;
    delay = LeakDC.ar(delay);
    sig = sig + delay;
    Out.ar(0, sig);
}).add;
)

Synth(\comb, [freq: 4]); // slower echo

Synth(\comb, [freq: 14]); // faster echo

Synth(\comb, [freq: 40]); // 40 Hz tone sensation

Synth(\comb, [freq: 120]); // 120 Hz tone sensation
```

An all-pass filter (`AllpassN/AllpassL/AllpassC`) is a close relative of the comb filter. At first glance, it appears nearly identical: it is a delay line with feedback and includes all the same arguments as the comb filter family. Its name refers to the fact that an all-pass filter passes all frequencies with equal gain (though this name does not do an ideal job of conveying its general purpose). Simplifying somewhat, the all-pass filter differs from the comb filter in that it involves a feedback path that scales the delayed signal by a coefficient, and a feedforward delay path that scales the signal by the same coefficient, but with the opposite sign. The consequence of this design is that an all-pass filter has a perfectly flat frequency response, thus counteracting the natural resonance and "twangy" sound of a comb filter. All-pass filters have useful applications in artificial reverberation design, as they help create a diffuse, uncolored sound. Companion Code 6.3 explores the use of delays, particularly comb filters and all-pass filters, to create reverberation effects based on M.R. Schroeder's 1961 article, "Natural Sounding Artificial Reverberation."[3]

6.4 Real-Time Granular Synthesis

Chapter 4 introduced granular synthesis as a generative process, but it can also be used as a signal processing effect, applied to a live signal. Thus, we can access the usual palette of granular flavors—dense soundscapes, pointillistic textures, pitch-shifting, and time stretching—without needing to store the source sound in a buffer ahead of time. There are limitations, of course. Notably, we can't look into the future and granulate sound that has not yet happened!

We can only create grains from sound that is happening now, or sound that has already happened. Nonetheless, real-time granular synthesis provides options for decorating and enhancing live sound in exotic ways.

GrainIn is the simplest option for live granular synthesis. It is essentially a pared-down version of **GrainBuf**, designed to operate on a live signal instead of one that is read from a buffer. As previously discussed, SoundIn and GrainIn should be deployed in two separate SynthDefs and pass signal via a bus for optimal modularity/flexibility. In Code Example 6.23, they are merged into one UGen function for the sake of brevity. GrainIn is somewhat boring in isolation. Because there are no controls for playback rate or grain start position, the grains are perfectly synchronized with the input signal, and the effect is uninteresting. In fact, GrainIn is virtually indistinguishable from a retriggerable envelope generator. A nearly identical result, pictured in Code Example 6.24, can be achieved using EnvGen/Env.

CODE EXAMPLE 6.23: SIMPLE GRANULATION OF A LIVE SIGNAL USING GRAININ.

```
(
{// FEEDBACK WARNING — use headphones
    var sig = SoundIn.ar(0);
    sig = GrainIn.ar(
        numChannels: 1,
        trigger: Dust.kr(16),
        dur: 0.04,
        in: sig
    ) ! 2;
}.play;
)
```

CODE EXAMPLE 6.24: SIMPLE GRANULATION OF A LIVE SIGNAL USING A RETRIGGERABLE ENVELOPE.

```
(
{// FEEDBACK WARNING — use headphones
    var sig = SoundIn.ar(0);
    sig = sig * Env.sine(0.04).ar(gate: Dust.ar(16)) ! 2;
}.play;
)
```

GrainIn naturally pairs with delay lines, demonstrated in Code Example 6.25, which can be inserted before granulating to desynchronize the grains from the input signal, producing a granulated echo effect. Many variations are possible, such as adding parallel delays with different delay times, or using a delay line with feedback, such as CombN. The delayed signals can also be further processed before or after granulation (filters, amplitude modulation, reverb, etc.) to create a more complex effect.

CODE EXAMPLE 6.25: A GRANULATED ECHO EFFECT USING DelayN AND GrainIn.

```
(
{// FEEDBACK WARNING — use headphones
    var sig = SoundIn.ar(0);
    sig = DelayN.ar(sig, 0.2, 0.2) * 0.7;
    sig = GrainIn.ar(1, Dust.kr(16), 0.04, sig) ! 2;
}.play;
)
```

In contrast, GrainBuf provides a more sophisticated interface, though the setup is more involved. Broadly, the process involves recording a live signal into a buffer (looping and overwriting old samples in cyclic fashion), while simultaneously generating grains from the same buffer. This approach necessitates a periodic ramp signal, used as a recording pointer for BufWr. GrainBuf relies on this same pointer signal for determining grain start positions but subtracts some amount so that the grain pointer consistently lags behind the record pointer by a fraction of the buffer's length.

Code Example 6.26 demonstrates live granulation using GrainBuf. A buffer holds the three most recent seconds of a live microphone signal. Phasor generates the pointer signal, which BufWr uses to index into the buffer. GrainBuf subtracts a durational value (0.2 seconds) from this pointer signal. Converting the pointer values is the only tricky part: the Phasor signal represents a frame count, our delay argument is measured in seconds, and GrainBuf expects a normalized value between zero and one for the grain start position. To provide GrainBuf with an appropriately lagged pointer signal, we must convert seconds to samples, subtract this value from the pointer signal, and divide by the number of frames in the buffer.

CODE EXAMPLE 6.26: GRANULATION OF A LIVE SIGNAL USING GRAINBUF.

```
b = Buffer.alloc(s, s.sampleRate * 3); // three-second buffer

(
SynthDef(\livegran, {
    arg buf = 0, rate = 1, ptrdelay = 0.2;
    var sig, ptr, gran;
    sig = SoundIn.ar(0);
    ptr = Phasor.ar(0, BufRateScale.ir(buf), 0, BufFrames.ir(buf));
    BufWr.ar(sig, buf, ptr);
    sig = GrainBuf.ar(
        numChannels: 2,
        trigger: Dust.kr(16),
```

```
        dur: 0.04,
        sndbuf: buf,
        rate: rate,
        pos: (ptr - (ptrdelay * SampleRate.ir)) / BufFrames.ir(buf)
    );
    Out.ar(0, sig);
}).add;
)

// FEEDBACK WARNING - use headphones
Synth(\livegran, [buf: b]);
```

A potential pitfall revolves around the fact that as the playback/record pointers move through the buffer, there is always a discontinuity at the record pointer. This pointer indicates the "now" moment, where the current sample from our live signal overwrites the oldest sample in the buffer (see Figure 6.6). Care should be taken to avoid generating grains that contain this discontinuity, as they may produce an audible click, producing inferior sound quality.

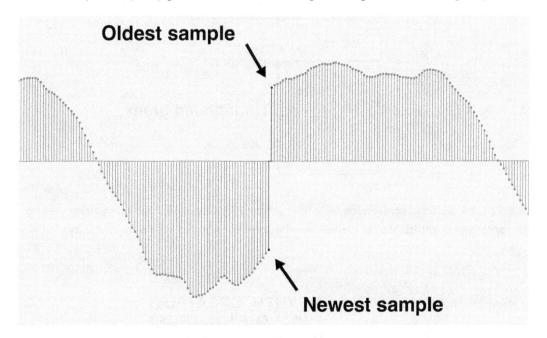

FIGURE 6.6 A close-up of the buffer discontinuity produced by recording new samples over old samples.

Pitch-shifting, if not done carefully, can produce grains that overlap with this discontinuity. Consider a grain playback rate of two, which specifies that a grain should be transposed up one octave, pictured in Figure 6.7. To achieve the correct grain duration and playback rate, GrainBuf extracts a section of the buffer that is twice the specified grain duration, and then time-compresses it by a factor of two. If the time delay between the record/playback pointers is too small, the grain will contain the discontinuity. Downward transpositions, by comparison, are not problematic, because they extract a section of the buffer that is smaller than the desired grain size, and time-expand it. In this case, there is no risk of including the discontinuity as long as the specified grain duration is smaller than the distance between the record/playback pointers. Code Example 6.27 provides an example in which an upward transposition and short pointer delay captures the discontinuity in each grain, producing clicky, glitchy audio.

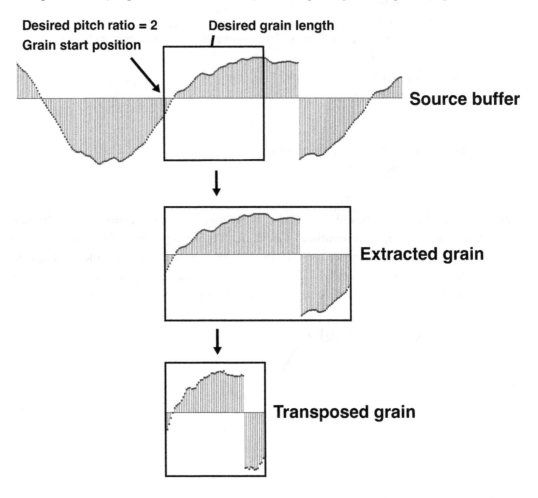

FIGURE 6.7 A grain that contains the buffer discontinuity because of upward pitch-shifting, despite the appearance of sufficient distance between the grain start position and the discontinuity.

CODE EXAMPLE 6.27: A SYNTH, CREATED FROM THE SYNTHDEF IN CODE EXAMPLE 6.26, THAT PRODUCES CLICKY GRAINS THAT EACH CONTAIN THE BUFFER DISCONTINUITY.

```
(
// FEEDBACK WARNING — use headphones
b.zero;
Synth(\livegran, [buf: b, ptrdelay: 0.005, rate: 4.midiratio]);
)
```

A general solution, pictured in Code Example 6.28, is to constrain one parameter based on the value of another, like proportionally decreasing grain duration as grain playback rate increases. Specifically, we can set the maximum allowable grain duration equal to pointer delay divided by playback rate. For the actual grain duration, we consider the maximum grain duration and the user-provided duration, and use whichever value is smaller.

CODE EXAMPLE 6.28: AVOIDING THE BUFFER DISCONTINUITY BY CONSTRAINING GRAIN DURATION BASED ON POINTER DELAY AND PLAYBACK RATE.

```
b = Buffer.alloc(s, s.sampleRate * 3);

(
SynthDef(\livegran, {
    arg buf = 0, rate = 1, ptrdelay = 0.2;
    var sig, ptr, gran, maxgraindur;
    sig = SoundIn.ar(0);
    ptr = Phasor.ar(0, BufRateScale.ir(buf), 0, BufFrames.ir(buf));
    BufWr.ar(sig, buf, ptr);
    maxgraindur = ptrdelay / rate;
    sig = GrainBuf.ar(
        numChannels: 2,
        trigger: Dust.kr(16),
        dur: min(0.04, maxgraindur),
        sndbuf: buf,
        rate: rate,
        pos: (ptr - (ptrdelay * SampleRate.ir)) / BufFrames.ir(buf)
    );
    Out.ar(0, sig);
}).add;
)

(
// FEEDBACK WARNING — use headphones
b.zero;
Synth(\livegran, [buf: b, ptrdelay: 0.05, rate: 7.midiratio]);
)
```

A possible side-effect of this approach is that large upward pitch-shifts or small pointer delays can produce extremely short grains, which have a "clicky" character (despite avoiding the discontinuity) and may not be desirable. In most cases, specifying a sufficiently long delay between the recording pointer and grain pointer—at least 0.03 seconds or so—helps provide some wiggle room for pitch shifting and avoids excessively short grains.

Though this GrainBuf example sounds like the GrainIn examples, it enables musical flexibility that GrainIn cannot easily provide. Beyond pitch-shifting, this approach invites random/nonlinear grain pointer movement for real-time "scrambling" effects and offers the ability to pause the recording pointer to create a granular "freeze" effect. These and other ideas are explored in Companion Code 6.4.

Notes

1 A target for a new Node may also be an integer, in which case it is interpreted as the Node ID of the desired target. Whenever a Synth or Group is created, it automatically receives a Node ID, which is an incremented integer that starts at 1,000 and counts upward as new Nodes are created. We rarely provide Node IDs ourselves, and instead let the ID allocator handle this process automatically. In many cases, we won't know the Node ID of a Synth or Group offhand, so we don't typically rely Node IDs as targets. Node IDs are visible on the Node tree window and also in Figure 6.4.
2 DelayN (and other delay UGens that dynamically allocate real-time memory) automatically increase the user-provided "maxdelaytime" argument to a value that corresponds to a number of samples equal to the next-highest power of two. Thus, these UGens often allow delay times that are somewhat larger than the user-provided maximum. For practical reasons, though, it is sensible to treat the maximum delay time as a true maximum, even if longer delay times are technically possible.
3 Manfred R. Schroeder, "Natural Sounding Artificial Reverberation," *Journal of the Audio Engineering Society*, Vol. 10, no. 3 (1962 July): 219–223.

CHAPTER 7

EXTERNAL CONTROL

7.1 Overview

A self-contained SC project can be compelling and expressive on its own, but typing and evaluating code as the sole means of interaction can feel like a limiting experience. SC can communicate with a variety of external devices, including MIDI keyboards, game controllers, other computers running SC, and more. External controllers enhance creative options by inviting new modes of interaction and alternative approaches to composition, performance, and improvisation.

7.2 MIDI

The MIDI (Musical Instrument Digital Interface) communication protocol was publicly released in 1983 and rapidly became a centerpiece of the digital audio world. Today, it remains a ubiquitous option for sending and receiving data, built into virtually every DAW and audio programming environment. Though MIDI was created with music in mind, the protocol is largely music-agnostic; MIDI messages are merely control data that exist as sequences of bytes, with no active knowledge of the sound they may be controlling. It's the responsibility of a receiving device to translate MIDI data into relevant musical actions. This flexibility allows MIDI to be used in many different contexts, some of which are completely unrelated to sound.

The full collection of MIDI messages is relatively large, but in practical use, only a handful of "channel voice" messages are encountered. These messages include note-on, note-off, control change (CC), program change, pitch bend, and aftertouch. Even within this small collection, note-on/off and CC are arguably the most commonly used. A data component of a message contains 7 bits, which represent $2^7 = 128$ discrete values. Thus, there are 128 possible MIDI note numbers, 128 possible note velocities, 128 unique controller numbers, and so on. Despite this relatively low resolution, the dataspace provided by MIDI is sufficient to accommodate many different types of projects.

7.2.1 RECEIVING MIDI

If one or more MIDI devices are connected to and recognized by your computer before launching SC, you can initialize MIDI functionality by evaluating:

```
MIDIClient.init;
```

which makes SC aware of available MIDI devices and displays a list of MIDI sources and destinations in the post window. From here, the quickest way to connect to all available MIDI sources is to evaluate:

```
MIDIIn.connectAll;
```

Note that `MIDIIn.connectAll` indirectly calls `MIDIClient.init` if needed, so the first of these two expressions can be omitted. At this point, the incoming data can be visualized with a built-in debugging utility that prints all incoming MIDI messages. This is often a helpful first step in confirming data flow and understanding the inner workings of your MIDI device(s). Debugging is activated/deactivated with:

```
MIDIFunc.trace(true);
```

```
MIDIFunc.trace(false);
```

`MIDIdef` is a primary class for defining an action to be performed in response to incoming data. A MIDIdef is created using one of several class methods, such as `noteOn`, `cc`, etc., which determines the type of message to which the MIDIdef will respond. At minimum, a MIDIdef expects two arguments: a symbol, which serves as a unique identifier key for the MIDIdef (like the first argument of `SynthDef.new`), and a function, evaluated whenever SC receives the relevant type of message. Arguments declared within this function represent the data contained in the MIDI message. Functions for some MIDI messages expect three arguments (value, channel, source ID), while others expect four arguments (value, number, channel, source ID). These arguments can be freely named but are always interpreted in one of these two orders. The "channel" argument refers to the MIDI channel associated with the transmitted message, relevant if working with a multi-channel MIDI setup. There are sixteen possible MIDI channels, commonly represented as 1–16 for human readability, but SC interprets these channels as 0–15. A message's "source ID" is a unique integer that identifies a specific transmitting device, relevant only if necessary to distinguish identical messages from two different sources. The meanings of "value" and "number" vary depending on message type. Table 7.1 provides a descriptive list of expected arguments and their meanings for common message types, and Code Example 7.1 creates a MIDIdef that plays a short tone in response to note-on messages, whose frequency and amplitude are determined by note number and velocity.

TABLE 7.1 MIDIdef creation methods, their expected function arguments, and interpreted meaning of value/number arguments.

MIDIdef Creation Method	Function Arguments	Meaning of val/num
noteOn	val, num, chan, src	note velocity/note number
noteOff	"	release velocity/note number
cc	"	controller value/controller number
polytouch	"	aftertouch pressure value/note number
touch	val, chan, src	maximum aftertouch pressure value
program	"	program or patch number
bend	"	pitch bend amount

CODE EXAMPLE 7.1: USING `MIDIdef` TO PLAY A SHORT TONE WHENEVER A NOTE-ON MESSAGE IS RECEIVED.

```
s.boot;

MIDIIn.connectAll;

(
MIDIdef.noteOn(\simpleNotes, {
    |val, num, chan, src| // chan & src declared but not used
    {
        var sig, freq, amp;
        freq = num.midicps;
        amp = val.linexp(1, 127, 0.01, 0.25);
        sig = SinOsc.ar(freq * [0, 0.1].midiratio) * amp;
        sig = sig * Env.perc.kr(2);
    }.play;
});
)
```

MIDIdef is a subclass of **MIDIFunc**, from which it inherits its functionality. MIDIFunc can be used to achieve the same results as MIDIdef with a slightly different syntax. The benefit of MIDIdef is that each instance can be dynamically replaced with a new MIDIdef, without inadvertently creating a duplicate. For instance, if you replace the SinOsc in Code Example 7.1 with a different oscillator and re-evaluate the code, a new MIDIdef replaces the older one, and is stored at the same key.

Once created, a MIDIdef can be referenced by its key, using the same proxy syntax that appears in Code Example 5.38:

```
MIDIdef(\simpleNotes);
```

A MIDIdef can be temporarily deactivated and reactivated with **disable/enable**:

```
MIDIdef(\simpleNotes).disable; // bypassed

MIDIdef(\simpleNotes).enable; // reactivated
```

By default, [cmd]+[period] destroys MIDIdefs, which is sometimes but not always desirable. A MIDIdef can be made to survive [cmd]+[period] by setting its **permanent** attribute to true (similar to making a TempoClock permanent):

```
MIDIdef(\simpleNotes).permanent_(true); // now immune to
[cmd]+[period]
```

A MIDIdef can be permanently destroyed with **free**. If multiple MIDIdef objects exist, they can all be destroyed at once using the class method **freeAll**:

```
MIDIdef(\simpleNotes).free; // remove this MIDIdef

MIDIdef.freeAll; // remove all MIDIdefs
```

When working with MIDI note messages, we typically want a MIDIdef to respond to all note numbers, so that the entire keyboard of a piano-type controller is playable. With control change messages, however, we usually want more selective behavior, that is, a MIDIdef that only responds to one specific controller, rather than all possible CC messages. To filter out undesirable messages, we can provide an integer as a third MIDIdef argument. This value is compared against incoming messages. If the number of an incoming message number does not match, the message is ignored. This argument can also be an array of integers, in which case the MIDIdef ignores any message whose number does not match any number contained in the array. It's possible to create the same filtering behavior by implementing conditional logic inside the MIDIdef function, but providing a message-filtering argument is usually simpler. Code Example 7.2 creates a second MIDIdef that updates a cutoff frequency whenever a CC message from controller number one is received. The cutoff is incorporated into the note-on MIDIdef, which passes a sawtooth wave through a resonant low-pass filter. The modulation wheel, a standard feature on many keyboard controllers, is conventionally designated controller number one. If your keyboard has a mod wheel, it will likely influence the filter value in Code Example 7.2. This example is relatively simple in that the cutoff value is only applied at the moment a new Synth is created; moving the mod wheel does not influence Synths that have already been created and are currently sounding (Companion Code 7.1 demonstrates how to dynamically influence existing Synths with real-time control data).

CODE EXAMPLE 7.2: USING TWO MIDIDEFS TO PLAY TONES AND DETERMINE A CUTOFF FREQUENCY, APPLIED WHEN A SYNTH IS CREATED.

```
(
~filtCutoff = 200;

MIDIdef.cc(\filtControl,
    {
        |val, num, chan, src|
        ~filtCutoff = val.linexp(1, 127, 200, 10000);
    }, ccNum: 1 // only respond to CC#1 messages
);

MIDIdef.noteOn(\simpleNotes,
    {
        |val, num, chan, src|
        {
```

```
            arg cf = 200;
            var sig, freq, amp;
            freq = num.midicps;
            amp = val.linexp(1, 127, 0.01, 0.25);
            sig = Saw.ar(freq * [0, 0.1].midiratio) * amp;
            sig = RLPF.ar(sig, cf, 0.1);
            sig = sig * Env.perc.kr(2);
        }.play(args: [\cf, ~filtCutoff]);
    }
);
)
```

MIDI is commonly used to trigger samples instead of controlling synthesis algorithms. In Code Example 7.3, a MIDIdef is used to play built-in samples, and uses note number to transpose the sample pitch. Note number 60 (middle C) is treated as the root key.

CODE EXAMPLE 7.3: USING MIDIDEF TO PLAY AND TRANSPOSE SAMPLES.

```
(
b = Buffer.read(s, Platform.resourceDir ++ "/sounds/a11wlk01.wav");

MIDIdef.freeAll;

MIDIdef.noteOn(\sampler, {
    |val, num, chan, src|
    {
        var sig, rate, amp;
        rate = (num - 60).midiratio;
        amp = val.linexp(1, 127, 0.1, 0.7);
        sig = PlayBuf.ar(
            1, b, BufRateScale.ir(b) * rate, startPos: 85000
        );
        sig = sig * Env.perc.kr(2) * amp ! 2;
    }.play;
});
)
```

Although MIDI messages are often used to make a MIDI controller to behave like a musical instrument, this is not a requirement. The action function of a MIDIdef can contain any valid SC code. The MIDIdef in Code Example 7.4 will post a random number in response to note 60, play a short noise burst in response to note 61, and note 62 will quit the audio server! Messages from other note numbers are ignored.

CODE EXAMPLE 7.4: **USING A MIDIDEF TO TRANSLATE INCOMING MESSAGES INTO ARBITRARY ACTIONS.**

```
(
MIDIdef.freeAll;

MIDIdef.noteOn(\weird, {
    |val, num, chan, src|
    case
    {num == 60} {exprand(1, 100).postln}
    {num == 61} {
        {PinkNoise.ar(0.1 ! 2) * Line.kr(1, 1, 0.1, doneAction:2)}.play
    }
    {num == 62} {s.quit};
}, noteNum: [60, 61, 62]
);
)
```

MIDI controllers come in many varieties; the examples presented here may require some tweaking to work with your specific MIDI device. Incorporating additional features, like listening for note-off messages and applying pitch bend information, requires a bit more work and is explored in Companion Code 7.1. In contrast, Companion Code 7.2 demonstrates a fundamentally different application: using a MIDIdef to facilitate text entry of pitch information into arrays and patterns.

7.2.2 SENDING MIDI

In addition to receiving, SC can also send MIDI to external devices. This can be useful for controlling a hardware synthesizer, piping an algorithmic MIDI sequence into a DAW, or sending synchronization cues to another computer. As was the case with receiving, the first step in transmitting MIDI data is to initialize the MIDIClient class, to make SC aware of available devices:

```
MIDIClient.init;
```

An array of available MIDI destinations can be generated with

```
MIDIClient.destinations;
```

Each destination will have a device name and a port name, both represented as strings. Code Example 7.5 shows an example of what a destinations array might look like. Some devices may have multiple input ports, in which case each port will appear as a unique destination.

> **CODE EXAMPLE 7.5:** **AN EXAMPLE OF THE ARRAY RETURNED BY EVALUATING `MIDIClient.destinations`.**
>
> ```
> -> [
>     MIDIEndPoint("IAC Driver", "IAC Bus 1"),
>     MIDIEndPoint("IAC Driver", "IAC Bus 2"),
>     MIDIEndPoint("UltraLite mk3 Hybrid", "MIDI Port 1")
>     MIDIEndPoint("UltraLite mk3 Hybrid", "MIDI Port 2")
>     MIDIEndPoint("OSCulator In (8000)", "OSCulator In (8000)"),
>     MIDIEndPoint("Oxygen 49", "Oxygen 49"),
> ]
> ```

A connection to a MIDI destination can be established by creating a new instance of **MIDIOut**. The most reliable and cross-platform friendliest way to specify a destination is to provide the device and port name via the **newByName** method:

```
m = MIDIOut.newByName("UltraLite mk3 Hybrid", "MIDI Port 2");
```

Alternatively, a MIDIOut object can be specified via **new**, along with the array index of the desired destination. However, the array order may be different if your setup changes, so this is not as reliable as **newByName**[1]:

```
m = MIDIOut.new(3); // item in MIDIClient.destinations at index 3
```

After creating a new instance of MIDIOut, we can apply instance methods to generate and send messages to the target device. For instance, the following line will generate a note-on message on channel 0, corresponding to note number 72 with a velocity of 50 (keep in mind that most receiving devices envision MIDI channels as being numbered 1–16, and will interpret channel n from SC as equivalent to channel $n + 1$. If the receiving destination is a sound-producing piece of hardware or software, and is actively "listening" for MIDI data, the following line should play a sound:

```
m.noteOn(0, 72, 50);
```

At this point, from the perspective of the MIDI destination, the situation is no different from a user holding down key 72. This imaginary key can be "released" by sending an appropriate note-off message (note that the release velocity may be ignored by some receiving devices):

```
m.noteOff(0, 72, 50);
```

The process of sending a sequence of MIDI messages can be automated by constructing and playing a routine, pictured in Code Example 7.6.

> **CODE EXAMPLE 7.6: USING A ROUTINE TO AUTOMATE THE PRODUCTION AND TRANSMISSION OF MIDI MESSAGES TO AN EXTERNAL DEVICE.**
>
> ```
> (
> // assumes 'm' is an appropriate instance of MIDIOut
> r = Routine({
>     inf.do({
>         var note = rrand(40, 90);
>         m.noteOn(0, note, exprand(20, 60).asInteger);
>         (1/20).wait;
>         m.noteOff(0, note);
>         (3/20).wait;
>     });
> }).play;
> )
>
> r.stop;
> ```

This routine-based approach works well enough, but if the routine is stopped between a note-on message and its corresponding note-off, the result is a "stuck" note. Obviously, [cmd]+[period] will have no effect because the SC audio server is not involved. One solution is to use iteration to send all 128 possible note-off messages to the receiving device:

```
(0..127).do({ |n| m.noteOff(0, n) });
```

This solution can be enhanced by encapsulating this expression in a function and registering it with the **CmdPeriod** class, so that the note-off action is performed whenever [cmd]+[period] is pressed. This action can be un-registered at any time by calling **remove** on CmdPeriod (see Code Example 7.7).

> **CODE EXAMPLE 7.7: AUTOMATING THE REMOVAL OF STUCK NOTES USING CMDPERIOD.**
>
> ```
> (
> ~allNotesOff = {
>     "all notes off".postln;
>     (0..127).do({ |n| m.noteOff(0, n) });
> };
> CmdPeriod.add(~allNotesOff);
> )
>
> CmdPeriod.remove(~allNotesOff); // un-register this action
> ```

Events provide a more elegant interface for sending MIDI messages to external devices. In Chapter 5, we introduced note- and rest-type Events. There is also a built-in **midi** type event, whose keys include **\midiout** and **\midicmd**, which specify the instance of MIDIOut to be used, and the type of message to be sent. We can view valid options for **\midicmd** by evaluating:

```
Event.partialEvents.midiEvent[\midiEventFunctions].keys;
```

The type of MIDI message being sent determines additional keys to be specified. For example, if we specify **\noteOn** as the value for the **\midicmd** key, the Event will also expect **\chan**, **\midinote**, **\amp**, **\sustain**, and **\hasGate**. A value between 0 and 1 should be provided for **\amp**, which is automatically multiplied by 127 before transmission. When **\hasGate** is true (the default), a corresponding note-off message is automatically sent after **\sustain** beats have elapsed. If **\hasGate** is false, no note-off message will be sent. Code Examples 7.8 and 7.9 demonstrate the use of Events to send MIDI data to an external destination.

CODE EXAMPLE 7.8: SENDING A NOTE-ON AND AUTOMATIC NOTE-OFF MESSAGE TO AN EXTERNAL DEVICE BY PLAYING AN EVENT.

```
(
(
    type: \midi,
    midiout: m,
    midicmd: \noteOn,
    chan: 0,
    midinote: 60,
    amp: 0.5,
    sustain: 2 // note-off sent 2 beats later
).play;
)
```

CODE EXAMPLE 7.9: USE OF PBIND TO CREATE A STREAM OF MIDI-TYPE EVENTS.

```
(
t = TempoClock.new(108/60);

p = Pbind(
    \type, \midi,
    \dur, 1/4,
    \midiout, m,
    \midicmd, \noteOn,
```

```
        \chan, 0,
        \midinote, Pseq([60, 72, 75],inf),
        \amp, 0.5,
        \sustain, 1/8,
    );

    ~seq = p.play(t);
)

~seq.stop;
```

7.3 OSC

Open Sound Control (OSC) is a specification for communication between computers, synthesizers, and other multimedia devices, developed by Matt Wright and Adrian Freed at UC Berkeley CNMAT in the late 1990s, and first published in 2002.[2] Designed to meet the same general goals of MIDI, it allows devices to exchange information in real-time, but offers advantages in its customizability and flexibility. In contrast to MIDI, OSC supports a greater variety of data types, and includes high-resolution timestamps for temporal precision. OSC also offers an open-ended namespace using URL-style address tags instead of predetermined message types (such as note-on, control change, etc.), and is optimized for transmission over modern networking protocols. It's a common choice for projects involving device-to-device communication, such as laptop ensembles, multimedia collaborations, or using a smartphone as a multitouch controller.

Little needs to be known about the technical details of OSC to use it effectively in SC. To send a message from one device to another, the simplest option is for both devices to be on the same local area network, which helps avoid security and firewall-related obstacles. The sending device needs to know the IP address of the receiving device, as well as the network port on which that device is listening. The structure of an OSC message begins with a URL-style address, followed by one or more pieces of data. Code Example 7.10 shows an example of an OSC message, as it would be displayed in SC, which includes an address followed by three numerical values.

CODE EXAMPLE 7.10: AN EXAMPLE OF AN OSC MESSAGE IN SC.

```
['/sine/freqs', 220, 220.3, 221.05]
```

Since its creation, OSC has been incorporated into many creative audio/video software platforms. SC, in particular, is deeply intertwined with OSC. In addition to being able to exchange OSC with external devices, OSC is also how the language and server communicate with each other. Any code that produces a server-side reaction (adding a SynthDef, allocating a Buffer, creating a Synth, etc.) is internally translated into OSC messages.

7.3.1 THE TRIVIAL CASE: SELF-SENDING OSC IN THE LANGUAGE

To begin demonstrating the basics, it's instructive to have the SC language send an OSC message to itself. In SC, **NetAddr** is the class that represents a network device, defined by its IP address (a string), and the port (an integer) on which it listens. You can look up your computer's local IP address in your network settings, or you can use the self-referential IP address "127.0.0.1". By default, the language listens for OSC data on port 57120, or sometimes 57121. The incoming OSC port can be confirmed by evaluating:

```
NetAddr.langPort;
```

The following NetAddr represents the instance of the SC language running on your computer:

```
~myself = NetAddr.new("127.0.0.1", NetAddr.langPort);
```

OSCdef is a primary class for receiving OSC messages, generally similar to MIDIdef in behavior and design. At minimum, an OSCdef expects (1) a symbol, serving as a unique identifier for the OSCdef, (2) a function, evaluated in response to a received OSC message, and (3) the OSC address against which incoming messages are compared (non-matching addresses are ignored). Inside the function, four arguments can be declared: the OSC message, a timestamp, a NetAddr representing the sending device, and the port on which the message was received. Often, we only need the first of these four arguments. OSC addresses begin with a forward slash, and symbols in SC often begin with a backslash. SC can't parse this combination of characters, which is why symbols are typically expressed using single-quote enclosures in the context of OSC.

```
\/test; // invalid
```

```
'/test'; // valid
```

Code Example 7.11 shows the essentials of sending an OSC message to/from the SC language. After creating instances of NetAddr and OSCdef, we can send an OSC message to ourselves with **sendMsg**, and including the OSC address tag, followed by any number of comma-separated pieces of data. The message is represented as an array when received by the OSCdef, so we can use an expression like **msg[2]** to access a specific piece of data within the message.

> **CODE EXAMPLE 7.11:** THE BASIC STRUCTURE FOR SENDING AN OSC MESSAGE FROM THE LANGUAGE, TO BE RECEIVED BY THE LANGUAGE. THE `OSCdef` RESPONDS BY INDEXING INTO THE MESSAGE AND PRINTING THE RANDOM VALUE.
>
> ```
> (
> ~myself = NetAddr("127.0.0.1", NetAddr.langPort);
>
> OSCdef(\receiver,
>     {
>         |msg, time, addr, port|
>         ("random value is " ++ msg[2]).postln;
>     },
>     '/test'
> );
> )
>
> ~myself.sendMsg('/test', 5, exprand(100,200), -9); // send a message
> ```

7.3.2 SENDING OSC FROM THE LANGUAGE TO THE SERVER

Though it's possible to explicitly send OSC from the language to the server, this is rarely necessary or advantageous, because these OSC messages are already encapsulated in higher-level classes that are more intuitive (Synth, SynthDef, Buffer, etc.). Nonetheless, simulating the "behind-the-scenes" flow of OSC data from language to server may provide clarity on fundamental concepts. With the server booted, consider the two expressions in Code Example 7.12. We can produce the same result by sending OSC messages explicitly.

> **CODE EXAMPLE 7.12:** CREATING A SYNTH AND SETTING AN ARGUMENT VIA THE SYNTH CLASS, IMPLICITLY SENDING OSC MESSAGES TO THE SERVER.
>
> ```
> x = Synth(\default, [freq: 300], s, \addToHead);
>
> x.set(\gate, 0);
> ```

By default, the audio server listens for OSC messages on port 57110, and automatically has an instance of NetAddr associated with it, accessible via `s.addr`. The server is programmed to create a new Synth in response to messages with the '/s_new' address. Following the address, it expects the SynthDef name, a unique node ID (assigned automatically when using the Synth class), an integer representing an addAction (0 means \addToHead), the node ID of the target Group or Synth (the default Group has a node ID of 1), and any number of comma-separated pairs, representing argument names and values. Messages with the '/n_set' address tag are equivalent to sending a set message to a Node (either a Synth or Group). It requires the node ID, followed by one or more argument-value pairs. Code Example 7.13 performs the same actions as Code Example 7.12, but builds the OSC messages from scratch. Note that we don't need to use **s.addr** to access the NetAddr associated with the server; **sendMsg** can be directly applied to the instance of the localhost server.

CODE EXAMPLE 7.13: CREATING A SYNTH AND SETTING AN ARGUMENT BY EXPLICITLY SENDING OSC MESSAGES TO THE SERVER.

```
s.sendMsg('/s_new', "default", ~id = s.nextNodeID, 0, 1, "freq", 300);

s.sendMsg('/n_set', ~id, "gate", 0);
```

Documentation of OSC messages the server can receive are detailed in a help file titled "Server Command Reference." Keep in mind it's almost always preferable to use Synth and other language-side classes that represent server-side objects, rather than manually writing and sending OSC messages. The primary goal of this section is simply to demonstrate the usefulness and uniformity of the OSC protocol.

7.3.3 SENDING OSC FROM THE SERVER TO THE LANGUAGE

Sending data from the server to the language involves a little more work but is considerably more useful. For example, we might want to know the current value of a UGen on the server, so that we can incorporate that value into a new Synth. The **SendReply** UGen is designed to do exactly this. It sends an OSC message to the language when it receives a trigger. To continuously capture values from a UGen, the trigger source can be a periodic impulse generator, and its frequency determines the "framerate" at which OSC messages are generated (a frequency between 10–30 Hz is sensible). The trigger signal, SendReply, and the UGen being captured should all be running at the same rate (audio or control). In the UGen function at the top of Code Example 7.14, a low-frequency noise generator drives the center frequency of a band-pass filter, and SendReply transmits this value back to the language twenty times per second. Below, a language-side OSCdef listens for messages with the appropriate address. When this code is evaluated, a stream of data will appear in the post window. The raw message generated by SendReply is verbose; it contains the address, the node ID, a reply ID (–1 if unspecified), and finally, the signal value of the UGen. In most cases, only the UGen value is relevant, which we can access by returning the message item at index three. Once the Synth and OSCdef are created, we have a "live" language-side value that follows the noise generator, which can be freely incorporated into other processes. A third block of code plays a short sine tone whose frequency mirrors the real-time filter frequency.

CODE EXAMPLE 7.14: USING `SendReply` AND `OSCdef` TO SEND A SERVER-SIDE VALUE TO THE LANGUAGE, WHICH IS THEN INCORPORATED INTO A DIFFERENT SOUND.

```
(
{
    var sig, freq, trig;
    trig = Impulse.kr(20);
    freq = LFDNoise3.kr(0.2).exprange(200, 1600);
    SendReply.kr(trig, '/freq', freq);
    sig = PinkNoise.ar(1 ! 2);
    sig = BPF.ar(sig, freq, 0.02, 4);
}.play;
)

(
OSCdef(\getfreq, {
    arg msg;
    ~freq = msg[3].postln;
}, '/freq');
)

(
{// evaluate repeatedly
    var sig = SinOsc.ar(~freq * [0, 0.2].midiratio);
    sig = sig * Env.perc.kr(2) * 0.2;
}.play;
)

(
s.freeAll; // cleanup
OSCdef.freeAll;
)
```

7.3.4 EXCHANGING OSC WITH OTHER APPLICATIONS

Beyond SC, many software platforms are either natively OSC-compliant or augmentable with external OSC libraries. Other audio languages such as Max, Pd, Kyma, ChucK, and Csound have built-in OSC capabilities, and OSC libraries exist for general-purpose languages such as C++, Java, and Python. Some DAWs can also be manipulated with OSC. Mobile apps like TouchOSC and Lemur transform a smartphone or tablet into a customizable multitouch controller. Though the design specifics for these platforms vary, general OSC principles remain the same. In the TouchOSC Mk1 editor software, for example, the OSC address and numerical data associated with a graphical widget appears in the left-hand column when it is selected (see Figure 7.1). In this example, we have a knob that sends values between 0 and 1, which arrive with the '/1/rotary1' OSC address.

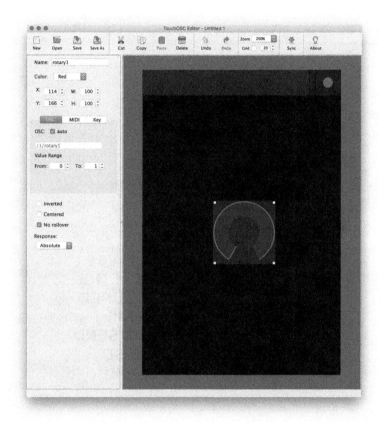

FIGURE 7.1 A screenshot of the TouchOSC Mk1 Editor software, displaying a graphical knob that transmits values that have the address "/1/rotary1."

To send OSC to SC from TouchOSC on a mobile device, it should be on the same local network as your computer and needs the IP address and port of your computer, which it considers to be its "host" device. This information can be configured in the OSC settings page of the mobile TouchOSC app, pictured in Figure 7.2 (note that the self-referential IP address "127.0.0.1" cannot be used here, since we are dealing with two separate devices). The final step is to create an OSCdef to receive the data, shown in Code Example 7.15, after which data should appear in the post window when interacting with the TouchOSC interface. To send OSC data from SC to TouchOSC, we create an instance of NetAddr that represents the mobile device running TouchOSC, and send it a message, for example, one that randomly moves the knob. If OSC data doesn't appear, **OSCFunc.trace(true)** can be used as a debugging tool that prints all incoming OSC messages. Accidentally mistyping the OSC address or IP address is a somewhat common source of problems that may likely cause OSC transmission to fail.

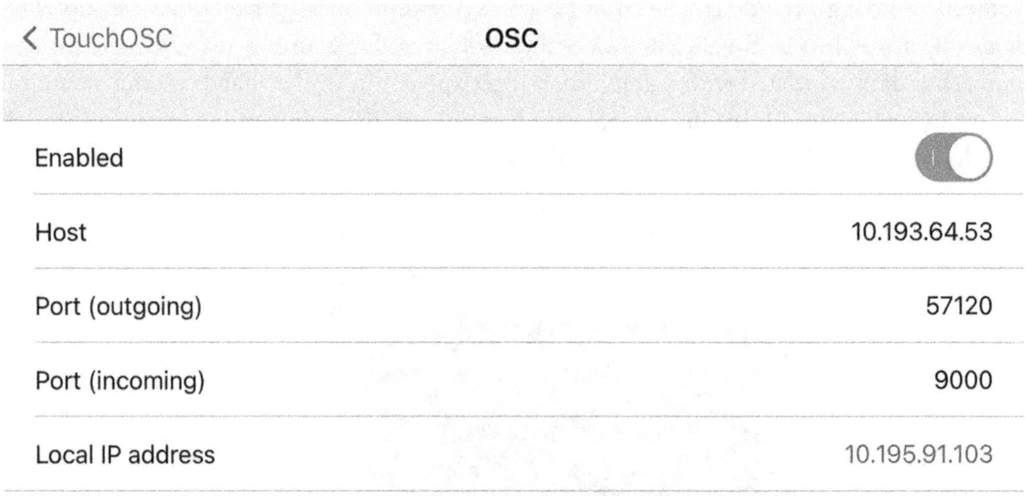

‹ TouchOSC	OSC
Enabled	⬤
Host	10.193.64.53
Port (outgoing)	57120
Port (incoming)	9000
Local IP address	10.195.91.103

FIGURE 7.2 OSC configuration settings in the TouchOSC Mk1 mobile app.

CODE EXAMPLE 7.15: AN OSCDEF THAT RECEIVES AND PRINTS DATA FROM THE GRAPHICAL KNOB PICTURED IN FIGURE 7.1, AND A PAIR OF EXPRESSIONS THAT SEND A MESSAGE FROM THE SC LANGUAGE TO TOUCHOSC.

```
(
OSCdef(\fromTouchOSC, { |msg|
    "data received: ".post;
    msg[1].postln;
}, '/1/rotary1');
)

~touchOSC = NetAddr("10.195.91.103", 9000);

~touchOSC.sendMsg('/1/rotary1', rrand(0.0, 1.0));
```

7.3.5 SENDING OSC TO ANOTHER COMPUTER RUNNING SC

Sending OSC from one instance of the SC language to another is similar to previous examples and involves the same general principles: both computers should be on the same local network, and the sending computer must know the IP address and port of the receiving computer. The receiver should create an appropriate OSCdef, and the sender should create an appropriate NetAddr and use **sendMsg** to transmit messages. The receiver can create as many OSCdefs as needed to accommodate a larger collection of addresses and data, or include conditional logic in an OSCdef in order to create different logical branches. Data "sanitization" may be appropriate in some cases; in Code Example 7.16, the receiving device uses conditional logic and **clip** to avoid bad values.

CODE EXAMPLE 7.16: A SIMPLE STRUCTURE FOR SENDING OSC MESSAGES FROM THE LANGUAGE TO ANOTHER INSTANCE OF THE SC LANGUAGE RUNNING ON A DIFFERENT COMPUTER.

```
(
// On the receiving computer:
OSCdef (\receiver, { |msg|
    var freq;
    if(msg[1].isNumber, {
        freq = msg[1].clip(20,20000);
        {
            var sig = SinOsc.ar(freq) * 0.2 ! 2;
            sig = sig * XLine.kr(1, 0.0001, 0.25, doneAction:2);
        }.play(fadeTime:0);
    });
}, '/makeTone');
)

// On the sending computer:
~sc = NetAddr("192.168.1.15", 57120); // local IP/port of receiver

~sc.sendMsg('/makeTone', 500);
```

Though it's possible to send OSC data from the language to an audio server running on a separate computer, this may not necessarily be the simplest option, for reasons explained in Section 7.3.2. From a practical perspective, you may find that sending data from language to language is a more straightforward option (albeit less direct), in which the receiving computer creates Synths and other server-related actions within the function of an OSCdef. For the interested reader, information on sending OSC directly to a remote audio server can be found in a pair of guide files in the help documentation, titled "Server Guide" and "Multi-client Setups."

7.4 Other Options for External Control

MIDI and OSC are commonly used and cover a lot of ground, but these protocols are not the only options for external device communication. This section briefly details serial communication and the HID specification, which provide two additional options. Relative to MIDI/OSC, these options are encountered less often, and may not feel as user-friendly. However, they are essential when using certain types of control interfaces.

7.4.1 SERIAL COMMUNICATION

The **SerialPort** class provides an interface for communicating with certain types of devices connected to a USB port on your computer. Serial port communication can be useful for reading sensor data from microcontrollers and prototyping kits, such as Arduino and Raspberry Pi. In these types of projects, the workflow involves programming your microcontroller to output the desired data, and specifying a baudrate, that is, the rate at which data is transferred. A baudrate of 9,600 bits per second is common, but other options exist. The Arduino code in Figure 7.3 reads and digitizes the value from its 0th analog input and writes it to the serial port 9,600 times per second. The "a" character is used as a delimiter to mark the end of one number and the beginning of the next.

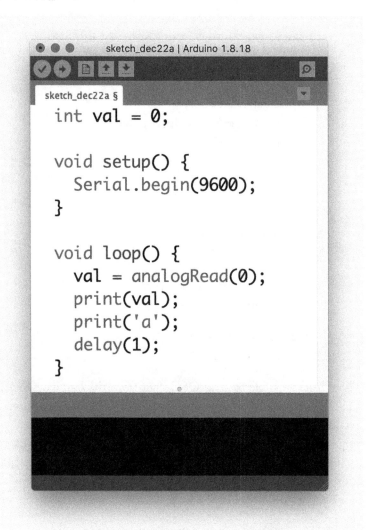

FIGURE 7.3 A simple Arduino program that writes analog input values to its serial output port.

A random segment of the data stream resulting from the Arduino code in Figure 7.3 will look something like this:

```
...729a791a791a792a793a792a...
```

Once your controller is connected to your computer's USB port, you can evaluate **SerialPort.devices** to print an array of strings that represent available serial port devices. Using this information, the next step is to create an instance of SerialPort that connects to the appropriate device, by providing the name and baudrate. Identifying the correct device name may involve some trial-and-error if multiple devices are available:

```
~port = SerialPort.new("/dev/tty.usbmodem14201", 9600);
```

The final step, shown in Code Example 7.17, is to build a looping routine that retrieves data from the serial port by repeatedly calling **read**, and storing the returned value in a global variable. The details may involve some experimentation, depending on how the transmitted data is formatted. For example, when an Arduino sends a number to the serial port, it writes the data as ASCII values that represent each character in sequence. So, if the Arduino sends a value of 729, it arrives as the integers 55, 50, and 57, which are the ASCII identifiers for the characters "7," "2," and "9." In each routine loop, we read the next value from the serial port and convert it to the symbol it represents, and then we perform a conditional branch based on whether it is a number or the letter "a." If it's a number, we add the number to an array. If it's the letter "a," we convert the character array to an integer and empty the array. While the routine plays, **~val** is repeatedly updated with the latest value from the USB port, which can be used elsewhere in your code. Interestingly, we have a looping routine with no wait time, yet SC does not crash when it runs. This is because **read** pauses the routine thread while waiting for the Arduino to send its next value. Because the Arduino waits for one millisecond between sending successive values (see Figure 7.3), this wait time is effectively transferred into the routine.

CODE EXAMPLE 7.17: SC CODE THAT READS DATA FROM THE USB PORT AND CONVERTS IT INTO USEABLE DATA. NOTE THAT THE DOLLAR SIGN DESIGNATES A CHARACTER (AN INSTANCE OF THE Char CLASS).

```
(
// assumes ~port is a valid instance of SerialPort
var ascii = 0, chars = [];
r = Routine({
    loop{
        ascii = ~port.read.asAscii;
        if(ascii.isDecDigit) {chars = chars.add(ascii)};
        if(ascii == $a) {
            ~val = chars.collect({ |n| n.digit}).convertDigits;
            chars = [];
        };
    };
}).play;
)
```

7.4.2 HUMAN INTERFACE DEVICES

The Human Interface Device (HID) specification exists to standardize and simplify communication between computers and various types of peripheral devices. Common HIDs include game controllers, joysticks, and computer keyboards/mice, but numerous others exist. A guide file titled "Working with HID" details its implementation and related classes. Notably, at the time of writing this chapter, HID functionality is not yet fully implemented on Windows. Other cross-platform discrepancies and permission issues may also arise (on macOS, for instance, you may need to be logged in as a root-level user and/or adjust access permissions in your security and privacy settings). Despite being a bit unwieldy compared to MIDI/OSC, HID is an essential tool for interaction between SC and certain control devices.

Communication with an HID begins by finding and posting information about available devices, which is done by evaluating the following two lines:

```
(
HID.findAvailable;
HID.postAvailable;
)
```

If, for example, you have an external mouse connected to your computer, information about that device should appear, and may look something like this:

```
9:      Usage name and page: Keyboard, GenericDesktop
        Vendor name:
        Product name: HID Gaming Mouse
        Vendor and product ID: 7119, 2232
        Path: USB_1bcf_08b8_14200000
        Serial Number:
        Releasenumber and interfaceNumber: 256, -1
```

A connection to an HID can be established using **open**, and specifying the device's Vendor ID and Product ID:

```
~device = HID.open(7119, 2232);
```

Keep in mind your device may cease its normal functions while this connection remains open! A connection can be closed with the **close** method, or by using the class method **closeAll**:

```
~device.close;

HID.closeAll;
```

An HID encompasses some number of HID elements, which represent individual aspects of the device, such as the state of a button, or the horizontal position of a joystick. Once a connection has been opened, the following statement will print a line-by-line list of all the device's elements:

```
~device.elements.do({ |n| n.postln});\
```

For instance, a gaming mouse with several different buttons may print something like this:

```
a HIDElement(0: type: 2, usage: 9, 1)

a HIDElement(1: type: 2, usage: 9, 2)

a HIDElement(2: type: 2, usage: 9, 3)

a HIDElement(3: type: 2, usage: 9, 4)

...etc...
```

Figuring out which elements correspond to which features may involve some trial-and-error. The process begins by creating an **HIDdef**, much like creating a MIDIdef/OSCdef. An HIDdef's action function expects a relatively large argument list, but the first two values (the normalized value and raw value of the element) are usually the most relevant. An integer, which follows the function as the third argument for HIDdef, determines the element to which the HIDdef is listening. This message-filtering behavior is essentially the same as getting the first MIDIdef in Code Example 7.2 to respond only to the mod wheel.

CODE EXAMPLE 7.18: AN HIDdef THAT PRINTS THE NORMALIZED AND RAW VALUES OF ELEMENT ZERO OF A CONNECTED DEVICE.

```
(
HIDdef.element(\getElem0, { |val, raw|
    [val, raw].postln;
}, elID: 0 // only respond to element 0
);
)
```

Once an HID element has been identified, the HIDdef function can be dynamically changed and re-evaluated to accommodate the needs of a particular project. Like MIDIdef and OSCdef, an HIDdef can be destroyed with **free**, or all HIDdef objects can be collectively destroyed with **HIDdef.freeAll**.

Notes

1 For Linux users, additional steps are required to connect an instance of MIDIOut to a target destination, because of how MIDI is handled on this operating system. Detailed information is available in the MIDIOut help file, under a section titled "Linux specific: Connecting and disconnecting

ports." This section of the help file recommends reliance on **MIDIOut.newByName** for maximizing cross-platform compatibility.

2. Matthew J. Wright and Adrian Freed, "Open SoundControl: A New Protocol for Communicating with Sound Synthesizers," in *Proceedings of the 1997 International Computer Music Conference*, Proceedings of the International Computer Music Association (San Francisco: International Computer Music Association, 1997).

CHAPTER 8

GRAPHICAL USER INTERFACES

8.1 Overview

A Graphical User Interface (GUI) refers to an arrangement of interactive objects, like knobs and sliders, that provides a system for controlling a computer program and/or displaying information about its state. Because SC is a dynamically interpreted language that involves real-time code evaluation, a GUI may not always be necessary, and may even be a hindrance in some cases. In other situations, building a GUI can be well worth the effort. If you are reverse-engineering your favorite hardware/software synthesizer, emulating an analog device, sending your work to a collaborator who has minimal programming experience, or if you simply want to conceal your scary-looking code, a well-designed GUI can help.

Older versions of SC featured a messy GUI "redirect" system that relied on platform-specific GUI classes that were rife with cross-platform pitfalls. Since then, the SC development community has unified the GUI system, which now uses Qt software on all supported operating systems, resulting in more simplicity and uniformity.

8.2 Basic GUI Principles

8.2.1 WINDOWS

A GUI begins with a new **Window**, a class that provides a rectangular space on which other elements can be placed. A newly created window is invisible by default, but can be made visible by calling **front** on the instance:

```
Window.new().front;
```

On creation, a new window accepts several arguments, shown in Code Example 8.1. The first argument is a string that appears in the window's title bar. The second, **bounds**, is an instance of **Rect** (short for rectangle) that determines the size and position of the window relative to your computer's screen. A new Rect involves four integers: the first two determine the horizontal/vertical pixel distance from the bottom-left corner of your screen, and the second two integers determine pixel width/height. Two additional Booleans determine whether a window can be resized and/or moved. Setting these to false prevents the user from manipulating the window with the mouse, which is useful when the window is meant to remain in place. Experimenting with these arguments (especially the bounds) is a great way to understand how they work. A window can be destroyed with **close**, and multiple windows can be closed with **Window.closeAll**.

CODE EXAMPLE 8.1: CREATION OF A NEW WINDOW WITH CUSTOM ARGUMENTS.

```
(
w = Window(
    name: "Hello World!",
    bounds: Rect(500, 400, 300, 400),
    resizable: false,
    border: false
).front;
)

w.close;
```

The class method **screenBounds** returns a Rect corresponding to the size of your computer screen. By accessing certain attributes of this Rect, a window can be made to appear in a consistent location, irrespective of screen size. The instance method **alwaysOnTop** can be set to a Boolean that determines whether the window will remain above other windows, regardless of the window that currently has focus. Making this attribute true keeps the window visible while working in the IDE, which can be desirable during GUI development to avoid having to click back and forth between windows. Code Example 8.2 demonstrates the use of these two methods.

CODE EXAMPLE 8.2: CREATION OF A CENTERED WINDOW THAT ALWAYS REMAINS ON TOP OF OTHER WINDOWS.

```
(
w = Window(
    "A Centered Window",
    Rect(
        Window.screenBounds.width / 2 - 150,
        Window.screenBounds.height / 2 - 200,
        300,
        400
    )
)
.alwaysOnTop_(true)
.front;
)
```

8.2.2 VIEWS

View is the parent class of most recognizable/useful GUI classes, such as sliders, buttons, and knobs, and it's also the term used to describe GUI objects in general. Table 8.1 provides a descriptive list of commonly used subclasses. The View class defines core methods and behaviors, which are inherited by its subclasses, establishing a level of behavioral consistency across the GUI library. At minimum, a new view requires a parent view, that is, the view on which it will reside, and a Rect that determines its bounds, relative to its parent. Unlike windows, which are positioned from the bottom-left corner of your screen, a view's coordinates are measured from the top-left corner of its parent view. If two views are placed on a window such that their bounds intersect, the view created second will be rendered on top of the first, partially obscuring it (this may or may not be desirable, depending on context). Once a view is created, it can be permanently destroyed with **remove**. Code Example 8.3 demonstrates these techniques by placing a slider on a parent window. Note that the rectangular space on the body of a window is itself a type of view (an instance of **TopView**, accessible by calling the **view** method on the window). In the Qt GUI system, the distinction between a window and its TopView is minimal, and both are valid parents.

CODE EXAMPLE 8.3: PLACEMENT OF A SLIDER ON A WINDOW.

```
(
w = Window("A Simple Slider", Rect(500, 400, 300, 400))
.alwaysOnTop_(true).front;
x = Slider(w, Rect(40, 40, 40, 320));
)

x.remove; // remove the slider

w.close; // close the window
```

TABLE 8.1 A list of commonly used View classes and their descriptions.

Class Name	Description
Button	multi-state button
Knob	rotary controller
ListView	display list of items
MultiSliderView	array of multiple sliders
NumberBox	modifiable field for numerical values
PopUpMenu	drop-down menu for selectable items
RangeSlider	slider with extendable handle on either end
Slider	linear controller
Slider2D	two-dimensional slider
StaticText	non-editable text display
TextField	simple editable text display
TextView	editable, formattable, multi-line text display

8.2.3 LAYOUT MANAGEMENT

Without tools for managing the placement and organization of views, building a GUI in SC quickly devolves into tedious pixel-hunting. Layout classes, discussed in the "Layout Management" guide file, help avoid this drudgery by automatically making smart choices about how child views should be placed on a parent. These tools are **HLayout** and **VLayout**, which organize views in horizontal and vertical lines, **GridLayout**, which organizes views in a two-dimensional arrangement of rows and columns, and **StackLayout**, which overlays multiple views in the same space while allowing the user to specify the topmost element. Code Example 8.4 demonstrates the use of these layout tools and highlights the fact that we can "nest" a layout class within another to create more complex arrangements. Notably, when using these layout classes to organize views, we don't have to specify the parent view (because the **layout** method is already attached to the parent), nor do we have to specify bounds, which are inferred based on the type of view and the available space on the parent. These layout classes enlarge a window if it's too small to accommodate its child views, prevent a window from becoming too small to render its views, and dynamically adjust views' bounds if the parent window is resized. There are some situations (featured in some Companion Code files for this chapter), where a high degree of pixel precision is needed, in which case we may decide not to use layout classes and instead manually specify bounds information. When pixel precision is not an issue, however, we can offload the pixel-hunting onto these layout tools, which saves quite a bit of time.

CODE EXAMPLE 8.4: USE OF LAYOUT MANAGEMENT CLASSES TO AUTOMATE THE PLACEMENT OF VIEWS ON A WINDOW.

```
(
Window("Layout Management", Rect(100, 100, 250, 500)).front
.layout_(
    VLayout(
        HLayout(Knob(), Knob(), Knob(), Knob()),
        HLayout(Slider(), Slider(), Slider(), Slider()),
        Slider2D(),
        Button()
    )
);
)
```

8.2.4 GETTING AND SETTING GUI ATTRIBUTES

Getting and setting attributes, introduced in Chapter 1, is one of the primary ways we design and interact with GUIs during development. Views are defined by their attributes, accessible via method calls, which determine their appearances and behaviors. Some attributes are common to all views, while others are specific to individual classes. For instance, every view has a **visible** attribute, which determines whether it will be displayed, and an **enabled** attribute, which determines whether the user can interact with the view. Most views also have a **background** attribute, which determines a background color. As a reminder: to "get" an attribute, we call the method, and the attribute's value is returned. To "set" an attribute to a new value, we can assign the value using an equals symbol or the underscore syntax, both demonstrated in Code Example 8.5. Recall that the underscore setter is advantageous because it returns the receiver and lets us chain setter commands back-to-back in a single expression. Note that the underscore syntax and setter-chaining have already appeared in Code Example 8.2.

CODE EXAMPLE 8.5: GETTING AND SETTING ATTRIBUTES OF A VIEW.

```
(
~slider = Slider();
w = Window("A Slider", Rect(500, 400, 100, 400)).front
.alwaysOnTop_(true)
.layout_(HLayout(~slider));
)

~slider.visible; // get attribute (returns "true")

~slider.visible = false; // set attribute (make invisible)

// set multiple attributes (visible, non-interactable, and yellow)
~slider.visible_(true).enabled_(false).background_(Color(1, 1, 0));
```

As a side note, color is expressed using the **Color** class, which encapsulates four floats between 0 and 1. The first three are red, green, and blue amounts, and the fourth is a transparency value called **alpha**. The alpha value defaults to 1, which represents full opacity, while 0 represents full transparency.

TIP.RAND(); EXPRESSING COLOR

The **Color** class features a flexible variety of creation methods, detailed in its help file. In addition to a handful of convenience methods for common colors (e.g., **Color.red, Color.cyan**), color can also be specified as follows:

```
Color.new255(250, 160, 20); // RGB integers between 0-255

Color.fromHexString("BF72C4"); // hexidecimal string

Color.hsv(0.1, 0.6, 0.9); // hue, saturation & value
```

8.2.5 VALUES AND ACTIONS

GUIs are not just meant to look nice, they're designed to perform specific actions in response to input from the user. For example, Code Example 8.6 demonstrates a simple approach to controlling the amplitude of a signal using a slider. Here, the methods **value**, **action**, and **valueAction** come into play, which are directly linked to a view's state and behavior.

The **value** attribute stores the state of a view. In the case of a slider or knob, its value is a float between 0 and 1. The value of a button is an integer corresponding to the index of its current state (for instance, a toggle button has two states, with indices 0 and 1). A view's **action** attribute references a function that is evaluated in response to user interaction. An argument declared inside an action function represents the view instance itself, thus enabling access to other view attributes inside the function (this is essential, for instance, when we want a toggle button to perform one of two actions based on its value).

When the user interacts with a slider by clicking and dragging the mouse, its value attribute is updated, and the action is performed for each value change. We can also simulate user interaction by calling the **valueAction** setter, which updates the value and performs the action. By contrast, if we use the **value** method as a setter, the view's value is updated, but the action is not performed. This approach is useful for "silently" updating a view's state.

CODE EXAMPLE 8.6: USING A SLIDER AND BUTTON TO CONTROL THE AMPLITUDE OF A SOUND.

```
s.boot;

(
~amp = 0.3;
~synth = { |amp, on = 0|
    var sig = LFTri.ar([200, 201], mul: 0.1);
    sig = sig * amp.lag(0.1) * on;
}.play(args: [amp: ~amp]);

~slider = Slider()
.value_(~amp)
.action_({ |v|
    ~amp = v.value;
    ~synth.set(\amp, ~amp);
});

~button = Button()
.states_([
    ["OFF", Color.gray(0.2), Color.gray(0.8)],
    ["ON", Color.gray(0.8), Color.green(0.7)]
])
.action_({ |btn| ~synth.set(\on, btn.value) });
```

```
Window("Amplitude Control", Rect(500, 400, 100, 400))
.layout_(VLayout(~slider, ~button))
.onClose_({~synth.release(0.1)})
.alwaysOnTop_(true)
.front;
)

~slider.valueAction_(rrand(0.0, 1.0)); // simulate random user
interaction
```

The code in Code Example 8.6 has a few noteworthy features. Our button has two states, defined by setting the **states** attribute equal to an array containing one internal array for each state. Each internal array contains three items: a string to be displayed, the string color, and the background color. The **lag** method is applied to the amplitude argument, which wraps the argument in a **Lag** UGen, whose general purpose is to smooth out discontinuous changes to a signal over a time interval (in this case, a tenth of a second). Without lagging, any large, instantaneous, or fast changes to the slider may result in audible pops or "zipper" noise (if you remove the lag, re-evaluate, and rapidly move the slider with the mouse, you'll hear a distinct "roughness" in the sound). Finally, the **onClose** attribute stores a function to be evaluated when the window closes, useful for ensuring sound does not continue after the window disappears.

Although all views understand **value**, not all views respond to this method in a meaningful or useful way. Some classes rely on one or more alternative method calls. For instance, text-oriented objects such as **StaticText** and **TextView** consider their text to be their "value," which they return in response to **string**. Likewise, **Slider2D** returns its values as two independent coordinates through the methods **x** and **y**.

Companion Code 8.1 combines several of the techniques presented thus far and expands upon Table 8.1 by providing an interactive tour of several different types of views.

8.2.6 RANGE-MAPPING

A numerical range between 0 and 1 is acceptable for signal amplitude but unsuitable for frequency, MIDI data, decibels, and many other parameters. Even when the default range is suitable, the inherent linear behavior of sliders and knobs may not be. Suppose we want our slider to control frequency instead of amplitude. To produce a sensible frequency range, one option is to apply a range-mapping method such as **linexp** before the value is passed to a signal algorithm. Range-mapping can alternatively be handled with **ControlSpec**, a class designed to map values back and forth between 0 and 1, and another custom range, using the methods **map** and **unmap**. A ControlSpec requires a minimum value, a maximum value, and a warp value, which collectively determine its range and curvature. The warp value may be a symbol (e.g., \lin, \exp), or an integer (similar to Env curve values). Code Example 8.7 demonstrates the use of ControlSpec.

CODE EXAMPLE 8.7: USE OF CONTROLSPEC TO MAP SLIDER VALUES TO AN APPROPRIATE FREQUENCY RANGE.

```
(
~freqspec = ControlSpec(100, 2000, \exp);
~freq = ~freqspec.map(0.2);
~synth = { |freq, on = 0|
    var sig = LFTri.ar(freq.lag(0.1) + [0, 1], mul: 0.05);
    sig = sig * on;
}.play(args: [freq: ~freq]);

~slider = Slider()
.value_(0.2)
.action_({ |v|
    ~freq = ~freqspec.map(v.value);
    ~synth.set(\freq, ~freq);
});

~button = Button()
.states_([
    ["OFF", Color.gray(0.2), Color.gray(0.8)],
    ["ON", Color.gray(0.8), Color.green(0.7)]
])
.action_({ |btn| ~synth.set(\on, btn.value) });

Window("Frequency Control", Rect(500, 400, 100, 400))
.layout_(VLayout(~slider, ~button))
.onClose_({~synth.release(0.1)})
.front;
)
```

Several pre-built ControlSpecs are available, and can be viewed with:

```
ControlSpec.specs.keys;
```

And, a ControlSpec can be created by calling **asSpec** on the relevant symbol:

```
~freqspec = \freq.asSpec; // -> a ControlSpec suitable for frequency
```

As an exercise to help you understand these fundamental techniques more deeply, consider combining the frequency and amplitude GUIs in Code Examples 8.5 and 8.6 into a single GUI with a pair of sliders and an on/off button.

8.3 Intermediate GUI Techniques

8.3.1 KEYBOARD AND MOUSE INTERACTION

On a basic level, sliders, knobs, and other "moveable" views are pre-programmed to respond to input from your mouse and keyboard. Clicking and dragging has a predictable response, as does pressing the arrow keys on your keyboard. A few other built-in keyboard actions exist as well: pressing [r] will randomize a slider or knob, [c] will center it, and [n] and [x] will set the view to its mi*n*imum/ma*x*imum. Pressing [tab] cycles focus through focusable views, and pressing [spacebar] when a button is in focus has the same effect as clicking it. Still, manipulating GUIs with only these elementary modes can be a limiting experience. Notably, the mouse can only interact with one view at a time. Catching and processing a greater variety of keyboard and mouse input can enhance the user experience.

Table 8.2 lists some common methods that register actions to be performed in response to keyboard/mouse input. These actions exist alongside a view's normal action function and are defined by setting the attribute to a function. In contrast to a normal action, mouse/keyboard functions accept a longer list of arguments. Keyboard functions are passed arguments that represent:

1. the view instance;
2. the character that was pressed;
3. information on which modifier keys were held;
4. a unicode integer;
5. a hardware-dependent keycode; and
6. a key integer defined by the Qt framework.

The sixth argument is described in the SC help documents as being the "most reliable way to check which key was pressed." Mouse functions accept arguments that represent some combination of the following:

1. the view instance;
2. the horizontal pixel position of the mouse, relative to the view;
3. the vertical pixel position of the mouse, relative to the view;
4. information on which modifier keys were held;
5. an integer corresponding to the mouse button that was pressed; and
6. a click count within your system's double-click timing window.

One of the best ways to understand these functions and their arguments is to create an empty view that posts argument values, as demonstrated in Code Example 8.8.

TABLE 8.2 A descriptive list of methods for defining keyboard/mouse actions.

Method	Description
`.mouseDownAction`	evaluated when a mouse button is clicked on the view
`.mouseUpAction`	evaluated when a mouse button is released on the view
`.mouseMoveAction`	evaluated when the mouse moves after clicking/holding on the view
`.mouseOverAction`	evaluated when the mouse moves over the view, regardless of clicks (requires `acceptsMouseOver` to be true)
`.mouseEnterAction`	evaluated when the mouse moves into the view's bounds
`.mouseLeaveAction`	evaluated when the mouse moves out of the view's bounds
`.keyDownAction`	evaluated when the view is in focus and a key is pressed
`.keyUpAction`	evaluated when the view is in focus and a key is released

CODE EXAMPLE 8.8: A VIEW THAT POSTS INFORMATION ABOUT KEY PRESSES AND MOUSE CLICKS.

```
(
w = Window("Keyboard and Mouse Data").front
.layout_(VLayout(
    StaticText()
    .align_(\center)
    .string_("press keys/click the mouse")
));

w.view.keyDownAction_({ |view, char, mod, uni, keycode, key|
    postln("character: " ++ char);
    postln("modifiders: " ++ mod);
    postln("unicode: " ++ uni);
    postln("keycode: " ++ keycode);
    postln("key: " ++ key);
    "".postln;
});

w.view.mouseDownAction_({ |view, x, y, mod, button, count|
    postln("x-position: " ++ x);
    postln("y-position: " ++ y);
    postln("modifiers: " ++ mod);
    postln("button ID: " ++ button);
    postln("click count: " ++ count);
    "".postln;
});
)
```

As a practical example of incorporating keystrokes into a GUI, Companion Code 8.2 builds a virtual piano keyboard that can be played using the computer keyboard.

8.3.2 CONTROLLING GUI WITH MIDI/OSC

External devices that send MIDI or OSC data can be used to control a GUI. For the most part, the process is simple: the action function of a MIDI/OSC receiver should call the appropriate GUI commands. However, MIDIdef/OSCdef functions cannot directly interact with windows and views, because MIDIdef and OSCdef functions are considered to exist outside of the "main application context." This limitation can be overcome by enclosing problematic code in curly braces and applying the **defer** method, which passes the task of evaluation to the **AppClock**, a low-priority scheduler capable of interacting with GUIs. Code Example 8.9 demonstrates this technique by displaying incoming MIDI note numbers in a **NumberBox**. If the **defer** enclosure is removed, SC will produce an error when a note-on message arrives.

CODE EXAMPLE 8.9: DEFERRING A FUNCTION TO CONTROL A GUI WITH INCOMING MIDI MESSAGES.

```
(
MIDIIn.connectAll;

w = Window("MIDI Control").front
.layout_(VLayout(
    StaticText().align_(\center)
    .string_("press a key on your MIDI controller"),

    ~numbox = NumberBox().align_(\center)
    .enabled_(false)
    .font_(Font("Arial", 40));
));

MIDIdef.noteOn(\recv, { |vel, num| {~numbox.value_(num)}.defer });
)
```

Companion Code 8.3 reinforces these techniques by creating an interface that can dynamically "learn" MIDI inputs and assign their data to control specific GUI objects.

8.3.3 GUI AND CLOCKS

Some GUIs involve timing elements, such as a clock that shows elapsed time, or a button with a "cooldown" period that prevents multiple presses within a time window. Generally, these situations are addressable by playing a routine from within a view's action function. However, code scheduled on TempoClock or SystemClock is (like MIDIdef/OSCdef) considered to exist outside the main application context and must be deferred to the AppClock. Code Example 8.10 creates a button with a cooldown to demonstrate timing considerations. When clicked, the button disables itself and plays a routine that decrements a counter. Once the counter has reached a threshold, the button is re-enabled. As an alternative to wrapping GUI code in a deferred function, we can explicitly play the routine on the AppClock. Also, note that the **val** counter serves two purposes: it is part of the conditional logic that determines when to exit the **while** loop and simultaneously influences the button's background color during the cooldown period.

CODE EXAMPLE 8.10: USING APPCLOCK TO SCHEDULE A "COOLDOWN" PERIOD FOR A BUTTON.

```
(
~button = Button()
.states_([["Click Me", Color.white, Color(0.5, 0.5, 1)]])
.action_({ |btn|
	btn.enabled_(false);
	Routine({
		var val = 1;
		while({val > 0.5}, {
			btn.states_([
				[
					"Cooling down...",
					Color.white,
					Color(val, val, 1)
				]
			]);
			val = val - 0.01;
			0.05.wait;
		}
		);
		btn.enabled_(true);
		btn.states_([
			[
				"Click Me",
				Color.white,
				Color(val, val, 1)
			]
		]);
	}).play(AppClock);
});
w = Window("Cooldown Button", Rect(100, 100, 300, 75)).front
.layout_(VLayout(~button));
)
```

▶ Companion Code 8.4 reinforces these timing techniques by creating a simple stopwatch.

8.4 Custom Graphics

SC supports the creation of simple custom graphics, both static and animated. Although a project's needs are often met by the core collection of built-in GUI objects, it may be desirable or practical to add custom graphical features to a GUI in order to add emphasis, mimic the design of another interface, or create a more inviting appearance.

8.4.1 LINES, CURVES, SHAPES

UserView is a class that provides a blank rectangular canvas on which shapes can be drawn using the **Pen** class. Instructions for what to draw on a UserView are contained in a function, stored in the UserView's **drawFunc** attribute. Inside this function is the only place the Pen class can be used. Pen is an unusual class in that we don't create new instances of it. Instead, the class itself serves as a singular, imagined drawing implement, manipulated through method calls. Its methods manage things like setting colors, changing stroke width, and performing various drawing tasks.

When using Pen, there is a distinction between constructing a shape and rendering a shape. Construction specifies shape existence but does not actualize it. Rendering, executed by calling **fill**, **stroke**, **fillStroke**, or a related method, is what produces visible results. Code Example 8.11 demonstrates the use of UserView and Pen by creating some basic shapes. Note that because most Pen methods return the Pen class itself, methods can often be chained together into compound expressions. Methods that alter an aspect of Pen persist through the drawFunc until they are changed. For example, because **strokeColor** remains unchanged after being set for the first shape, the same color is used when **fillStroke** renders the third shape. Code Example 8.11 also indirectly introduces the **Point** class, frequently used in GUI contexts to represent a point on the Cartesian plane. A point can be created via **Point.new(x, y)**, or written more concisely using the syntax shortcut **x @ y**. For example, the **addArc** method constructs all or part of a circular arc and needs to know the x/y coordinates of the center pixel, which are specified as a Point. The help file for the Pen class documents a large collection of useful and interesting methods, accompanied by numerous code examples. Table 8.3 provides a partial list of Pen methods.

CODE EXAMPLE 8.11: CONSTRUCTING AND RENDERING BASIC SHAPES USING PEN, USERVIEW, AND DRAWFUNC.

```
(
u = UserView().background_(Color.gray(0.2))
.drawFunc_({
    Pen.width_(2) // set Pen characteristics
    .strokeColor_(Color(0.5, 0.9, 1))
    .addArc(100 @ 100, 50, 0, 2pi) // construct a circle
    .stroke; // render the circle (draw border, do not fill)

    Pen.fillColor_(Color(0.9, 1, 0.5)) // set Pen characteristics
    .addRect(Rect(230, 90, 120, 70)) // construct a rectangle
    .fill; // render the rectangle (fill, do not draw border)
```

```
    Pen.width_(6)
    .fillColor_(Color(0.2, 0.8, 0.2))
    .moveTo(90 @ 250) // construct a triangle, line-by-line
    .lineTo(210 @ 320).lineTo(90 @ 320).lineTo(90 @ 250)
    .fillStroke; // render the triangle (fill and draw border)

    Pen.width_(2)
    .strokeColor_(Color(1, 0.5, 0.2));
    8.do({
        Pen.line(280 @ 230, 300 @ 375);
        Pen.stroke;
        Pen.translate(10, -5); // 'translate' modifies what Pen
perceives as its origin by a horizontal/vertical shift. You can
imagine translation as shifting the paper underneath a pen.
    });
});
w = Window("Pen", Rect(100, 100, 450, 450))
.front.layout_(HLayout(u));
)
```

TABLE 8.3 A selection of Pen methods and their descriptions.

Pen Method	Description
`.width_(n)`	Set the line/curve thickness to **n** pixels.
`.strokeColor_(a Color)`	Set the color of drawn lines/curves.
`.fillColor_(a Color)`	Set the color used to fill closed paths.
`.moveTo(x @ y)`	Move the pen to the point **(x, y)**.
`.lineTo(x @ y)`	Construct a line from the current pen position to the point **(x, y)**. After this, the pen position is **(x, y)**.
`.line(x @ y, z @ w)`	Construct a line between two specified points. After this, the pen position is **(z, w)**.
`.addArc(x @ y, r, p, q)`	Construct a circular arc around the point **(x, y)** with radius **r** (pixels), starting at angle **p** and rotating by **q** (radians).
`.addRect(a Rect)`	Construct the specified rectangle.
`.stroke`	Render all lines, curves, arcs, etc. previously constructed.
`.fill`	Render the insides of paths. An unclosed path will be filled as if its endpoints were connected by a straight line.
`.fillStroke`	Combination of **stroke** and **fill**.

Companion Code 8.5 explores these techniques by creating a custom transport control interface (i.e., a bank of buttons with icons representing play, pause, stop, etc.).

8.4.2 ANIMATION

A UserView's drawFunc executes when the window is first made visible and can be re-executed by calling **refresh** on the UserView. If a drawFunc's elements are static (as they are in Code Example 8.11), refreshing has no discernible effect. But, if the drawFunc includes dynamic elements (such as randomness or some "live" element), refreshing will alter its appearance. A cleverly designed drawFunc can produce animated effects.

There is no need to construct and play a routine that repeatedly refreshes a UserView. Instead, this process can be handled internally by making a UserView's **animate** attribute true. When animation is enabled, a UserView automatically refreshes itself at a frequency determined by its **frameRate**, which defaults to 60 frames per second. This value cannot be made arbitrarily high and will be constrained by your computer screen's refresh rate. In many cases, a frame rate between 20 and 30 provides an acceptable sense of motion.

By default, when a UserView is refreshed, it will clear itself before redrawing. This behavior can be changed by setting **clearOnRefresh** to false. When false, the UserView will draw each frame on top of the previous frame, producing an accumulation effect. By drawing a semi-transparent rectangle over the entire UserView at the start of the drawFunc, we can produce a "visual delay" effect (see Code Example 8.12) in which moving elements appear to leave a trail behind them.

CODE EXAMPLE 8.12: AN ANIMATED "TUNNEL" EFFECT.

```
(
var win, uv, inc = 0;
win = Window("Tunnel Vision", Rect(100, 100, 400, 400)).front;

uv = UserView(win, win.view.bounds)
.background_(Color.black)
.drawFunc_({ |v|
    // draw transparency layer
    Pen.fillColor_(Color.gray(0, 0.05))
    .addRect(v.bounds)
    .fill;

    // green color gets brighter as arcs get "closer"
    Pen.width_(10)
    .strokeColor_(Color.green(inc.linlin(0, 320, 0.2, 1)))

    // draw random arc segments with increasing radii
    .addArc(
        200 @ 200,
        inc.lincurve(0, 320, 0, 320, 6),
        rrand(0, 2pi),
        rrand(pi/2, 2pi)
    ).stroke;
```

```
    inc = (inc + 5) % 320;         // counter increases by 5 each frame
                                   // and resets to zero when it reaches 320
})
.clearOnRefresh_(false)
.frameRate_(30)
.animate_(true);
)
```

Bear in mind that SC is not optimized for visuals in the same way it is optimized for audio. A looping process that calls screen updates may strain your computer's CPU, significantly so if it performs intensive calculations and/or has a relatively high frame rate. It's usually best to have a somewhat conservative attitude toward animated visuals in SC, rather than an enthusiastically decorative one! To conclude this chapter, Companion Code 8.6 creates an animated spectrum visualizer that responds to sound.

PART III
LARGE-SCALE PROJECTS

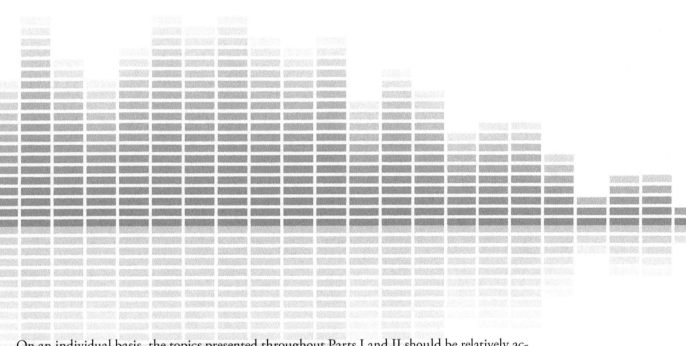

On an individual basis, the topics presented throughout Parts I and II should be relatively accessible and learnable for a newer SC user. With a little dedication and practice, you will soon start to feel increasingly comfortable creating and adding SynthDefs, working with buffers, playing Synths and Pbinds, and so on. Putting all of these elements together into a coherent and functional large-scale structure, however, often poses unique and unexpected challenges to the user, sometimes manifesting confounding problems with elusive solutions. The beauty (and perhaps, the curse) of SC is that it is a sandbox-style environment, with few limitations placed on the user, and no obvious guideposts that direct the user toward a particular workflow. These final chapters seek to address these challenges by introducing tips and strategies for building an organized performance structure from individual sounds and ideas, and examining specific forms these projects might take.

CHAPTER 9

CONSIDERATIONS FOR LARGE-SCALE PROJECTS

9.1 Overview

SC naturally invites a line-by-line or chunk-by-chunk approach to working with sound. If you're experimenting, sketching out new ideas, or just learning the basics, this type of interaction is advantageous, as it allows us to express ideas and hear the results with ease. Nearly all the previous examples in this book are split into separate chunks; for example, one line of code boots the server, a second block reads audio files into buffers, another block adds SynthDefs, and so on. However, as your ideas grow and mature, you may find yourself seeking to combine them into a more robust and unified structure that can be seamlessly rehearsed, modified, performed, and debugged. A scattered collection of code snippets can certainly get the job done, and in fact, there is a pair of keyboard shortcuts ([cmd]+[left square bracket] and [cmd]+[right square bracket]), which navigate up and down through parenthetically-enclosed code blocks. However, the chunk-by-chunk approach can also be unwieldy, time-consuming, and prone to errors. It's arguably preferable to write a program that can be activated with a single keystroke, and which includes intuitive mechanisms for adjustment, navigation, and resetting.

It should be noted that not all project types will rely on SC as a real-time performance vehicle. Some projects may only need its signal-generating and signal-processing capabilities. A common example is the use of SC as a "rendering farm" for sonic material (making use of real-time recording features discussed in Section 2.9.6), while using multitrack software for assembly, mixing, and fine-tuning. This is a perfectly sensible way to use SC, particularly for fixed-media compositions, but it forgoes SC's rich library of algorithmic tools for interactivity, indeterminacy, and other dynamic mechanisms.

All things considered, when tackling a big project in SC, it's a good idea to have a plan. This is not always possible (and experimentation is part of the fun), but even a partially formed plan can supply crucial guidance on the path forward. For example, how will the musical material progress through time? Will the music advance autonomously and deterministically, along a predetermined timeline? Or will a hardware interface (the spacebar, a MIDI controller) be used to advance from one moment to the next? Or is the order of musical actions indeterminate, with some device for dynamic interaction? Will a GUI be helpful to display information during performance? Plunging ahead into the code-void without answers to these types of questions is possible but risks the need for major changes and significant backtracking later.

In recognition of the many divergent paths a large-scale SC project might take, this chapter focuses on issues that are widely applicable to large-scale performance structures, regardless of finer details. Specifically, this chapter focuses on the importance of order of execution, which in this context means the sequence in which setup- and performance-related actions must be taken. This concept is relevant in all programming languages; when a program is compiled, an interpreter parses the code in the order it is written. Variables must be declared before they can be used, memory must be allocated before data can be stored there, and functions/routines must be defined before they can be executed. In SC, which exists as a client-server duo communicating via OSC, the order in which setup actions take place is perhaps even more important, and examples of pitfalls are plenty: a Buffer must be allocated before samples can be recorded into it, a SynthDef must be fully added before a corresponding Synth can be spawned, and of course, the audio server must be booted before any of this can happen.

9.2 waitForBoot

If one of our chief goals is to be able to run an arbitrarily complex sound-generating program with a single keystroke, then a good first step is to circumvent the inherently two-step process of (1) booting the server and (2) creating sound after booting is complete. Sound-generating code can only be called after the booting process has completely finished, and a direct attempt to bundle these two actions into a single chunk of code will fail (see Code Example 9.1), a bit like pressing the accelerator pedal in a car at the instant the ignition begins to turn, but before the engine is actually running.

CODE EXAMPLE 9.1: A FAILED ATTEMPT TO BOOT THE SERVER AND PLAY A SOUND IN ONE CODE EVALUATION.

```
s.quit; // quit first to properly demonstrate

(
s.boot;
{PinkNoise.ar(0.2 ! 2) * XLine.kr(1, 0.001, 2, doneAction: 2)}.play;
)
```

The essence of the problem is that the server cannot receive commands until booting is complete, which requires a variable amount of time, usually at least a second or two. The language, generally ignorant of the server's status, evaluates these two expressions with virtually no time between them. The **play** method, seeing that the server is not booted, posts a warning, but there is no inherent mechanism for delaying the second expression until the time is right. Instead, the pink noise function is simply not received by the server.

The **waitForBoot** method, demonstrated in Code Example 9.2, provides a solution. The method is applied to the server and given a function containing arbitrary code. This method will boot the server and evaluate its function when booting is complete.

> **CODE EXAMPLE 9.2:** USING `waitForBoot` TO BOOT THE SERVER AND PLAY A SOUND IN ONE CODE EVALUATION.
>
> ```
> s.quit; // quit first to properly demonstrate
>
> (
> s.waitForBoot({
>     {PinkNoise.ar(0.2 ! 2) * XLine.kr(1, 0.001, 2, doneAction: 2)}.play;
> });
> )
> ```

In practice, a waitForBoot function usually contains a combination of server-side setup code, such as creating Groups, adding SynthDefs, allocating Buffers, and instantiating signal-processing Synths.

9.3 Asynchronous Commands

Packing all your server-side code into a waitForBoot function is tempting, but this alone will not guarantee that your program will work correctly. Within a waitForBoot function, some code might rely on the completion of previous code, for example, the creation of a Synth is only possible if its corresponding SynthDef has already been built and added to the server. Like booting the server, building a SynthDef requires a variable amount of time that depends on the number of UGens in the SynthDef, and the complexity of their interconnections. Code Example 9.3 demonstrates an example of this problem.

> **CODE EXAMPLE 9.3:** A FAILURE TO CREATE A NEW SYNTH, RESULTING FROM THE FACT THAT ITS CORRESPONDING SYNTHDEF IS NOT YET FULLY ADDED TO THE SERVER WHEN SYNTH CREATION IS ATTEMPTED.
>
> ```
> s.quit; // quit first to properly demonstrate
>
> (
> s.waitForBoot({
>     SynthDef(\tone_000, {
>         var sig = SinOsc.ar([350, 353], mul: 0.2);
>         sig = sig * XLine.kr(1, 0.0001, 2, doneAction: 2);
>         Out.ar(0, sig);
>     }).add;
>
>     Synth(\tone_000);
> });
> )
> ```

When the language tries to create the Synth, the server has not yet finished building the SynthDef, and produces a "SynthDef not found" error. On second evaluation, the code in Code Example 9.3 will work properly, because enough time will have passed to allow the SynthDef-building process to finish. This issue can be a common source of confusion, resulting in code that always fails on the first try, but works fine on subsequent tries.

This example highlights the difference between synchronous and asynchronous commands, discussed in a guide file titled "Synchronous and Asynchronous Execution." In the world of digital audio, certain actions must occur with a high level of timing precision, such as processing and playing audio signals. Without sample-accurate timing, audio samples get dropped during calculation, producing crackles, pops, and other unacceptable glitches. These time-sensitive actions are referred to as "synchronous" in SC and receive the highest scheduling priority. Asynchronous actions, on the other hand, are those that require an indeterminate amount of time to complete, and which generally do not require precise timing or high scheduling priority, such as adding a SynthDef or allocating a Buffer.

The problem of waiting for the appropriate duration while asynchronous tasks are underway is solved with the **sync** method, demonstrated in Code Example 9.4. When the language encounters **s.sync**, it sends a message to the server, asking it to report back when all of its ongoing asynchronous commands are complete. When the server replies with this confirmation, the language then proceeds to evaluate code that occurs after the sync message. Note that although the SynthDef code remains the same in Code Example 9.4, its name has been changed so that the server interprets it as a brand new SynthDef that has not yet been added.

CODE EXAMPLE 9.4: USING sync TO ALLOW ASYNCHRONOUS TASKS TO COMPLETE BEFORE PROCEEDING.

```
s.quit; // quit first to properly demonstrate

(
s.waitForBoot({
    SynthDef(\tone_001, {
        var sig = SinOsc.ar([350, 353], mul: 0.2);
        sig = sig * XLine.kr(1, 0.0001, 2, doneAction: 2);
        Out.ar(0, sig);
    }).add;

    s.sync;

    Synth(\tone_001);
});
)
```

Because a sync message involves suspending and resuming code evaluation in the language, it can only be called from within a routine, or inside a method call (such as waitForBoot) that implicitly creates a routine. Thus, the code in Code Example 9.5 will fail, but will succeed if enclosed in a routine and played.

CODE EXAMPLE 9.5: A FAILURE PRODUCED BY CALLING sync OUTSIDE OF A ROUTINE.

```
(
// audio server assumed to be already booted
SynthDef(\tone_002, {
    var sig = SinOsc.ar([350, 353], mul: 0.2);
    sig = sig * XLine.kr(1, 0.0001, 2, doneAction: 2);
    Out.ar(0, sig);
}).add;

s.sync; // -> ERROR: yield was called outside of a Routine.

Synth(\tone_002);
)
```

Liberal usage of sync messages is generally harmless but does not provide any benefits. For example, if adding several SynthDefs to the server, there is no need to sync between each pair; a SynthDef is an independent entity, whose existence does not rely on the existence of other SynthDefs. Similarly, there's is no need to sync between a block of buffer allocations and a block of SynthDefs, since these two processes do not (or at least should not) depend on each other. Generally, a sync message is only necessary before running code that depends on the completion of a previous asynchronous server command.

9.4 Initialization and Cleanup Functions

The [cmd]+[period] shortcut is useful when composing, testing, and experimenting, and provides an essential "panic button." The downside of this keystroke is that it indiscriminately wipes out every Synth and Group on the server. This behavior can be annoying when working on a project that involves one or more signal-processing Synths, such as reverbs or delays. When the audio server is wiped with [cmd]+[period], these Synths must be re-instantiated before rehearsal or performance can resume. Without taking steps to automate this process, re-instantiation becomes laborious, and may require lots of scrolling up and down through your code. Consider the following example, in which we allocate a bus, create a source/reverb SynthDef pair, and instantiate a reverb Synth. After evaluating the setup code block, we can begin a "performance" by creating a source Synth and routing it to the bus (see Code Example 9.6). If we press [cmd]+[period] while the sound is playing, both Synths are destroyed, and a re-instantiation of only the source Synth will produce silence since it relies on the reverb as part of its output path. As a result, we must first navigate back to our setup code and re-evaluate it (or at least, re-instantiate the reverb Synth) to hear sound again. Though not a huge chore in this specific case, this back-and-forth becomes tedious in a more complex project.

> **CODE EXAMPLE 9.6: INITIALIZING THE SERVER WITH AN AUDIO BUS AND A PAIR OF SOURCE/REVERB SYNTHS.**
>
> ```
> s.quit; // quit first to properly demonstrate
>
> (
> s.newBusAllocators;
> ~bus = Bus.audio(s, 2);
>
> s.waitForBoot({
>     SynthDef(\source, { |out = 0|
>         var sig, env, freq, trig;
>         trig = Trig.kr(Dust.kr(4), 0.1);
>         env = EnvGen.kr(Env.perc(0.001, 0.08), trig);
>         freq = TExpRand.kr(200, 1500, trig);
>         sig = SinOsc.ar(freq ! 2, mul: 0.2);
>         sig = sig * env;
>         Out.ar(out, sig);
>     }).add;
>
>     SynthDef(\reverb, { |in = 0, mix = 0.2, out = 0|
>         var sig, fx;
>         sig = In.ar(in, 2);
>         fx = FreeVerb2.ar(sig[0], sig[1], 1, 0.85);
>         sig = sig.blend(fx, mix);
>         Out.ar(out, sig);
>     }).add;
>
>     s.sync;
>
>     ~reverb = Synth(\reverb, [in: ~bus]);
> });
> )
>
> Synth(\source, [out: ~bus, freq: exprand(200, 1500)]);
> ```

ServerBoot, **ServerTree**, and **ServerQuit** are classes that allow automation of server-related tasks. Each class is essentially a repository where specific action functions can be registered, and each class evaluates its registered actions when the audio server enters a particular state. ServerBoot evaluates registered actions when the server boots, ServerQuit does the same when the server quits, and ServerTree evaluates its actions when the node tree is reinitialized, that is, when all nodes are wiped via [cmd]+[period] or by evaluating **s.freeAll**. Actions are registered by encapsulating the desired code in a function, and **add**ing the function to the appropriate repository. Code Example 9.7 demonstrates a simple example of making SC say "good-bye" whenever the server quits.

CODE EXAMPLE 9.7: USE OF `ServerQuit` TO POST A GOOD-BYE MESSAGE WHEN THE SERVER QUITS.

```
(
~quitMessage = {
    " **************** ".postln;
    " *** good-bye! *** ".postln;
    " **************** ".postln;
};
ServerQuit.add(~quitMessage);
)

s.boot;

s.quit; // message appears in post window
```

A specific action can be removed from a repository with the **remove** method:

```
ServerQuit.remove(~quitMessage);
```

Or, all registered actions can be removed from a repository with **removeAll**:

```
ServerQuit.removeAll;
```

TIP.RAND(); RISKS OF REMOVING ALL ACTIONS FROM A SERVER ACTION REPOSITORY

Most of the time, calling **removeAll** on a repository class will not disrupt your workflow in a noticeable way. However, when SC is launched, these three repository classes may have one or more functions that are automatically attached to them. At the time of writing, ServerBoot includes automated actions that allow the spectrum analyzer (**FreqScope.new**) and Node proxies (discussed in Chapter 12) to function properly. If you evaluate **ServerBoot.removeAll** and reboot the server, you'll find that these objects no longer work correctly. If you ever need to reset one or more repositories to their default state(s), the simplest way to do so is to recompile the SC class library, which can be done with [cmd]+[shift]+[L]. Alternatively, you can avoid the use of removeAll and instead remove custom actions individually.

Care should be taken to avoid accidental double-registering of functions. If the code in Code Example 9.8 is evaluated multiple times, ServerTree will interpret **~treeMessage** as a new function on each evaluation, even though the code is identical. As a result, pressing

[cmd]+[period] will cause the message to be posted several times. For functions that only post text, duplicate registrations clog the post window, but don't do any real harm. However, if these functions contain audio-specific code, duplicate registrations can have all sorts of unexpected and undesirable effects. A safer approach is to remove all actions before re-evaluating/re-registering, as depicted in Code Example 9.9.

CODE EXAMPLE 9.8: CODE THAT INADVERTENTLY RE-REGISTERS A FUNCTION TO A REPOSITORY WHEN EVALUATED A SECOND TIME.

```
(
s.waitForBoot({
    ~treeMessage = {"Server tree cleared".postln};
    ServerTree.add(~treeMessage);
});
)

// press [cmd]+[period] to see the message
```

CODE EXAMPLE 9.9: CODE THAT AVOIDS ACCIDENTAL RE-REGISTERING OF SERVER REPOSITORY FUNCTIONS.

```
(
s.waitForBoot({
    ServerTree.removeAll;
    ~treeMessage = {"Server tree cleared".postln};
    ServerTree.add(~treeMessage);
});
)

// press [cmd]+[period] to see the message
```

TIP.RAND(); INITIALIZING THE NODE TREE

Initializing the Node tree is an inherent part of the server-booting process, so any actions registered with ServerTree will occur when the server boots. For example, if you run the code in Code Example 9.9, and then quit and reboot the server, "Server tree cleared" will appear in the post window, despite the fact that we did not press [cmd]+[period] or evaluate **s.freeAll**.

Registered repository actions can be manually performed by calling **run** on the repository class:

```
ServerTree.run;
```

Calling **run** only evaluates registered actions and spoofs the normal triggering mechanism (e.g., evaluating **ServerBoot.run** does not actually boot the server—it only evaluates its registered functions).

Armed with these new tools, Code Example 9.10 improves the audio example in Code Example 9.6. Specifically, we can automate the creation of the reverb Synth by adding an appropriate function to ServerTree. To avoid accidental double-registrations, we also define a cleanup function that wipes Nodes and removes all registered actions. This cleanup function is called once when we first run the code, and also whenever we quit the server.

CODE EXAMPLE 9.10: INITIALIZING THE SERVER WITH THE HELP OF SERVER ACTION REPOSITORY CLASSES.

```
(
s.newBusAllocators;
~bus = Bus.audio(s, 2);

~cleanup = {
    s.freeAll;
    ServerBoot.removeAll;
    ServerTree.removeAll;
    ServerQuit.removeAll;
};
~cleanup.();
ServerQuit.add(~cleanup);

s.waitForBoot({
    SynthDef(\source, { |out = 0|
        var sig, env, freq, trig;
        trig = Trig.kr(Dust.kr(4), 0.1);
        env = EnvGen.kr(Env.perc(0.001, 0.08), trig);
        freq = TExpRand.kr(200, 1500, trig);
        sig = SinOsc.ar(freq ! 2, mul: 0.2);
        sig = sig * env;
        Out.ar(out, sig);
    }).add;

    SynthDef(\reverb, { |in = 0, mix = 0.2, out = 0|
        var sig, fx;
        sig = In.ar(in, 2);
        fx = FreeVerb2.ar(sig[0], sig[1], 1, 0.85);
        sig = sig.blend(fx, mix);
        Out.ar(out, sig);
    }).add;
```

```
        s.sync;

        ~makeReverb = {~reverb = Synth(\reverb, [in: ~bus])};
        ServerTree.add(~makeReverb);
        ServerTree.run;
    });
)

Synth(\source, [out: ~bus, freq: exprand(200, 1500)]);
```

In this improved version, pressing [cmd]+[period] no longer requires jumping back to our setup code. Instead, a new reverb Synth automatically appears to take the place of its predecessor, allowing us to focus our creative attention exclusively on our sound-making code. At the same time, we've taken appropriate precautions with our cleanup code, so that if we do re-evaluate our setup code (intentionally or unintentionally), it does not create any technical problems. When we're finished, we can quit the server, which removes all registered actions.

9.5 The Startup File

If you have code that you want to be evaluated every time you launch SC, you can include it in the language startup file, detailed in a reference file titled "Sclang Startup File." When SC is launched, it looks for a file named "startup.scd" in your user configuration folder, which is located at the path returned by **Platform.userConfigDir**. If a properly named file exists at this location, the interpreter evaluates its contents on startup (technically, this file is evaluated whenever the class library is recompiled, which is one of several actions that occur at startup). Though we're accustomed to seeing an outermost pair of parentheses around a code block, these parentheses are mainly a convenience for being able to evaluate code with [cmd]+[return] and need not be included in the startup file.

If you find yourself running the same code at the start of every session, consider moving it to the startup file to save time and space. Common startup actions include setting the server's sample rate, selecting a hardware device for audio input/output, registering actions with ServerTree, or just booting the server. The startup file might also include actions that occur post-boot, like adding SynthDefs or allocating buffers. Any valid code is fair game.

Remember that your startup file is specific to your computer. If you move a code project from one computer to another, the startup file does not automatically accompany it. So, if you're working on a project that will eventually be run on a different machine, using the startup file might not be a good choice. However, if your work will always be performed on the same computer, the startup file may be beneficial and is worth considering.

9.6 Working with Multiple Code Files

A large body of code stored in a single file becomes more cumbersome to navigate as it grows, even with impeccable organization. The IDE has a few features that facilitate navigation. For example, the "Find" function allows quick jumping to a specific piece of text (particularly useful if you leave unique combinations of characters as "bookmarks" for yourself). Similarly, the "split" feature allows multiple parts of the same document to be displayed simultaneously (see Figure 9.1). Still, even with the advantages of these features, there are limits to what the interpreter can handle. If you try to evaluate an enormous block of code that contains thousands of nested functions, you may even encounter the rare "selector table too big" error message.

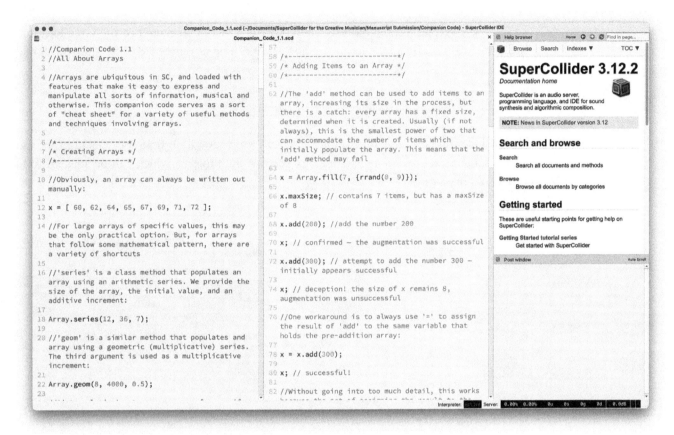

FIGURE 9.1 Viewing two parts of the same code file in the IDE using a split view. Split options are available in the "View" drop-down menu.

For large or even medium-sized projects, partitioning work into separate code files has distinct advantages. Modularization yields smaller files that focus on specific tasks. These files are generally easier to read, understand, and debug. Once a sub-file is functional and complete, you can set it aside and forget about it. In some cases, some of your sub-files may be general-purpose enough to be incorporated into other projects (for example, a sub-file that contains a library of your favorite SynthDefs).

Code in a saved .scd file can be evaluated by calling **load** on a string that represents the absolute path to that file. If your code files are all stored in the same directory, the process is even simpler: you can call **loadRelative** on a string that contains only the name and extension of the file you want to run. The loadRelative method requires that the primary file and the external file have previously been saved somewhere on your computer. Otherwise, the files don't technically exist yet, and SC will have no idea where to look for them.

You can create a simple demonstration of loadRelative as follows. First, save a SC document called "external.scd" that contains the following code:

```
s.waitForBoot({
    {
        var sig = SinOsc.ar([500, 503], mul: 0.2);
        sig = sig * Env.perc.kr(2);
    }.play;
});
```

Then, save a second SC file named "main.scd" (or some other name) in the same location. In the main file, evaluate the following line of code. The server should boot, and you should hear a tone.

```
"external.scd".loadRelative;
```

To conclude this chapter, Companion Code 9.1 brings several of these concepts together and presents a general-purpose template for large-scale SC projects, which can be adapted for a variety of purposes.

CHAPTER 10

AN EVENT-BASED STRUCTURE

10.1 Overview

One advantage of creating music with SC is its potential to introduce randomness and indeterminacy into a composition, enabling musical expression that is difficult to achieve in other contexts. In other words, choices about certain musical elements can be driven by algorithms, without having predetermined orders or durations, allowing the composer to take a higher-level approach to music-making. However, algorithmic composition introduces new layers of open-endedness that can prove challenging for composers who are new to this kind of approach.

As an entryway into algorithmic composition, this chapter focuses on structuring a composition that follows a chronological sequence of musical events. We begin with structures that are completely deterministic, that is, those that produce the exact same result each time. Toward the end of the chapter, we add some indeterminate elements that leverage SC's algorithmic capabilities, while maintaining an overall performance structure that remains ordered.

10.2 Expressing Musical Events Through Code

In the context of musical performance, what exactly do we mean by "musical event"? In short, this term refers to some discrete action, occurring at a distinct point in time, which produces some musically relevant result (note that we are not referring to the **Event** class). Some examples of musical events might include the production of a sound, the articulation of a musical phrase or sequence, or the onset of some parameter trajectory, such as vibrato or a timbral shift. With varying degrees of complexity, virtually any piece of music can be represented as a sequence of discrete events. The ability of music to be discretized in this manner is, in part, what enables us to represent music via score notation, and it is also a fundamental principle behind the MIDI protocol, similarly designed to represent a musical performance through discrete messages.

Thinking broadly and simply about musical events, we could perhaps group them into the following six categories:

1. Create a new sound.
2. Modify a parameter of an existing sound.
3. Terminate an existing sound.
4. Create/Enable a new signal-processing effect.
5. Modify a parameter of an existing signal-processing effect.
6. Terminate/Disable an existing signal-processing effect.

In practice, a musical event may be treated as a singular unit but may comprise several different simultaneous events from this list. For example, an event might create ten or 100 new sounds at once, or an event might simultaneously terminate one sound while creating another. Further still, an event might initiate a timed sequence of sounds whose onsets are separated in time (such as an arpeggiated chord). Even though multiple sounds are produced, we can still conceptualize the action as a singular event.

So how are these types of musical events represented in code? A Synth is arguably the most basic unit of musical expression. When a new Synth is created, a signal-calculating unit is born on the server. Other times, we play a Pbind to generate a sequence of Synths. Thus, categories (1) and (4) can be translated into the creation of Synths and/or the playing of Pbinds. For categories (2) and (5), a **set** message is a logical translation, which allows manipulation of Synth arguments in real-time. Alternatively, we might iterate over an array of Synths, or issue a **set** message to a Group, to influence multiple Synths at once. In the context of Pbind, we might call upon a Pdefn to modify some aspect of an active EventStreamPlayer. Lastly, categories (3) and (6) might translate into using **free** to destroy one or more Synths, or more commonly, using a **set** message to zero an envelope gate to create a smooth fade, or we might update a Pdefn to gradually fade the amplitude values of an EventStreamPlayer.

Musical events can also be categorized as "one-shots" or "sustaining" events. In a one-shot event, all generative elements have a finite lifespan and terminate themselves automatically, usually as a result of a fixed-duration envelope or finite-length pattern. The Synths and Pbinds in a one-shot event typically do not need to be stored in named variables, because they are autonomous and there is rarely a need to reference them after creation. Sustaining events, on the other hand, have an indefinite-length existence, and rely on a future event for termination. Unlike one-shots, sound-generating elements in sustaining events must rely on some storage mechanism and naming scheme, so that they can be accessed and terminated later.

The first step toward building a chronological event structure is to express your musical events as discrete chunks of code. In other words, determine what's going to happen and when, and type out the code that performs each step. In early stages of composing, this can be as easy as putting each chunk of code in its own parenthetical enclosure, so that each event can be manually evaluated with [cmd]+[return]. As an initial demonstration, consider the code in Code Example 10.1, which represents a simple (and uninspired) event-based composition.

CODE EXAMPLE 10.1: A SIMPLE EVENT-BASED COMPOSITION, EXPRESSED AS DISCRETE CHUNKS OF CODE. SEVERAL SUBSEQUENT CODE EXAMPLES IN THIS CHAPTER RELY ON THESE TWO SYNTHDEFS.

```
s.boot;

(
SynthDef(\sine, {
    arg atk = 1, rel = 4, gate = 1,
    freq = 300, freqLag = 1, amp = 0.1, out = 0;
    var sig, env;
    env = Env.asr(atk, 1, rel).kr(2, gate);
    sig = SinOsc.ar(freq.lag(freqLag) + [0, 2]);
    sig = sig * amp * env;
    Out.ar(out, sig);
}).add;
```

```
SynthDef(\noise, {
    arg atk = 1, rel = 4, gate = 1,
    freq = 300, amp = 0.2, out = 0;
    var sig, env;
    env = Env.asr(atk, 1, rel).kr(2, gate);
    sig = BPF.ar(PinkNoise.ar(1 ! 2), freq, 0.02, 7);
    sig = sig * amp * env;
    Out.ar(out, sig);
}).add;
)

(
// event 0: create sine synth
~sine0 = Synth(\sine, [freq: 60.midicps, amp: 0.05]);
)

(
// event 1: create two noise synths
~noise0 = Synth(\noise, [freq: 75.midicps, amp: 0.15]);
~noise1 = Synth(\noise, [freq: 53.midicps, amp: 0.3]);
)

(
// event 2: modify frequencies of noise synths
~noise0.set(\freq, 77.midicps);
~noise1.set(\freq, 56.midicps);
)

(
// event 3: modify frequency of sine synth
~sine0.set(\freq, 59.midicps);
)

(
// event 4: fade all synths
[~sine0, ~noise0, ~noise1].do({ |n| n.set(\gate, 0) });
)
```

Though devoid of brilliance and nuance, this example illustrates the essential technique of discretizing a musical performance into individual actions. In practice, your events may likely be substantially larger and more complex, involving dozens of Synths and/or Pbinds. Your SynthDefs, too, may also be larger, more developed, and more numerous.

In this current form, our "composition" is performable, but involves some combination of mouse clicking, scrolling, and/or keyboard shortcuts. We can improve the situation by loading these event chunks into an ordered structure, explored in the next section.

10.3 Organizing Musical Events

SC offers various options for organizing a sequence of musical events. The **Collection** class, for instance, is a parent class of several useful subclasses. The **Array** class naturally rises to the surface as a simple, effective solution. A non-ordered collection, such as a **Dictionary**, offers some benefits that arrays do not provide. Further still, a stream generated from a **Pseq** provides an elegant solution as well.

10.3.1 AN ARRAY OF MUSICAL EVENTS

Consider the even-simpler event sequence depicted in Code Example 10.2, which includes a version of the "sine" SynthDef from Code Example 10.1, modified with a fixed-duration envelope. The first event creates a one-shot Synth, and the next event creates another.

CODE EXAMPLE 10.2: A SIMPLE PERFORMANCE SEQUENCE CONSISTING OF TWO GENERATIVE ONE-SHOT EVENTS.

```
(
SynthDef(\simple, {
    arg atk = 0.2, rel = 1, gate = 1,
    freq = 300, freqLag = 1, amp = 0.1, out = 0;
    var sig, env;
    env = Env.linen(atk, 1, rel).kr(2);
    sig = SinOsc.ar(freq.lag(freqLag) + [0, 2]) * amp * env;
    Out.ar(out, sig);
}).add;
)

Synth(\simple, [freq: 330, amp: 0.05]); // event 0

Synth(\simple, [freq: 290, amp: 0.05]); // event 1
```

Code Example 10.3 shows a tempting but erroneous attempt to populate an array with these two events. When the array is created, both sounds play immediately. An attempt to access either item returns the Synth object, but no sound is produced. This behavior is a byproduct of the separation between the language and the server. To create the array, the language must interpret the items it contains. But, once the language interprets a Synth, an OSC message to the server is automatically generated, and the Synth comes into existence.

CODE EXAMPLE 10.3: AN INCORRECT ATTEMPT TO POPULATE AN ARRAY WITH MUSICAL EVENTS, RESULTING IN THE SOUNDS BEING HEARD IMMEDIATELY.

```
(
~events = [
    Synth(\simple, [freq: 330, amp: 0.05]),
    Synth(\simple, [freq: 290, amp: 0.05])
];
)

~events[0]; // returns the Synth, but no sound is produced
```

The solution is to wrap each event in a function, shown in Code Example 10.4. When the interpreter encounters a function, it only sees that it is a function, but does not "look inside" until the function is explicitly evaluated.

CODE EXAMPLE 10.4: A VALID APPROACH FOR CREATING AND PERFORMING AN ARRAY OF MUSICAL EVENTS.

```
(
~events = [
    {Synth(\simple, [freq: 330, amp: 0.05])},
    {Synth(\simple, [freq: 290, amp: 0.05])}
];
)

~events[0].(); // play 0th event

~events[1].(); // play 1st event
```

If the array is large, we can avoid dealing with a long list of evaluations by creating a global index and defining a separate function that evaluates the current event and increments the index, demonstrated in Code Example 10.5. If the index is beyond the range of the array, access attempts return nil, which can be harmlessly evaluated. The index can be manually reset to zero to return to the beginning, or some other integer to jump to a point in the middle of the sequence.

CODE EXAMPLE 10.5: USING AN INDEX THAT IS AUTOMATICALLY INCREMENTED WHENEVER AN EVENT IS PERFORMED.

```
(
~index = 0;
~events = [
    {Synth(\simple, [freq: 330, amp: 0.05])},
    {Synth(\simple, [freq: 290, amp: 0.05])},
    {Synth(\simple, [freq: 420, amp: 0.05])},
    {Synth(\simple, [freq: 400, amp: 0.05])}
];

~nextEvent = {
    ~events[~index].();
    ~index = ~index + 1;
};
)

~nextEvent.(); // evaluate repeatedly

~index = 0; // reset to beginning
```

Code Example 10.5 essentially reinvents the behaviors of **next** and **reset** in the context of routines (introduced in Section 5.2), but without the ability to advance through events automatically with precise timing. If precise timing is desired, we can bundle event durations into the array and play a simple routine that retrieves these pieces of information from the array as needed. In Code Example 10.6, each item in the event array is an array containing the event function and a duration.

CODE EXAMPLE 10.6: USING A ROUTINE TO AUTOMATICALLY ADVANCE THROUGH AN ARRAY OF MUSICAL EVENTS WITH SPECIFIC TIMING.

```
(
~index = 0;
~events = [
    [{Synth(\simple, [freq: 330, amp: 0.05])}, 2],
    [{Synth(\simple, [freq: 290, amp: 0.05])}, 0.5],
    [{Synth(\simple, [freq: 420, amp: 0.05])}, 0.25],
    [{Synth(\simple, [freq: 400, amp: 0.05])}, 0],
];
```

```
~seq = Routine({
    ~events.do({
        ~events[~index][0].();
        ~events[~index][1].wait;
        ~index = ~index + 1;
    });
});
)

~seq.play;
```

As an exercise for the reader, consider converting the performance events in Code Example 10.1 into either the array or routine structures that appear in Code Examples 10.5 and 10.6.

10.3.2 A DICTIONARY OF MUSICAL EVENTS

Dictionary is an unordered collection. At first glance, it seems like an odd choice for storing a chronological musical sequence. Instead of a numerical index, each item in a dictionary is paired with a symbol, which allows a more verbose and human-readable naming scheme.[1] Basic usage appears in Code Example 10.7. When using an array, it can be difficult to remember exactly what happens at each index (consider, for example, the meaninglessness of **~events[37]**), which can pose difficulties in making changes or debugging. A naming scheme such as **~events[\modulateSubTone]** tends to be more meaningful and memorable.

CODE EXAMPLE 10.7: USING A DICTIONARY TO STORE AND PERFORM A SEQUENCE OF MUSICAL EVENTS.

```
(
~events = Dictionary()
.add(\play330sine -> {Synth(\simple, [freq: 330, amp: 0.05])})
.add(\play290sine -> {Synth(\simple, [freq: 290, amp: 0.05])});
)

~events[\play330sine].();

~events[\play290sine].();
```

The decision of whether to use a dictionary or array is a matter of taste, and perhaps also dictated by the nature of the project; it depends on whether the familiarity of named events outweighs the convenience of numerical ordering. Though the ability to name events is useful, using a dictionary is somewhat more prone to human error (e.g., accidentally using the same name twice). Arguably, a similar effect can be achieved with arrays by strategically placing comments at points throughout your code. Or, perhaps your memory is sharp enough to recall events by number alone!

10.3.3 A STREAM OF MUSICAL EVENTS

We typically use **Pseq** in the context of Pbind, but it has an application here as well. As we saw in Chapter 5, a pattern responds to **asStream** by returning a routine. Code Example 10.8 revisits the code in Code Example 10.1 and uses Pseq to express these events as a stream.

CODE EXAMPLE 10.8: THE MUSICAL EVENTS FROM CODE EXAMPLE 10.1, EXPRESSED AND PERFORMED AS A STREAM CREATED FROM A Pseq. THIS EXAMPLE RELIES ON THE SYNTHDEFS IN CODE EXAMPLE 10.1.

```
(
~events = Pseq([
    {
        ~sine0 = Synth(\sine, [freq: 60.midicps, amp: 0.05])
    },
    {
        ~noise0 = Synth(\noise, [freq: 75.midicps, amp: 0.15]);
        ~noise1 = Synth(\noise, [freq: 53.midicps, amp: 0.3]);
    },
    {
        ~noise0.set(\freq, 77.midicps);
        ~noise1.set(\freq, 56.midicps);
    },
    {
        ~sine0.set(\freq, 59.midicps);
    },
    {
        [~sine0, ~noise0, ~noise1].do({ |n| n.set(\gate, 0) });
    }
], 1).asStream;
)

~events.next.(); // evaluate repeatedly;

~events.reset; // reset to beginning
```

When using Pseq, we don't need to maintain an event index, and instead merely need to call **next** on the stream to retrieve the next function. The stream can also be **reset** at will. Once the stream is reset, we can jump to a point along the event timeline by extracting a certain number of events from the stream, but not evaluating them, as shown in Code Example 10.9.

> **CODE EXAMPLE 10.9:** A TECHNIQUE FOR SKIPPING AHEAD IN A STREAM OF MUSICAL EVENTS.
>
> ```
> (
> ~events.reset;
> 1.do({~events.next}); // retrieve the first event but do not evaluate
> )
>
> ~events.next.(); // retrieve and evaluate the next event
> ```

Retrieving without evaluating is a useful technique, but it reveals a problem. In a chronological event-based composition, it's common to have events that depend on the execution of previous events. For example, the penultimate event in Code Example 10.8 sets the frequency of a Synth created during the first event. If we skip to this event by changing **1.do** to **3.do** in Code Example 10.9, the next event produces no sound, and we'll see a failure message in the post window. Solutions to this problem are explored in the next section.

10.4 Navigating and Rehearsing an Event-Based Composition

For timeline-based compositions, the ability to "skip ahead" is essential for rehearsal and troubleshooting. If there's a problem at the eleventh minute, you shouldn't have to sit through ten minutes of music to get there! Notated scores have measure numbers and rehearsal marks for this purpose, and in DAWs and waveform editors, we can click or drag the playback cursor to a desired location or set timeline markers. In a programming language like SC, a bit of work is needed to address this issue.

It can be tempting to ignore the need for rehearsal cues, and simply accept the fact that some sounds may be absent or inaccurate if we start in the middle. This approach is sometimes workable, but highly impractical in other cases. For example, if the first musical event of a composition plays a sustained sound, and the remaining events manipulate this sound, then no events will do anything unless the first event is executed.

Another tempting option is to quickly "mash" through earlier events to arrive at a target location. Doing so ensures that preceding events are performed in order, but the accelerated timing may produce unpleasantly loud or distorted sound, and/or overload your CPU. Some preceding sounds may also be one-shots with long durations, and we'll have to wait for them to end.

A better approach is to identify key moments that serve as useful starting points, and build a special collection of rehearsal cues, which each place the program in a specific state when executed. Generally, rehearsal cues create Synths and/or play Pbinds, while supplying parameter values that are appropriate for that specific moment. Code Example 10.10 depicts a dictionary of rehearsal cues named **~startAt**, meant to accompany the musical events in Code Example 10.8. Pseq is not the best option for rehearsal cues, because we may want to "jump around" from one rehearsal cue to another in non-chronological order, so **next** is of little use to us. An array would be slightly better, but the number of rehearsal cues may not match the number of events, in which case numerical indexing is unhelpful. Therefore, we use a dictionary for storing rehearsal cues, for the ability to give each cue a meaningful name.

CODE EXAMPLE 10.10: A Dictionary OF REHEARSAL CUES THAT AUGMENTS THE MUSICAL EVENTS IN CODE EXAMPLE 10.8, MEANT TO FACILITATE PLAYING THE COMPOSITION FROM ARBITRARY POINTS ALONG ITS TIMELINE. THIS EXAMPLE RELIES ON THE SYNTHDEFS IN CODE EXAMPLE 10.1 AND THE ~events STREAM FROM CODE EXAMPLE 10.8.

```
(
~startAt = Dictionary()
.add(\event1 -> {
    ~events.reset;
    1.do({~events.next});
    ~sine0 = Synth(\sine, [freq: 60.midicps, amp: 0.05]);
})
.add(\event2 -> {
    ~events.reset;
    2.do({~events.next});
    ~sine0 = Synth(\sine, [freq: 60.midicps, amp: 0.05]);
    ~noise0 = Synth(\noise, [freq: 75.midicps, amp: 0.15]);
    ~noise1 = Synth(\noise, [freq: 53.midicps, amp: 0.3]);
})
.add(\event3 -> {
    ~events.reset;
    3.do({~events.next});
    ~sine0 = Synth(\sine, [freq: 60.midicps, amp: 0.05]);
    ~noise0 = Synth(\noise, [freq: 77.midicps, amp: 0.15]);
    ~noise1 = Synth(\noise, [freq: 56.midicps, amp: 0.3]);
})
.add(\event4 -> {
    ~events.reset;
    4.do({~events.next});
    ~sine0 = Synth(\sine, [freq: 59.midicps, amp: 0.05]);
    ~noise0 = Synth(\noise, [freq: 77.midicps, amp: 0.15]);
    ~noise1 = Synth(\noise, [freq: 56.midicps, amp: 0.3]);
});
)
```

```
~events.reset;

~events.next.(); // evaluate repeatedly

// press [cmd]+[period], then cue an event
~startAt[\event3].value;

~events.next.(); // play the new "next" event
```

With this improvement, if we interrupt a performance with [cmd]+[period], we can call a rehearsal cue, which transports us to a specific moment in time. For example, the function stored in **~startAt[\event3]** navigates to the appropriate stage within the **~events** stream, creates all three Synths, and provides appropriate frequency values for the noise Synths (which are normally set by the previous event).

This approach of building rehearsal cues is no different for larger and more complex pieces. At its core, it involves identifying useful rehearsal points, identifying active musical processes at these moments, and building a collection of functions that construct these moments. To this end, creating a spreadsheet, or even using pencil and paper, can be helpful for sketching out a "map" of events, which may help clarify exactly what musical processes occur, when they occur, and how long they last. Not every moment in a composition is a practical place for a rehearsal cue, much in the same way it can be awkward for an instrumental ensemble to begin rehearsing in the middle of a musical phrase. There is also a point of diminishing returns for rehearsal cues; beyond a certain quantity, additional rehearsal cues require time and effort to code, but they do not provide much practical benefit. So, it's wise to be judicious in selecting moments for rehearsal cues.

10.5 Indeterminacy in an Event-Based Composition

An event-based composition can be identical with each performance but doesn't need to be. As discussed at the start of this chapter, we have the option of introducing randomness and other algorithmic techniques to produce a composition that remains chronological when viewed as a whole, but which has varying degrees of unpredictability in its lower-level details.

The simplest and most obvious way to add randomness to a composition is to build random features into the event code itself. For example, we might have an event that creates (and another that later fades) a random collection of pitches from a scale, or a one-shot pattern that produces a tone burst with a random number of articulated notes (see Code Examples 10.11 and 10.12).

CODE EXAMPLE 10.11: A MUSICAL EVENT THAT PLAYS A CLUSTER OF SYNTHS WHOSE PITCHES ARE RANDOMLY SELECTED FROM A SCALE. THIS EXAMPLE RELIES ON THE "NOISE" SYNTHDEF IN CODE EXAMPLE 10.1.

```
(
var scl = [0, 3, 5, 7, 9, 10];
var oct = [72, 72, 84, 84, 84, 96];
var notes = oct.collect({ |n| n + scl.choose});
~synths = ([60] ++ notes).collect({ |n|
    // MIDI note 60 is prepended to avoid randomizing the bass note
    Synth(\noise, [freq: n.midicps, amp: 0.15]);
});
)

~synths.do({ |n| n.set(\gate, 0)});
```

CODE EXAMPLE 10.12: A MUSICAL EVENT THAT PLAYS A PATTERN WITH A RANDOM NUMBER OF NOTES. THIS EXAMPLE RELIES ON THE "SINE" SYNTHDEF IN CODE EXAMPLE 10.1.

```
(
Pfin(
    exprand(3, 15).round, // creates between 3-15 synths
    Pbind(
        \instrument, \sine,
        \dur, 0.07,
        \scale, [0, 3, 5, 7, 9, 10],
        \degree, Pbrown(10, 20, 3),
        \sustain, 0.01,
        \atk, 0.002,
        \rel, 0.8,
        \amp, 0.03
    )
).play;
)
```

Randomness can also be implemented at a higher level, influencing the sequential arrangement of events. In Code Example 10.13, a Pseq is nested inside the outermost Pseq to randomize the number of tone burst patterns that are played before the filtered noise chord is faded out. The noteworthy feature of this inner Pseq is that the **repeats** value is expressed as a function, guaranteeing that the number of repeats will be uniquely generated each time the sequence is performed. Using a similar technique, we can randomize the order in which certain events occur. Code Example 10.14 uses **Pshuf** to randomize the order of the first two events, so that either the tone bursts or the filtered noise chord may occur first.

CODE EXAMPLE 10.13: USING AN INSTANCE OF PSEQ INSIDE THE EVENT SEQUENCE TO RANDOMIZE THE NUMBER OF TIMES AN EVENT REPEATS BEFORE MOVING ON.

```
(
~events = Pseq([
    {
        // create cluster chord
        var scl = [0, 3, 5, 7, 9, 10];
        var oct = [72, 72, 84, 84, 84, 96];
        var notes = oct.collect({ |n| n + scl.choose});
        ~synths = ([60] ++ notes).collect({ |n|
            Synth(\noise, [freq: n.midicps, amp: 0.15]);
        });
    },

    // repeat a pattern a random number of times
    Pseq([
        {
            Pfin(
                exprand(3, 15).round,
                Pbind(
                    \instrument, \sine,
                    \dur, 0.07,
                    \degree, Pbrown(10, 20, 3),
                    \scale, [0, 3, 5, 7, 9, 10],
                    \sustain, 0.01,
                    \atk, 0.002,
                    \rel, 0.8,
                    \amp, 0.03
                )
            ).play;
        }
    ], {rrand(3, 5)}), // <- produces 3, 4, or 5 tone burst events
```

```
		// fade cluster chord
		{~synths.do({ |n| n.set(\gate, 0) })}
	], 1).asStream;
)

~events.next.();

~events.reset;
```

CODE EXAMPLE 10.14: USING PSHUF TO RANDOMIZE THE ORDER OF CERTAIN MUSICAL EVENTS.

```
(
~events = Pseq([
	Pshuf([
		{
			var scl = [0, 3, 5, 7, 9, 10];
			var oct = [72, 72, 84, 84, 84, 96];
			var notes = oct.collect({ |n| n + scl.choose });
			~synths = ([60] ++ notes).collect({ |n|
				Synth(\noise, [freq: n.midicps, amp: 0.15]);
			});
		},
		
		Pseq([
			{
				Pfin(
					exprand(3, 15).round,
					Pbind(
						\instrument, \sine,
						\dur, 0.07,
						\degree, Pbrown(10, 20, 3),
						\scale, [0, 3, 5, 7, 9, 10],
						\sustain, 0.01,
						\atk, 0.002,
						\rel, 0.8,
						\amp, 0.03
					)
				).play;
			}
		], {rrand(3, 5)})
	], 1),
```

```
        {~synths.do({ |n| n.set(\gate, 0) })}
], 1).asStream;
)

~events.next.();

~events.reset;
```

Companion Code 10.1 synthesizes these techniques for structuring event-based compositions and, building upon foundational techniques from the previous chapter, presents a somewhat larger and more complex event-based project.

Note

1 It should be noted that **Dictionary** is a distant superclass of **Event**. Dictionaries cannot be "played" like Events, nor are they deeply intertwined with Patterns and Streams. In the context of storing functions that perform arbitrary actions, however, these two classes are largely interchangeable, with minor syntax differences. The reader may even find Events to be the more practical option. In this section, Dictionary is only favored to avoid potential confusion between the abstract notion of a musical "event" and the "Event" class.

CHAPTER 11

A STATE-BASED STRUCTURE

11.1 Overview

State-based composition represents a different way of thinking about musical structure. Instead of relying on a predetermined timeline, we rely on a collection of sounds that can be activated and deactivated at will, in any order or combination.

Imagine four sound-generating "modules" named A, B, C, and D. In this context, a module might be a Synth, or an EventStreamPlayer created by playing a Pbind. You might spontaneously decide to start a performance by activating modules B and D. After fifteen seconds, you might activate module A, and, ten seconds later, deactivate module B. Module C might remain inactive for the entire duration of the performance (an imagined "score" for this performance is depicted in Figure 11.1). Performed on a different day, your choices might be entirely different. The term "state-based" refers to the fact that at any point during a performance, the program is in a particular "state." States themselves can involve sounds that are static or dynamic, dense or sparse, regular or unpredictable. With a large collection of sound-generating modules, dozens or even hundreds of combinations are possible.

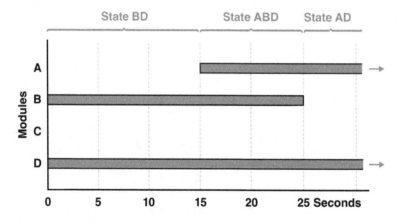

FIGURE 11.1 A partial imagined "score" for a state-based composition involving four sound-generating modules.

Why pursue a state-based approach instead of a chronological one? A state-based approach encourages a mindset more oriented toward improvisation and discovery, rather than precise sounds that happen at precise times, allowing sounds to be mixed-and-matched as the mood strikes. It's like improvising on an acoustic instrument, or a conductor cueing members of an improv ensemble; we know in advance a good deal about what types of sounds might occur, but decisions about when and if these sounds occur are made in real-time, as a performance unfolds. A state-based approach pairs well with GUIs, MIDI controllers, and other "playable" interfaces. A state-based approach is also a solid choice for sound installations that run autonomously over long durations. This approach invites flexibility in terms of audience experience as well as duration; listeners can engage by coming and going as they please, by moving around a performance space, or simply listening with an "in-the-moment" mentality.

Because states can theoretically occur in any order/combination, it's important to design state-change actions to avoid conflicting or contradictory behavior. In other words, state-change actions should be state-aware on some level. For example, an attempt to activate sound module B should have no effect if module B is already playing. Similarly, an attempt to modify the sound of a module that is not playing should be ignored.

A timeline is a bedrock design feature of DAWs and waveform editing software. Creating music without one can feel disorienting! You might feel adrift in a sea of timeless musical possibilities. To help bridge the gap, it can be helpful to first envision a rough order in which your states will occur—maybe even create a simple score for yourself to follow—but then venture outside the boundaries of your plan once you start refining and rehearsing. With the flexibility to dynamically reorder your ideas, you might stumble upon unexpectedly interesting sequences and combinations.

11.2 Simple State Control

Let's first consider a minimal state-based structure with a straightforward means of on/off control for individual modules, which are individual Synths in this section. As we have seen, a gated amplitude envelope with a non-freeing doneAction gives us the ability to fade a Synth without terminating it. Frequently, we use doneAction: 0 (the default) for this purpose, but Synths with this feature are always active (thus consuming CPU power), even when silent. If your composition uses lots of complex Synths, your computer may struggle to handle the computation load. This being the case, we have an opportunity to introduce the technique of pausing and unpausing Synths. When a Synth is paused, signal calculation stops, but the Synth is not destroyed. A Synth can be paused and unpaused using the **run** method and supplying a Boolean argument that represents whether we want the Synth to be actively running. A new Synth can be instantiated in a paused state using **newPaused**. Relatedly, if a UGen contains doneAction: 1, the enclosing Synth will pause itself when the UGen finishes.

In Code Example 11.1, we create three Synths in a paused state, with an initially closed gate. Each Synth can be faded in by opening its gate and unpausing. When the gate is closed and the fade-out is complete, the Synth automatically re-pauses itself. This approach allows us to create many sounds that are always available for activation, but which consume virtually no resources when silent. After evaluating the setup code, the six lines at the bottom of this example can be run in any sequence or combination. Running any individual statement multiple times in succession has no negative consequences.

CODE EXAMPLE 11.1: A SIMPLE STATE-BASED COMPOSITION INVOLVING THREE SOUND-GENERATING MODULES THAT CAN BE ACTIVATED/ DEACTIVATED IN ANY ORDER.

```
(
s.waitForBoot({
    SynthDef(\pulse_noise, { |gate = 0|
        var sig, env;
        env = Env.asr(5, 1, 5, [2, -2]).kr(1, gate);
        sig = BPF.ar(PinkNoise.ar(1 ! 2), 1600, 0.01, 3);
        sig = sig * env * LFPulse.kr(8, width: 0.2);
        Out.ar(0, sig);
    }).add;
    SynthDef(\beating_tone, { |gate = 0|
        var sig, env;
        env = Env.asr(5, 1, 5, [2, -2]).kr(1, gate);
        sig = SinOsc.ar([250, 251], mul: 0.1) * env;
        Out.ar(0, sig);
    }).add;
    SynthDef(\crackle, { |gate = 0|
        var sig, env;
        env = Env.asr(5, 1, 5, [2, -2]).kr(1, gate);
        sig = Dust.ar(8 ! 2, 0.2) * env;
        Out.ar(0, sig);
    }).add;

    s.sync;

    ~a = Synth.newPaused(\pulse_noise);
    ~b = Synth.newPaused(\beating_tone);
    ~c = Synth.newPaused(\crackle);
});
)

~a.set(\gate, 1).run(true); // pulsed filtered noise
~a.set(\gate, 0);

~b.set(\gate, 1).run(true); // beating tones
~b.set(\gate, 0);

~c.set(\gate, 1).run(true); // subtle crackles
~c.set(\gate, 0);
```

We can reduce the performance code in Code Example 11.1 from six lines to three. Instead of using a pair of statements for on/off functionality, we can define a toggle function that turns a module on if it is off, and vice-versa. This improvement makes use of the **Event** class, which allows us to bundle additional information with each Synth. Specifically, we include a Boolean for tracking each Synth's paused status. After running the setup code in Code Example 11.1, Code Example 11.2 can be used as performance code. The three toggle statements at the bottom of Code Example 11.2 can be run in any order/combination.

CODE EXAMPLE 11.2: USING A TOGGLE FUNCTION TO TURN MODULES ON/OFF IN A STATE-BASED COMPOSITION. THIS EXAMPLE RELIES ON THE SETUP CODE IN CODE EXAMPLE 11.1.

```
(
~a = (synth: Synth.newPaused(\pulse_noise), running: false);
~b = (synth: Synth.newPaused(\beating_tone), running: false);
~c = (synth: Synth.newPaused(\crackle), running: false);

~toggle = { |module|
    if(
        module[\running],
        {module[\synth].set(\gate, 0)},
        {module[\synth].set(\gate, 1).run(true)}
    );
    module[\running] = module[\running].not;
};
)

~toggle.(~a);
~toggle.(~b);
~toggle.(~c);
```

This approach can be applied to generative SynthDefs of all different kinds, as long as they include a gated, pausing envelope that affects the overall amplitude of the output signal. The SynthDefs in this section include only a gate argument, but other arguments can be added if desired. A Synth can still receive a **set** message while paused, but the message will not take effect until it is unpaused. Code Example 11.3 provides a brief example based on a SynthDef from Code Example 11.1, which adds a frequency argument. Though not demonstrated here, adding arguments for envelope attack and release times can be helpful to control transition timings during state changes (in this example, they are hard-coded as five seconds each).

> **CODE EXAMPLE 11.3:** THE BEHAVIOR OF SETTING SYNTH ARGUMENTS WHILE THE SYNTH IS PAUSED.
>
> ```
> (
> SynthDef(\beating_tone, { |freq = 250, freqlag = 0, gate = 0|
>     var sig, env;
>     env = Env.asr(5, 1, 5, [2, -2]).kr(1, gate);
>     sig = SinOsc.ar(freq.lag(freqlag) + [0, 1], mul: 0.1) * env;
>     Out.ar(0, sig);
> }).add;
> )
>
> ~b = (synth: Synth.newPaused(\beating_tone), running: false);
>
> ~toggle.(~b); // fade in
>
> ~b[\synth].set(\freq, 350, \freqlag, 1); // update frequency
>
> ~toggle.(~b); // fade out
>
> // wait until silent...
>
> ~b[\synth].set(\freq, 450, \freqlag, 5); // update while paused
>
> ~toggle.(~b); // fade in, new values take effect when unpaused
> ```

Adding lots of SynthDef arguments is fine, though perhaps not totally in the "spirit" of state-based composition. Having many individually controllable parameters invites a mindset oriented toward precise individual adjustments, and also can lead to large, unwieldy performance interfaces. It is arguably better to create generative SynthDefs that exhibit complex and evolving behaviors on their own, without reliance on manipulation from an external source. For example, if you find yourself relying heavily on **set** messages, consider replacing those arguments with control rate UGens that produce similar effects. Ideas for complex generative materials are presented throughout Chapters 3 and 4. This being said, there are no hard rules in state-based composition, and these are only suggested guidelines. Your sounds are yours to craft!

11.3 Composite States

In practice, a state-based composition might include tens or hundreds of generative modules. With so many sounds to choose from, it may be cumbersome to operate on a Synth-by-Synth basis, especially if states involve specific Synth combinations. To activate/deactivate multiple modules with a single command, it is helpful to prepare presets, using higher-level functions that transition from one composite state to another. Imagine, for example, that we have five generative modules named A through E, and that we envision three possible composite states defined as follows:

State 0:   Modules A, C, and E are active
State 1:   Modules B, C, and D are active
State 2:   Modules A and B are active

When a state change occurs from a previous state, the logic is as follows: if a module is included in the current state but not in the previous state, turn it on. If a module is not included in the current state, but was specified in the previous state, switch it off.

Code Example 11.4 creates five different generative SynthDefs and five paused Synths. Synths are stored in an Event, at keys corresponding to our A–E naming scheme. Each state is represented as an array of keys corresponding to modules that should be activated when that state is recalled. Finally, we build a function that handles state changes. It accepts an integer that represents a state index, and, in response, it updates current/previous state information and relays gate/run messages to Synths. The three **~playState** lines near the bottom of the example can be evaluated in any order to move from one state to another.

CODE EXAMPLE 11.4: AN APPROACH FOR MANAGING A STATE-BASED COMPOSITION IN WHICH EACH STATE IS COMPOSED OF A COMBINATION OF INDIVIDUAL MODULES.

```
(
s.waitForBoot({
    SynthDef(\pulse_noise, { |gate = 0|
        var sig, env;
        env = Env.asr(5, 1, 5, [2, -2]).kr(1, gate);
        sig = BPF.ar(PinkNoise.ar(1 ! 2), 1600, 0.005, 4);
        sig = sig * env * LFPulse.kr(8, width: 0.2);
        Out.ar(0, sig);
    }).add;
    SynthDef(\beating_tone, { |gate = 0|
        var sig, env;
        env = Env.asr(5, 1, 5, [2, -2]).kr(1, gate);
        sig = SinOsc.ar([250, 251], mul: 0.08) * env;
        Out.ar(0, sig);
    }).add;
    SynthDef(\crackle, { |gate = 0|
        var sig, env;
        env = Env.asr(5, 1, 5, [2, -2]).kr(1, gate);
        sig = Dust.ar(8 ! 2, 0.2) * env;
        Out.ar(0, sig);
    }).add;
    SynthDef(\buzzy, { |gate = 0|
        var sig, env, fb;
        env = Env.asr(5, 1, 5, [2, -2]).kr(1, gate);
        fb = LFNoise1.kr(3 ! 2).range(1.9, 2.1);
        sig = SinOscFB.ar([60, 60.2], feedback: fb, mul: 0.008) * env;
```

```
            Out.ar(0, sig);
        }).add;
        SynthDef(\windy, { |gate = 0|
            var sig, env, cf;
            env = Env.asr(5, 1, 5, [2, -2]).kr(1, gate);
            cf = LFNoise1.kr(0.2 ! 2).range(400, 800);
            sig = WhiteNoise.ar(0.2 ! 2);
            sig = BPF.ar(sig, cf, 0.05) * env;
            Out.ar(0, sig);
        }).add;

        s.sync;

        ~modules = (
            a: Synth.newPaused(\pulse_noise),
            b: Synth.newPaused(\beating_tone),
            c: Synth.newPaused(\crackle),
            d: Synth.newPaused(\buzzy),
            e: Synth.newPaused(\windy)
        );
        ~states = [
            [\a, \c, \e],
            [\b, \c, \d],
            [\a, \b],
            [] // state 3 (everything off)
        ];

        ~currState = [];
        ~playState = { |selection|
            ~prevState = ~currState;
            ~currState = ~states[selection];
            ~modules.keys.do({ |module|
                if(
                    ~currState.includes(module) &&
                    ~prevState.includes(module).not,
                    {~modules[module].set(\gate, 1).run(true)}
                );
                if(
                    ~currState.includes(module).not &&
                    ~prevState.includes(module),
                    {~modules[module].set(\gate, 0)}
                );
            });
            // return the state so it appears in the post window
            ~states[selection];
        };
    });
)
```

```
~playState.(0);
~playState.(1);
~playState.(2);

(
Routine({// clean up when finished:
    ~playState.(3);
    5.wait;
    ~modules.do({ |n| n.free });
}).play;
)
```

The code in Code Example 11.4 is meant to demonstrate an efficient and scalable management strategy for a state-based composition with composite states. Our single-character module naming scheme (A–E) is chosen for brevity, but more descriptive names can be substituted. Also, bear in mind that the number of SynthDefs need not match the number of modules (a well-designed SynthDef can spawn multiple Synths that sound quite different from each other). Adapting this example to a larger and more interesting SynthDef collection is left as an open exercise for the reader.

11.4 Patterns in a State-Based Composition

Patterns, like Synths, can be easily activated and deactivated at will. At a basic level, an EventStreamPlayer can be switched on and off with **play/stop** messages. To produce a gradual fade, **Pseg** can be used to change amplitude values over time. Wrapping a Pseg within **Pdefn** allows us to apply such changes in real-time.

Code Example 11.5 reuses the "beating_tone" SynthDef as the basis for three different EventStreamPlayer modules, named A, B, and C. Additionally, we envision three possible states: AB, AC, and BC. Modules and states are stored as they were in the previous section, and the conditional logic also remains the same. The **~playState** lines at the bottom can still be evaluated in any order, and the crossfade durations can be altered as well. A few structural changes are necessary and worth discussing:

- doneAction: 1 is useful for pausing individual Synths, but a poor choice when used with Pbind, because it results in an accumulation of Synths that are paused but never destroyed. Even though paused Synths do not demand signal calculation resources, there is an upper limit to the number of nodes allowed on the server at one time, accessible via **s.options.maxNodes**. So, the hard-coded doneAction is replaced with an argument, to provide flexibility.
- Each Pbind is followed by a slightly unusual-looking "**.play.pause**" message combination. The play message returns an EventStreamPlayer, which is immediately put into a paused state.
- Each Pbind amplitude value is scaled by a Pdefn. Each Pdefn name is identical to the module it belongs to, which helps make our **~playState** function slightly more concise. For simplicity and consistency, Pdefn values are treated as normalized scalars, ranging between zero and one.

- When a stream reaches its end, it does not produce further output unless reset. When we fade an EventStreamPlayer using Pseg, the amplitude value stream—and by extension, the EventStreamPlayer itself—becomes finite. As a result, once the fade-out is complete, we must **reset** the EventStreamPlayer before it will play again.
- As a small enhancement, the **~playState** function can now accept a crossfade duration as its second argument, allowing us to specify the duration of each state change.

> **CODE EXAMPLE 11.5: AN APPROACH FOR MANAGING A STATE-BASED COMPOSITION WHOSE STATES INCLUDE EVENTSTREAMPLAYERS.**

```
(
s.waitForBoot({
    SynthDef(\beating_tone, {
        arg freq = 250, amp = 0.1, atk = 0.02,
        rel = 0.2, gate = 1, done = 2;
        var sig, env;
        env = Env.asr(atk, 1, rel, [2, -2]).kr(done, gate);
        sig = SinOsc.ar(freq + {Rand(-2.0, 2.0)}.dup(2)) * env * amp;
        Out.ar(0, sig);
    }).add;

    s.sync;

    ~modules = (
        a: Pbind(
            \instrument, \beating_tone,
            \dur, 0.2,
            \degree, Prand([-9, -5, -1], inf),
            \atk, 1,
            \sustain, 1,
            \rel, 1,
            \done, 2,
            \amp, 0.04 * Pdefn(\a, 1),
        ).play.pause,
        b: Pbind(
            \instrument, \beating_tone,
            \dur, Pexprand(0.001, 1),
            \freq, Phprand(3000, 8000),
            \atk, 0.001,
            \sustain, Pexprand(0.002, 0.015),
            \rel, 0.001,
            \amp, 0.015 * Pdefn(\b, 1),
        ).play.pause,
        c: Pbind(
            \instrument, \beating_tone,
```

```
            \dur, 0.5,
            \degree, 10,
            \atk, 0.04,
            \sustain, 0.05,
            \rel, 0.3,
            \amp, Pseq(Array.geom(7, 0.1, 0.5), inf) * Pdefn(\c, 1),
        ).play.pause
    );

    ~states = [
        [\a, \b],
        [\a, \c],
        [\b, \c],
        []
    ];
    ~currentState = [];
    ~playState = { |selection, fadedur = 5|
        ~prevState = ~currState;
        ~currState = ~states[selection];
        ~modules.keys.do({ |module|
            if(
                ~currState.includes(module) &&
                ~prevState.includes(module).not,
                { // fade in
                    Pdefn(
                        module,
                        Pseq([
                            Env([0, 1], [fadedur]).asPseg,
                            Pseq([1],inf)
                        ], 1)
                    );
                    ~modules[module].reset.play;
                }
            );
            if(
                ~currState.includes(module).not &&
                ~prevState.includes(module),
                // fade out
                {Pdefn(module, Env([1, 0], [fadedur]).asPseg)}
            );
        });
        // return the state so it appears in the post window
        ~states[selection];
    }
});
)
```

```
~playState.(0, 10); // change to state 0 over 10 seconds
~playState.(1, 2);
~playState.(2, 5);
~playState.(3, 5); // when finished
```

If you switch back and forth between certain states quickly enough, you will see an "already playing" message appear in the post window. This occurs because SC attempts to play an EventStreamPlayer that is still actively fading out from a previous state and thus still considered to be playing. These messages are harmless and can be ignored.

The generative modules in this example are all EventStreamPlayers, but it is possible to compose a state-based work involving a combination of EventStreamPlayers and Synths in your module collection. In this case, the only additional requirement is that the **~playState** function must include an additional layer of conditional logic to separate EventStreamPlayers from Synths, because they require different types of commands for fading in and out.

11.5 One-Shots in a State-Based Composition

One-shot modules are those that are inherently finite, autonomously terminating themselves at a point in the future. They are fully independent of other processes and therefore easily incorporated into a state-based composition, often as decorative elements to be layered atop existing states. Because they do not need to be manually turned off, one-shots are even easier to store and manage than sustaining modules and states.

Code Example 11.6 demonstrates an approach for storing and recalling one-shots. The SynthDefs are modified from versions appearing earlier in this chapter. The primary difference is that their amplitude envelope has been made finite and self-terminating. One-shots are stored as functions in an Event, similar to the Dictionary approach from Section 10.3.2. To perform a one-shot module, we simply evaluate the function stored at the desired key.

CODE EXAMPLE 11.6: DEFINING, STORING, AND RECALLING ONE-SHOT MODULES IN A STATE-BASED COMPOSITION.

```
(
s.waitForBoot({
    SynthDef(\crackle_burst, { |length = 3|
        var sig, env;
        env = Env.perc(0.01, length, curve: [0, -4]).kr(2);
        sig = Dust.ar(XLine.kr(30, 1, length) ! 2, 0.6) * env;
        sig = LPF.ar(sig, ExpRand(2000, 6000));
        Out.ar(0, sig);
    }).add;
    SynthDef(\buzzy_burst, {
        arg atk = 0.01, rel = 0.5, freq = 80, fb = 2, amp = 1;
```

```
            var sig, env;
            env = Env.perc(atk, rel, curve:[2, -2]).kr(2);
            fb = fb + LFNoise1.kr(3 ! 2, 0.2);
            sig = SinOscFB.ar(freq + [0, 1], feedback: fb, mul: 0.015);
            sig = sig * env * amp;
            Out.ar(0, sig);
        }).add;

        s.sync;

        ~oneShots = (
            a: { Synth(\crackle_burst, [length: rrand(3, 6)]) },
            b: {
                [55, 58, 60, 65, 69].do({ |n|
                    Synth(\buzzy_burst, [
                        atk: 3,
                        rel: 3,
                        freq: n.midicps,
                        fb: rrand(1.6, 2.2),
                        amp: 1/3
                    ]);
                });
            },
            c: {
                Pfin({rrand(9, 30)}, Pbind(
                    \instrument, \buzzy_burst,
                    \dur, Pexprand(0.01, 0.1),
                    \amp, Pgeom(1, {rrand(-1.5, -0.7).dbamp}),
                    \midinote, Pbrown(35, 110.0, 7),
                    \fb, Pwhite(1.5, 2.6)
                )).play;
            }
        );
    });
)

~oneShots[\a].();
~oneShots[\b].();
~oneShots[\c].();
```

These one-shot functions are static in the sense that we cannot influence their sound, only trigger them. If we want to pass custom argument values to a one-shot in order to modify its behavior at runtime, we can declare one or more arguments at the top of the corresponding one-shot function (stored in the **~oneShots** Event) and provide specific values when the one-shot is called. For example, Code Example 11.7 provides an alternate version of the first one-shot in the previous example, which allows the duration of the crackle burst to be customized.

> **CODE EXAMPLE 11.7:** A MODIFIED VERSION OF THE FIRST ONE-SHOT FUNCTION FROM CODE EXAMPLE 11.6, WHICH CAN NOW BE GIVEN AN ARBITRARY LENGTH.
>
> ```
> ~oneShots[\a] = {arg len = 5; Synth(\crackle_burst, [\length, len])};
>
> ~oneShots[\a].(1.5); // short
> ~oneShots[\a].(8); // long
> ```

11.6 Signal Processing in a State-Based Composition

So far, all the sound in this chapter has been purely generative. The next logical question might be: How do we incorporate signal processing effects into a state-based composition?

The guidelines for adding effects here are virtually identical to the general considerations we have already discussed in Chapters 6 and 9. Signal flow should be conceptualized ahead of time. How many effects will there be? Will they be arranged in series, parallel, or some combination? Will your effects follow an insert model (one output UGen per SynthDef), or an auxiliary send model (multiple output UGens per SynthDef)? Many options are possible, but these questions must be answered to properly allocate busses and create groups on the server.

A recommended practice is to instantiate effect Synths at the start of the performance and leave them in active states for the entire duration. Though this approach requires more processing power than pausing or freeing effect Synths when you don't need them, it requires less mid-performance micromanagement. This is particularly true if your effect SynthDefs include a bypass feature, or if your signal flow follows a pre-fader auxiliary send model (in which the direct send and effect send levels can be independently controlled). If your effect Synths are not too computationally intensive, they can remain active throughout a performance, providing an additional layer of options for musical expression.

Code Example 11.8 demonstrates a basic approach to incorporating effects into a state-based composition. In addition to two generative SynthDefs, we also have a simple reverb SynthDef. The reverb SynthDef is designed to output only the processed signal, that is, there is no internal option to blend the dry/wet signals. Instead, both generative SynthDefs have a pair of outputs, one for signal that goes directly to hardware outputs, while the other passes signal to the reverb effect. Relying on concepts from Section 9.4, ServerTree automates the instantiation of nodes on the server and resets the current state whenever [cmd]+[period] is pressed. The states in this example are intentionally simple but can be expanded as additional generative SynthDefs are added. Additionally, we create a Group to contain all source modules, so that we can easily communicate with all of them at once. Some examples of performance actions involving signal processing effects are included in Code Example 11.9.

CODE EXAMPLE 11.8: AN EXAMPLE OF SETUP CODE FOR A STATE-BASED COMPOSITION INVOLVING SIGNAL-PROCESSING EFFECTS.

```
(
ServerTree.removeAll;
s.newBusAllocators;
~bus = Bus.audio(s, 2);
s.waitForBoot({
    SynthDef(\pulse_noise, {
        arg out = 0, auxout = 0, auxamp = 0, lag = 1, gate = 0;
        var sig, env;
        env = Env.asr(5, 1, 5, [2, -2]).kr(1, gate);
        sig = BPF.ar(PinkNoise.ar(1 ! 2), 1600, 0.005, 4);
        sig = sig * env * LFPulse.kr(8, width: 0.2);
        Out.ar(out, sig);
        Out.ar(auxout, sig * auxamp.varlag(lag));
    }).add;
    SynthDef(\crackle, {
        arg out = 0, auxout = 0, auxamp = 0, lag = 1, gate = 0;
        var sig, env;
        env = Env.asr(5, 1, 5, [2, -2]).kr(1, gate);
        sig = Decay2.ar(Dust.ar(8 ! 2), 0.0005, 0.005, SinOsc.ar(900));
        sig = Splay.ar(sig, 0.6) * env * 0.2;
        Out.ar(0, sig);
        Out.ar(auxout, sig * auxamp.varlag(lag));
    }).add;
    SynthDef(\reverb, { |in = 0, out = 0|
        var sig, fx;
        sig = In.ar(in, 2);
        sig = FreeVerb2.ar(sig[0], sig[1], 1, 0.85);
        Out.ar(out, sig);
    }).add;

    s.sync;

    ~makeNodes = {
        ~srcGroup = Group();
        ~reverb = Synth.after(~srcGroup, \reverb, [in: ~bus]);
        ~modules = (
            a: Synth.newPaused(\pulse_noise, [auxout: ~bus], ~srcGroup),
            b: Synth.newPaused(\crackle, [auxout: ~bus], ~srcGroup),
        );
        ~currState = [];
    };
```

```
        ServerTree.add(~makeNodes);
        ServerTree.run;
        ~states = [
            [\a, \b],
            []
        ];
        ~playState = { |selection|
            ~prevState = ~currState;
            ~currState = ~states[selection];
            ~modules.keys.do({ |module|
                if(
                    ~currState.includes(module) &&
                    ~prevState.includes(module).not,
                    {~modules[module].set(\gate, 1).run(true)}
                );
                if(
                    ~currState.includes(module).not &&
                    ~prevState.includes(module),
                    {~modules[module].set(\gate, 0)}
                );
                ~states[selection];
            });
        }
    });
)
```

CODE EXAMPLE 11.9: SOME EXAMPLES OF PERFORMANCE ACTIONS THAT CAN BE TAKEN AFTER EVALUATING THE SETUP CODE IN CODE EXAMPLE 11.8.

```
~playState.(0); // play state zero

~srcGroup.set(\auxamp, -22.dbamp, \lag, 2); // subtle reverb, 2 second fade

~srcGroup.set(\auxamp, -3.dbamp, \lag, 5); // heavy reverb, 5 second fade

// fade out module 'b' reverb send over 5 seconds:
~modules[\b].set(\auxamp, 0, \lag, 5);
```

```
(
// fade out module 'a' reverb send, fade in module 'b' reverb send
~modules[\a].set(\auxamp, 0, \lag, 5);
~modules[\b].set(\auxamp, -3.dbamp, \lag, 5);
)

~srcGroup.set(\auxamp, 0, \lag, 8); // fade all reverb, 8 second fade

(
Routine({// clean up when finished
    ~playState.(1); // everything off
    5.wait; ~modules.do({ |n| n.free});
    3.wait; ~reverb.free;
}).play;
)
```

11.7 Performing a State-Based Composition

Manual code evaluation may not be the most optimal or preferable way to perform a state-based composition. If the work will be presented as an installation over a long period of time, we need an alternative approach. If real-time human interaction is not part of the picture, we can automate the progression of the piece by constructing a routine that moves from one state to another, governed by some algorithm. If human interaction is the goal, a GUI can provide a clean and intuitive control scheme. Because GUI design was discussed in Chapter 8, this section focuses on algorithmic control, but both options are explored in the Companion Code files that accompany this chapter.

For the sake of brevity, this chapter section omits SynthDefs and other sound-specific code, and only presents the most relevant parts in order to convey key concepts. These examples assume you are following models presented earlier in the chapter, that is, using an Event to contain individual generative modules, an array of states, and a **~playState** function that recalls states when evaluated and provided with a state index.

To start, imagine working with three sound-generating states, plus an "everything off" state. Code Example 11.10 provides an example of what our **~states** array might look like.

CODE EXAMPLE 11.10: AN EXAMPLE OF AN ARRAY OF STATES FOR A STATE-BASED COMPOSITION.

```
~states = [
    [\tone, \grains, \noise],       // state 0
    [\crunchy, \grains, \pad],      // state 1
    [\tone, \pad],                  // state 2
    []                              // state 3
];
```

Examples of algorithms for progressing through states might include cycling through states in a specific order or choosing states at random. These options are elegantly handled with patterns. Code Example 11.11, which could be included within a block of setup code, defines algorithms for selecting states and durations, and a routine that performs them. Pattern substitutions are possible. For example, Pshuf will determine a random order that repeats, while Pxrand will move randomly from one state to another without ever selecting the same state twice in a row.

CODE EXAMPLE 11.11: A PATTERN-BASED ALGORITHM FOR AUTONOMOUSLY MOVING FROM ONE STATE TO ANOTHER. THIS CODE COULD BE PAIRED WITH, FOR EXAMPLE, THE SETUP CODE AND CLEANUP CODE IN CODE EXAMPLE 11.4.

```
(
~stateStream = Pseq([0, 1, 2], inf).asStream;
~durStream = Pwhite(20, 80, inf).asStream;
~statePerformer = Routine({
    loop{
        ~playState.(~stateStream.next);
        ~durStream.next.wait;
    }
});
)

~statePerformer.play;
```

For a more complex state sequence, Markov chains are a popular choice. A Markov chain describes a sequence of states in which the probability of selecting a particular state depends on the previous state. If we are currently in state zero, we might want a 30% chance of moving to state one, and a 70% chance of moving to state two. A complete hypothetical flowchart appears in Figure 11.2.

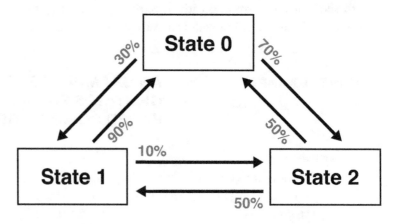

FIGURE 11.2 A flowchart depicting a Markov chain that governs the probabilities of moving from one state to another in a small state-based composition.

Implementing a Markov chain involves adding a second array (of the same size as the array of states) that describes the possible target states from a given state, as well as the probabilities of moving to each of those states. Using an Event allows us to provide meaningful names for the data, shown in Code Example 11.12. In this example, if we start in state zero, there is a 0% chance of staying in state zero, a 30% chance of moving to state one, and a 70% chance of moving to state two. Note that if we were to start in state three (the "everything off" state), all three of the other states are equally likely, but the Markov chain will never return to state three, since the probability of moving to state three is 0% for all four states. In fact, the last item in the Array could be removed completely; if state three represents the end of the performance, there is no need to store information about what comes next.

CODE EXAMPLE 11.12: AN ARRAY THAT DEFINES THE PROBABILITIES OF MOVING TO PARTICULAR STATES WHILE IN A SPECIFIC STATE. THE FIRST ITEM IN THE ARRAY, FOR EXAMPLE, DESCRIBES PROBABILITIES THAT ARE RELEVANT WHILE IN STATE ZERO.

```
~targets = [
    (states: [0, 1, 2, 3], weights: [0, 0.3, 0.7, 0]),
    (states: [0, 1, 2, 3], weights: [0.9, 0, 0.1, 0]),
    (states: [0, 1, 2, 3], weights: [0.5, 0.5, 0, 0]),
    (states: [0, 1, 2, 3], weights: [1/3, 1/3, 1/3, 0])
];
```

Using this Markov chain approach, a performance routine (pictured in Code Example 11.13) might begin by selecting a random state, after which it enters a loop. In this loop, it plays the next state, determines where to go next, and waits for one minute. This example also includes a second block of code that can be used to end the performance.

CODE EXAMPLE 11.13: A ROUTINE THAT APPLIES MARKOV CHAIN PROBABILITIES AND AUTOMATES A PERFORMANCE.

```
(
~statePerformer = Routine({
    var next = [0, 1, 2].choose;
    loop{
        ~playState.(next);
        next = ~targets[next][\states].wchoose(~targets[next][\weights]);
        wait(60);
    };
});
)
```

```
~statePerformer.play;

(
var off = ~states.collect({ |state| state == [] }).indexOf(true);
~statePerformer.stop;
~playState.(off);
)
```

In this specific example, we know that state three is the empty state, so it's true that we could stop the performance routine and simply run `~playState.(3)`. However, this expression would need to change if we added or removed states later. So instead, we use iteration to determine the index of the empty state, and then play it. If there is at least one empty state in the `~states` array, the block of code at the end of Code Example 11.13 will always stop the piece, regardless of the order or number of states.

A separate looping routine, running in parallel, can also be used to algorithmically activate one-shots. Code Example 11.14 assumes your one-shots follow the model from Section 11.5, stored as functions inside an Event. The loop begins with a wait, to avoid always triggering a one-shot at the instant the routine begins.

CODE EXAMPLE 11.14: A SEPARATE ROUTINE DESIGNED TO PLAY RANDOM ONE-SHOTS FROM A COLLECTION.

```
(
~oneShotPerformer = Routine({
    loop{
        exprand(5, 60).wait;
        ~oneShots.choose.();
    }
});
)

~oneShotPerformer.play;
```

We have options for automating one-shots beyond this simple example of random play-and-wait. You may, for example, want to associate certain one-shots with certain states, so that each state only permits randomization within a particular subset of one-shots. Code Example 11.15 demonstrates an example of how to apply such restrictions. In the `~oneShotTargets` array, "foo" and "bar" are defined as valid one-shot options while in state 0, while only "foo" is possible in state 1 and only "bar" is possible in state 2. No one-shots are possible in the empty state. Because our `~playState` function automatically updates the current state and stores it in the `~currState` variable, we can rely on it when selecting one-shots. The routine in Code Example 11.15 identifies the index of the current state, selects a one-shot based on the current state, and plays it.

CODE EXAMPLE 11.15: AN APPROACH FOR PERMITTING ONLY CERTAIN ONE-SHOTS TO BE PLAYED DURING CERTAIN STATES.

```
(
~oneShotTargets = [
    [\foo, \bar], // valid options while in state 0
    [\foo], // ... state 1
    [\bar], // ... state 2
    [] // no one-shots are allowed in the empty state
];

~oneShotPerformer = Routine({
    var currIndex, selectedOneShot;
    loop{
        exprand(5, 45).wait;
        currIndex = ~states.collect({ |n|
            n == ~currState;
        }).indexOf(true);
        selectedOneShot = ~oneShotTargets[currIndex].choose;
        ~oneShots[selectedOneShot].();
    }
});
)

~oneShotPerformer.play;
```

To conclude, this chapter offers two Companion Code bundles that synthesize concepts from this chapter into a complete state-based composition. Companion Code 11.1 relies on a fully automated Markov chain approach, while Companion code 11.2 uses a GUI for real-time human interaction.

CHAPTER 12

LIVE CODING

12.1 Overview

Live coding is an improvisatory performance practice that emerged in the early 2000s and remains an area of active development and exploration today. It encompasses a diverse set of styles and aesthetics that extend beyond the boundaries of music and into the broader digital arts, unified by the defining characteristic of creating the source code for a performance in real-time, as the performance is happening. Since the inception of live coding, practitioners have established various organizations (notably TOPLAP) for the purposes of promoting, disseminating, and celebrating the practice.[1] SC is one of a growing collection of software platforms that pair nicely with live coding, alongside ChucK, FoxDot, Hydra, ixi lang, Sonic Pi, TidalCycles, and others (notably, many of these platforms actually use the SC audio server as their backend synthesis engine). Like playing a musical instrument, live coding is an embodied, public-facing practice; it involves a human performer onstage, almost always accompanied by a projected computer screen display. Live coding is also a natural fit for livestreams and other online venues.

Overall, live coding is a fundamentally different approach to music-making than the event- and state-based approaches explored in previous chapters. It demands focus and preparation from the performer, and blurs the distinction between composing and performing. While live coding bears a slight resemblance to state-based composition (in the sense that we build an interface and then have the option to make improvisatory choices during performance), these similarities are few and superficial. In a live coding context, we are not simply manipulating pre-made code but also writing it from scratch. It's a bit like performing on a musical instrument while simultaneously building and modifying that instrument, all in front of a live audience! The coding environment itself becomes the performance interface. In a sense, we're also taking a step back from the highly "prepared" approaches of the previous two chapters and returning to a more dynamic (and sometimes messy) approach of running code on a line-by-line and chunk-by-chunk basis.

Why pursue live coding? In addition to being fun and exciting, it's also a totally new mindset for most artists. It pushes you out of your comfort zone and demands a more time-sensitive decision-making process, but as a result, tends to elicit sounds and ideas that might otherwise go undiscovered. It's a different sort of experience for audience members, too, who get to hear your sounds while watching your code evolve. Live coding can feel challenging and perhaps a bit awkward for a newcomer, but it's important not to get discouraged. To develop a sense of confidence and personal style, live coding requires an investment of time, practice, and dedication, plus a solid familiarity with the tools at your disposal—just like learning to play a musical instrument.

Among compelling and memorable quotes on live coding is one from Sam Aaron, the creator of Sonic Pi, who reassures us that "there are no mistakes, only opportunities," meaning that you might begin a live coded performance with some pre-formed musical ideas, but during the course of active listening, spontaneous choices, and a few inevitable missteps, you might find yourself on an unpredictable and discovery-rich musical journey.[2] It's all part of the experience!

12.2 A Live Coding Problem and Solution

12.2.1 THE PROBLEM: MUSICAL CHOICES MADE IN REAL-TIME

Live coding involves making real-time musical decisions, which requires the ability to modify our sounds as the mood strikes us, preferably without disruption. To illuminate some fundamental limitations more clearly, we'll first attempt to use "conventional" SC techniques for live coding. Suppose we boot the server, build a UGen function, and play it:

```
s.boot;

~fn = {BPF.ar(PinkNoise.ar(0.1 ! 2), 700, 0.01, 20)};

x = ~fn.play;
```

And, suppose we want to change this sound while it's playing (maybe adjust the filter frequency or reduce the amplitude). Well, it's a bit late for that. We should have planned ahead! This UGen function has no arguments, just a handful of constant values, so sending **set** messages won't accomplish anything. It's also important to realize that redefining the UGen function while the sound is playing also has no effect:

```
~fn = {BPF.ar(PinkNoise.ar(0.1 ! 2), 1050, 0.01, 20)}; // no change
```

The sound remains the same because the function **~fn** that defines the algorithm is totally independent from the Synth **x** that executes the algorithm. The former exists in the language, and the latter on the audio server. Redefining one has no effect on the other. So, with this approach, our best option is probably to remove the current Synth and create another:

```
x.release(3);

x = ~fn.play;
```

However, this is awkward, disruptive, and the continuity is artificial. The question becomes: How can we change a live sound in real-time, without having to plan all the moves in advance?

12.2.2 THE SOLUTION: JITLIB AND PROXIES

The Just-In-Time Programming Library, or JITLib, is a collection of tools that provide support for live coding in SC.[3] At the heart of JITLib is the concept of a "proxy," typically described as a placeholder for an object. The central purpose of a proxy is to allow the object it represents to be used as a component of a larger structure as if it had a meaningful value—even when it doesn't! In short, proxies allow us to build things and make sounds spontaneously, without knowing all the details ahead of time.

Proxies were briefly mentioned in Section 5.5, in order to introduce the pattern proxies Pdef, Pbindef, and Pdefn (subclasses of PatternProxy), which facilitate real-time changes to event streams and value streams. This chapter focuses on two additional classes, **NodeProxy** and **TaskProxy**, which let us apply proxy functionality to Synths and routines. This chapter aims to outline the essential features of JITLib and get you tinkering with live coding as quickly as possible. In the SC help documentation, there are several JITLib tutorial files, notably the four-part "JITLib basic concepts" series, which are full of interesting code morsels and worth reading for those seeking more depth.[4]

12.3 NodeProxy

An important note before you approach this section: If you've called **ServerBoot.removeAll** during your current session, you must either recompile the class library, or quit and restart SC. On startup, **ServerBoot** automatically includes registered actions which, if absent, will prevent some JITLib features from working correctly.

12.3.1 NODEPROXY BASICS

NodeProxy is one of the primary live coding classes under the JITLib umbrella. It acts as a wrapper for a sound process on the server, creating an intermediary layer that facilitates language-side communication and makes "smart" decisions about information that hasn't been provided by the user. For example, we can play a NodeProxy, even before we've decided what it should sound like:

```
s.boot;

~n = NodeProxy.new;

~n.play;

~n.isPlaying; // -> true (we're live!)
```

Every proxy has a **source**, which is the content for which the proxy serves as a placeholder. Initially, a NodeProxy's source is **nil**, which results in silence when played:

```
~n.source; // -> nil
```

A NodeProxy's source is usually a UGen function, similar to the content of a SynthDef. However, in the case of NodeProxy, there's no need to use **In/Out** UGens (in fact, doing so may create problems). As we'll see shortly, routing is automatically and dynamically handled by internal NodeProxy mechanisms. The following two expressions each define a different source. Assuming you've evaluated the previous lines, you can run the following two lines repeatedly, in any order, and as many times as you like. There's no risk of creating awkward gaps of silence or redundant copies of the proxy.

```
~n.source = {PinkNoise.ar(0.1 ! 2)};

~n.source = {SinOsc.ar([300, 301], mul: 0.2)};
```

Throughout this chapter, keep in mind that live coding is a dynamic, improvisatory experience. A book isn't an optimal venue for conveying the "flow" of a live coding session, because it can't easily or concisely capture code modifications and deletions that take place over time. When changing a proxy's source, you might type out a new line (as pictured above), or you might simply overwrite the first line. In any case, you're encouraged to improvise and explore as you follow along with these examples and figure out a style that suits you!

On a basic level, we've solved the problem presented in the previous section. Instead of having to remove an old Synth and create a new one, we now have a singular object, whose content can be spontaneously altered. However, this change is abrupt, and this might not be what we want. Every NodeProxy also has a **fadeTime** that defaults to 0.02 seconds, which defines the length of a crossfade that is applied whenever the source changes:

```
~n.fadeTime = 1;

~n.source = {PinkNoise.ar(0.1 ! 2)};

~n.source = {SinOsc.ar([300, 301], mul: 0.2)};
```

If the source of a new NodeProxy is an audio rate signal, it automatically becomes an audio rate proxy, and the same is true for control rate sources/proxies. When a NodeProxy's source is defined, it automatically plays to a private audio bus or control bus. This bus index, too, is selected automatically. When we **play** a NodeProxy, what we're actually doing is establishing a routing connection from the private bus to hardware output channels, and as a result, we hear the signal. The **stop** message undoes this routing connection but leaves the source unchanged and still playing on its private bus. The **stop** method accepts an optional fade time. The **play** method also accepts a fade time, but because it's not the first argument, it must be explicitly specified by keyword if provided all by itself:

```
~n.stop(3);

~n.play(fadeTime: 3);
```

> ### TIP.RAND(); WHEN TO PLAY A NODEPROXY
>
> Don't get into the habit of instinctively calling **play** on every NodeProxy you create. It's rarely a good idea to play a control rate proxy, even though this is technically possible (the control rate signal will be upscaled to the audio rate using linear interpolation). Proxies that represent control rate signals, such as LFOs, are generally not signals we want to monitor, because their numerical output ranges often extend well beyond ±1, and may result in loud, distorted sound. You should only call **play** on proxies meant to be heard directly!

The **clear** message, which also takes an optional fade time, will fully reset a NodeProxy, severing the monitoring connection and resetting its source to nil:

```
~n.clear(3);
```

12.3.2 NODEPROXY ROUTING AND INTERCONNECTIONS

In previous chapters, we've relied on manual bus allocation and the use of input/output UGens to route signals from one Synth to another, while carefully managing node order on the server. When using NodeProxy, the process is simpler and more intuitive. In particular, instances of NodeProxy can be nested inside of other NodeProxy sources. Let's have a look at a few examples, starting with a simple square wave:

```
~sig = NodeProxy().fadeTime_(3).play;

~sig.source = {Pulse.ar([100, 100.5], mul: 0.03)};
```

Suppose we want to pass this oscillator through a low-pass filter. While it's true that we could just redefine the source to include a filter, this approach doesn't showcase the modularity of NodeProxy. Instead, we'll create and play a second proxy that represents a filter effect:

```
~filt = NodeProxy().fadeTime_(3).play;
```

And now, with **~sig** still playing, we define the source of the filter proxy and supply the oscillator proxy as the filter's input. We also stop monitoring the square wave proxy, which is now being indirectly monitored through the filter proxy. These two statements can be run simultaneously, or one after the other. How you evaluate these statements primarily depends on how/whether you want the filtered and unfiltered sounds to overlap.

```
(
~filt.source = {RLPF.ar(~sig.ar(2), 800, 0.1)};
~sig.stop(3);
)
```

When we nest a NodeProxy inside of another, best practice is to supply the proxy rate and number of channels. Providing only the name (e.g., **~sig**) may work in some cases but may produce warning messages about channel size mismatches in others.

Let's add another component to our signal flow, but in the upstream direction instead of downstream: we'll modulate the filter's cutoff frequency with an LFO. The process here is similar: we create a new proxy, define its source, and plug it into our existing NodeProxy infrastructure. This new proxy automatically becomes a control rate proxy, due to its control rate source. Note that we don't **play** the LFO proxy; its job is not to be heard, but rather to influence some parameter of another signal.

```
~lfo = NodeProxy();

~lfo.source = {SinOsc.kr(0.5).range(55, 80).midicps};

~filt.source = {RLPF.ar(~sig.ar(2), ~lfo.kr(1), 0.1)};
```

With these basic concepts in mind, now is an excellent time to take the wheel and start modifying these sounds on your own! Or, if you're finished, you can simply end the performance:

```
~filt.clear(3); // fade the source signal first;

(
~sig.clear; // then clean up the others
~lfo.clear;
)
```

12.3.3 NDEF: A STYLISTIC ALTERNATIVE

Practically speaking, using NodeProxy requires the use of environment variables to maintain named references. With this approach, there is always a risk of accidentally overwriting a variable with a new NodeProxy assignment, in which case the old proxy remains alive but becomes inaccessible. For example, if we evaluate `~n = NodeProxy().play` twice in a row, we'll create two instances of NodeProxy, but the variable name `~n` only refers to the second version, and this might become a problem later on.

Ndef is a subclass of NodeProxy, which thus inherits all of NodeProxy's methods and behaviors while offering a more concise syntax style that avoids the need for environment variables. Ndef follows the same syntax of other "def-style" classes in SC (e.g., MIDIdef, OSCdef, Pdef), involving a symbol name and the object it represents. If the content for an existing Ndef is redefined, the new data replaces the old data stored in that existing Ndef (instead of creating a new, additional Ndef).

Code Example 12.1 replicates the filter/LFO example from the previous section, using Ndef instead of NodeProxy. Once again, note the syntax for providing the rate and channel count when nesting one Ndef inside of another. As with other def-style classes, it's possible to access every instance of Ndef with **all**, which allows the use of iteration for wide message broadcasts, such as clearing every proxy.

CODE EXAMPLE 12.1: USING **Ndef** TO RECREATE THE INTERCONNECTED NODEPROXY EXAMPLE PRESENTED IN PIECES THROUGHOUT THE BEGINNING OF CHAPTER 12.

```
// play the square wave proxy
Ndef(\sig, {Pulse.ar([100, 100.5], mul: 0.03)}).fadeTime_(3).play;

// play the filter proxy, nesting the oscillator proxy inside
Ndef(\filt, {RLPF.ar(Ndef.ar(\sig, 2), 800, 0.1)}).fadeTime_(3).play;
```

```
// stop playing the original proxy
Ndef(\sig).stop(3);

// create the LFO proxy (but don't play it)
Ndef(\lfo, {SinOsc.kr(0.5).range(55, 80).midicps});

// patch the LFO into the filter proxy
Ndef(\filt, {RLPF.ar(Ndef.ar(\sig, 2), Ndef.kr(\lfo, 1), 0.1)});

// fade everything over 5 seconds
Ndef.all.do({ |n| n.clear(5) });
```

12.3.4 PROXYSPACE: ANOTHER STYLISTIC ALTERNATIVE

If you've been following along with this book, you've probably come to rely on environment variables, i.e., the often-called "global" variables that begin with a tilde and don't require a separate declaration step. Technically, these named containers are not global but are local to the environment in which they were created. They only seem global because there's rarely a need to change from one environment to another.

An **Environment** is a collection-type class that functions as a space in which language-side data can be stored by name. It is the immediate parent class of the **Event** class, to which it is nearly identical. The current environment SC is using is accessible through the special keyword **currentEnvironment**, demonstrated in Code Example 12.2.

CODE EXAMPLE 12.2: CREATION OF TWO ENVIRONMENT VARIABLES, AND ACCESS OF THE CURRENT ENVIRONMENT IN WHICH THEY ARE STORED.

```
(
~a = 5; // create two environment variables
~b = 7;
)

currentEnvironment; // ~a and ~b live here, possibly other items too
```

It's possible to create and use a different environment to manage a totally separate collection of variables, and then return to the original environment at any time, where all of our original variables will be waiting for us. Environments let us compartmentalize our data, instead of having to messily stash everything in one giant box.

A good way to think about managing multiple environments is to imagine them in a spring-loaded vertical stack, with the current environment on the top, as illustrated in

Code Example 12.3. At any time, we can **push** a new environment to the top of the stack, pressing the others down, and the new topmost environment becomes our current environment. When finished, we can **pop** that environment out of the stack, after which the others rise to fill the empty space, and the new topmost environment becomes our current environment.

```
CODE EXAMPLE 12.3: MANAGING MULTIPLE
                   ENVIRONMENTS BY PUSHING
                   AND POPPING.

e = Environment().push; // create and push to the top of the stack

(
~apple = 17; // store some data
~orange = 19;
)

currentEnvironment; // check the data: only ~apple and ~orange live here

e.pop; // pop it from the stack

currentEnvironment; // we've returned to our previous environment
```

What does all this have to do with live coding? A **ProxySpace** is a special type of environment that facilitates the use of NodeProxy objects. We start by pushing a new ProxySpace to the top of the stack:

```
p = ProxySpace().push;
```

Inside of a ProxySpace, every environment variable is an instance of NodeProxy, created as soon as its name is queried:

```
~sig; // -> a NodeProxy
```

Instead of setting fade times on an individual basis, we can set a fade time for the ProxySpace itself, which will be inherited by all proxies within the environment, although we retain the ability to override the fade time of an individual NodeProxy:

```
p.fadeTime = 3; // all NodeProxies adopt a 3-second fade time
```

Code Example 12.4 recreates the square wave/filter/LFO example using ProxySpace. Note that all proxies in a ProxySpace can be simultaneously cleared by sending a **clear** message to the environment itself.

> **CODE EXAMPLE 12.4: USING ProxySpace TO RECREATE THE INTERCONNECTED NDEF EXAMPLE PRESENTED IN THE PREVIOUS SECTION.**
>
> ```
> p = ProxySpace().fadeTime_(3).push; // (if not already inside a ProxySpace)
>
> ~sig.play;
>
> ~sig.source = {Pulse.ar([100, 100.5], mul: 0.03)};
>
> ~filt.play;
>
> ~filt.source = {RLPF.ar(~sig.ar(2), 800, 0.1)};
>
> ~sig.stop(3);
>
> ~lfo.source = {SinOsc.kr(0.5).range(55, 80).midicps};
>
> ~filt.source = {RLPF.ar(~sig.ar(2), ~lfo.kr(1), 0.1)};
>
> p.clear(5);
>
> p.pop;
> ```

The beauty of ProxySpace is that it provides full access to the NodeProxy infrastructure without us ever having to type "NodeProxy" or "Ndef". The primary disadvantage of using ProxySpace, however, is that every environment variable is an instance of NodeProxy, and therefore they cannot be used to contain other types of data, like Buffers or GUI classes, because these types of objects are not valid sources for a NodeProxy. For example, the following line of code looks perfectly innocent, but fails spectacularly while inside of a ProxySpace:

```
~b = Buffer.read(s, Platform.resourceDir +/+ "sounds/a11wlk01.wav");
```

Luckily, the global interpreter variables (lowercase letters a through z) can still be used normally inside of a ProxySpace. There are only twenty-six of these, so using them on an individual basis is not sustainable! Instead, Code Example 12.5 demonstrates a better approach, involving the creation of a multilevel collection-type structure, such as nested Events, all contained within a single interpreter variable.

> **CODE EXAMPLE 12.5:** USING NESTED EVENTS STORED WITHIN A SINGLE INTERPRETER VARIABLE WHILE INSIDE A PROXYSPACE, TO CONTAIN DATA THAT ARE INVALID PROXY SOURCES.
>
> ```
> b = (); // main structure
>
> b[\buf] = (); // a "subfolder" named 'buf'
>
> // inside this subfolder, a buffer named '0'
> b[\buf][\0] = Buffer.read(s, Platform.resourceDir +/+ "sounds/allwlk01.wav");
>
> b[\buf][\0].play; // it is accessible and playable
>
> b[\chords] = (); // another subfolder named 'chords'
>
> b[\chords][\major] = [0, 4, 7]; // store a chord in this subfolder, etc.
> ```

When finished using a ProxySpace, it's always a good idea to pop it from the stack and return to the previous environment:

```
p.pop;

currentEnvironment; // back where we started
```

> ### TIP.RAND(); SIMILARITIES BETWEEN NDEF AND PROXYSPACE
>
> The Ndef and ProxySpace styles are not actually that different from each other. When using an Ndef-based approach, there is a singular instance of ProxySpace used by all Ndefs, which resides in the background. This ProxySpace is accessible by calling **proxyspace** on any Ndef. You can then chain additional methods that would ordinarily be sent to an instance of ProxySpace, like setting a global fadeTime for all Ndefs. The following example demonstrates these similarities:
>
> ```
> Ndef(\a).proxyspace.fadeTime_(5);
>
> Ndef(\a).fadeTime; // -> all Ndefs (current and new) have a
> 5-second fade time
>
> Ndef(\b).fadeTime; // -> 5
> ```

Whichever of these three styles (NodeProxy, Ndef, ProxySpace) you decide to use is ultimately a matter of individual preference. Speaking from personal experience, most users seem to prefer Ndef, perhaps for its concise style and avoidance of environment variables, while retaining the ability to freely use environment variables as needed. Keep in mind, however, that these styles aren't amenable to a "mix-and-match" approach. For a live coding session, it's necessary to pick one style and stick with it.

12.4 Additional NodeProxy Features

The techniques in the previous section should be enough to get you started with some live coding experiments of your own. NodeProxy has some additional features that may be useful in some situations, detailed here.

12.4.1 NODEPROXY ARGUMENTS

Like a SynthDef, the source of a NodeProxy can include a declaration of arguments, which will respond to **set** messages, demonstrated in Code Example 12.6. We also have the option of calling **xset**, which uses the proxy's fade time to crossfade between argument values.[5] An argument can be set to a number (as is typical) or another NodeProxy object. Note that once a proxy argument has been set, it will "remember" its value, even if the source is redefined.

CODE EXAMPLE 12.6: USING THE set/xset METHODS WITH NODEPROXY.

```
Ndef(\t).fadeTime_(2).play;

(
Ndef(\t, {
    arg freq = 200, width = 0.5;
    VarSaw.ar(freq + [0, 2], width: width, mul: 0.05);
});
)

Ndef(\t).set(\freq, 300); // immediate change

Ndef(\t).xset(\freq, 400); // crossfaded change

(
// after a source change, freq remains at 400, even though the default is 200
Ndef(\t, {
    arg freq = 200, width = 0.5;
    var sig = SinOsc.ar(freq + [0, 2], mul: 0.1);
    sig = sig * LFPulse.kr(6, 0, 0.3).lag(0.03);
});
)
```

```
(
Ndef(\lfo, {LFTri.kr(0.25).exprange(300, 1500)});
Ndef(\t).xset(\freq, Ndef(\lfo));
)


Ndef.all.do({ |n| n.clear(2) });
```

12.4.2 CLOCKS AND QUANTIZATION

We saw in parts of Chapter 5 that a Pbind or routine can be rhythmically quantized when played, which guarantees proper timing alignment. A nearly identical process can be applied to a NodeProxy. Each NodeProxy has a pair of attributes named **clock** and **quant**, which determine the timing information for source changes. Code Example 12.7 demonstrates the usage of these attributes.

CODE EXAMPLE 12.7: NODEPROXY QUANTIZATION TECHNIQUES.

```
(
// first, create a clock at 108 bpm and post beat information
t = TempoClock(108/60);
t.schedAbs(0, {t.beats.postln; 1;});
)


// play a proxy and specify timing information
Ndef(\p).fadeTime_(0).clock_(t).quant_(4).play;

(
// now, any source change to the proxy will be quantized:
Ndef(\p, { |freq = 1000|
    var trig, sig;
    trig = Impulse.kr(t.tempo);
    sig = SinOsc.ar(freq) * 0.1 ! 2;
    sig = sig * Env.perc(0, 0.1).kr(0, trig);
});
)

(
Ndef(\p).clear; // clean up
t.stop;
)
```

Note that using clock and quant does not require a fadeTime of 0, but is used here to create a quantized source change that occurs precisely on a desired beat. If a source change occurs and the fadeTime is greater than zero, the crossfade will begin on the next beat specified by quant.

When using ProxySpace instead of Ndef, the instance of ProxySpace can be assigned clock and quant values, and all of the proxies within that space automatically inherit this information. At the same time, we retain the ability to override an individual proxy's attributes to be different from that of its environment. These techniques are demonstrated in Code Example 12.8.

CODE EXAMPLE 12.8: QUANTIZING PROXIES WHILE INSIDE A PROXYSPACE.

```
(
// create a clock, post beats, and push a new ProxySpace
t = TempoClock(108/60);
t.schedAbs(0, {t.beats.postln; 1;});
p = ProxySpace(clock: t).quant_(8).push; // all proxies inherit clock/quant
)

~sig.play;

(
// source changes are quantized to the nearest beat multiple of 8
~sig = {
    var freq, sig;
    freq = ([57, 60, 62, 64, 67, 69, 71]).scramble
    .collect({ |n| n + [0, 0.1] }).flat.midicps;
    sig = Splay.ar(SinOsc.ar(freq)) * 0.05;
};
)

~sig.quant_(0); // override quant for this proxy

(
// change now occurs immediately
~sig = {
    var freq, sig;
    freq = ([57, 60, 62, 64, 67, 69, 71] - 2).scramble
    .collect({ |n| n + [0, 0.1] }).flat.midicps;
    sig = Splay.ar(SinOsc.ar(freq)) * 0.05;
};
)

(
p.clear;
t.stop;
)

p.pop;
```

12.4.3 "RESHAPING" A NODEPROXY

Every NodeProxy has a channel size, stored in its **numChannels** attribute. Often, the channel size of a NodeProxy is determined automatically, based on the channel size of the source. Other times, the channel size (and rate) of a NodeProxy can be provided at creation time, while its source is still nil. If a NodeProxy is created without a source and without specifying a channel size, it defaults to two channels if running at the audio rate, and one channel if running at the control rate. If we play a proxy, we are implicitly telling SC it should run at the audio rate. But, regardless of how a proxy's channel size is determined, a good question is: What happens if we change the source such that its channel size is different from that of its proxy?

Code Example 12.9 demonstrates the use of an attribute called **reshaping**, which determines a NodeProxy's behavior in response to such a change. By default, reshaping is nil, which means the NodeProxy will not adapt to accommodate a differently sized source. If the new source has more channels than available in the proxy, excess channels are mixed with lower-numbered channels, in order to match the proxy's size. If reshaping is set to the symbol **\elastic**, it will grow or shrink to accommodate the channel size of its new source, if different from the previous source. If reshaping is **\expanding**, the proxy will grow, but not shrink, to accommodate a differently sized source.

CODE EXAMPLE 12.9: THE reshaping BEHAVIOR OF NODEPROXY IN RESPONSE TO DIFFERENTLY SIZED SOURCES.

```
Ndef(\sines).play;

Ndef(\sines).numChannels; // -> 2

Ndef(\sines).reshaping; // -> nil (no reshaping)

(
// Define a 2-channel source
Ndef(\sines, {
    var sig = SinOsc.ar([425, 500]);
    sig = sig * Decay2.ar(Impulse.ar([2, 3]), 0.005, 0.3, 0.1);
});
)

(
// Define a 4-channel source. No reshaping is done, and excess
channels are mixed with the lowest two. A notification appears in
the post window.
Ndef(\sines, {
    var sig = SinOsc.ar([425, 500, 750, 850]);
    sig = sig * Decay2.ar(Impulse.ar([2, 3, 4, 5]), 0.005, 0.3, 0.1);
});
)
```

```
Ndef(\sines).numChannels; // -> 2

Ndef(\sines).reshaping_(\elastic); // change reshaping behavior

(
// Defining a 4-channel source now reshapes the proxy. All four
// signals are on separate channels. If working with only two
// speakers, we'll only hear the first two channels.
Ndef(\sines, {
    var sig = SinOsc.ar([425, 500, 750, 850]);
    sig = sig * Decay2.ar(Impulse.ar([2, 3, 4, 5]), 0.005, 0.3, 0.1);
});
)

Ndef(\sines).numChannels; // -> 4

(
// An elastic proxy will shrink to accommodate a smaller source
Ndef(\sines, {
    var sig = SinOsc.ar([925, 1100]);
    sig = sig * Decay2.ar(Impulse.ar([6, 7]), 0.005, 0.3, 0.1);
});
)

Ndef(\sines).numChannels; // -> 2

Ndef(\sines).clear;
```

12.4.4 PBIND AS A NODEPROXY SOURCE

Strange though it may seem, a Pbind is a valid NodeProxy source, demonstrated in Code Example 12.10. An EventStreamPlayer is not technically a type of Node, but is a process that often generates a timed sequence of Synths, and can therefore be treated similarly. Attributes such as **fadeTime** and **quant** can still be used and have predictable results. A NodeProxy that has a Pbind source can be used as part of another NodeProxy's source, without the need for any special steps or precautions.

CODE EXAMPLE 12.10: USING PBIND AS A NODEPROXY SOURCE.

```
(
b = Buffer.read(s, Platform.resourceDir +/+ "sounds/a11wlk01.wav");

SynthDef(\play, {
    arg atk = 0.002, rel = 0.08, buf = 0,
```

```
        rate = 1, start = 0, amp = 0.5, out = 0;
        var sig, env;
        env = Env.perc(atk, rel).ar(2);
        sig = PlayBuf.ar(
            1, buf, rate * BufRateScale.kr(buf), startPos: start
        );
        sig = sig * env * amp ! 2;
        Out.ar(out, sig);
}).add;

t = TempoClock(108/60);
t.schedAbs(0, {t.beats.postln; 1;});
)

// create a proxy and provide an initial source
Ndef(\a).fadeTime_(0).clock_(t).quant_(4).play;

(
// source change occurs on a quantized beat
Ndef(\a, Pbind(
    \instrument, \play,
    \dur, 1/2,
    \buf, b,
    \amp, 0.2,
    \start, 36000,
));
)

// set a crossfade time of four beats
Ndef(\a).fadeTime_(t.beatDur * 4);

(
// pattern-based proxies are crossfaded as expected
Ndef(\a, Pbind(
    \instrument, \play,
    \dur, 1/4,
    \buf, b,
    \amp, 0.3,
    \start, Pwhite(50000, 70000),
    \rate, -4.midiratio,
));
)

// create an effect and route the first proxy through it
Ndef(\reverb).fadeTime_(5).play;

(
Ndef(\reverb, {
```

```
    var sig;
    sig = Ndef.ar(\a, 2);
    sig = LPF.ar(GVerb.ar(sig.sum, 300, 5), 1500) * 0.2;
});
)


(
// clean up:
Ndef.all.do({ |n| n.clear });
t.stop;
)
```

12.5 TaskProxy

TaskProxy serves as a proxy for a routine (introduced in Section 5.2), allowing us to manipulate a timed sequence in real-time, even when that sequence isn't fully defined.[6] Though it's possible to use TaskProxy directly (similar to using NodeProxy), here we will only focus on its subclass Tdef, which (like Ndef) inherits all the methods of its parent and avoids the need to use environment variables. Note that a Tdef's source should not be an instance of a routine, but rather a function that would ordinarily appear inside of one.

Code Example 12.11 provides a basic demonstration. If a TaskProxy is in a "playing" state when its source is defined, it will begin executing its source function immediately. If the source stream is finite, the proxy will remain in a playing state when finished and will begin executing again as soon as a new source is supplied—even if the new source is identical to the previous one. Similarly, if a TaskProxy has reached its end, the **play** message will restart it. Like routines, an infinite loop is a valid source for a TaskProxy (just be sure to include a wait time!). When paused and resumed, a TaskProxy "remembers" its position and continues from that point. When stopped, it will start over from the beginning when played again. Like other proxies, **clear** will stop a TaskProxy and reset its source to nil.

CODE EXAMPLE 12.11: BASIC USAGE OF TaskProxy, ACCESSED THROUGH ITS SUBCLASS, Tdef.

```
Tdef(\t).play;

(
// a finite-length source – execution begins immediately
Tdef(\t, {
    3.do{
        [6, 7, 8, 9].scramble.postln;
        0.5.wait;
    };
    "done.".postln
});
)
```

```
Tdef(\t).play; // do it again

(
// a new, infinite-length source
Tdef(\t, {
    ~count = Pseq((0..9), inf).asStream;
    loop{
        ~count.next.postln;
        0.25.wait;
    };
});
)

Tdef(\t).pause;

Tdef(\t).resume; // continues from pause location

Tdef(\t).stop;

Tdef(\t).play; // restarts from beginning

Tdef(\t).clear;
```

Every TaskProxy runs on a clock and can be quantized, as shown in Code Example 12.12. If unspecified, a Tdef uses the default TempoClock (60 beats per minute) with a quant value of 1. Usage is essentially identical to Ndef. Like **\dur** values in a Pbind, wait times in a Tdef are interpreted as beat values with respect to its clock.

CODE EXAMPLE 12.12: SPECIFYING CLOCK AND QUANTIZATION INFORMATION FOR A TDEF.

```
(
// create a verbose clock at 108 bpm
t = TempoClock(108/60);
t.schedAbs(0, {t.beats.postln; 1;});
)

// create a task proxy and set clock/quant values
Tdef(\ticks).clock_(t).quant_(4).play;

(
// post a visual effect, execution begins on next quantized beat
Tdef(\ticks, {
    loop{
        4.do{ |n|
            "*---".rotate(n).postln;
```

```
                0.25.wait;
            }
        }
    });
)

(
// clean up
Tdef(\ticks).clear;
t.stop;
)
```

Code Examples 12.11 and 12.12 aim to demonstrate basic usage, but mainly post values and don't really do anything useful. How might a Tdef be used in a practical setting? Whenever you have some sequence of actions to be executed, Tdef is always a reasonable choice, especially if you envision dynamically changing the sequence as it runs. One option is to automate the sending of set messages to a NodeProxy. In Code Example 12.13, we have an Ndef that plays a sustained chord. Instead of repeatedly setting new note values ourselves, we can delegate this job to a Tdef.

CODE EXAMPLE 12.13: USING TDEF TO AUTOMATE THE PROCESS OF UPDATING A NODE PROXY WITH set MESSAGES.

```
Ndef(\pad).fadeTime_(3).play;

(
Ndef(\pad, { |notes = #[43, 50, 59, 66]|
    var sig;
    sig = notes.collect({ |n|
        4.collect({
            LFTri.ar(
                freq: (n + LFNoise2.kr(0.2).bipolar(0.25)).midicps,
                mul: 0.1
            );
        }).sum
    });
    sig = Splay.ar(sig.scramble, 0.5);
    sig = LPF.ar(sig, notes[3].midicps * 2);
});
)
```

```
(
Tdef(\seq, {
    var chords = Pseq([
        [48, 55, 62, 64],
        [41, 48, 57, 64],
        [55, 59, 64, 69],
        [43, 50, 59, 66],
    ], inf).asStream;
    loop{
        Ndef(\pad).xset(\notes, chords.next);
        8.wait;
    }
}).play
)

(
// clean up
Tdef(\seq).stop;
Ndef(\pad).clear(8);
)
```

> **TIP.RAND(); ARRAY ARGUMENTS IN A UGEN FUNCTION**
>
> It is possible for an argument declared in a UGen function (e.g., in a SynthDef or NodeProxy function) to be an array of numbers, as is the case in Code Example 12.13. However, once an array argument is declared, its size must remain constant. Additionally, the argument's default value must be declared as a literal array, which involves preceding the array with a hash symbol (#). Literal arrays were briefly mentioned in Section 1.6.9, but not discussed in detail.

12.6 Recording a Live Coding Performance

What options do we have for capturing a live coding session? We could evaluate **s.makeGui** and record the audio straight to our hard drive, but this only captures the sound, and not the code, which is arguably a crucial element of the performance. If at some point mid-performance, we happened to make some truly impressive sound, the code that generated it might be lost in the process; for example, it may have been deleted or overwritten in the heat of the moment. We could alternatively use screen recording software to capture the visual elements, but video files tend to be relatively large, and piling this recording task on top of real-time audio processing might strain your computer. Plus, we'd still need to copy the code manually when watching the video later.

The **History** class, demonstrated in Code Example 12.14, provides a lightweight solution for recording code as it is evaluated over time. When a history session is started, it captures every subsequent piece of code that runs, exactly when it runs, until the user explicitly ends the history session.

Once a history session has ended, we have the option of recording the code history to a text file, so that it can be studied, sent to a collaborator, or replayed. The **saveCS** method (short for "save as compile string," writes a file to a path as a **List** of individual code evaluations, formatted as strings, which can be loaded in as the current history using **History.loadCS**, and played back automatically with **History.play**. This will feel as if a "ghost" version of yourself from the past is typing at your keyboard! If desired, a history playback can be stopped partway through with **History.stop**. Alternatively, a history can be saved with **saveStory**, which produces a more human-readable version, complete with commented timestamps. This type of save is meant to be played back manually and is well-suited for studying or editing.

CODE EXAMPLE 12.14: USE OF THE **History** CLASS TO RECORD AND REPLAY CODE EVALUATION.

```
History.start; // start a history session

// now, run a sequence of code statements:

s.boot;

Ndef(\k).fadeTime_(1).play;

Ndef(\k, {SinOsc.ar([200, 201], mul: 0.1)});

Ndef(\k, {SinOsc.ar([250, 253], mul: 0.1)});

(
Ndef(\k, {
    var sig, mod;
    mod = LFSaw.kr(0.3, 1).range(2, 40);
    sig = LFTri.ar([250, 253], mul: 0.1);
    sig = sig * LFTri.kr(mod).unipolar(1);
});
)

Ndef(\k).clear(3);

s.quit;

History.end; // stop the session
```

```
// save to your home directory
History.saveCS("~/myHistoryCS.scd".standardizePath);

History.clear; // clear the history, to demonstrate properly

History.play; // confirm history is currently empty

History.loadCS("~/myHistoryCS.scd".standardizePath); // load re-
corded history

History.play; // replay

// save to your home directory in "story" format
History.saveStory("~/myHistoryStory.scd".standardizePath);
```

Companion Code 12.1 features a live coding demonstration/performance, which exists in both history formats and a live screen recording.

Notes

1. https://toplap.org/about/.
2. https://sonic-pi.net/tutorial.html.
3. https://doc.sccode.org/Overviews/JITLib.html.
4. https://doc.sccode.org/Tutorials/JITLib/jitlib_basic_concepts_01.html.
5. Technically, when calling **xset** on a NodeProxy, this method does not directly "crossfade" between two argument values (which would create a glissando or something similar); rather, an **xset** message instantiates a new source Synth using the updated argument value and crossfades between it and the older Synth. This behavior can be confirmed by visually monitoring the Node tree.
6. **TaskProxy** is a reference to the **Task** class, a close relative of routines. Don't be distracted by the fact that this class is not named "RoutineProxy"—routines and tasks are very similar, and both are subclasses of **Stream**. Though tasks and routines are not identical nor fully interchangeable, it is rare during practical usage to encounter an objective can be handled by one but not the other.

INDEX

For the benefit of digital users, indexed terms that span two pages (e.g., 52–53) may, on occasion, appear on only one of those pages.

Page numbers followed by *f* refer to figure; *t* to table; *c* to code example; *tr* to tip.rand().

absolute file paths. *See* resolving relative file paths
actions of GUI elements, 238–39
addActions for Nodes, 195, 196
ADSR envelope, 52
aliasing, 37–38, 92–93
all-pass filter. *See* delay effect (with feedback)
amplitude, 40, 41, 44*tr*, 52, 71, 81, 104, 162–63
animation of GUI elements, 247–48
AppClock, 243–44
arguments
   for functions, 24–25
   for methods, 8
   for NodeProxies, 308–9
   for UGens, 40–42
   for UGen functions, 43–45
   in a SynthDef, 68–69, 123
   trigger-type, 59*c*, 59, 126
Array, 22–24. *See also* dup
   as storage mechanism for Buffers, 119
   as storage mechanism for musical events, 266–69
   arguments in a SynthDef or NodeProxy, 317, 317*tr*
audio setup, 35, 41, 41*tr*, 185–86

binary operators, 18, 18*t*
bitcrushing, 112–13
Blip, 82
block size. *See* control block
Boolean values, 21, 123
bouncing to disk. *See* recording to an audio file
brown noise, 99
bufnum, 117
BufRd, 127–28
BufWr, 134–38
busses, 183–88
   resetting allocation counter, 188

classes, 6
client, the. *See* language, the
clipping, 109
   smooth variants, 110–11
CmdPeriod, 218
color, 237
comb filter. *See* delay effect (with feedback)
command-period (keyboard shortcut), 42
comments, 12–13

control block, 38, 193
ControlSpec, 239–41
conversions
   decibels to amplitude, 71
   MIDI note numbers to Hertz, 71
   semitones to frequency ratios, 71

debugging. *See* polling a UGen; *see* postln; *see* trace
   MIDI data, 212
default SynthDef, the, 162
defer. *See* AppClock
delay effect, 133, 137, 199–200
   with feedback, 203–4
Dictionary
   as storage mechanism for musical events, 269–70
digital audio, 37–38
doneActions, 54, 124, 279
dup, 23, 60
DynKlang, 83
DynKlank, 108
echo. *See* delay effect

effects
   inserts vs. sends, 183
enclosures, 7, 9
Env, 55–59, 142, *See also* Pseg
EnvGen, 55–59
Environment, 304–5
escape character, 20*c*, 20
evaluating code
   multi-line block, 9
   single line, 7
Event
   as module in a state-based composition, 281
   as playable action, 160–66
   as storage mechanism, 120, 160
   midi type, 219–20
   note type, 161–66
   rest type, 170–73
EventStreamPlayer, 167, 285–88
exclamation mark. *See* dup

fadeTime, 46, 301. *See also* release
feedback
   acoustic, 190, 190–91*tr*
   delay lines, 203

filters, 102–6
    quality, 103, 104, 105–6
    types, 102–3, 105–6
flanger effect, 202
Float, 18
folding, 109
foldover. *See* aliasing
free
    a Group, 198
    an HIDdef, 231
    a MIDIdef, 214
    a Synth, 45
freeAll
    applied to a Group, 198
    applied to HIDdef, 231
    applied to MIDIdef, 214
FreqScope, 73*f*, 74–75
frequency, 37–38, 39, 40–41, 71, 92, 163–64
Function, 24–25, 267
function-dot-play, 42, 46, 65–66
gated envelopes, 57, 165–66
getting an attribute, 26
    of a GUI element, 236–37

GrainBuf, 140–42
Group, 195–98
    default Group, the, 195

help browser, the, 3*f*, 4, 13–15
HID, 230–31
History, 318–19

IDE, 3*f*, 4
if-then-else, 30
In. *See* inputting a signal; *see also* SoundIn
inputting a signal, 184, 190, *See also* busses
instances, 6
Integer, 18
Integrated Development Environment. *See* IDE
interaction with GUIs
    using MIDI/OSC, 243
    using the keyboard/mouse, 241–43
interpreter, the, 4–5
iteration
    for additive synthesis, 81–82
    for reading audio files into Buffers, 120, 121–22*c*
    for sequencing, 149–50

JITLib, 299–300

Klang, 82–83
Klank, 108

Lag (UGen), 239, 282, 282*c*
language, the, 4–5
Latch, 113
layout management of GUIs, 236
LFO, 84, 105–6, 202
literals, 26–27
loading external code files, 261–62

looping
    a Routine, 150
    a sample, 124, 128
low-frequency noise generators, 101–2
low-frequency oscillator. *See* LFO

Markov chain, 294–95
memory allocation (for delay lines), 200–1
messages. *See* methods
methods, 6
MIDIdef, 212–16
modulation, 49, 84
    amplitude, 85–86
    frequency, 88–90
    ring, 86–87
mul/add, 41–42
multichannel expansion, 60–63
multichannel mixing. *See* Splay

Ndef, 303–4
NetAddr, 221–23
nil, 22
Node, 195
node tree, the, 73*f*, 75–76, 192
noise, 99–102
normalization, 115
notes. *See* Event (note type)
Nyquist frequency, 37–38, 39

objects, 6
object-oriented programming, 5–6
one-shot sample playback, 127
OOP. *See* object-oriented programming
order of execution
    for signal processing, 192–95
    for server actions, 252
order of operations, 19
Osc (oscillator UGen), 94
OSCdef, 221–22
oscilloscope. *See* Stethoscope
Out. *See* outputting a signal. *See also* busses
outputting a signal, 66–68, 184, 188–89, 193
overdubbing, 131–32, 138
overloading, 20

panning, 60, 64
PathName, 120
pattern types, 159*t*
pausing a Synth, 279–82
Pbind, 166–70, 285–88
    as NodeProxy source, 312–14
Pbindef, 180–82
Pdef, 179–80
Pdefn, 177–79
Pen, 245–48
phase, 40–41
Phasor, 128, 136
pink noise, 37*t*, 99
pitch, 34, 71, 124–25, 129, 163–64
pitch-shifting
    delay-based, 202

granular, 207–10
play
    a Buffer, 115–16
    an Event, 160
    a NodeProxy, 300, 301
    a Pbind, 167
    a Routine, 149–50, 153
    a UGen function. *See* function-dot-play
playback speed, 124–26
PlayBuf, 122–27
plotting
    Buffers, 115–16
    UGen functions, 73–74
Point, 245
polling a UGen, 72–73
polymorphism, 6
postln, 12, 161, 161*tr*
ProxySpace, 305–7
proxy objects, 176, 299–300
Pseg, 285, 285*c*, 287

quantization, 154–55, 169, 178, 309

range-mapping
    for GUI elements, 239–41
    for UGens. *See* UGen ranges
read
    an audio file into a Buffer, 115–18
    data from a USB device, 229
readChannel, 118, 139
receiver, 7
RecordBuf, 130–33
recording
    to an audio file, 75
    a live coding performance, 317–19. *See also* History
Rect, 233
Ref, 82–83
release, 46, 52, 68
reshaping a NodeProxy, 311–12
resolving relative file paths, 121–22
resonator. *See* delay effect with feedback
Resonz, 107
rests. *See* Event (rest type)
returning a value, 7–8
reverberation, 194, 204
Ringz, 107

sample rate, 37, 39–40
sclang. *See* language, the
scsynth. *See* server, the
SendReply, 223–24
SerialPort, 228–29
server, the, 4, 5
    meters, 60, 61*f*, 73*f*
ServerBoot/ServerQuit/ServerTree, 256–60
set message
    applied to Synths, 43–44, 281–82
    applied to Groups, 198
    applied to NodeProxies, 308. *See also* xset

setting an attribute, 26, 178
    of a GUI element, 236–37
Shaper, 96
Signal, 94
signal generators. *See* UGen (common examples)
sine wave oscillator. *See* SinOsc
SinOsc, 40, 40*f*
SoundIn, 192
spectrum analyzer. *See* FreqScope
Splay, 65
Stethoscope, 73*f*, 74
stop
    an EventStreamPlayer, 168–69
    a NodeProxy, 301
    a Routine, 150
    a TempoClock, 155
    all sound. *See* command-period. *See also* free
Stream, 146
    as storage mechanism for musical events, 270–71
String, 20
sustain, 166, 219. *See also* gated envelopes
Symbol, 21
sync, 254–55
synchronized sample playback, 129

targets for Nodes, 195
TempoClock, 152–56
    permanence, 155
TGrains, 143
trace, 168*tr*
tremolo, 85

UGen
    common examples, 37*t*
    ranges, 50, 51*t*, 112
    rates, 38–40
unary operators, 18, 18*t*
USB communication. *See* SerialPort
UserView, 245–48

variables, 9
    environment, 11–12
    interpreter, 11–12
    local, 10
vibrato, 88
View, 234–35
    common types, 235*t*
volume, 41, 41*tr*, 73*f*, 75
VOsc, 95–96

Warp 1, 143–44
waveshaping, 96–97
while, 148
white noise, 37*t*, 99
Window, 233–34
wrapping, 109

xset, 308